Teen Astrology

Other Titles by M. J. Abadie

The Everything Tarot Book
Awaken to Your Spiritual Self
Healing Mind, Body, Spirit
Your Psychic Potential
Love Planets (with Claudia Bader)
Finding Love (with Sally Jessy Raphael)
Multicultural Baby Names
Child Astrology
The Everything Herbal Remedies Book
The Everything Angels Book

This book is dedicated to all teens everywhere
and to those special teens in my own life:

Megan Elizabeth Abadie
Charles Hedrick Abadie
Caroline Rose Abadie

and to my beloved niece and goddaughter Kathleen Victoria Abadie.

Teen Astrology

The Ultimate Guide to

Making Your Life Your Own

M. J. Abadie

Bindu Books
Rochester, Vermont

Bindu Books
One Park Street
Rochester, Vermont 05767
www.InnerTraditions.com

Bindu Books is a division of Inner Traditions International

Library of Congress Cataloging-in-Publication Data

Abadie, M. J. (Marie-Jeanne)
    Teen astrology : the ultimate guide to making your life your own / M. J.
Abadie.
        p. cm.
    ISBN 978-0-89281-823-5 (alk. paper)
        1. Astrology. 2. Teenagers—Miscellanea. I. Title.

    BF1729.T44 A23 2001
    133.5—dc21

                                                            00-053011

Printed and bound in India by Replika Press Pvt. Ltd.

10 9 8 7 6 5
Text design and layout by Kristin Camp
This book was typeset in Apollo, with Neuland as a display face

Contents

Part One Getting to Know You

Part Four The Parent Trap

Acknowledgments

Writing a book is a solitary task, but the process of getting it published in final form involves many people. I want to thank the following especially for their vital contributions to this complex process:

First and foremost, my deepest appreciation goes to Laura Schlivek, the book's project editor, whose enormous task it was to coordinate all the parts and make them come out as a whole. A more magnificent job could not have been done and she did it with grace and good humor in spite of the many difficulties encountered. Not only did she serve as a compassionate adviser, but she coped with mountains of details. It's said "The devil is in the details," and Laura's patience with the tedious work of organizing countless details was nothing short of magnificent. My good fortune in having her as my editor is equal only to my gratitude for the splendid manner in which she held everything together on its long route to the printing press.

My thanks, too, to Priscilla Baker for her good eye in the final stages of typesetting.

Jon Graham is thanked for his enthusiasm for *Teen Astrology*, which made it a reality.

The support of the publisher, Ehud Sperling, was, of course, invaluable.

To my long-time friend, H. M. Frombaugh, I am grateful for the delightful illustrations of the astrological animal symbols that add so much to the book's visual appearance.

Anne Sellaro, my agent and dear friend, was—as always—there for me when I needed business advice or just a shoulder to lean on. I feel blessed indeed to have Anne's counsel and understanding.

For kindly allowing me to excerpt some passages from her book *Changing Your Destiny,* I am indebted to my friend and fellow astrologer Mary Orser.

My assistant, Will Varley, was a treasure who cheerfully took on a multitude of chores, no matter how dull or exacting, with unfailing good humor and thoroughness.

Chris Santini, best of friends, gave aid and comfort throughout the long process, always cheering me on and reminding me to call on the angels when I needed help.

A group of young teenage friends lent their comments along the way and I thank them all for their useful input.

Last but not least, I thank you, the reader, for being the indirect inspiration for *Teen Astrology,* which was conceived and written with you in mind. My hope is that it will serve you as a valuable guide during your teen years.

Why an Astrology Book Just for Teens?

As a teen, you are presumed to be *different* from an adult—and many adults, if not all of them, assume that young people are something *other* than themselves, something basically alien. The reverse is also true—parents can seem to their teenage children to be of another species entirely.

The truth of the matter is that as a teen you are *not an adult;* you are *in the process of becoming an adult.* The difference between you, a teen, and adults is that you are "a work in progress," and nothing that exists as potential has yet crystallized into permanent form. The teen years are crucial to the human development process, for during them there is more room for experimentation and exploration of who you are and how you want to live your life than you will have as you grow older.

The purpose of astrology is *not* to predict the future—that is, fortune-telling. Put simply, astrology is the best tool we have, or have ever devised, including psychology, for understanding an individual's inner dynamics and for making the best of them.

Since the teen years are of primary importance in forming the adult you will become, it's an ideal time to enhance your own understanding of yourself. And astrology can give you insights—available through no other method—into yourself and your relationships with other people, including love interests, parents, and friends.

My inspiration for writing this book came directly from my work on *Child Astrology,* a book for *parents* about their children. Through exploring how parents can best raise their children, I realized that as children reach their teen years they are in a position different from that of younger children. Teens stand on the brink of adulthood—they just aren't quite there yet.

My own teen years were extremely difficult, and since I became a professional astrologer there have been many times I wished achingly that I'd known astrology when I was a teen. What a difference it would have made! For example, I never could relate to myself as my Sun Sign, and so I thought astrology—as I knew it from columns in magazines and newspapers—was all bunk. I wasn't at all like those columns described my Sun Sign, and that confused me.

Later, when I studied astrology and found out that there are *ten* Planets, not just the Sun, a world of wonder opened up for me and I began to understand myself in a way that before had been impossible. When I discovered that in addition to the ten Planets I had an *Ascendant,* or rising, Sign, and I found out what it was, a lot of the confusion about who I was cleared up like a strong north wind blowing the sky clean of clouds and revealing the clear blue filled with sunshine.

That's why this book is written especially for the teenage reader. It addresses the concerns particular to your age period and tells you how to find out about your complete self—not just your Sun Sign, which is only one-tenth of your entire astrological picture.

At the same time, it's a book you can show your parents—and you can learn things about your parents that will help you make sense of them and their actions, especially when there is conflict between you. This book will help you to understand yourself as you are now and to peek into the future to see how you might develop your individuality. In addition to covering the basic fundamentals—who you are and how you relate to the world—it also is about *choices,* because making choices is a major part of becoming an adult. Right choices made early prevent regrets arriving later. Wrong choices made early can color an entire life, sometimes ruining it. This is especially true in the case of relationships involving love and sex. Right choices, made with a full knowledge of yourself and your potential, can lead to a happy and successful adult life.

Although *Teen Astrology* is written in plain, nontechnical English, it is not a simplified or watered-down version of astrology, as are many astrology books written for adults. It's serious, because life is serious business. Sure, being a kid is supposed to be a time to have fun—but as every kid knows there's a lot of stuff to deal with that isn't fun at all. There's pain and stress, emotional and physical trauma, anxiety and lack of self-confidence, worry about school and learning, and wondering if you're "doing it right."

Therefore, this book is about *self-understanding,* which ultimately is your own responsibility. The sooner you undertake it, the better off you will be. Knowing your Planetary energy patterns and how they work will put you ahead in the game of life. Difficult patterns can be minimized and used constructively when you know about them in advance. Positive patterns can be maximized.

The main purpose of this book—written especially for you as a teen—is to help you learn who you really are, what your potentials are, and how to accept yourself without being judgmental. When you have a clear mental picture of who you are and what you have the possibility to become, then you can make choices about how you will use your energies. You can change or modify any facet of yourself once you know what it is and how it operates. However, if you accept someone else's evaluation of what you *ought* to be, you will discover in time that you cannot live up to an image that others have pasted on you. You may try to fake it and pretend to be what you aren't, but this way lies disaster. If you try to be someone you are not, you will never be happy or complete as an adult. The *only* person you can be adequately is *yourself.*

The reason you have to take on the task of understanding yourself is clear: no one else can do it for you, and if you accept someone else's definition of who you are or ought to be, you are doomed to unhappiness. Most adults view children in one of two ways: either they are naturally good and virtuous until they get messed up by a bad society, or they are naturally like wild beasts that must be tamed and civilized through rigid authoritarian systems of education and religion. Neither of these views is correct. Children, and especially teenage children, have exactly the same needs and drives as do adults. They are neither perfect nor bestial, and they will do whatever they must in order to survive in the world both as biological entities and as distinct personalities. The principle difference is that the young person does not know as much about the so-called "real world" and, therefore, cannot manipulate it as successfully as a fully formed adult with extensive worldly experience. This difference often causes problems between teens and adults, since many adults presume that they know better. Usually they do know *more,* but more is not always better. That's why self-understanding is an important part of a teen's survival kit.

During the teen years, when emotions are in a heightened state of importance, what may seem all-encompassing—like the breakup of a relationship—takes on more intensity because it involves your identity, and a teen's identity is not yet on solid ground. This is not to say that adults don't have emotional explosions as well, only that they handle them from a different perspective. Astrology can provide that necessary perspective and help ease you through the difficult transitions in your journey from teen to adult.

You need absolutely no previous knowledge of astrology to use this book. Everything you need is provided, including the tables in which you can look up your Planetary placements and those of your parents. Who you are is important—important to *you*. Who you will become is vital, and you are ultimately in charge of that outcome. Your stars can be your trusted and faithful guides along the way.

ONE

Getting to Know You

Why You Are More Than Your Sun Sign

*The advantages of an astrological viewpoint begin
with living in tune with nature rather than
in alienation from it.*

Thomas Moore,
The Re-Enchantment of Everyday Life

What *is* a Sun Sign? Chances are you already know your Sun Sign and those of the people close to you. Your Sun Sign is what you answer with when someone asks, "What's your Sign?"

There are twelve Signs in the entire Zodiac. They are named for the constellations that form the Zodiac, which—to put it as simply as possible—is a band of the sky that has our Sun at its center.

Your Sun Sign tells which of the twelve sections of the Zodiac the Sun was moving through on the day you were born, no matter what year. The Sun takes an entire year to make its way through all twelve Signs of the Zodiac.

You will notice that there are two different possible dates for the beginning and end of each period. The reason for this is the same reason that we have leap years: each of our days is actually four minutes longer than twenty-four hours. If you were born at the beginning or end date of any Sign, you may need a computer-generated chart to be

How to Find Your Sun Sign

The following table shows which days the Sun occupies each of the twelve Signs of the Zodiac.

♈	**Aries**	March 21–22—April 19–20
♉	**Taurus**	April 20–21—May 20–21
♊	**Gemini**	May 21–22—June 21–22
♋	**Cancer**	June 22–23—July 22–23
♌	**Leo**	July 23–24—August 23–24
♍	**Virgo**	August 23–24—September 22–23
♎	**Libra**	September 23–24—October 23–24
♏	**Scorpio**	October 24–25—November 21–22
♐	**Sagittarius**	November 22–23—December 21–22
♑	**Capricorn**	December 22–23—January 19–20
♒	**Aquarius**	January 20–21—February 18–19
♓	**Pisces**	February 19–20—March 20–21

certain what your Sun Sign is. See appendix 2 for sources of accurate computerized astrological charts.

Get Acquainted with All Ten Planets

Astrology is primarily about the relationship of the *Planets* to one another at the exact time and place of a person's birth. Although the Sun and Moon are not actually Planets (astrologers call them "lights"), for the sake of convenience we are grouping them with the Planets. Using this method, the Planets are as follows, listed in order of their distance from the Sun—Mercury being closest to the Sun and so on.

Sun	Jupiter
Moon	Saturn
Mercury	Uranus
Venus	Neptune
Mars	Pluto

By including the Sun and the Moon in the planetary lineup, there is a total of *ten* Planets in every person's astrological chart, or horoscope. (The word *horoscope* is derived from the Greek word for *hour*.) As everyone has *all* ten Planets influencing his or her horoscope, you can easily see that *you are more than your Sun Sign.*

This is not to say that the Sun Sign isn't important—only that it isn't the total picture, which is what the popular newspaper and magazine horoscope columns and many oversimplified astrology books lead us to believe.

As you study this book, bear in mind that astrology is not destiny. It is an excellent tool for self-understanding, as is psychology, but neither practice is foolproof. That's why astrology is known as an *intuitive art,* even though it is based on strict mathematical calculations that give the precise relationships of the Planets to one another at the time of our birth. Astrology has been studied and practiced for centuries because people learned a very long time ago that certain characteristics of human beings could be related to the position of the Planets when they were born. *How* this works is still something of a mystery, just as the workings of the human mind remain mostly unknown despite constant and intense research. However, we know that astrology *works*—just as we know that the mind works, even if we don't know everything about its complexity.

You can use astrology to make your life work better in all areas. Also, getting acquainted with your Planets and your horoscope is lots of fun, and it will give you an advantage others don't have—and a jump on the competition in this very competitive world.

Astrology Is Earth Centered

It's important to know that everything in the sky is in constant movement, just as the Earth is always moving. The relationship of the Earth to the Signs of the Zodiac is the basis of astrology. We call this *geocentric,* which means "earth centered," because we treat the celestial objects— planets and stars—by what we see from our position on Earth, even though we know scientifically that the Sun is the center of our planetary system. If we were standing on the Sun, the Moon, or any of the Planets, we would see the sky differently than we see it from Earth.

Astrology in Ancient Times

With astrology, we have *centuries* of research and accumulated data, for the ancient peoples of Babylon, Egypt, Greece, and India were fascinated by what they saw in the sky at night. In those past times, astrology was one of the most important sciences. It was so important that only kings and emperors had their individual charts calculated, and their royal courts employed astrologers in the same way that we today employ government officials to predict the weather, look after the nation's health, and manage the country.

The Sun

The Sun is represented by a *glyph,* or picture, as a circle with a dot at the center. The circle is a symbol for eternity, for what has no beginning and no end, and it stands for the unity of everything in the universe. The dot at the center stands for the individual person, who is the point through which the universal energy (call it God, the One, the Source, or whatever suits your belief system) manifests into life. In other words, the dot stands for you as the center of your own life contained within the circle of the universe.

Sun

The Sun is the center of the chart, the core of who you are in *essence.* However, the Sun represents where you are going; it doesn't say how you are going to get there. That's the function of the other personal Planets.

Your Sun Sign says a lot about your *potential,* about what you can do with your life, but it doesn't tell you *what* to do. Each Sun Sign carries certain definite characteristics, but these are *inner,* not *outer,* facets of your emerging personality.

Your Sun Sign can give some overall clues about your identity, but it's important to remember that your Sun Sign is just one part of the total picture. Even though you may get a hit now and then from reading the Sun Sign horoscope columns in newspapers or magazines, those columns are much too generalized to relate to any specific individual. And you are an individual, not a generality!

Your Sun Sign functions primarily as your *sense of yourself*—your core identity. It is plain, however, that the process of growing and developing from a child through the teen years into a full-fledged adult is a complex matter involving many factors. Some of these are strictly internal—how you feel, what you want, what motivates you, what your learning patterns are—while others are external, such as where you live, what your parents are like, what religious training you do or don't receive, what teachers you have, who your friends and peers are, and what others expect of you. As a teenage person, you are in the process of learning about who you are and what you want to do with your life.

This process of growing into yourself and fulfilling the possibilities of your Sun Sign lasts a lifetime. It's not like getting a high school diploma or a college degree—once done, it's over. You are *always* growing toward what your Sun Sign represents and what it offers you. This is a slow process, and for this reason the standard characteristics of any one of the twelve Sun Signs may not show clearly at an early age. In fact, one of the reasons I took up the study of astrology was because I just could not identify with my Sun Sign. What I read about my Sign didn't seem to have much to do with what I knew about myself. Only after I realized that there's a lot more to astrology than the Sun Sign did I begin to understand who I was and what I might be able to do with my life. The same holds true, to one degree or another, for everyone.

Your Sun Sign is not a static quality in your life—as you get older you will express different aspects of your Sun Sign at different times. There's a lot to the Sun Sign, but it is not always obvious how it's operating at any one particular moment. That's because of all the other Planets and their influences, and that's why following astrological advice based solely on the Sun Sign is a big mistake. Trying to understand yourself—or anyone else—by just the Sun Sign is like wearing blinders. It's as if you walk into a living room and sit on the couch but don't see the table or the vase of flowers on it, ignore the bookcase, and don't look at the book titles. When you leave the room, you may know the couch is covered with blue-and-green plaid fabric that's a bit scratchy and that the cushions are soft, but you will have missed the entirety of the total room.

Put another way, your Sun Sign is what might be called your "I-consciousness," how you view the world from your standpoint as an

Sun Key Characteristics

Individuality	Egotism
The Father	Authority
Consciousness	Logic
Physical vitality	Left brain
Will	Lack of sensitivity
Ambition and drive	Pride
Creative potential	Self-consciousness

Key Words for the Sun in the Twelve Signs

The Sun expresses itself:

In **Aries,** through *action.*

In **Taurus,** through *stability.*

In **Gemini,** through *thinking.*

In **Cancer,** through *feeling.*

In **Leo,** through *creativity.*

In **Virgo,** through *practicality.*

In **Libra,** through *uniting.*

In **Scorpio,** through *desire.*

In **Sagittarius,** through *learning.*

In **Capricorn,** through *usefulness.*

In **Aquarius,** through *humanity.*

In **Pisces,** through *imagination.*

individual. Thus, the Sun in your chart represents or symbolizes *your conscious purpose in life,* or what you feel you are here on Earth to do and accomplish. Note that this is only your *potential*—there's no promise or guarantee implied. For example, the Sun in Capricorn suggests worldly success, but not every Capricorn Sun Sign is a corporate executive or a high-ranking military commander. Capricorn's energy definitely relates to the world stage, but how it plays out in an individual life is colored by multiple influences that we will be discussing throughout this book.

Moon

The Moon is best understood in terms of basic emotional needs, habit patterns, bodily rhythms, and what makes us feel comfortable. It represents what we *need* at a deep emotional level (as opposed to what we merely want). Your Moon shows what makes you feel *loved* and *cared for,* and it indicates what kind of environment makes you feel most *comfortable*—especially at home. Your Moon tells you what gives you a sense of personal security.

The Moon in the sky illuminates what is naturally dark, the night; the Moon in our *charts* reveals our inner emotional nature, which is often invisible even to ourselves. That part of ourselves that is often unseen in the bright light of day, when we are involved with external activities, comes alive in us at night, when the Moon sheds her gentle light. Then doors open to magical realms of the imagination and human creativity, often through the medium of dreams. Usually we dream when the Moon reigns over the world, and from our dreaming comes poetry, literature, art, music, and dance.

As with the Sun, other factors in addition to the Moon Sign must be considered. However, the more knowledge you have of your Moon, the better you will understand your inner, emotional self.

Your Moon needs are vital to your health and well-being. When they are not met, you become unhappy at the deepest core of your being. Illness can result, sometimes of the sort called *psychomatic.* These Moon needs stem from the time when you were in the cradle and dependent on others to provide what you needed for survival: nourishment, warmth, cleanliness, a sense of security, and most importantly,

The Moon

The Moon's glyph is a semicircle that looks like an open bowl. This shows the Moon as the *receptive* principle of the universe. If the Sun's circle represents your potential that has yet to come into being, then the Moon's semicircle represents what's already there—the physical body and your reactions to your environment, as well as your emotions and your natural tendencies to behave as you do.

Imagine that the Sun's circle is a reel of film. The inner dot is the projector. The lens and the beam of light allowing the projector to throw an image on the screen is the Moon (often called the soul).

love and affection. If you were deprived of these vital necessities, you will likely have emotional problems. The Moon is a knee-jerk place within us that sets off old behavioral and psychological patterns.

If our Moon needs are neglected or denied, we get out of balance. Sadly, because we live in a solar-dominated world (Sun=masculine) where paying attention to Moon needs is considered to be "sissy" or unimportant, especially for boys, problems can result.

The Moon represents your feelings. It is vitally important for you to get to know, respect, and honor them. Because the teen years are always full of emotional turmoil and confusion, teens especially can benefit from knowing their Moon Sign characteristics. They—often quite correctly—believe that others, especially their parents, don't understand them. All children need to feel nurtured, cared for, connected, and protected. In fact, one of the major causes of personal unhappiness is a sense of aloneness and isolation and a lack of feeling loved and cared for. Unfortunately, many teens do not get that fundamental caring and must learn to meet their needs themselves. Luckily, with Moon knowledge this can be done. Getting acquainted with your Moon will give you a powerful means of interpreting your inner world to yourself and communicating it to others.

Moon Key Characteristics

Feelings	Moods
Sensitivity	Femininity
The Mother	Dependency
Nurturing	Neediness
Changeability	Emotion
Food and cravings	Self-indulgence
Home and family	Attachment
Subconsciousness	Intuition

Exercise for Getting in Touch with Your Moon Self

Choose an hour of the day—say, from three to four in the afternoon—and sit quietly in a room by yourself with no distractions (such as music or TV). See what comes to your mind, how you feel, what you think, where your mind goes naturally.

Afterward, take that same hour in the *night* (or early morning) and repeat the procedure. Notice the differences between your sense of yourself during the day hour and your experience in the night hour.

If you let yourself be in tune with the celestial forces, you will *feel* your Moon's energies, for they are not only "out there," they are *in you!*

Key Words for the Moon in the Twelve Signs

The Moon expresses a need:

In **Aries,** for *activity.*
In **Taurus,** for *security.*
In **Gemini,** for *lightness.*
In **Cancer,** for *nurturing.*
In **Leo,** for *attention.*
In **Virgo,** for *orderliness.*
In **Libra,** for *harmony.*
In **Scorpio,** for *intensity.*
In **Sagittarius,** for *freedom.*
In **Capricorn,** for *results.*
In **Aquarius,** for *friendship.*
In **Pisces,** for *sensitivity.*

Mercury

Mercury's glyph is a combination of the cross of matter and the circle of spirit, plus the semicircle of the Moon. A complex symbol, it stands for the principle of active intelligence, for the circle is the activating force behind Mind. The semicircle indicates that we can receive information from two sources, the conscious and the unconscious, the rational and the intuitive.

Mercury

The fastest-moving of the Planets, Mercury is popularly considered a lightweight, partly because of his natural multiciplicity. Like quicksilver (another name for mercury, the metal), he can be all over the place at the same time. This quality has given Mercury a reputation for frivolity.

In his pure state, Mercury is the ultimate collector of information for its own sake. However, Mercury has more depth than most astrologers grant him. He deals with the various aspects of writing, speaking, learning, commerce, and message relaying. He is also Thoth, bringer of divine wisdom. In fact, Mercury is so many-leveled that being in his company is like riding a fast elevator past floor after floor offering thousands of things—some trivial and merely entertaining, others deep and profound. Where Mercury occupies the chart and how he relates to the other planets will indicate which of these thousands of things will most attract our interest and where we will put our energies regarding them.

Mercury is particularly relevant to teenagers who are just discovering the wonders of their minds and the power of their thoughts. Mercury is the Planet to consult about mental matters, especially now in this highly technological age. Not everyone is—or wants to be—a "techie," but knowing your Mercury characteristics will give you important clues about how to make the best of your natural mental abilities. Your Mercury can tell you what and *how* you learn, which in turn will give you a valuable tool for your education.

Mercury represents not only *how the mind works* and *how we learn* but also *how we comunicate*. As ruler of the thinking process that we call "rational," Mercury is the lens through which we focus our creative powers. The Sign position reveals our psychological cast of mind, while the House position (to be discussed in chapter 2) tells us where we are most activated in our thinking processes.

Mercury Key Characteristics

Communications	Technologies
Logic and analysis	Intellectualizing
Thinking	Cleverness
Messenger	Gossip
Learning	Superficiality
Adaptability	Nervousness
Ideas	Lack of focus

Key Words for Mercury in the Twelve Signs

Mercury expresses thinking:

In **Aries,** through *quickness.*

In **Taurus,** through *thoroughness.*

In **Gemini,** through *multiplicity.*

In **Cancer,** through *sensitivity.*

In **Leo,** through *dramatics.*

In **Virgo,** through *analysis.*

In **Libra,** through *harmony.*

In **Scorpio,** through *depth.*

In **Sagittarius,** through *learning.*

In **Capricorn,** through *organizing.*

In **Aquarius,** through *association.*

In **Pisces,** through *intuition.*

Mercury: Messenger of the Gods

In Greek mythology, Mercury was known as the messenger of the gods, which is why we see him represented with wings on his feet and cap. He was always depicted as a youth who was gifted with swiftness, and in his role as carrier of the gods' communications with one another he was honored as the patron of thought and its source, the human mind. Mercury has a special relationship with young people.

Venus

It will come as no surprise that the planet Venus relates to matters of love and romance, beauty and art. The mere mention of the word conjures up images, from the classically beautiful naked Greek statues to the busty and blond movie queens of whom the legendary Marilyn Monroe is the prime example.

But the goddess Venus, called Aphrodite by the Greeks, is a lady of great power, not some vapid cutie longing for love. Love is itself a powerful emotion. It is not to be taken lightly or to be confused with the sentimentality of Valentines. Our Venus natures are at the very core of our being.

Playing with love is like playing with fire—it's very exciting but can be dangerous. Teens especially can be hurt when they don't take love seriously enough and use the idea of it to fill in gaps in their lives instead of realizing that this powerful force needs to be handled with respect.

Falling in love with love is not the same as falling in love with a *person*. Unfortunately, too often teens make that mistake and come up either burned or empty-handed. That's why it is vital for you as a teenager to get to know and understand your inner Venus nature.

After the Sun and the Moon, Venus is the brightest object in the sky. And, like the Moon, she goes through "phases," from crescent to full. Perhaps the most interesting phenomenon about Venus is that she appears as the Morning Star during part of her cycle and as the Evening Star during the remainder of it.

Although Venus is our nearest planetary neighbor, she remains a mystery, resisting our scientific telescopic probes with a great mantle

Venus

Venus's glyph, or symbol, is a circle above a cross. Just like the circle of the Sun, the circle of Venus represents eternity. The cross stands for matter, or the earth. Together these represent the harmonious union of heaven and earth, or of the masculine and feminine principles. It's important to keep in mind that *both* sexes possess a Venus nature.

of clouds that veils her. Thus, her physical reality is the same as her effect on human emotions. Put simply, there's a lot we don't know!

So how do we interpret this goddess in the horoscope?

Venus represents the *affections;* she tells you about what you hold dear and describes your social nature.

Her process is *relating through the emotions.* This is generally expressed as love between the sexes, but that's not its only form. Appreciation of music and art, how we dress, what attracts us naturally, and sensuality (the use of all five of our physical senses: what we like to see, hear, smell, taste, and feel) are all Venus functions.

You can see that Venus represents *how we express love, what we want, our taste,* and *what makes us feel loved.*

Venus Key Characteristics

Beauty	Vanity
Affections	Sentimentality
Artistic sense	Superficiality
Social activities	Dependency
Sexual love	Promiscuity
Romance	Self-indulgence
Harmony	Cravings
Charm	Laziness

Key Words for Venus in the Twelve Signs

Venus expresses *love:*

In **Aries,** with *enthusiasm.*

In **Taurus,** with *sensuality.*

In **Gemini,** with *superficiality.*

In **Cancer,** with *nurturing.*

In **Leo,** with *dramatics.*

In **Virgo,** with *discrimination.*

In **Libra,** with *cooperation.*

In **Scorpio,** with *intensity.*

In **Sagittarius,** with *objectivity.*

In **Capricorn,** with *caution.*

In **Aquarius,** with *detachment.*

In **Pisces,** with *sensitivity.*

Mars

The glyph for Mars is a circle with an arrow protruding from it. The circle, as we have seen with the Sun and Venus, symbolizes the universal source. The arrow is energy being projected outward from it into physical life. As God of War, Mars is seen carrying a shield and a lance, and his symbol reflects this. It can also be read as a symbol for sexual arousal in both sexes.

Mars

Mars is entirely different from Venus, even though astrologers consider them as a pair (as will be seen in chapter 4). But Mars's function is to create *separation,* while Venus wants to create unity.

Known as the God of War, Mars is primarily *energy,* and especially sexual energy. Mars is about physical energy, not emotional energy. He represents everything we traditionally consider to be masculine. Qualities such as assertiveness, aggressiveness, action, drive, ambition, initiative, combativeness, and courage are Mars's territory.

This does not mean that girls and women don't have these qualities or are unable to express them. Anyone who has watched women's sports has seen female Mars energy in action. And there are lots of everyday activities in which females use their Mars energy, such as working out, making decisions, taking action of any kind, and, of course, being sexual, a topic we will discuss at length in chapter 4.

When we feel angry, we are feeling our Mars energy. But Mars isn't really a bad guy; just misunderstood and, often, misused. If we look

Key Words for Mars in the Twelve Signs

Mars expresses *action:*

In **Aries,** by being *heroic.*

In **Taurus,** by being *deliberative.*

In **Gemini,** by being *mental.*

In **Cancer,** by being *protective.*

In **Leo,** by being *courageous.*

In **Virgo,** by being *impersonal.*

In **Libra,** by being *diplomatic.*

In **Scorpio,** by being *determined.*

In **Sagittarius,** by being *uninhibited.*

In **Capricorn,** by being *serious.*

In **Aquarius,** by being *unconventional.*

In **Pisces,** by being *idealistic.*

at Mars as purely *energy*, we can understand that it can be used well or badly, just like nuclear energy can provide electricity or fuse bombs.

It's our Mars energy that gets things done. In fact, without the get-up-and-go energy of Mars, we'd all be lying down on the beach soaking up the sun, and no one would be playing beach volleyball. Or we'd be lolling around in the backyard with grass growing up around our ears. So we *need* Mars—but we need to learn to use his energy correctly.

Mars can make war or he can make love—it's the same basic energy in both cases. Mars says, "I will," and does it. Mars shows your heroic aspect. He shows how you *act*.

Jupiter

The largest Planet in the solar system is great Jupiter, as big as thirteen hundred Earth-sized bodies. It takes him twelve years to cycle through the twelve Signs. In Roman times, the god Jupiter was considered to be the defender of truth and justice.

Astrologers say that Jupiter is the "second Sun," which means he is a helpful Planet, bestowing generosity and good fortune. Jupiter represents the principle of *expansion*. (Interestingly, physically Jupiter is a big ball of gas—and gases tend to expand!)

Since Jupiter stays in one Sign for an entire year, everybody born during that year will have him in the same Sign as everybody else. So why is he important, especially to teens? It's because Jupiter is a *social* Planet. As the first not-strictly-personal Planet (because of his longer journey through the Signs), Jupiter is considered to be beyond merely physical matters and signals the first step into spirituality.

In spite of his high-mindedness, Jupiter is not unapproachable. *Your* Jupiter will be different from every one else's because he will be in your chart, and no two charts are exactly alike. We'll discuss individual Jupiter placements in chapter 6.

Jupiter's effect on you can be either personal or impersonal. Either way, he can indicate where your good fortune will come from and tell you about yourself as a spiritual person.

Teenagers need to know about their Jupiter in order to achieve the greatest success in adult life. This is because Jupiter's placement in your chart shows *how you grow beyond the personal sphere*. Once you leave school you have to deal with the world "out there," or society as a

Mars Key Characteristics

Motivation	Self-projection
Drive	Aggression
Physicality	Impetuousness
Action	Violence
Sexuality	Hostility
Bold	Anger
Up-front	Argumentative

Jupiter

Jupiter's glyph combines the semicircle of the Moon (soul) rising above the cross of matter. The significance of this symbol is that the human spirit can triumph over mere matter and understand universal law. Broadly speaking, universal law includes human law and higher education as well as religion, philosophy, and the ability to judge impartially.

Jupiter Key Characteristics

Expansiveness	Overexpansion
Optimism	Foolhardiness
Abundance	Exaggeration
Ethics	Judgment
Enthusiasm	Unrealistic
Principles	Dogma
Society	Hypocrisy

whole. All of your growing-up years are preparation for being an adult and functioning as a productive member of your society. That's where Jupiter comes in as a helper.

This is associated with the process of learning, but in a different way from Mercury, which is how you *personally* learn best. Jupiter represents the *function* of learning and is the ideological basis for systems of thought, whether philosophical or religious, orthodox or unorthodox. The beginning of the second Jupiter cycle starts your teen years, and by the end of it, you will be twenty-four years old. These are crucial years in your development, as they take you from puberty into full legal adulthood.

Key Words for Jupiter in the Twelve Signs

Jupiter expresses how we *integrate* what we learn about the world into our personal philosophy of life.

We integrate our learning:

In **Aries,** *immediately.*

In **Taurus,** *deliberately.*

In **Gemini,** *logically.*

In **Cancer,** *personally.*

In **Leo,** *self-referringly.*

In **Virgo,** *sequentially.*

In **Libra,** *indecisively.*

In **Scorpio,** *perceptively.*

In **Sagittarius,** *philosophically.*

In **Capricorn,** *conservatively.*

In **Aquarius,** *impersonally.*

In **Pisces,** *idealistically.*

Saturn

Saturn is Father Time as the old man with the scythe. But Saturn is also represented as a newborn babe. A major factor in career choice and development, Saturn is especially important to the late teenage years, when college or entering the workforce looms large on the horizon. There are many important choices to make, and teens can find themselves bewildered by them.

Even with parental help, you have to make your own decisions—and suffer the consequences if you make a mistake. This is where Saturn comes in as the Great Teacher. Saturn shows how and where you learn the lessons of dealing with the practical reality of life.

There is no escaping Saturn and his lessons, so it's best to be forearmed with knowledge about him and how he operates in your chart.

You may want to fly, but if you leap off the roof you will crash to the ground. You can, of course, fly in an airplane, but you walk its aisles just as you walk on the earth, held tight in position by gravity.

Saturn

Saturn's glyph is made up of the same two components found in Jupiter's—the semicircle and the cross—except that the two are inverted. While Jupiter's emblem symbolizes expansion, Saturn's represents the opposite principle of *contraction*. Thus, we think of Saturn as the Planet of restrictions and limitations imposed by physical reality.

Key Words for Saturn in the Twelve Signs

Your greatest lessons come:

In **Aries,** through *leadership.*

In **Taurus,** through *possessions.*

In **Gemini,** through *socializing.*

In **Cancer,** through *attachments.*

In **Leo,** through *pride.*

In **Virgo,** through *orderliness.*

In **Libra,** through *relationships.*

In **Scorpio,** through *sexuality.*

In **Sagittarius,** through *travel abroad.*

In **Capricorn,** through *ambition.*

In **Aquarius,** through *experimentation.*

In **Pisces,** through *spirituality.*

Saturn Key Characteristics

Discipline	Restriction
Practicality	Limits
Structure	Rigidity
Time-consciousness	Fear
Conservatism	Confines
Maturity	Caution
Wisdom	Restraint

(Don't be surprised if this list makes you think of your father—Saturn is a stand-in for the father principle.)

Uranus

Uranus's glyph looks something like a TV antenna—two out-facing semicircles are connected to the arms of a cross with a small circle at its bottom. The two semicircles represent the human and the divine, linked together by the cross of matter, or Earth. The small circle represents the energy force that makes it all happen.

Although you can jump out of a plane with a parachute and free-fall for a few minutes, you are always going down toward the ground. That's Saturn for you. He is the Planet that keeps you grounded. As I said, there's no escaping him. That's why it's a good idea to make friends with him early on in your life. Reality never goes away: it's always there to deal with.

Saturn does not really *limit* us—he only makes certain that we realize that limitations are inevitable in human life. He teaches us that personal growth and personal satisfaction are possible only through the fulfillment of our earthly obligations and responsibilities.

As a teen, you are required to go to school. Of course, you can drop out or just resist learning by refusing to do your homework. But if you do, you will suffer later unless you develop skills through some channel other than regular school.

School can be a bore and a chore, but it can't be avoided one way or another. So, no matter what choice you make, you will still be learning the lessons of Saturn.

Uranus

Uranus was the first of the "modern" Planets discovered since the invention of the telescope. The astronomer William Herschel spotted Uranus in the winter of 1781 as it passed through the constellation of Gemini—which may account for it being considered the "higher octave" of Mercury, which rules Gemini! Uranus is also called "the Higher Mind."

The lower octave Planets already discussed are concerned with the physical and material world, but Uranus, Neptune, and Pluto relate to humanity's spiritual evolution. This is because they take a long time to pass through all the Signs of the Zodiac—Uranus, for example, takes eighty-four years. Because of this, the slow-moving Planets affect the development of entire generations.

Although Uranus isn't a personal Planet, some astrologers (myself included) think that Uranus is indicative of the unique task each person has been given to fulfill during his or her lifetime on Earth.

Uranus symbolizes the urge for freedom from Saturn's restrictions. He shows us our free-spirited nature and how we express it. Primarily mental and *experimental*, Uranus indicates where we are original and innovative.

Most of today's teenage population belongs to either the generation with Uranus in Sagittarius (1981–1988) or Uranus in Capricorn (1988–1996). Children born between 1996 and 2004 will have Uranus in Aquarius, which he rules. They will be an interesting group of teenagers!

The Sagittarius generation came of age at just about the time of the new millennium—the year 2000. If you are one of these, you will question all previously accepted notions of society, including religion. Your generation is freedom-loving and attracted to new and innovative *ideas*. As a group, you will demand the right to think as you please and overthrow old ways of doing things.

If you belong to the Capricorn generation, you are part of a group that will also question all authority, but you will do it in an extremely practical and down-to-earth way. You will want to make changes, but you will be concerned about *how* to make those changes, in a manner that will *work*. You won't want to overthrow the government unless you have something better to put in its place!

Uranus Key Characteristics

Intuition	Undisciplined
Innovation	Rebellion
Unexpected	Spontaneity
Liberation	Explosive
Humanitarian	Activism
Revolution	Destruction
Insight	Originality

Neptune

Discovered on September 23, 1846, during the reign of Britain's Queen Victoria, who gave her name to an age in which lots of things were kept secret—especially sex—Neptune ushers us into the realm of mystery and illusion, deception and confusion. Representing all that is invisible and inspirational, mystical and otherworldly, Neptune is the *creative principle*. Where do ideas come from? Who knows? They materialize "out of the blue," which is where Neptune resides, far from our sight. Neptune is so far from Earth that he can be seen only with the aid of a very powerful telescope.

Neptune is like a marvelous singer of songs and teller of stories whose creations simply *flow out*. Being visionary, he doesn't much care if his visions are made concrete or "real," for unreality *is* his reality.

Older teenagers belong mostly to the tail-end part of the generation born while Neptune was in Sagittarius (1970–1984). Because of the length of time involved, social factors have to be considered, but in general, your generation has brought into being young persons who need to find positive expression for their higher spiritual values. Interestingly, filmmaker George Lucas's *Star Wars* was a major source

Neptune Key Characteristics

Imagination	Escapism
Inspiration	Confusion
Spirituality	Muddle-headedness
The Artist	Visionary
Creativity	Undisciplined
Dreamer	Substance abuse
Idealism	Self-delusion

Neptune

Neptune's glyph is a trident, just like the one that mythological Neptune carries in his undersea home. Known as the Lord of the Oceans, or King of the Seas, Neptune has always been involved with water. The trident is like a three-pronged fork. Each prong represents a part of human consciousness: the physical body with its five senses; the emotions and desires; and the mental processes that produce thoughts. Neptune unites these three elements to produce unity on the spiritual level, which gives rise to inspiration and visions. Hence, Neptune is the patron Planet of filmmakers, artists, poets, and dreamers of all kinds.

of inspiration to the Sagittarius generation of kids, and his new work continues that trend.

Those reaching teenhood recently belong to the generation born with Neptune in Capricorn (1984–2000), and they will be in their teen years during the first part of the new century, an awesome time! If you belong to this generation, you will face many challenges resulting from bad public policies of the past.

Children born after the new millennium (2000–2014) will belong to the long-awaited generation with Neptune in Aquarius. They will have the opportunity to create a truly new civilization, and their teen years will be important ones because of all the new technologies on the horizon. Many of them will experience extraordinary abilities, such as clairvoyance, at an early age. They will become seers.

Pluto

The most recently discovered inhabitant of our solar system was discovered only in 1930, which has not given astrologers much time to study it thoroughly. However, the general consensus is that Pluto has to do with the process of *regeneration,* which means the renewal of life. We can see this process all around us—vegetation decays and brings forth new growth; the caterpillar bursts out of its cocoon and turns into a beautiful butterfly; we make compost out of our kitchen scraps to provide nutrients for our gardens; the snake sheds its skin annually in order to keep growing larger, just as the crab and the lobster go through a "soft shell" period for the same reason. Everywhere we look, life is transforming itself from one form into another. And that's why Pluto is known as The Transformer. He brings about the end of one form so that a new form can be brought into existence. This process happens not only on the physical level, as described above, but emotionally and spiritually as well. All around us, all the time, change is happening both on the outside and on the inside. This is what transformation means. As you grow, you are gradually transformed from an infant to a toddler to a preschooler to a preteen to, finally, a teenager, who will one day become an adult. Pluto is the planet that oversees this process, which is fundamental to all life on Earth.

Pluto takes 244 years to circle the Zodiac, so no one ever experiences more than a small slice of this powerful Planet. But even that tiny fragment can cause major changes in your life. Every time Pluto touches anything in the chart, he releases powerful energies that can change a person's life dramatically, sometimes instantly!

Many of today's teens belong to the generation of Pluto in Scorpio (1984–1995), the Sign Pluto rules. There is a lot of intensity in those of you born during this period, and it may be difficult for your parents—born with Pluto in soft Libra—to understand how deeply you feel about things. So you need to get to work understanding yourself *now!*

The next generation of teens will have Pluto in the lighter sign of Sagittarius (1996–2007), and they will benefit from the preceeding generation's work. As you attain adulthood and infuse the world with your energies, you will set the stage for those who follow to bring forth new forms of religion and new ways of attaining freedom.

Pluto Key Characteristics

Revitalization	Change
Endings and beginnings	Destruction
Basic drives	Sexuality
Elimination	Obsessions
Transformation	Compulsions
Renewal	Cruelty
Destiny	Power

Pluto

Pluto's usual glyph is a simple symbol P, derived from the initials of Percival Lowell, the man whose mathematical calculations led to the discovery of the distant planet. However, Pluto has a second glyph also. It is a semicircle mounted on a cross, with a small circle floating within the half-circle. This glyph has ancient symbolic meanings. The semicircle (soul) is linked with the cross of matter (Earth), and hovering above the two is the circle of eternity. This combination says *universality*, and it suggests the entire cycle of birth-death-rebirth, or the continuity of life.

Practice Exercise: The Planets

List what you have learned about each of the Planets' characteristics below.

Sun _____

Moon _____

Mercury _____

Venus _____

Mars _____

Jupiter _____

Saturn _____

Uranus _____

Neptune _____

Pluto _____

The Planets I like best are _____

The Planets I like least are _____

The Planets I want to know more about are _____

The Signs of the Zodiac

The twelve signs of the zodiac lay down twelve different "paths" of life. . . . Every sign has its own manner of expression, both in a higher and in a lower sense, and it depends on the person which options to take and how to use them.

Karen Hamaker-Zondag,
Astro-Psychology

The *Zodiac* is a band of the sky divided into twelve sections, known as the *Signs,* which are named for constellations. As the *Planets* move on their individual paths across the sky, called "orbits," each one passes in turn through each of the Signs.

It's important to understand that every Planet is at all times occupying one or another sign of the Zodiac—which is like a great wheel of stars in the sky.

The Natural Order of the Signs

Each of the twelve Signs symbolizes certain unique characteristics. The Signs have a "natural" order that never varies, as shown below.

1. Aries symbolizes *beginnings*.
2. Taurus symbolizes *manifestation*.
3. Gemini symbolizes *mentality*.
4. Cancer symbolizes *emotions*.
5. Leo symbolizes *ego development*.
6. Virgo symbolizes *perfection*.
7. Libra symbolizes *relationships*.
8. Scorpio symbolizes *regeneration*.
9. Sagittarius symbolizes *idealization*.
10. Capricorn symbolizes *reality*.
11. Aquarius symbolizes *experimentation*.
12. Pisces symbolizes *spirituality*.

Remember that the Signs apply to *all ten Planets*, not just the Sun. Whether you have Planets in any specific Sign or not, your chart contains all twelve Signs just as it contains all ten Planets. Depending on which Planet (or Planets) is found in any Sign, you will be more or less typical of that Sign's general characteristics. Two or more Planets in the same Sign increase that Sign's emphasis. However, even if you have a dominant Sign, you will still express the energies of Planets in other Signs.

As an example of the above, suppose you have the Sun, Moon, and Mercury in the Sign of Aries. As these are all highly *personal* Planets, you would exhibit many of Aries's characteristics. Let's say you have the Planet Venus in the Sign of Cancer. While you might appear to be typical of Mars-ruled Aries, your inner love nature (Venus) would be soft and domestic (Cancer).

Each Sign has a planetary ruler. When a Planet is in the Sign that rules it, the influence of the Sign is increased.

Sign	Ruler
Aries	Mars
Taurus	Venus
Gemini	Mercury
Cancer	Moon
Leo	Sun
Virgo	Mercury
Libra	Venus
Scorpio	Pluto
Sagittarius	Jupiter
Capricorn	Saturn
Aquarius	Uranus
Pisces	Neptune

In addition to the Signs each having a planetary ruler, some Planets are considered to be "exalted," or "in honor," in some Signs. As there are twelve Signs and only ten Planets, not every Sign has an exalted Planet. A planet in the Sign of its exaltation is in its most powerful position and influences, the meaning of that Sign. For example, the Moon is exalted in Taurus, giving Taurus a strong connection to Moon ideas and symbols.

Sign	Exalted Planet
Aries	Sun
Taurus	Moon
Cancer	Jupiter and Neptune
Leo	Pluto
Virgo	Mercury*
Libra	Saturn
Scorpio	Uranus
Capricorn	Mars
Pisces	Venus

Each Sign has both a *symbol,* usually an animal (Aries's symbol is the Ram), and a *glyph,* which is a shorthand way of writing the Sign.

*Astrologers disagree about Mercury's exaltation. Some place it in the Sign of Aquarius. The entire subject of exaltations, and another classification known as "dignity," is complex and beyond the scope of this book. If you are interested further, consult *Horoscope Symbols* by Robert Hand, pp. 201–210.

♈ ARIES

"I seek my *Self.*"

Aries Key Characteristics

Outgoing	Aggressive
Active	Pushy
Adventurous	Rash
Pioneering	Self-centered
Energetic	Impulsive
Independent	Headstrong
Enthusiastic	Impetuous

The glyph for Aries can be interpreted as the horns of the Ram, seen charging. It indicates a person who is aware of being different and separate from the rest of humanity. Aries is the individual—it stands for the sense of "I am."

Aries symbolizes beginnings, and the person influenced by Aries acts like the Ram, Aries's symbolic animal. Thus, Planets in Aries express themselves by rushing out into the world headfirst, ready for adventure without much thought for the consequences. They seek what is new and exciting and like to start things (but aren't much interested in finishing what they start!).

Any Planet in Aries will exhibit some of these typical characteristics. As an example, if you have the Moon in Aries, your emotional nature will be impulsive and forthright; if Mars, Aries's ruling Planet, is found in his own Sign, you will be particularly headstrong and aggressive whether you are a boy *or* a girl. Girls may find it difficult to deal with this energy because it's not considered "nice."

I was born under the Sign of Aries.
I accept all its power, potential, and gifts.
I am the Pioneer of the Zodiac.
I accept my energy and ability
to launch new actions
for the betterment and benefit of myself
or for others.

☉ TAURUS

"I seek my Self through what I *have.*"

The glyph for Taurus is a semicircle (the Moon), which can also be read as the horns of the Bull, the animal that symbolizes Taurus, atop a circle representing the Earth.

Taurus is connected to all things of the Earth; its time is spring, when the soil is warming so that seeds can begin growing. A very relaxed Sign, Taurus has plenty of stamina for the long haul. The open bowl of the symbol indicates a vessel waiting to be filled.

Often the crescent, or cup, is filled with gold, for Taurus is the Sign of the wealth of the Earth—think of oil, minerals, and gemstones, all of which come out of the Earth's depths. The circle represents material abundance, and many Taureans become wealthy.

Taurus is shown as a great Bull—generally a placid creature unless he is taunted or disturbed at his grazing. An angry bull can be fierce and dangerous. Luckily, he will put up with a lot before charging.

In Taurus all planetary action, even fleet-footed Mercury, is slowed down and bent toward practical objectives.

Taurus Key Characteristics

Stable	Persistent
Steady	Determined
Reliable	Stubborn
Practical	Thorough
Productive	Wealthy
Sensuous	Nature-loving

I was born under the Sign of Taurus.
I accept all its power, potential, and gifts.
I am the Settler of the Zodiac;
I use stability and persistence
for the benefit of myself and others.

GEMINI

"I seek my Self through what I *think*."

Gemini Key Characteristics

Quick-witted	Versatile
Inquisitive	Many-sided
Flexible	Variety-seeking
Adaptable	Changeable
Talkative	Superficial
Intelligent	Nervous

The symbol for Gemini looks like the Roman numeral II, which perfectly describes the dualistic nature of this multilevel Sign. Gemini is a pair of Twins.

Known for its changeability, curiosity, quickness of mind, and rapid movement, Gemini typically speeds up any Planet in its Sign. As a mental Sign, it has the effect of "mentalizing" the Planets concerned with feelings, like the Moon and Venus. When in Gemini, these Planets behave unlike their usual selves, which can cause problems.

Venus, for example, is often fickle in Gemini and will act the flirt just for the fun of it. Gemini Planets don't like being serious and can lack persistence. This can undermine the standard serious Planets, such as Saturn and Mars.

No matter which Planets you have in Gemini, they will exhibit a dual nature, even if it's unnatural for them to do so. Having several Planets in Gemini makes it hard for people to commit to anything for any length of time. They always want to move on to something else, or else to be doing two or more things at the same time.

I was born under the Sign of Gemini.
I accept all its power, potential, and gifts.
I am the Twin Eyes of perception.
My keen perceptive intuition is
all that is needed
for the evolution of myself and others.

CANCER

"I seek myself through what I *feel.*"

The glyph for Cancer indicates the merger of the genetic material of the two sexes to produce children. It can also be seen as the Crab symbol. Cancer represents motherhood and nurturing. Moon-ruled, it is the feminine principles of home and family, which are based on emotional connection.

Obviously, Planets having to do with emotions—the Moon, Venus, Neptune—are comfortable in Cancer, which is personal and subjective. The energies of masculine-oriented Planets like Mars are watered down in this Sign and may seem weak, especially in boys' charts.

Cancer emotionalizes, but when mental faculties are colored by emotional response, rational judgment may be lacking. Mercury and Uranus have a hard time in Cancer because its watery nature interferes with their clear mental observation and detachment. Cancer, however, has the beneficial effect of softening the harsher Planetary energies.

Cancer Key Characteristics

Sensitive	Oversensitive
Nurturing	Dependent
Intuitive	Irrational
Traditional	Living in the past
Comfort-loving	Acquisitive
Food-oriented	Self-indulgent
Tenacious	Clinging

I was born under the Sign of Cancer.
I accept all its power, potential, and gifts
for I am the star in a sea of stars,
I am Water and the Moon,
I provide the haven, the safe haven, in the
universe.

LEO

"I seek my Self through what I *create.*"

Leo Key Characteristics

Dramatic	Attention-seeking
Generous	Dominant
Honorable	Keeping up appearances
Courageous	Self-glorifying
Fun-loving	Self-centered
Self-expressive	Insensitive
Warm	Overbearing

The glyph for Leo represents the heart and its functions. Leo's animal symbol, the Lion—king of the jungle—says it all! Leo is about self-confidence and ego development. Any Planet in Leo has strong needs for self-expression and requires admiration. Leo Planets exhibit personal integrity.

Leo's effect on Planets is a stabilizing influence, but it also makes normally impersonal Planets, like Mercury, self-referring. Planets in Leo need acknowledgment from others; the Leo Moon in particular needs a lot of feedback or else it becomes terribly insecure.

This need for personal recognition is sometimes interpreted as showing off, but Planets in Leo absolutely require themselves to be seen as impressive, and they will work hard to get that result!

However, there's no real arrogance to this need, for Leo naturally sees itself as the center of the universe, since its ruler is the great Sun—without which we'd all be dead. However, like the Sun, Leo's generosity gives off warmth.

I was born under the Sign of Leo.
I accept fully all its great power,
potential, and regal gifts.
I am the Monarch of the universe, I am
the Heart of hearts.
I am the heart of Creative Energy.

♍ VIRGO

"I seek my Self through what I *learn.*"

The symbol for Virgo is the Goddess of the Harvest, a maiden holding a sheaf of wheat. Its glyph is representative of the coils of energy within the bounty of food from the Earth.

On the nonphysical plane, Virgo is about the quest for perfection, which is harvested from the fields of experience. Virgo's aim is to be effective in the real world of practical results.

Although associated with the Earth, Virgo is really a *mental* Sign, but its mentality is related to the practical side of life, not the abstract.

Virgo's effect on Planets makes them work with precision and care, even if it goes against their nature. Virgo tones down the more active Planetary energies (like Mars) and harnesses them to the task of productivity. Mercury, Virgo's ruler, works well in this Sign, but the Moon is not at its happiest here.

Virgo Key Characteristics

Detail-oriented	Sensible
Helpful	Duty-bound
Work-oriented	Practical
Unassuming	Shy
Accurate	Fussy
Orderly	Criticizing
Precise	Neat

I was born under the Sign of Virgo.
I accept all its power, potential, and gifts.
I am the Magician of the universe.
I accept the healing and magical powers I
*   have or will use.*
The key for tapping into my deeper
*   resources is*
the ever-increasing acceptance of who I
*   am now.*

LIBRA

"I seek my Self through what I *unite.*"

Libra Key Characteristics

Relationship-oriented	Sociable
Needs partnership	Approval-seeking
Cooperative	Indecisive
Charming	Fawning
Refined	Judgmental
Companionable	Can't be alone

The glyph of two separate lines for Libra indicates the higher and the lower planes of duality, or the divine and the human spheres of life. Its symbol, the Scales, shows the effort to balance the two.

Libra is a complex Sign. Relating to marriage and the uniting of all opposites, its effect on the Planets is to bend them to its desire for harmony, balance, getting along, and being in a relationship that's not too heavy. This works well for Venus, Libra's ruler, and for the Moon, but Mars in Libra is a difficult placement, for Mars's natural aggressiveness is muted. It may go underground and surface as resentment. This placement indicates someone who is likely to create the kind of intimate, one-on-one relations that thrive on being combative or that flip-flop between passive and aggressive.

Although Saturn is exalted in Libra, he's not truly relationship-oriented—but then, he isn't exactly individualistic, either. His traditional role is in the obligation to the social world, through marriage.

I was born under the Sign of Libra.
I accept fully all its power, potential,
     and gifts.
I hold the celestial balance in my hands;
I am the Cosmic Judge.
I am the artist and the lover,
Peacemaker of the Heavens.

♏ SCORPIO

"I seek my Self through what I *desire.*"

The glyph for Scorpio can represent the coils of the Serpent, one of its symbolic animals, or the Scorpion, with its barbed tail raised to strike. The most complex of the Signs, Scorpio is full of mystery. It relates to both sex and death as well as to regeneration.

Its effect on the Planets is as intense as the Sign itself, and Planets in Scorpio operate with unusual emotional fervor. Even the most light-hearted, like Mercury, take on a dark coloration. Scorpio is anything but detached! Even loving Venus can sting viciously when placed in Scorpio. His influence on Planets is deep, and they demand privacy.

This makes Planets in Scorpio hard to understand, both for the person experiencing them and for those on the outside. A Scorpio Moon especially tends toward secrecy.

Having more than two Planets in Scorpio will make people prone to heavy-duty emotionalism, reluctant to communicate their feelings to anyone they don't completely trust, and wary of trusting because of being hurt. Teens especially have difficulty with Planets in Scorpio.

Scorpio Key Characteristics

Intense	Passionate
Secretive	Determined
Mysterious	Compulsive
Sexual	Vindictive
Regenerative	Destructive
Healing	Sarcastic

I was born under the Sign Scorpio
and I fully accept all its power, potential,
*   and gifts.*
As one of the most mysterious and power-
*   ful members of the Zodiac*
I am the Transformer,
I am the Keeper of Mysteries,
I am the Mystic.

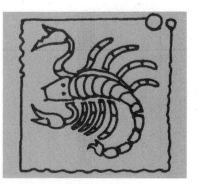

SAGITTARIUS

"I *seek,* therefore I am."

Sagittarius Key Characteristics

Enthusiastic	Outgoing
Optimistic	Eager
Independent	Loner
Ethical	Philosophical
Exploratory	Risk-taking
Travel-oriented	Restless
Straightforward	Blunt

The glyph for Sagittarius, an arrow split by a line on its shaft, illustrates a duality different from Gemini's—the problem of correctly aiming its tremendous physical and mental power. The Archer is also the *centaur*—half horse, half man. The horse part refers to the human instinctive nature.

Planets in Sagittarius express a desire for *freedom*. Sagittarius likes to be on the move constantly, either mentally or physically—or both!

Relationship-oriented Planets, like Venus and the Moon, can reverse themselves entirely when in Sagittarius and go out of their way to avoid relationship entanglements in order to preserve their precious freedom.

The physically oriented Planets do well in Sagittarius, which likes the outdoor life with plenty of exercise. At the same time, Jupiter-ruled Sagittarius loves learning and likes to travel as a learning experience. You can count on it: any Planet in the Sign of Sagittarius will be interesting, but it may cause the person to shy away from making a long-term commitment.

I was born under the Sign of Sagittarius.
I fully accept its power, potential, and
     gifts.
I am the Sage of the universe.
I am the Seer of the Zodiac.
I see the future now.
I remember the future.

♑ CAPRICORN

"I seek my Self through what I use."

The glyph for Capricorn represents its symbolic animal, the Mountain Goat, who is ever striving to reach the heights. Capricorn's ability to hang in there when the going gets tough is legendary.

Planets in Capricorn take on a seriousness that can be profound. Those that do best in the Sign are natural workaholics, like Saturn. Relationship Planets can feel restricted by Capricorn's relentless materialism. For example, Venus in Capricorn is likely to marry for money, not love. Mercury learns for practical ends.

Interestingly, Mars, exalted in Capricorn, doesn't get blocked but rather becomes disciplined and lends his energy to worldy achievement. Having several Planets in Capricorn will make a person dedicated to getting to the top of the heap, no matter how much effort it takes, or how long.

Capricorn Key Characteristics

Serious	Practical
Hard-working	Down-to-earth
Realistic	Disciplined
Focused	Responsible
Authoritative	Dominating
Decisive	Rigid
Traditional	Conservative
Trustworthy	Severe

I was born under the Sign of Capricorn.
I accept fully the potential, power, and gifts of
my Sign.
Like a growing crystal I initiate cosmic order.
I am enterprising, the Builder, the Organizer
who looks toward higher orders, greater
justice,
constantly building relationships, families,
communities, and countries.

AQUARIUS

"I seek my Self through Humanity."

The glyph for Aquarius is two jagged lines, representing waves. Alone of the Signs, the symbol for Aquarius is human—the "Waterbearer," a man pouring liquid out of a jug, which represents the divine spirit watering the Earth. This is an important Sign for the twenty-first century, which will usher in the long-awaited "Age of Aquarius."

Aquarius is the most emotionally cool of the Signs, known for its detachment from the messy emotional sphere. Having planets in Aquarius will make a person shy away from emotional involvement at any deep level. Aquarius would rather think *abstractly* about emotions than go to the bother of feeling them. For this reason, Planets concerned with emotions and relationships do poorly in this emotionally detached sign. Venus here tends toward buddies rather than lovers.

The Moon in Aquarius is an oddball, often hardly recognizable, but Mercury is totally at home here, along with Jupiter and, of course, Uranus, the ruler of Aquarius. Self-centered Mars has a problem in this humanitarian Sign.

Aquarius Key Characteristics

Friendly	Noncomforming
Scientific	Innovative
Humanitarian	Detached
Likes new ideas	Uninvolved
Group-oriented	Rebellious
Abstract thinker	Eccentric

I was born under the Sign of Aquarius.
I fully accept all its potential, powers, and gifts.
I am the promised power of the new age.
I am the Truth Sayer, the Scientist, the Revolutionary.
I am the genius Sign of the Zodiac.

♓ PISCES

"I seek my Self when I don't seek my Self."

Pisces's glyph is two semicircles connected by a crossbar, which suggests its self-contradictory nature—as does its symbol, two fish swimming in opposite directions.

Planets in Pisces find it difficult to live on the material plane (which, alas, can't be avoided!). They want to be somewhere out there in the stratosphere—where the atmosphere is unfettered by the necessities of ordinary life, such as having to feed, wash, and take care of a body—which can produce escapist tendencies involving drugs and alcohol.

Ultrasensitive Pisces affects its Planets with otherworldly notions sometimes quite out of keeping with the Planet's basic nature. Even the action Planets take on a dreamy, fantasy-prone quality under Pisces's influence. Mars, for example, has his energy sapped by Pisces's desire to merge with the entire universe. He can become quite muddled by it all, in the same way a big, strong man turns to melted butter when a sweet, innocent child crawls into his lap. Relationship Planets are extremely idealistic

Pisces Key Characteristics

Sensitive	Oversentimental
Imaginative	Overimaginative
Sympathetic	Prone to tears
Compassionate	Self-sacrificing
Artistic	Dreamy
Inspired	Self-deceiving
Introverted	Self-pitying

I was born under the Sign of Pisces.
I accept fully the potential, power, and gifts
  of my Sign.
The Cosmic Dreamer,
I am the Beloved, I am the Loving, I am
  the Poet.
I am the Divine Dark Warrior, I am the
  Divine White Healer.

The Zodiac Signs: Practice Exercise

Without looking back over the preceding chapter, how many of the Signs of the Zodiac can you list?

1. _____

2. _____

3. _____

4. _____

5. _____

6. _____

7. _____

8. _____

9. _____

10. _____

11. _____

12. _____

Now, go back and look up any that you missed and fill in the blanks. Then arrange them all in their "natural order," as listed on page 47.

Without looking up at any of your planetary placements, list the Signs that you feel best match your personality. (You probably already know your Sun Sign: does it seem true to who you are now?)

Meet the Ruler of Your Chart

There was a time when adults believed children were blank paper on which the parents could write what they liked, and this mistaken idea has caused enormous problems for generations of children. The fact is that every child is born into this world with distinct needs, desires, opinions, and tendencies. As anyone who has been in the presence of an infant or toddler for even a short time can readily tell, children have quite definite personalities. They are not little empty vessels waiting for parents, teachers, and others to fill them.

Although preverbal children can express their opinions and reactions only through immature means, express them they do! Whether by crying in despair, yelling with fury, gurgling with pleasure, or sleeping serenely, they do not fail to let others know their state of mind.

Later, when they begin to acquire a vocabulary, they use their few words most forcefully: *No! Me want! Go 'way! Mine!* are just a few definite and quite unmistakable expressions. These are usually accompanied by the appropriate body language, which enforces the child's expression.

How does it happen that even a tiny newborn is already a *person* to be reckoned with?

The flag-bearer for these inner traits is found in a point on the horoscope chart known as the *Ascendant* (ASC), which is the ruler of the entire chart. Another term for the Ascendant is the *Rising Sign*.

Having left childhood and reached your teen years, you have much more sophisticated means of letting others know what you want, what you feel, what you think, how you react. You can talk, reason, sulk, balk, cooperate, argue, cause trouble, or express yourself in any number of ways. Often, this is your Ascendant at work.

Because it is determined by the exact *time* and *place* you were born, the Ascendant is the *most personal* point in your chart and therefore one of the most important factors. It symbolizes the cosmic gate through which you entered life, and its qualities are as much a part of you as are your Planets' characteristics.

As the most personal point in the chart, the Ascendant is of equal importance to the Sun Sign. It can even be so strong as to overshadow the Sun.

In fact, as a teen you may find your Ascendant describes you better than your Sun Sign. It is an indication of your immediate reactions to new situations, and it shows *how you view the world from within yourself*. You *always* see the outside world through the lens of your Ascendant.

Naturally, babies and small children can express their Ascendant only by reacting, but as a child gets older, he or she uses the Ascendant differently.

Here's a brief overview of how your Ascendant is likely to behave in the different Signs:

Aries Ascendant is open and direct, taking the initiative and displaying energy and enthusiasm. Its key word is *action*.

Taurus Ascendant is pleasant but waits for the reactions of others, displaying sensuality and practicality. Its key word is *slowly*.

Gemini Ascendant is talkative, a conversation starter who displays wit and curiousity. Its key word is *communication*.

Cancer Ascendant is sensitive to the mood of the situation, feels shy, and displays warmth and caring. Its key word is *nurturing*.

Leo Ascendant is always up-front, is personally engaging, and displays generosity and style. Its key word is *attention-getting*.

Virgo Ascendant is restrained but analytical of the situation, displaying intelligence and seriousness. Its key word is *analyzing*.

Libra Ascendant is nice, polite, and harmonizing and displays diplomacy, tact, and good manners. Its key word is *socializing*.

Scorpio Ascendant is smoldering, making direct eye contact, and displaying sexuality and perception. Its key word is *thoughtfulness*.

Sagittarius Ascendant is humorous and full of high spirits, displaying playfulness and knowledge. Its key word is *outgoing*.

Capricorn Ascendant is managerial and matter-of-fact but reticent, displaying capability and integrity. Its key word is *serious*.

Aquarius Ascendant is open, shows interest in others, and displays humanitarianism and being unusual. Its key word is *friendly*.

Pisces Ascendant is shy while tuning in to the feel of a situation, displaying compassion and sensitivity. Its key word is *feeling*.

The flip side of the coin of the Ascendant is that it also shows how the world views you. You carry your Ascendant up front, like a waving banner going before you. Astrologer Robert Hand has termed the Ascendant the "outermost aspect of one's inner being."

Thus, the Ascendant is the most *visible* part of your total self—what you present, and what others see first. The Ascendant can also be used as a shield to protect those parts of your inner self you feel insecure about or don't want to exhibit.

What Is the Ascendant?

The Ascendant is the Sign of the Zodiac that was rising on the eastern horizon at the time and place you were born. The Planet that rules that Sign is the ruler of your chart. For example, if you were born with a Scorpio Ascendant, the ruler of your chart would be Pluto, which rules Scorpio.

Ascendant Key Characteristics

Personality	Self-observation
Physical body	Self-consciousness
Personal vitality	Self-awareness
The Mask	Self-image
Conscious focus	Self-expression
Appearance	Self-acceptance
Facial structure	Self-analysis

Key Words for the Ascendent in the Twelve Signs

The Ascendent expresses its first response to a new situation:

In **Aries,** by *acting.*

In **Taurus,** by *waiting.*

In **Gemini,** by *talking.*

In **Cancer,** by *nurturing.*

In **Leo,** by *leading.*

In **Virgo,** by *helping.*

In **Libra,** by *relating.*

In **Scorpio,** by *being intense.*

In **Sagittarius,** by *enjoying.*

In **Capricorn,** by *managing.*

In **Aquarius,** by *detaching.*

In **Pisces,** by *feeling.*

A mathematically correct horoscope (plotted for both the exact time and the exact geographical location of birth) identifies the precise *degree* of the Sign appearing on the horizon at the moment of birth. This is important, for the Ascendant acts to set up the division of the chart into its twelve houses, which we will discuss in the next chapter.

In addition, the Ascendant fixes the Planetary relationships permanently—like a snapshot of the heavens at the moment of birth. The astrological chart becomes your own celestial fingerprint, unique to you alone, for no two charts are exactly alike.

It's important to understand that the Ascendant is not a Planet: it is a point in time and space. Nonetheless, understanding it is vital to your ability to understand yourself.

Putting the matter another way, the Ascendant is the mask that we wear in public. It is what comes naturally when we are required to deal with any new social situation. If you're alone and get a flat tire, your Mars or Moon might come leaping forward. But if you are with someone you don't know well, the Ascendant will step in and handle the situation.

Sometimes we feel we have to "put on a front," and the Ascendant is that front. This is not to say it is a false front, for the Ascendant is as much a part of you as are your Sun and Moon and other Planets. It's just that the Ascendant is what is immediately apparent about you.

Sometimes you might want to conceal your Moon nature, because that's the most sensitive, innermost area of life, or you might have a hard time revealing your Sun nature, because that's the deep core of who you are. But your Ascendant will always be up front and right there for all to see. And you will always view the world through the perspective of your Ascendant.

The Ascendant:
Practice Exercise

1. Without first looking up your Ascendant Sign, see if you can figure out what it is by reading the preceding descriptions of how the Ascendant causes you to act.
2. Next, find your Ascendant using the instructions on pages 44–45 and see if you got it right.
3. Practice this on people you know and soon you'll become an expert at correctly guessing the Ascendant sign just by careful observation of another person.

The Natural Order of the Signs

♈	Aries	♎	Libra
♉	Taurus	♏	Scorpio
♊	Gemini	♐	Sagittarius
♋	Cancer	♑	Capricorn
♌	Leo	♒	Aquarius
♍	Virgo	♓	Pisces

How to Find Your Ascendant Sign

By using your Sun Sign, you can find your Ascendant (or rising Sign) with the following simplified method. Bear in mind that this is only an approximation, as it is not possible to determine the exact degree of the Ascendant without complex mathematical calculations that are beyond the scope of this book.

The numbered pie-shaped slices of the wheel opposite correspond to times as shown below. The horizontal line that begins the section marked "1" is the point of the Ascendant, or "cusp" of the first House of the chart. The Ascendant is not a *body* in space, but a *point* on the horizontal plane across the chart from the Descendant—its opposite point. These points are less like energies and more like places where energies can manifest.

1	=	4:00 A.M.–6:00 A.M.
2	=	2:00 A.M.–4:00 A.M.
3	=	MIDNIGHT–2:00 A.M.
4	=	10:00 P.M.–MIDNIGHT
5	=	8:00 P.M.–10:00 P.M.
6	=	6:00 P.M.–8:00 P.M.
7	=	4:00 P.M.–6:00 P.M.
8	=	2:00 P.M.–4:00 P.M.
9	=	NOON–2:00 P.M.
10	=	10:00 A.M.–NOON
11	=	8:00 A.M.–10:00 A.M.
12	=	6:00 A.M.–8:00 A.M.

To use this method, first find your Sun Sign using the table on page 4. Then write your Sun Sign in the section of the chart that corresponds to your birth time, taking daylight saving time into consideration if it applies. For example, if you were born between 2:00 and 4:00 A.M. and your Sun is in the sign of Capricorn, you would write "Capricorn" in the 2:00–4:00 A.M. section of the wheel, or House number 2.

You can photocopy the larger blank wheel on page 47 and use it to find Ascendants for different people.

Next, using the natural order of the Signs, as given at left, place a Sign in each section moving in a counterclockwise direction. In my example, Capricorn in the 2:00–4:00 A.M. section would be followed by Aquarius in the midnight–2:00 A.M. space and Pisces in the 10:00 P.M.–midnight section, and so forth. When you reach Pisces, start with Aries and so on until you have a Sign in each section. The Sign that falls in the first House, marked with a "1", will be the Rising Sign. In the sample given, the Rising Sign would be Sagittarius.

For most people this method will work satisfactorily; however, for some people there will be two possible Rising Signs—one Sign forward or one Sign back—if the birth time is very close to the beginning or ending time segment. If, for instance, birth time was 5:45 A.M., your Ascendent could be the Sign in the 6:00 A.M. to 8:00 A.M. section; and if time of birth is 6:10 A.M. it could be the Sign in the 4:00 A.M.– 6:00 P.M. section. The rising Sign could also be one Sign forward or back if the birth date is at the very beginning or at the very end of the Sun Sign. If the Rising Sign is in doubt, read the descriptions of the two signs that were rising during the applicable time span. It may be obvious which applies.

If the rising Sign is on the borderline between two Signs, or if the Sun Sign is in doubt, resolve the problem with a computerized chart. See appendix 2, Computer Resources.

Note:

The horizontal line across the chart represents the actual horizon—Planets below the line, that is, in the first through sixth Houses, have not yet risen (hence, "Rising Sign"); Planets above the line have already risen and are above the horizon. The twelfth House shows the Planets that rose in the two hours before dawn; the Houses in descending numerical order (eleven, ten, etc.) indicate how long before dawn the Planets rose. It is, of course, actually the Sign that is rising, but as the Planets always occupy one or another Sign, they perforce rise when the Sign rises, with the result that all the Planets (and the Moon) can rise at any time of day or night depending on the Sign they are occupying.

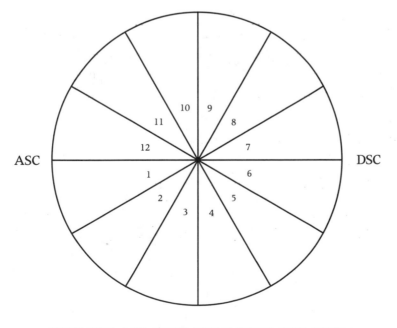

A Tour of Your Horoscope's Working Parts

The horoscope seems to act as a schematic diagram of one's intentions in life. It only shows what one is going to experience because one intends to experience it. It is a description not of what is going to happen (that is destiny), but of what one is and what shape one is going to give to one's life.

Robert Hand

Where It's Happening:
The Houses of Your Chart

Now that you know you have ten Planets and that each of your Planets is in one of the twelve Signs of the Zodiac, you need to understand *where* the action is taking place.

The Planet tells you *what kind of action,* and the Sign tells you the focus of the action. The Houses tell you *in what area of your life the action takes place.*

Think of the Houses as the stage settings where the Planets act out their energies. Just as every Planet is always in one of the Signs (in the sky as well as in your chart), every Planet is in one of the Houses of your chart. (There aren't any houses in the sky! This is "astro-speak.")

As you learned in the last chapter, your Ascendant Sign *begins* your chart, which means that it describes characteristics of your first House. That first House is your *personal* domain, unconnected with other people. It's where you express yourself.

Knowing your Ascendant Sign, you are now ready to find out what Houses each of your Planets falls in. (See the planetary tables in appendix 1 to find out which Signs your Planets occupied at the time you were born.) Using the blank horoscope form below, begin by placing your Ascendant Sign in the first House. Continue on, following the natural order of the Zodiac and put a Sign in each house. Then place each of your Planets in the appropriate House. You won't have a Planet in every House and you may have more than one Planet in any given House. Keep this completed chart as a reference as you read through this book to learn more about the Planets and how they operate.

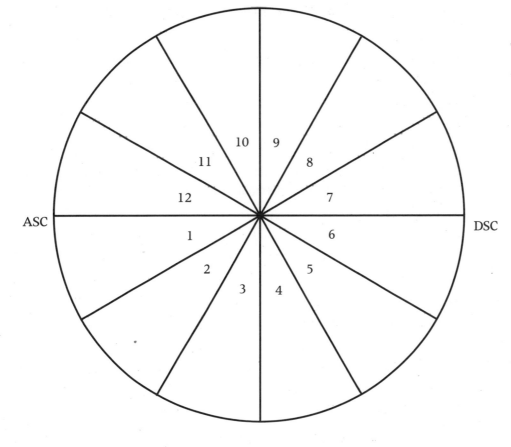

Natural Order of the Zodiac

♈	**Aries**
♉	**Taurus**
♊	**Gemini**
♋	**Cancer**
♌	**Leo**
♍	**Virgo**
♎	**Libra**
♏	**Scorpio**
♐	**Sagittarius**
♑	**Capricorn**
♒	**Aquarius**
♓	**Pisces**

Remember that the House position of the Planets is an important factor. For example, a first-House Sun will take on some of the characteristics of Aries, the "natural" Sign of the first House, exaggerating the Sun's already self-centered nature.

On the other hand, a first-House Moon will personalize your emotions to a much greater degree than would the Moon in another House. As you read through the significances of the Houses, look at where your Moon is and see if you can understand how your emotions are colored by the House position of your Moon, regardless of its Sign.

The Symbolic Meaning of the Twelve Houses

House One   Personality—how you interface with the world, your appearance, the impression you make, the image you project.

House Two   Your material resources and what you value, both materially and spiritually. Your personal possessions, your money or income, and your attitudes toward them.

House Three   Your connections with your immediate environment, neighbors, and relatives (except parents); daily communications; ordinary, regular travel and movement, such as going to school.

House Four   Your home and family, your base of operations, how you are nourished (food, love, approval), where your roots are, and what supports you.

House Five   What gives you pleasure, how you have fun, your sense of play and creativity, what you enjoy, what you find beautiful and pleasing, and your attitude toward children.

House Six   Your sense of yourself in terms of helping others, your health, your bodily functions, how you are effective in school, and how you accomplish your work.

House Seven   Your one-on-one relationships with your parents and friends, your romantic involvements, and your attitude toward partnerships, especially marriage.

The Houses: Practice Exercise

Once you have placed all your Planets in the Houses around your chart, make a list of them following in the example below. (Remember that you won't have a Planet in every house, and you may have more than one Planet in any given House.)

House 1 = _____

House 2 = _____

House 3 = (Moon) _____

House 4 = _____

House 5 = (Sun) _____

House 6 = _____

House 7 = _____

House 8 = (Mercury) _____

House 9 = _____

House 10 = (Mars) _____

House 11 = _____

House 12 = _____

After listing all your Planets through your Houses, use a separate piece of paper to write a brief description of how each of *your* Planets functions in its House. Describe how you feel each Planet affects your life by its House placement. *Example:* My third-House Moon means that I am emotionally connected to communication and my immediate environment. *Example:* I get emotional satisfaction when I send e-mail to my friends and siblings.

House Eight   Matters relating to the past, older relatives or wise teachers, money from other people, your inner resources, and your attitude toward mutual possessions.

House Nine   Your higher education, your attitude toward the larger world, how you broaden your horizons, and your attitude toward visiting foreign countries and meeting foreign people.

House Ten   Your connection to society at large; your public achievements, activities, and honors. Your vocation; authority figures in your life and your attitude toward them.

House Eleven   Your aspirations, your relationships with those with whom you share like interests, groups you belong to.

House Twelve   What's hidden from the rest of the world, your dreams and inner life, how you are imaginative, your religious point of view, and where you are addictive.

Helpers and Hindrances:
The Meaning of the Four Major Aspects

The Planets are always related to one another in some fashion because they are all part of the same solar system. The way they relate to one another is arrived at mathematically, and astrologers call these relationships *Aspects*. The Aspects formed when you were born are fixed in your natal, or birth, chart.

The Aspects refer to your personal dynamics. You might envison your horoscope as a crystal, and its faces are defined by the Aspect lines between each Planet. What shape is your crystal? The Aspects answer the question.

Aspects can also be seen geometrically as slices of the circle of the Zodiac. Since the Zodiacal circle is made up of 360 degrees, if you slice it in half you get two 180-degree sections, or half of the Zodiacal pie. Planets that are 180 degrees apart are said to be in *Opposition*. If you cut the circle into four equal parts, each will be 90 degrees, a right angle. This Aspect is called a *Square*.

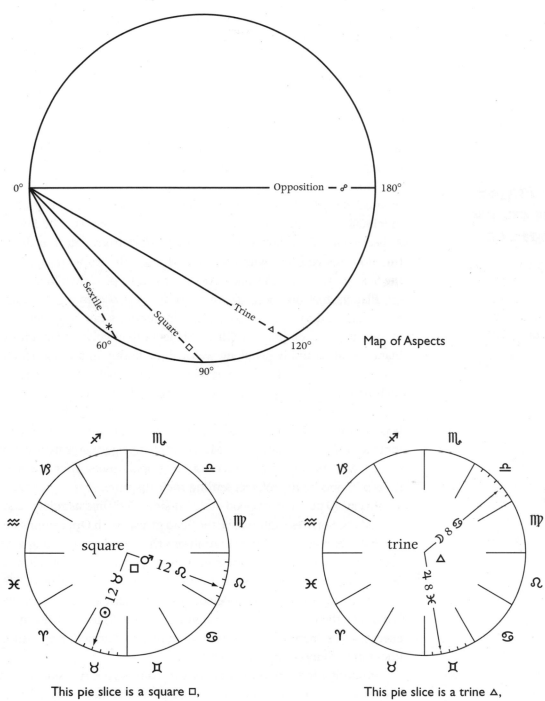

Map of Aspects

This pie slice is a square □,
¼ of the 360° circle (90°).

This pie slice is a trine △,
⅓ of the 360° circle (120°).

The Major Aspects by Degrees

Conjunction	0°
Sextile	60°
Square	90°
Trine	120°
Opposition	180°

Opposition and Square aspects are related in that they are considered "dynamic," which can also mean difficult. These two Aspects present challenges. With Oppositions and Squares, you have to *integrate* different energies, which isn't always an easy task. However, the act of integrating these parts of yourself strengthens you. Your Aspects make you who you are, whether you find them difficult or exhilarating.

If you divide the circle by three, you will obtain a 120-degree angle, which is called a *Trine*. Divide by six and you get half a Trine, or a 60-degree angle, which is called a *Sextile*.

Trines and Sextiles are similar Aspects. The Trine makes things easy, because Planets in Trine Aspects get along well together and work harmoniously without you having to put forth any effort. The Sextile Aspect is also easy, but it requires some effort from you in order to function. It's said that with the Trine, things fall into your lap; with the Sextile, you have to walk across the room to pick them up.

Planets that are close together—ordinarily occupying the same Sign—are said to be in *Conjunction*. Conjunctions can be either easy or difficult, depending on which Planets are involved. Obviously, Planets that naturally get along well will be happy in a Conjunction, while those that are at cross-purposes will fight each other's energies, each trying to dominate the other. For example, Sun conjunct Moon will mean that your outer and inner selves are comfortable together because they are cozily connected in the same Sign. But if Mars is conjunct Moon, trouble can result. Mars's outgoing, aggressive nature may disturb Moon's inner peace and cause emotional upsets. Then you have to step in and be the referee, settling their disputes.

Every Aspect has its good and bad side. Old-time astrology considered the Squares to always be the "bad guys," with Oppositions not much better regarded. Trines were always the "good guys," along with their sibling Sextiles. Now, however, astrologers are more sophisticated. We know that different Aspects are necessary to create a balanced life. Too many Trines can make a person lazy and colorless, for when life is too easy there's no reason to do anything. Many Squares create much energy, but sometimes it uses itself up in its own turmoil, like a storm knocking around things in its path.

Properly used, any Aspect can be turned to its positive side, which is why you need to know about *your* Aspects and how they operate. Aspects are a window into your personality and behavioral patterns.

Compatible Planets in Conjunction with one another usually express their energies positively. *Incompatible* Planets have a harder time combining their energies and may cause difficulties.

Study the key words for each aspect listed with the description of its symbolic meaning. You will notice that some key words are positive and some are negative. If you are currently expressing the energies of your Aspects in a negative manner, don't worry! That's why you are here on Earth—to learn how to express all of yourself in a positive manner.

To tune in to the positive energies of your Aspects, use the affirmations given for each Aspect.

Symbolic Meanings of the Aspects

Conjunction   The symbolic meaning is *an emphasized unit,* or two energies that reinforce each other and focus dynamic action. *Where* the action is focused depends on the House position; *how* it is focused depends on the Sign in which the Conjunction occurs. Note that it is possible for two Planets to be conjunct, or less than 10 degrees apart, while occupying adjacent Signs. When this type of Conjunction occurs, it is called an out-of-Sign Conjunction, and it not as strongly unified.

Affirmation for Positive Use of Conjunctions   I now express the power, potentials, gifts, and positive uses of my horoscope Conjunctions. Their concentrated and unified energies allow me to *initiate* and *fulfill* my aims and purposes

Square   The symbolic meaning of the Square Aspect (90 degrees apart) is *contrast between two different energies.* The Square gives a sharp awareness of difference and requires you to make choices. Sometimes you will prefer to use one of the energies over the other, and you might switch back and forth between the two at different times in your life.

Key Words for Conjunctions

Joins	Binds
Touches	Restricts
Strengthens	Overwhelms
Empowers	Conceals
Activates	Masks
Energizes	Overrides

Key Words for Squares

Challenges	Irritates
Motivates	Inhibits
Impassions	Blocks
Reorients	Obstructs
Tests	Frustrates
Disciplines	Delays

Squares in the chart are where we are challenged and tested, and although they can be difficult they also give us dynamism. If you are not aware of the sources of your inner conflicts, it is hard to resolve them. That's where astrological understanding can help. Once you know what's going on and where it's coming from, you are in a position to be in control. Squares are not "bad," but they do make you work!

Affirmation for the Harmonious Expression of Squares

I now express the power, potentials, gifts, and positive uses of my horoscope Squares. I meet challenges squarely and head-on, without fear. I choose wisely between possibilities with trust that I am making the right choice. I am motivated to find meaningful direction for my life. I develop my awareness more and more every day.

Key Words for Oppositions

Balances	Opposes
Cooperates	Restrains
Involves	Stresses
Controls	Confines
Makes aware	Restricts
Manifests	Limits

Opposition   The symbolic meaning of the Opposition Aspect (180 degrees) is the need for *balancing* two opposing energies, which requires the *interaction* of those energies. Like the Square, the Opposition is considered a difficult Aspect—its very name suggests conflict. Yet opposites also attract. They are reconcilable and can be complementary. Although the energies linked by the Opposition can produce seesaw-like instability, if you are willing to work with them you can get them to cooperate. Until you learn how to handle your opposition energies, though, you will probably swing back and forth between them. For example, a Jupiter/Saturn Opposition might make you go from generosity to stinginess and back again. To effect a balance, you'd have to curb your urge to be generous (Jupiter) with the reality (Saturn) of your resources so that you don't give away your lunch money and end up going hungry.

Below is a chart to show you quickly which Signs are in Opposition or Square Aspects to each other. From this chart you can determine which of *your Planets* (by their Sign position) are in either Opposition or Square Aspect.

Affirmation for the Harmonious Expression of Oppositions

I now express the power, potentials, gifts, and positive uses of my horoscope Oppositions. I am aware of different energies, both within myself and between myself and others. I experience myself through interaction with others, resolving tensions into harmonies creatively. My relationships with my inner energies in Opposition and with others are *creative partnerships*.

Determining Squares and Oppositions by Signs

Aries	*Opposite*	Libra
	Square	Cancer/Capricorn
Taurus	*Opposite*	Scorpio
	Square	Leo/Aquarius
Gemini	*Opposite*	Sagittarius
	Square	Virgo/Pisces
Cancer	*Opposite*	Capricorn
	Square	Aries/Libra
Leo	*Opposite*	Aquarius
	Square	Taurus/Scorpio
Virgo	*Opposite*	Pisces
	Square	Gemini/Sagittarius
Libra	*Opposite*	Aries
	Square	Cancer/Capricorn
Scorpio	*Opposite*	Taurus
	Square	Leo/Aquarius
Sagittarius	*Opposite*	Gemini
	Square	Virgo/Pisces
Capricorn	*Opposite*	Cancer
	Square	Aries/Libra
Aquarius	*Opposite*	Leo
	Square	Taurus/Scorpio
Pisces	*Opposite*	Virgo
	Square	Gemini/Sagittarius

How to Determine Trines by Signs

Any Planet that falls in any of the three groupings of Signs is automatically in a Trine Aspect by Sign to Planets in the other two Signs.

Aries, Leo, and Sagittarius all trine one another. For example, Mars in Leo is trine Moon in Sagittarius.

Taurus, Virgo, and Capricorn all trine one another. For example, Jupiter in Virgo is trine Saturn in Capricorn.

Gemini, Libra, and Aquarius all trine one another. For example, Mercury in Gemini is trine Sun in Aquarius.

Cancer, Scorpio, and Pisces all trine one another. For example, Venus in Cancer is trine Pluto in Scorpio.

Trine   The symbolic meaning of the Trine Aspect (120 degrees) is *stable and harmonious interaction between two energies*. The Trine Aspect allows a peaceful and natural harmony to flow between the Planets. With the Trine Aspect, you experience a smooth interaction of the Planets' energies.

Sextile   The symbolic meaning of the Sextile Aspect (60 degrees) is *opportunity for creative expression of your talents*. The Sextile Aspect provides energy for realization of your natural impulses toward insight and self-understanding. It also symbolizes where you function smoothly with yourself.

Key Words for Trines

Flows with	Indulges
Energizes	Lulls
Encourages	Promotes complacency
Works easily	Excessive
Benefits	Makes lazy

Affirmation for the Harmonious Expression of Trines

I now express the power, potentials, gifts, and positive uses of my horoscope Trines. My life *flows smoothly* through the *creative cooperation* of different energies. I affirm the blessing of this natural harmony in my life.

How to Determine Sextiles by Signs

As there are 30 degrees to each Sign, and as the Sextile Aspect represents Planets that are 60 degrees apart, every other Sign forms a Sextile Aspect to the Signs that fall before and after it. The following table shows the Sextiles for each Sign.

Sign	Sextiles
Aries	Gemini, Aquarius
Taurus	Cancer, Pisces
Gemini	Leo, Aries
Cancer	Virgo, Taurus
Leo	Libra, Gemini
Virgo	Scorpio, Cancer
Libra	Sagittarius, Leo
Scorpio	Capricorn, Virgo
Sagittarius	Aquarius, Libra
Capricorn	Pisces, Scorpio
Aquarius	Aries, Sagittarius
Pisces	Taurus, Capricorn

Key Words for Sextiles

Cooperates	Too easygoing
Helps	Makes no effort
Takes opportunities	Misses opportunities
Develops talents	Lacks drive
Thinks about	Intellectualizes
Informs	Overlooks

Affirmation for the Harmonious Expression of Sextiles

I now express the power, potentials, gifts, and positive uses of my horoscope Sextiles. I see *positive opportunities for the expression of my natural talents.* I use these opportunities when they appear to further my creative development. By using them, I am able to bring out my best.

Using the key words you have learned throughout this book for the Signs, Planets, and Houses, make *sentences* to express some of your Aspects. Following is a sample interpretation of an Opposition Aspect.

Sample Interpretation of an Aspect

Moon in	**Taurus** in the	**Seventh House**
Needs	Stable	One-to-one relationships
Emotions	Practical, Sensuous	Partners

OPPOSITE

Jupiter in	**Scorpio** in the	**First House**
Expansion	Intense	Personality
Generosity	Powerful	The Body
Optimism	Passionate	Self-projection

In the above example, Moon = *need;* Taurus = *stability;* seventh House = *relationship;* opposition = *stress;* Jupiter = *generosity;* Scorpio = *intensity;* first House = *personal way of expressing the self.*

Your sentence might read like this:

My need for stability in a relationship means that I feel stress between it and my generous, intense, personal way of expressing myself.

How would you work to solve this? Go back and look at the symbolic meaning of Oppositions. The key here is *balance.* You would need to balance your need for a close, personal relationship with your intense personality.

Exercise for Understanding Your Aspects

Figure out your Aspects using the tables on pages 55 and 57 and make sentences for all of them. Write down the sentences and study them to see how they relate to you and your feelings about yourself. Rewrite them so that they express how you see yourself, and then make a plan to work with your Aspects, and the Planets affected, to use them positively.

Your Personal Weather Forecast:
Your Elemental Type

Fire, Earth, Air, and Water—these are the *Elements* in astrology and in life on earth. You encounter them every day in ordinary life. For example, the heat of the sun comes from fire; we cook with fire and heat our homes with it. If you play with it carelessly, you can burn yourself. Forest fires destroy millions of dollars' worth of property annually. So, is Fire good or bad?

Clearly it has two sides, as do all the other Elements. And you have all four Elements in your chart and in your psyche. One or more of them will be emphasized. That's why as a teen you need to know your *Element type* and how the different types relate to one another.

Your basic elemental nature tells a lot about you, and it also tells a lot about those other people you interact with, like parents, friends, and teachers. Sometimes you will feel naturally comfortable with someone right away—usually because you are elementally compatible. On the other hand, you might meet someone and immediately back away. That's likely to be because you are elementally incompatible.

Elements that are alike get along together—Fire loves Fire, Earth and Earth never argue, Air feels comfortable with fellow Air, and Water flows easily with Water. *Different* Elements are either compatible or incompatible. Fire and Air get on well, while Earth and Water blend comfortably. Fire and Water irritate one another and Earth smothers Air.

There are four basic types related to Fire, Earth, Air, and Water. You may be a single type, a mixture of two types, or a multiple type.

You must determine your natural affinity for each of the four Elements in order to discover your type. Then you can tune in to your basic type and use its elemental energy to harmonize yourself and your relationships.

The Elements in the Signs

Fire—Aries, Leo, Sagittarius
Earth—Taurus, Virgo, Capricorn
Air—Gemini, Libra, Aquarius
Water—Cancer, Scorpio, Pisces

Finding Your Elemental Type

Here's a fun way for you to find out what your basic elemental type is. Treat this exercise like a game—have fun with it. Consider it an exploration of the unknown territory of your secret self. You may find emphasis on one type or another (especially if you are a mixed type) at different times of the month, day, or year, or over a lifetime.

From the word lists on the facing page, choose *only* the words that apply to you. Make four columns with headings that read "always," "often," "rarely," and "never" and rate the degree to which each word applies to you.

Using a set of colored pencils or markers, choose a color for each word and write it on your list in that color. You may find that you are consistently choosing the same or similar colors for words from a particular list or that certain words or groups of words seem to belong in a specific color. Don't try to think or decide what goes with which—just let the process flow from your interior self until you feel you have finished. Choose as many or as few words as you like. You don't have to work in any particular order—go back and forth between the lists if you like.

One way is to first read a list quickly and spontaneously choose words that produce a strong emotional charge, either positive—*Yes! Always*—or negative—*No! Never*—and afterward go back and rate those that fall into the *often* or *rarely* categories.

If you choose *only* words from a single list, you are a pure type (this is rare). Most people will have at least a few words from at least two elemental categories. To determine your type, first count the words *from each list* that you have placed into each column. The highest number of words from any one list in your *always* column determines your *primary type*.

For example, if you choose twenty words from the Fire category and place them in the *always* column, and the number of words in the *always* column from any or all the other lists is less than twenty, you are a Fire type.

Having determined your primary type, next count the words in your *often* column. If the highest number of these words comes from the *same* element as those in your *always* column, more emphasis is placed upon the primary type. If, however, an equal or greater number of words comes from a *different* list, you have a secondary type. For example, if you are a basic Fire type but the highest number of words in the *often* category come from the Water list, you are a mixed Fire-Water type.

The third step is to determine if you have a missing or inferior (de-emphasized) element. To do this, follow the same procedure outlined above for the *never* category, which will indicate the missing element if there is one, and from *rarely,* which will indicate the inferior element.

A missing or de-emphasized (*rarely*) element indicates that there is an imbalance, as ideally all four elements would be represented in your chart. When this occurs (and it is common) the missing element can be added by consciously seeking to tune in to it. For example, if Earth is missing, then earth-grounding can be added by planting a garden, working with the hands, or just sitting on the ground and tuning in to Mother Nature. Similarly, Water can be added by going to the seaside or lakeshore, taking long soaks in the tub, or walking in the rain.

Sometimes, we get elementally out of balance—such might be the case when a Water type is forced to go on a family camping trip in the mountains, or, conversely, if an Air type has to spend time in the wet air of a lakeside or beside the ocean. When imbalance occurs, and the stress of ordinary living

The Four Elemental Types

Fire	Earth	Water	Air
Self-starting	Organized	Feeling	Communicative
Self-confident	Serious	Sensitive	Quick-witted
Action-initiating	Practical	Sympathetic	Inquisitive
Decisive	Down-to-earth	Nostalgic	Adaptable
Outgoing	Realistic	Comfort-loving	Curious
Forceful	Ambitious	Security-oriented	Versatile
Driving	Hardworking	Domestic	Flexible
Active	Structured	Family-oriented	Variety-seeking
Strong	Methodical	Food-oriented	Relationship-oriented
Adventurous	Disciplined	Emotional	Cooperative
Self-expressive	Analytical	Intense	Sociable
Self-aware	Detail-oriented	Passionate	Companionable
Dramatic	Sensible	Secretive	Just
Playful	Sanitary	Mysterious	Balanced
Fun-loving	Stable	Compassionate	Tolerant
Powerful	Steady	Benevolent	Impartial
Impressive	Reliable	Sentimental	Intellectually detached
Enthusiastic	Productive	Intuitive	Friendly
Expansive	Persistent	Escapist	Innovative
Optimistic	Determined	Spacey	Independent
Generous	Deliberate	Impractical	Original
Blunt	Money-oriented	Unrealistic	Individualistic
Outdoors-oriented	Prudent	Artistic	Noncomformist
Travel-oriented	Cautious	Inspired	Charming
Careless	Economical	Receptive	Refined
Explosive	Self-controlled	Moody	Studious
Foolhardy	Reserved	Clinging	Babbling
Egotistical	Pessimistic	Brooding	Nervous
		Emotionally perceptive	Superficial
		Passive	Mentally organized

can cause this to happen, illness can follow. The best way to counteract this is to rebalance ourselves elementally.

When you have finished the word-association exercise, go over your chart to see what Signs your Planets occupy and review the elemental nature of each Sign. Then make a list of your Planets and identify each one by Element.

For example, if you have Sun in Leo and Moon in Taurus, you would write:

Sun = Fire

Moon = Earth

Now, total the number of Planets in each Element and see how good a match you have with your score from the exercise. This will show you how close to type you are and which Elements are most dominant.

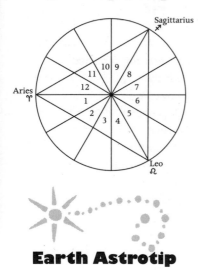

Fire Astrotip

Fire gets along best with other Fire types, as they replenish your energy. You get along with Air types, but they can irritate you with their endless mental speculations. Avoid Earth and Water types; Earth smothers you and Water drenches your Fire.

Fire Triplicity

Aries ♈

Leo ♌

Sagittarius ♐

Earth Astrotip

Fire people energize you, and you find Water types soothing. Other Earth types can be good friends, but too many makes the atmosphere heavy. Avoid Air types, whose lack of common sense annoys you.

The Fire Type

The energy of Fire is radiant. Your energy is flowing and you are excitable, enthusiastic, impatient, spontaneous, quick to react, self-centered, and overly objective. Your natural high spirits give self-esteem. Strength comes in spurts. A strong desire for self-expression and the need for freedom are your dominant characteristics.

Being cooped up depletes your life force; you need vigorous physical activity during the daytime, preferably out in the sunshine, with as much contact with the sun as possible. Winter in cold climates is hard on you, but sufficient outdoor activity during the hot summer months will allow you to store your elemental energy against the gloom of indoor winter months. Your energy goes down when the sun does. Early-to-bed, early-to-rise is a good health habit for you.

Illness, which can be brought on by overexcitement and a lack of proper rest, is difficult for you, as you dislike being confined and inactive. You need to develop patience with illness, for a premature return to activity can bring on a relapse. Restore balance by incorporating sunlight into your life as often as possible. You may suffer from seasonal affective disorder (SAD), caused by lack of sunlight. Light treatment can help.

You tend to suffer from headaches and injuries resulting from impulsive behavior. You may stress out as a result of overactivity and develop chronic back pain—often the product of lack of rest.

The Earth Type

The energy of Earth is closely related to the physical plane and the senses. Your energy is stable and you are patient, reliable, hardworking, commonsensical, practical, and stubborn, and you have extraordinary stamina. The desire for concrete results and the self-discipline needed to get them are your dominant characteristics.

You need to be in physical contact with your element, to get your hands and feet into the soil, handle growing things and the solid, basic material of the Earth, such as rocks and minerals. Rock or crystal collecting is a good hobby for Earth types.

Though you have great physical stamina, you are not inclined to physical exertion and need to push yourself to exercise regularly. You need to go at your own pace, especially in the matter of sleeping and waking. Being rushed can make you ill or delay recovery. When ill, you recuperate slowly but steadily and thoroughly.

You tend to have throat problems. You may get colds with sore throats as a result of emotional upsets or from pushing your endurance level beyond its limit by continuing activity long past the time to rest. You are prone to digestive upsets resulting from nerves and your desire for perfection. Bones and teeth can cause problems, so regular dental checkups are a must. Skin, too, is sensitive and can become dry and scaly or erupt in pimples if not cared for properly. Keep yourself balanced by tuning into your five senses. You need to touch and be touched—a furry pet is especially good! You derive relaxation as well as pleasure from well-prepared food. Learning to cook would be a good hobby. Aromatic bath products are good for your morale as well as for your skin. Listening to music rejuvenates your brain. And you should learn to appreciate art by looking at it.

The Air Type

The energy of Air is ephemeral. Your energy is constantly shifting and you are mental, abstract, detached, fair-minded, talkative, diplomatic, and multifaceted. A preference for detachment from the "messy" human emotions and an emphasis on theory and concepts are your dominant characteristics.

Prolonged contact with dampness depletes you, and in a humid climate you should have a dehumidifier in your room. You find emotional display upsetting; an atmosphere heavy with emotion can make you ill. Witnessing or coping with outbursts of weeping or temperament can bring on exhaustion. You prefer to talk about emotions rationally rather than actually dealing with them, but repressing your own emotions can cause illness.

You have nervous energy and need to dissipate it with mental activity in order to get a good night's sleep, but allow sufficient winding-down time before bed—it's a good time to spend a quiet half-hour in solitude. It's important for you to maintain a calm, restful environment to counteract your inclination to live in your busy head.

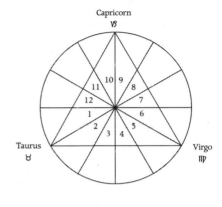

Earth Triplicity

Air Astrotip

Fellow Air types provide the mental stimulation and empathy you need; Fire types are energizing. Avoid Earth types—you find their practicality depressing—and Water types, whose emotionality gets on your nerves.

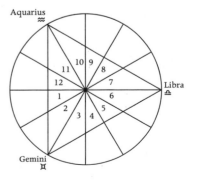

Air Triplicity

When ill, you hate being confined to bed, but you can deal with it if you have plenty of mental stimulation in a calm, unemotional atmosphere. Restore balance by frequent breathing exercises.

You are susceptible to respiratory ailments—especially those affecting the lungs, such as pneumonia. You are likely to throw out a shoulder, injure your hands (carpal tunnel syndrome from constant keyboarding at the computer is a risk) or arms, or sprain an ankle.

The Water Type

The energy of water is flowing. You are sensitive, intuitive, emotional, psychic, imaginative, and insecure, and various intangibles play a large part in your life. Exquisitely tuned in to feelings—your own and other people's—you can range from extreme compassion to total self-pity. You trust your inner promptings and act on them. When your feelings are blocked or repressed, you can suffer psychosomatic ailments. You need to express feelings freely, for if they stay inside they solidify into resentment and a bad temper, which can bring on ill health. When upset, relax in a warm bath until feelings have settled.

Your inner landscape is forever in flux, like the ocean tides. Waves of feeling wash over you constantly; if they are not expressed, trouble results. Do not accept criticism for being "overly sensitive."

Insisting on the right to express feelings in a nonjudgmental atmosphere will allow you to maintain your inner harmony and physical health. You need time and space to yourself. Privacy in which to sort out your feelings help you deal with stress.

When ill, you need a quiet, calm atmosphere and plenty of sleep. You respond to a spiritual environment. Spirituality and prayer come easily and are of utmost importance to your inner harmony, which can be enhanced by soft music and being near water—an ocean or a lake. Hot tubs are also good. Many of your complaints respond to a total-body immersion.

You can suffer immune system disorders, breast lumps, fluid retention, constipation, reproductive-system complaints, foot problems, and glandular imbalance.

Water Astrotip

Water benefits from the practical nature of Earth types. Other Water types are sympathetic but feed your self-pity. Avoid Fire, which boils the Water nature, and Air, which lacks empathy.

Water Triplicity

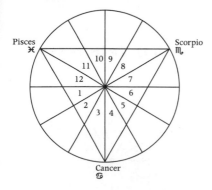

The Mixed Types

If you are a mixed type, the descriptions that follow allow you to *compare how each of the two Elements relates to each other within you.*

Fire/Earth   You mix practicality with impracticality, impulsiveness with patience. You can be the most reliable of persons who suddenly takes off without notice. You can make the visionary real. You mix strength and courage. Trouble results when you are insensitive to your environment or become self-centered to the point of hypochondria.

Fire/Air   You put ideas into action, join vision to logic. You are objective but can be affectionate as well. You like to gain knowledge about your own health and will seek out appropriate treatment from an intellectual standpoint. Trouble results when you disconnect from your spiritual needs and concentrate too narrowly on the intellectual level or when you exhaust yourself through restlessness and unrealistic adventures.

Fire/Water   You are the most intuitive of the mixed types. You're very fluid, and your connection to your inner realm is amazing. You get accurate hunches about what's wrong with you if you feel ill. Impressionable and sensitive, you respond well to visualizations to promote health and healing. Trouble results when you succumb to hysteria and overemotionalism or wall yourself off in your own private universe.

Earth/Air   Extremely efficient, you combine objectivity with practicality, and you are likely to be involved in your own health and health care, using conventional means of treatment for illness while being open to unorthodox methods. Trouble results when you fall prey to skepticism, pessimism, or a cynical view of life.

Earth/Water   Simultaneously sensitive and grounded, you are both intuitive and practical. You have a talent for accepting whatever cards life deals to you. When ill, you tend to feel your way into your own depths to find the cure. Trouble results when you overindulge, which can produce addictions, or use your depths as a means of escape.

Air/Water   Extremely sensitive, you combine compassionate feeling with objectivity. You can detach from your emotions and empathetic responses and analyze your experience coolly. You have both a logical mind and the ability to feel. Trouble results when you rely too heavily on your intellectual abilities, which make you high-strung and nervous.

Astrotip for Health

See pages 96–99 to discover the *self-nurturing* highlight for your elemental type and Moon Sign.

Practice Exercise

Write a short essay about your Element Type. If you are a Mixed Type, write about how the two Elements interact with each other and how you deal with these different—sometimes contradictory—energies within yourself. Tell your Modes what you think about them!

_____

_____

_____

_____

_____

_____

_____

_____

_____

_____

_____

_____

_____

_____

_____

_____

_____

Go-Getters, Stalwarts, and Chameleons

There are three basic ways that the Signs operate in terms of personality traits. These are called *Modes*. You're probably familiar with the term "M.O." for *modus operandi* or mode of operation. We all have our own personal M.O.s, and we are identifiable by them. One person's M.O. may be to head straight into a situation and stir things up to get them going, while another person's M.O. will be to keep the ship on course in as steady a manner as possible.

The Modes in astrological language are called *Cardinal, Fixed,* and *Mutable.* Like everything else in astrology, the Modes march around the Zodiac in a regular order so that each Mode has one Fire Sign, one Earth Sign, one Air Sign, and one Water Sign. (See table on page 70.) Each Sign in a Mode has its own distinctive personality.

Whichever Mode is dominant in your chart defines you as a *go-getter* (Cardinal), a *stalwart* (Fixed), or a *chameleon* (Mutable).

The function of the Cardinal Signs is to *initiate,* or to get things going. The Cardinal Signs—Aries, Cancer, Libra, and Capricorn—represent the month at the *beginning* of each season. Active and self-confident, often ambitious, usually self-motivated, Planets in Cardinal Signs give pizzazz to the personality and create a vivacious self-mover. However, if *most* of your Planets are in Cardinal Signs, you may be restless and overactive. You may constantly generate new ideas like popcorn leaping out of an uncovered pot—too many to put to practical use.

Cardinal Signs—Go-Getters of the Zodiac

Do you like to start things and get them going? Are you an active person who is always the first to volunteer for a new project at school? Do you like to be the one who begins the project, but don't much care about who finishes it? Do people see you as ambitious and self-confident? Is your M.O. to be the in the forefront of whatever's going on? If so, you are a go-getter, Cardinal Mode type.

Here's a brief overview of the go-getter, Cardinal Signs:

Aries (Fire) is the prime mover of the Zodiac, famous for starting things but not finishing them. Always on the lookout for new and exciting ideas, he thrusts forth his self-expression forcefully.

Cancer (Water) initiates *feelings* in order to express her moods and emotional needs. Although shy in other areas of life, she does not hesitate to make emotional contact to get feelings moving.

Libra (Air) is the initiator of relationships. Her function is to inspire human interactions, both intimate or personal and public or communal, by socializing and making sure everything goes smoothly.

Capricorn (Earth) is the initiator of practical activity. His nature is to be concerned with usefulness, material rewards, and social status. Capricorn finishes what he starts because that's practical.

The function of Fixed Signs is to *conserve* both energy and material goods. The Fixed Signs—Taurus, Leo, Scorpio, and Aquarius—represent the month in the middle of each season. They are conservative, reliable, and consistent. Planets in Fixed Signs give stability to the personality and create almost inexhaustible endurance, patience, and persistence. However, if *most* of your Planets are in Fixed Signs you may be stubborn to the point of being immovable, with an inclination to hold on long past the time to let go. This can result in extreme possessiveness, to the point of obsession.

Fixed Signs— Stalwarts of the Zodiac

Do you hate change? Are you the immovable object meeting the irresistible force head-on? Do people consider you stubborn? Once you've made up your mind, are you slow to change it? Do you like things to be in their proper place, where you can find them? Is your energy more concentrated than flowing? Are you known for your stamina and endurance? If so, you are a stalwart, or in the Fixed Mode.

Here's a brief overview of the stalwart, Fixed Signs:

Taurus (Earth), the most fixed of the Fixed Signs, represents a time when spring has sprung. There is tremendous activity in the material world. Nature's banker, Taurus acquires and increases material goods.

Leo (Fire) is that fixed, glaring eye of the Sun, merciless in its intensity, which illustrates Leo's strength of purpose. Just as the Sun rules the summer, Leo seeks to rule, but summer's a time for play and Leo loves to play.

Scorpio (Water) is the most intense of the Fixed Signs. He represents the concentration of Nature's power of regeneration, presiding over the annual "death" of plants so that new life may be brought forth the next spring.

Aquarius (Air) may seem like a contradiction in terms as a Fixed Sign because it is the nature of air to be in constant movement. Yet think of how one can be immobilized in the cold air! Mental in nature, Aquarius's concentration is so great that once his mind is made up, it is almost impossible to change it.

Mutable Signs— Chameleons of the Zodiac

Are you easy to get along with? Can you quickly and easily adapt to unexpected changes in your schedule or your life? Do you like to do a number of things at the same time or switch back and forth from one thing to another frequently? Can you carry on a conversation leaping from topic to topic without losing your train of thought? Do you love variety? Are you considered versatile? Do you automatically go with the flow in any situation? Does manipulation come easy to you? Can you talk your way out of almost any sticky situation? Do people accuse you of being scattered? If so, you are a chameleon, the Mutable type.

Here's a brief overview of the chameleon, Mutable Signs:

Gemini (Air) is the most mutable of the Mutables, who can change color quicker than the eye can follow. Flexible to the nth degree, his changeablity is mirrored in his season, that unpredictable time between spring and summer.

Virgo (Earth) is the most mental of the Mutable Signs. He is usually multitalented and can switch from one occupation to the next with ease. But Virgo doesn't change just for the novelty—he always seeks a practical end.

Sagittarius (Fire) signals the period of change from fall to winter. He likes to be on the move looking for adventure, especially outdoors. His mind is agile and questioning. He loves intellectual speculation.

Pisces (Water) signifies the time when winter changes to spring. It has the flowing, formless quality of the melting snow cascading down the mountains into rivers and streams. Like a leaf drifting on a current, he goes where his inner life leads.

CARDINAL Fire (Aries)	FIXED Fire (Leo)	MUTABLE Fire (Sagittarius)
CARDINAL Earth (Capricorn)	FIXED Earth (Taurus)	MUTABLE Earth (Virgo)
CARDINAL Air (Libra)	FIXED Air (Aquarius)	MUTABLE Air (Gemini)
CARDINAL Water (Cancer)	FIXED Water (Scorpio)	MUTABLE Water (Pisces)

The Modes and the Four Seasons

Examination of the cycle of Earth's seasons shows a close relationship between the Modes and the turning of our Planet in relation to our Sun, which is what gives us the four seasons—spring, summer, fall, and winter.

As you can see from the chart above, the Modes divide the twelve Signs into three groups of four each. These groups, called *quadruplicities*, are formed by the Square and Opposition Aspects.

Unlike the Element triplicities, which are compatible with each other, the Modes can be at odds within their own group. For example, in the Cardinal quadruplicity, Aries forms a *Square* to Cancer and Capricorn and an *Opposition* to Libra. (Refer to "Helpers and Hindrances: The Meaning of the Four Major Aspects" discussed earlier.)

Just how this affects your chart will depend on which Planets are in which Modes and on their House placements.

To understand how the mixed types work, read the characteristics of the two Modes involved and blend them together.

Cardinal/Fixed is a dynamic combination. You have strong opinions but switch between being a creative starter and getting stuck in a rut.

Cardinal/Mutable makes you a person full of new ideas and a variety of projects or activities. You are full of inspiration and prone to lightninglike changeability.

Fixed/Mutable is a curious contradiction. Sometimes you are flexibility itself; at other times you dig in your heels and refuse to budge. You may need help focusing on getting started.

Finding Your Dominant Mode

To find your dominant mode, simply count the number of Planets you have in each Mode, giving two points to the Sun and Moon, one point to the others. Add in the Mode of your Ascendant, giving it two points. If one Mode has more Planets than the other two, you are that Mode type. If you have an equal number of Planets in any two Modes, or if you have several Planets in one Mode and just one less in another Mode, you are a mixed type.

Now that you know all about your modes, write a short essay about how you feel they work in your chart. If you are a mixed-mode type, write about how they interact with each other.

_____

_____

_____

_____

_____

_____

_____

_____

_____

_____

_____

_____

_____

_____

_____

_____

_____

TWO

The Planetary Pairs

The Outer and Inner You:
Sun/Moon Pair

*Anyone seriously interested and willing to do a bit of system-
atic research can verify that the natal chart depicts the basic
psychological and emotional makeup of the individual . . . the
potential developmental patterns likely to evolve. [These] resonate with the individual's readiness.*

Edward C. Whitmont, M.D.,
The Alchemy of Healing

n chapter 1 you learned some basic ideas about the ten Planets and
their functions in your chart, and some key words as a kind of shorthand for getting to know your Planets. You now know the twelve Signs
of the Zodiac, how they operate, and what effect each has on the different Planets. You understand that every Planet is always occupying
one of the zodiacal Signs, and you have key words to help you quickly
get a handle on your Planets in the Signs.

The Sun represents the outer you, the one that functions in the
daytime, goes to school, plays sports, makes friends, and participates
in activities with other people.

Next, you're going to learn more extensively about how the Sun
operates in the different Signs during the teen years as you move forward into life and develop a sense of your purpose.

Meeting Your Destiny:
The Sun through the Signs

Sun in Aries

You are courageous, impulsive, innocent, humorous, vital, and enthusiastic. You can be aggressive, insensitive, and headstrong. *Independence* is your key word.

During your teens, you become even more independent and can be reckless. You anger easily and often rely on sarcasm to express your anger. Aware of your own courage, you seek challenges and take risks.

Aries—Likes and Dislikes

Some things you like are:

- Having your integrity trusted
- Getting information about sexuality
- Knowing the consequences of your actions
- Challenging authority by breaking the rules
- Being given answers to your questions
- Being treated honestly

Some things you dislike are:

- Being made fun of or humiliated
- Boring events or activities
- Getting hassled for telling the truth
- Restrictions of any kind
- Having to wait
- Having to finish what you start

Sun in Taurus

You are stable, security conscious, grounded, relaxed, conservative, and materialistic, and you love nature and beauty. When pushed, you get stubborn. *Stability* is your key word.

During your teens, you like privacy and are learning to handle your mood swings. Your social skills are good. You need affection and touching to fulfill your sensual nature. You like the familiar.

Taurus—Likes and Dislikes

Some things you like are:

- Information about your body's changes and grooming
- A generous allowance or adequate spending money
- Good food and knowledge of proper nutrition
- Lots of affection—hugs, back rubs, special food
- Privacy, physical comfort, a regular schedule
- Being allowed to do things at your own pace

Some things you dislike are:

- Being teased about how you look
- Being hurried or pushed against your will
- Not having enough of the food you like
- Being short of money or denied material possessions
- Chaos anywhere or sudden changes in plans
- Being accused of laziness or of being slow or possessive

Sun in Gemini

You are versatile, witty, verbal, logical, mentally changeable, social, and perceptive. You can be devious and inconsistent. *Versatility* is your key word.

   You are a social butterfly and you like to talk for hours, especially on the phone or by e-mail. You're eager to get information on topics that really interest you. Avoid the stress of over-extending yourself.

Gemini—Likes and Dislikes

Some things you like are:

- Information about many subjects
- Multiple sources of information—TV, the Net, books, etc.
- Learning what interests you
- Talking, talking, talking
- Freedom to do what you like and go where you choose

Some things you dislike are:

- Anything that bores you
- Anyone slow on the uptake
- Being accused of superficiality
- Being restricted to having only one of anything
- Repetitive tasks
- Lack of mental stimulation

Sun in Cancer

You are sensitive, shy, domestic, old-fashioned, nurturing, imaginative, home-loving, and security conscious. You can be crabby, tenacious, and insecure. *Sensitive* is your key word.

During your teens, changing moods perplex you. You may become moody and romantic or rebellious and sloppy. You suffer from being oversensitive to others' problems and may want to take care of everybody. If stressed, you overeat and crawl inside yourself to recover.

Cancer—Likes and Dislikes

Some things you like are:

- A secure home environment
- Lots of soft things, like pillows and quilts
- Encouragement and approval when you feel insecure
- Being able to talk things out with your mother or an older sympathetic woman
- Family reunions and knowing about your ancestors
- Children and the idea of having them one day.

Some things you dislike are:

- Feeling that you aren't needed
- Not being taken seriously
- Being accused of being over-emotional
- Being hassled for being moody and sensitive
- Teasing or being made to feel ashamed of your body
- When your mother doesn't pay enough attention to you

Sun in Leo

You are open, warmhearted, demonstrative, generous, playful, and loyal. You want to be the center of attention and you dramatize yourself to get it. *Dramatic* is your key word.

You are individualistic and courageous, sometimes loud and flamboyant, especially in your manner of dressing. You are a natural leader and may run for class president or be the lead in a school play.

Leo—Likes and Dislikes

Some things you like are:

- Attention, attention, and more attention
- Approval and the applause of the crowd
- Doing things your way and leading others
- Lots of feedback about your appearance and performance
- Opportunities to show your leadership abilities
- A positive, warm relationship with your father or a father figure

Some things you dislike are:

- Being ignored or excluded from group activities
- Being made to feel ashamed of your need for attention
- Keeping secrets or feeling disloyal
- Having your honor doubted or your pride hurt
- Wearing shabby or unstylish clothes
- Anyone making fun of your appearance

Sun in Virgo

You are practical, modest, hard-working, sensible, orderly, meticulous, and critical. You can be a perfectionist and extremely self-critical. *Analytical* is your key word.

During your teens, you tend to be shy and insecure, covering your uncertainty with a critical attitude. You avoid publicity but secretly long for recognition and for your efforts to be useful. You do well in school, but you risk feeling isolated because of your sense of modesty.

Virgo—Likes and Dislikes

Some things you like are:

- Advice and information about good nutrition
- Being allowed to make your own food choices
- Learning about your body and how to care for it
- Being taught social skills
- Being nursed gently and kindly when sick
- Being trusted with responsibility and duties

Some things you dislike are:

- Being prevented from finishing your work your own way
- A messy environment or any kind of disorder
- Not knowing exactly what is expected of you
- Exposing your body against your will
- Not being treated with seriousness and respect
- Being given information that doesn't make sense

Sun in Libra

You are gracious, kind, fair, diplomatic, affectionate, beauty loving, and sensitive. You can be vacillating, indecisive, and confused. *Relationship* is your key word.

During your teens, you are concerned with how you look, what people think of you, and most of all relationships. You want to get involved in a steady relationship as soon as possible. You are socially competent and make a nice personal impression, but you need to be careful not to be with someone just to avoid being alone.

Libra—Likes and Dislikes

Some things you like are:

- Being treated politely
- Playing the diplomat and resolving disputes
- Socializing in a calm and attractive environment
- Nice clothes that are classic rather than trendy
- Close relationships with family and friends
- Being given reasonable explanations and information

Some things you dislike are:

- Being forced to take sides
- Conflicts with others, especially loved ones
- Having to live in a disharmonious situation
- Not being allowed to create your own personal space
- Feeling isolated or unwanted
- Not being dealt with fairly

Sun in Scorpio

You are intense, private, committed, sexually oriented, and charismatic. You can be extreme, vengeful, suspicious, and distrustful of others' motives. *Intense* is your key word.

During your teens, you tend to be introspective, moody, and preoccupied with your body and its functions. You like to test yourself to the limit. You have self-control and can withstand extreme conditions. Personal privacy is a must because you want to explore your sexual nature thoroughly.

Scorpio—Likes and Dislikes

Some things you like are:

- Absolute privacy in your personal space
- Scaring yourself when no one is looking
- Exploring occult subjects, like astrology
- Wearing severe clothes, such as all-black outfits
- Shocking people with your extreme appearance
- Having and keeping deep, dark secrets

Some things you dislike are:

- Not being given thorough information about sex
- Being teased for being intense
- Having your privacy invaded by your parents
- Being accused of being compulsive or obsessive
- Ridicule for any reason whatsoever
- Being made to feel ashamed of your sexuality

Sun in Sagittarius

You are optimistic, adventurous, humorous, philosophical, open-minded, and frank. You can be blunt, clumsy, brash, or fanatical about your beliefs. *Freedom* is your key word.

During your teens, you want independence early and can become rebellious if you don't get it. You long to travel to faraway places and like to have foreign friends. You like outdoor sports you can do alone, such as hiking and rock climbing.

Sagittarius—Likes and Dislikes

Some things you like are:

- Freedom to do what you want and go where you like
- Being trusted to handle yourself responsibly
- Getting outdoors often, preferably on trips
- Having something to believe in—a personal ethic
- Learning about different countries and cultures
- Platonic friendships with both sexes

Some things you dislike are:

- Restrictions on your freedom of movement
- Having your integrity questioned
- Being required to be on time
- Injustice and hypocrisy
- Being accused of being scattered or superficial
- Being tied down to a rigid schedule

Sun in Capricorn

You are serious, responsible, organized, realistic, stoic, conservative, and productive. You can be uptight, repressed, and status-conscious. *Materialistic* is your key word.

During your teens, you are conscious of the rules and seek security through achievement. You are conscientious and thorough in whatever you do and a good scholar. You like to work hard because you aim at financial independence early.

Capricorn—Likes and Dislikes

Some things you like are:

- Responsibility for your own projects
- Being in a position of authority
- Receiving acknowledgment for your achievements
- Nondemanding relationships with both sexes
- Consistency, organization, and practicality
- Creating your own sense of value and self-esteem

Some things you dislike are:

- Being told how to do things
- Not knowing what the rules are
- Failing at any task
- Being accused of rigidity or being too practical
- Not being understood for who you are
- Being told you are too young to do something

Sun in Aquarius

You are unconventional, friendly, original, objective, unusual, and detached. You can be remote, unfeeling, cold, and rigid about your ideas. *Individualistic* is your key word.

During your teens, you become highly individualized. You express your personality however it suits you, even if you shock people. Extreme behavior appeals to you. As you get older, you begin to understand that being different isn't a matter of looking or acting weird or bizarre.

Aquarius—Likes and Dislikes

Some things you like are:

- Being treated as a unique individual
- Not being hassled about how you dress or act
- Having quiet time and mental freedom to think
- Learning social skills and joining groups
- Intellectual stimulation and scientific information
- People who listen to your ideas without prejudice

Some things you dislike are:

- Feeling trapped in any situation
- Dealing with life's ordinariness
- People who make fun of your ideas as being far-out
- Anyone who isn't an abstract thinker as you are
- Being considered weird
- Having your innovations ridiculed by those in authority

Sun in Pisces

You are sensitive, moody, introspective, dreamy, idealistic, creative, and compassionate. Impressionable and romantic, you live a fantasy life. *Imagination* is your key word.

During your teens, you are looking for something that you can hang your idealism on, and you may explore different spiritual paths. Be careful of using drugs or alcohol to alter your consciousness, because you could become addicted. Develop your artistic ability.

Pisces—Likes and Dislikes

Some things you like are:

- Having your own private space where you can sort things out
- Outlets for your creative impulses
- Understanding of your spiritual yearnings
- Discussing openly your feelings and dreams
- Having total emotional support from parents and peers
- Immersing yourself in music and art

Some things you dislike are:

- People who are totally materialistic and crass
- Insensitivity in any form
- Cruelty to animals, humans, or other life forms
- Insensitive people hurting your feelings
- Being accused of spaciness or impracticality
- Having to live in the world as it is

Your Emotional Nature:
The Moon through the Signs

The Moon is the second part of the threesome that shows your deepest and most real self. The Sun represents what you are growing into. The Ascendant is how you see the world and how it sees you. The Moon reveals your basic *needs*. It represents your emotional nature and shows what makes you feel comfortable, safe, secure, and loved.

Especially now, in your teen years, the Moon is of vital importance. You are learning—sometimes painfully—about your emotions and your rapidly changing body, which can seem to live a life of their own. The Moon is the receptive principle for your subconscious, behavioral instincts and the automatic functions of the body—your nervous system, digestion, breathing, the female menstrual cycle, the male hormone shifts. Although it is a feminine energy, boys as well as girls have the Moon in their charts.

Emotions just rise up in you. They don't first ask politely if you want to have them. Suddenly, seemingly for no apparent reason, you *feel* a strong emotion. It might be love or hate, exhilaration or despondency, optimism or despair, a positive reaction or a negative reaction.

Your emotions are just *there*. From deep inside you act (or react) in an automatic way. Long before you were able to think or express yourself in words, you could *feel* and *respond*. Much of how you understand yourself now was imprinted at an early age and has become automatic due to the *feeling tone* attached to both what you find pleasurable and what you find threatening. This early conditioning isn't something you are aware of; it simply *is*. As an illustration, think of something that automatically revolts you or attracts you. Where did that response come from? Were you repeatedly told that particular thing was bad for you or good for you? Chances are you are reacting to what you were taught in earliest childhood.

It is important for you to recognize your emotional reactions for what they are and honor how they affect you. They are built-in and cannot be discounted. They must be worked with at each stage of your development. The Moon is like an internal compass by which you navigate the sometimes rough waters of life. If you neglect or deny your

The Moon Speaks

Ruler of Blue shadows and
  moist silence in
The Bowl of Heaven.
I give form to creative
  force.
I rule the function and form
  of matter,
Rhythms of the body and
  fate of the soul,
Where one has been and
  what one has yet to face.

Moon energy—your inner lunar self—you throw yourself out of balance.

Becausee emotions are so basic, it's unfortunate that boys are taught not to show them. Little boys are told that "boys don't cry," which later has the negative effect of causing teenage boys (and adult men) to repress or hide their emotions for fear of being ridiculed as non-masculine.

Culturally, our society is almost completely male-oriented. In our race to reach it, we have abandoned what the Moon stands for. For this reason, many teens are disconnected from their inner Moon because of pressures to conform to the dominant masculine world around them, which prizes traditionally extroverted male Sun characteristics over more inward Moon qualities. Teens of both sexes with a sensitive Moon placement suffer from this especially. They feel out of step with others or what they think is supposed to be "normal."

It is important for you to realize that both boys and girls can be naturally more lunar than solar, or more Moonlike than Sunlike. This is not to say that having a sensitive Moon makes a boy or a man less masculine, or that having a strong Moon makes a girl or a woman more feminine. There's no right or wrong, no normal or not-normal involved in the Moon energies. Whatever Moon Sign you have is right for you.

Now, let's look at how the Moon shows your emotional nature in the twelve Signs. (You can find your Moon Sign placement in appendix 1, pages 273–285.)

Moon in Aries

Your emotional needs are to be active, adventurous, stimulated, direct, competitive, enthusiastic, first, and challenged. You *must* excel. Being first is emotionally important to you. With your active and vital nature, you rush headlong into activities and love to take chances. Easily bored, you need frequent changes in routine and are happiest when busy. Frustration and restrictions can upset you and bring on headaches. *Impatience* is your key word.

Your teen years can be tumultuous because you want to do everything *now*. When tired or stressed you tend to hide your hurt feelings under angry behavior. Fortunately, your anger evaporates as quickly as it comes and you don't bear grudges.

Astrotip for Moon in Aries

You think the best defense is a good offense, and you have a "live and let live" attitude. You want to win but won't cheat to do so. Your need for freedom and independence can make you testy and rash, and you prefer to make your own mistakes rather than being told what to do. You feel you know how to take care of yourself, and you need to learn to accept adult guidance without fearing it will make you dependent.

As you get older, your need for action may take the form of competitive sports that focus on a single goal, or you may find outlets to exert your natural leadership. Your trouble spots have to do with impulsive behavior, which can cause head injuries. Learning to think before you leap into action is your challenge.

Moon in Taurus

Your emotional needs are for stability, affection, touching, financial security, relaxation, peace, practical help, good food, and a sensual environment. Adequate physical comfort is a *must*. You are bodily based and get upset when you are deprived of physical comforts, including well-prepared food and clothes that make you feel good. You enjoy making others comfortable. Money in your pocket is extremely important; without funds you feel insecure. You dislike dealing with sudden changes in plans and find safety in the familiar. Avoid rigidity and relax more. *Comfort* is your key word.

Your teen years are usually fairly calm and stable, for you are looking forward to the world of work and preparing yourself to make money. Your possessions are your identity. You like to make sure everyone knows what is *yours*.

As you get older, you work hard if you see a tangible reward. You make long-term plans to use money for pleasure and relaxation. When you are rushed or pushed, stress makes you susceptible to sore throats. Learning to let go of overattachment to possessions is your challenge.

Moon in Gemini

Your emotional needs are for freedom, information from many sources, socializing, versatility, lack of routine, keeping busy, talking, and communicating freely. Mental stimulation is a *must*. You thrive on having lots going on at once, and your bright, quick, witty, changeable emotional nature can cause you to flip from mood to mood with astonishing speed. You can't tolerate being bored. Extremely curious, you thrive on diversity and distraction. Being confined, limited, or cut off from communication with others makes you irritable and nervous. *Versatility* is your key word.

Your teen years are full of activities and fun. You like school as long

Astrotip for Moon in Taurus

You think things as they are will never change and act accordingly. Your need for security makes you feel that if you don't watch out for yourself, you will run short of money one day. You believe only in what you can see, touch, smell, hear, or taste. Your earthiness needs some balance—try looking at the world in ways that are not physical.

Astrotip for Moon in Gemini

High spirits make you a sparkling conversationalist. Your basic attitude is that a rolling stone gathers no moss, and you live by the motto that it's hard to hit a moving target. You tend to think that whatever can't be explained or figured out mentally isn't worth bothering with anyway. Asking questions about emotions is a game you like to play, but you like to keep it light!

as your classes are interesting and challenging intellectually. You process information about the world mentally and then talk about what you know.

As you get older, your need for communication may lead you to take part in debating or speaking contests. You may drop projects that bore you. Your trouble spot is nervous exhaustion brought on by being "wired" or overtired. Your challenge is to have plenty of quiet time, especially before going to sleep.

Moon in Cancer

You are supersensitive emotionally. You need nurturing, emotional support, a secure home base, lots of comfort food, protection, and babying. Family ties are a *must*. You find separation painful. Independence comes late. Food represents comfort, home, and security. *Emotional* is your key word.

Your teen years can be filled with painful insecurity if you don't feel loved and secure. You cope with stress by eating, or overeating, and your sensitivity makes you shy away from all but intimate friends and your close family members.

As you get older, your security needs may lead to tight bonds with noncritical and caring friends whom you nurture and care for. You love animals and lavish your nurturing instinct on pets. Shy about your body, you seek approval for how you look. Your trouble spots come from your sensitivity to what others think and your fluctuating moods. Learning to not take things personally is your challenge.

Moon in Leo

Your emotional needs are for playfulness, attention, recognition of your talents, creativity, and grand gestures. Admiration is a *must*. You are warm and affectionate, so plenty of affection makes you feel wanted and important. A born ham, you need positive feedback. *Attention* is your key word.

Your teen years are full of exploring your creativity and having fun. As your warm emotional nature attracts people, you are seldom alone. You like to be the center of attention, doing almost anything to get yourself noticed and admired, and you attract admirers easily.

Astrotip for Moon in Cancer

You suffer from minor ailments brought on by excessive emotional stress but welcome the opportunity to cuddle up and cozy in while you pamper yourself, a sure cure. Your outlook on life is waiting for someone to rescue you or thinking there is only one person who can meet your needs. Your family is your main source of both pleasure and pain. Achieving independence is your main difficulty, for you cling to the past and yearn for unconditional love forever.

Astrotip for Moon in Leo

Your basic worldview is "All the world's a stage," and your rightful place is smack in the middle of it. Pushing your feelings right there out front is one way of getting the attention you demand, and your flair for the dramatic usually works in your favor. But don't push it too hard or you might find yourself resented for hogging the spotlight.

Astrotip for Moon in Virgo

You believe perfection is a worthy goal and anything can be fixed, but your self-critical nature can make you feel there's no point. Sometimes you feel you'll never get what you want or achieve your purposes. As a mental type, your emotions can make you feel inadequate, which makes you try harder. Criticism from others, if it is honest and true, helps you to keep on course, and you respect others' opinions.

As you get older, your need for attention and applause may lead you into theatrical activities or roles where you can display your natural leadership abilities. Extremely loyal, you expect loyalty in return and can be deeply hurt when betrayed. You're likely to choose people you admire as role models in order to get approval, support, and honest feedback from them. Trouble spots are lack of fun, praise, or acknowledgment, which can bring on a massive fit of the sulks. Your challenge is to share the spotlight gracefully.

Moon in Virgo

Your emotional needs are for modesty, usefulness, perfection, and neatness. Cleanliness and orderliness are vital. You *must* be helpful. Being orderly is emotionally important to you. With your careful nature, you want to be noticed for your effectiveness and for your skills. You need things in their proper places, and you want adults to make sense. You cultivate being self-sufficient, but if you get sick you need to be tenderly nursed. You are self-contained, careful, and precise. *Useful* is your key word.

Your teen years are calm if you can avoid disorder and dirt, have your efforts appreciated, and are given sensible information and explanations. You like knowing the rules and limits, and you rarely break them. Having lots of projects going at once keeps you busy and happy.

As you get older, your need for perfection may make you feel dissatisfied. Remember that perfection is not for this world! Your trouble spots are digestive upsets and worrying about your health. You either fuss over health or neglect hygiene. Getting in touch with your sensuousness and letting go of control is your challenge.

Moon in Libra

Your emotional needs are for peace and quiet in beautiful surroundings. You hate strife of any kind and will shrink from gross behavior and people. You seek balance and like refinement and harmony. You are likely either to be artistic or to enjoy the arts. Fairness is a *must*. You hate chaos or disharmony and will work to restore the balance.

Adept at diplomacy, you enjoy being the mediator and want to be appreciated for your social skills and respected for your judgment. *Harmony* is your key word.

Your teen years are very social, and you make friends easily by establishing and keeping things on an even keel. You enjoy using your negotiation abilities and may find yourself in the middle a lot. Being decorous and proper is important to you, especially in dress and manners.

As you get older, relationships become the focus of your life. You want to be in a relationship at all times, and broken ones upset you to the point of making you ill. Your trouble spot is refusal to face unpleasantness, which throws you off balance. Learning not to repress your anger is your challenge.

Moon in Scorpio

Your emotional needs are intense, deep, intimate, controlled, powerful, and perceptive. You *must* feel safe or you are extremely secretive about your inner self. You fear your intensity will drive others away and you may hide under another part of your chart, such as the Ascendant or Mars. Even under the best of circumstances, you have difficulty opening up about your deep internal feelings. You want to know that they will be respected and taken seriously or you will clam up. *Intensity* is your key word.

Your teen years can be challenging emotionally because you find it difficult to trust others with your inner life. This can make you feel lonely, isolated, and misunderstood. When you are angry, there's a powerful force behind the emotion that may frighten you and make you a loner.

As you get older, your sexuality merges with emotions, setting up a powerful force inside you that won't be denied. Experimental and fearless, you have trouble verbalizing your feelings because you hate hearing that you are too intense. Your trouble spot is hiding feelings, especially negative or unacceptable ones. Learning to trust is your challenge.

Astrotip for Moon in Libra

Without a relationship you find life sad and sour. Being alone is intolerable and brings on a sense of intense deprivation because basically you believe that you're nobody until somebody loves you. Appearances are your guide to who somebody is, which can be a mistake—you can't tell a book by its cover. Your need to be in a relationship can cause you to choose the wrong person over and over again.

Astrotip for Moon in Scorpio

You think that pain is just part of living and that suffering is a measure of love. Your basic attitude is "an eye for an eye," and you can extract vengeance when wounded. Being shamed or deprived of privacy will cause angry moods. You need to find friends who aren't scared of your intense emotions, and you like one or two close friends rather than the lighthearted, superficial banter of the crowd.

Moon in Sagittarius

Your emotional needs are to be adventurous, humorous, optimistic, playful, and allowed to roam free. You want to be noticed for your knowledge, and learning is vital to you. You expect everything to go well, and usually it does! You *must* have freedom to move about, and you'll want your driver's license as soon as possible, preferably with your own car! Humor is in your bones and you can be a practical joker, but you never mean any harm. Your characteristic bluntness may offend. *Freedom* is your key word.

Your teen years are usually a fun time because you like other people. Good at sports, you are an outdoor-type person who brightens up other people's lives with your good humor. Lots of friends are the norm, but you'll drop anyone who is not honest and forthright with you.

As you get older, your need for freedom will take you to as many places as you can get, preferably around the world. Endlessly curious, you want to learn everything and seek out answers to the universal philosophical questions. Although trustworthy, your trouble spot is in the details. Learning to thoroughly prepare is your challenge.

Moon in Capricorn

Your emotional needs are for organization, productivity, control, discipline, usefulness, ambition, and practicality. You *must* work hard toward useful ends, and you always strive to be the best you can be. You have a reserved and cautious nature to the point of austerity. Identification with material rather than spiritual values makes you uncomfortable with sloppy feelings, but you need love to thaw your cold emotions. *Responsibility* is your key word.

Your teen years are an active seeking of the means to earn money, which is an emotional anchor for you. Feeling poor is galling, and you will work extremely hard to prepare yourself because you have learned the old adage, "If you want something done well, do it yourself."

As you get older, you'll want to get good grades so you can go on to the best possible college and earn a degree that will bring good money. You like organizations and may take the leadership of some group. Inability to release stress and enjoy yourself are your likely trouble spots. Learning to have fun is your challenge.

Astrotip for Moon in Sagittarius

You think that bigger is better and that "all the world loves a clown," and you don't want anyone raining on your parade of good cheer. Limitations of any kind make you feel trapped and uneasy, and getting away is your therapy. Long trips are your meat and drink, even if they are imagined. You aren't inclined to fight, but you're not a coward. You believe implicitly in the natural goodness of people.

Astrotip for Moon in Capricorn

You think that "anything worth doing is worth doing well," and live by that motto. Trusting others isn't easy for you, and you need to develop faith in the Universal Plan. Cultivate a hopeful outlook. Pessimism brings with it the danger of giving up. Still, you usually press on no matter the obstacles because you are very goal oriented. You guard your privacy and need to spend time alone frequently.

Moon in Aquarius

Your emotional needs are to be unique, analytical, objective, detached, open-minded, sincere, rebellious, knowledgeable, and friendly in an impersonal way. You thrive on diversity and the unusual and can be unnervingly rational. You want to be appreciated for your intellect and seen as an unusual person. *Exploratory* is your key word.

Your teen years bring out your unusual personality, and you need freedom to be yourself and to experiment with the different facets of your personality. Emotional detachment is your hallmark. You'd rather rationalize your emotions than actually bother feeling them.

As you get older, you tend to express your difference from others forcefully, through dress or your behavior. You want to be noticed for being unusual and don't like rules that infringe on your self-expression. Emotional detachment and lack of personal involvement are likely trouble spots. Learning to become emotionally involved is your challenge.

Moon in Pisces

Your emotional needs are to be sensitive, devoted, inspired, imaginative, compassionate, attuned, merged, evasive, and escapist. You *must* operate intuitively. You soak up others' feelings, often negative ones. This can be dangerous to your health, because you often can't tell the difference between your own emotions and those of others around you. You are often vaguely ill, as you tend to float in and out of what we call reality, often being happiest in places where others cannot go. *Sensitive* is your key word.

Your teen years can be painful because of your extreme sensitivity. Negative vibrations from others and difficulty understanding what's "real" can make you seem spacey. Art and music are good outlets for you. Stay away from negative people and find time to spend by yourself to recoup.

As you get older, your emotional needs and sensitivity may draw you to people who need your help. Getting caught up in the net of self-sacrifice can be a trouble spot. You need to protect yourself and your creativity from intrusion by setting limits and boundaries. Frequent reality checks are your challenge. Don't become a rescuer!

Astrotip for Moon in Aquarius

You are almost exclusively cerebral, and the gyrations of abstract thinking can bring you to the point of exhaustion. Failure to manifest air-built castles in the real world can cause eruptions of impatience and despondency. You have to find a way to use your thinking processes without becoming identified with them to the exclusion of your feelings. Your motto is "One for all and all for one."

Astrotip for Moon in Pisces

You think relating to the real world is a drag, and you are susceptible to misusing drugs and alcohol. Easily hurt, you have neurotic tendencies. You need to balance your profound inner life with the demands of the material world without injuring your deepest emotional sensitivity. Remember that if you don't take care of yourself, you can't take care of anyone else.

Accepting the Animal Within

Here are some things you can do to honor your animal self:

- Trust your instincts. Learn to listen to your body. It has wisdom through and through. Never forget that your body is a wondrous thing, full of marvels. If you deny its perfection and ignore your instincts, you will be unhappy with your body and blame it for not feeling good or performing well. Learn that your body knows how to take care of itself if you will only allow it to guide you.

- Realize that your body is much more than its functions. It is not a machine but a living entity with intelligence and purpose. When you begin to relate to your body as having a soul, you appreciate its unique beauty and expressiveness.

- Learn to think with your heart as well as with your head. The heart may be just a muscle to the surgeon doing a bypass, but to you it is the seat of love and courage. Astrologically, the Sign of Leo rules the Sun, which represents both life purpose and the essence of human vitality. Leo the lion symbolizes the heart, the central pulse of one's being.

- Pay attention to symptoms. They are indications of a process deeper than mere physical discomfort. Ask yourself what it means when you don't feel well. Listen to the messages your body is sending you about what it needs.

- Don't accept the idea that your body is in any way disgusting. Its normal functions are entirely natural and necessary. Unfortunately, we have been convinced by the advertising industry that our necessary bodily activities, which keep us alive and healthy, are to be "corrected" by the use of some product, i.e., since we sweat, we must be deodorized. This false idea produces anxiety and shame. These are toxic feelings.

- Refuse to accept anyone else's standards of how you should use your body. Instead, pay close attention to your body and learn to live in harmony with it. You are one single entity— not a body and a brain/mind and a soul/spirit. You are all of these, but not separately.

- Learn to set your own pace for basic bodily needs like sleep, eating, and exercising. Do what is right for you. Eat when you are hungry. Sleep when you are tired. Exercise when you feel the need for movement. Don't feel you should follow somebody else's routine. The plain truth is that your body already knows what is best for you.

- Remember how you felt about your body as a child? Think of some of the things you did then that felt good. Make a list of things you would like to do again now. Think back to how you felt about your body as you entered puberty—what messages did you get about it? Were they negative or positive? Try to remember how you felt about your body as a small child. Did you like your body then, or did you have negative feelings early in your life? If you have become sexually active, are your feelings toward sexuality positive or negative? Do you need to correct a bad body image? Write a short essay with your body as a character. Let it express its feelings directly in dialogue.

- Find ways to enjoy your body. Pleasure nourishes the soul. Teens are often stressed out from doing too much—schoolwork, sports, clubs, and other activities. Often you use your body in ways that are painful—"No pain, no gain." Learn to treat your body with the compassion and understanding it deserves. Think of it as a library full of fascinating information.

Your Moon and Your Body

Your body is a visible record of your life and your experiences—wounds may have healed and left scars, you may have lost or gained weight, and you will have developed your own individual ways of walking, moving, gesturing, and using and caring for your body. The Moon tells how you feel about your body, how you treat its needs and functions.

Babies and small children take their bodies for granted—they experience the world through their bodily sensations, and unless they feel pain, they don't focus on their bodies or their natural bodily functions.

However, beginning at the time of puberty your body awareness increases dramatically. Your body is going through rapid changes in growth and hormonal development. It can be a time of confusion for a teenager. You may look in the mirror and wonder if what you see is *you* or someone you don't quite recognize. Unfortunately, during this time of bodily changes many teens become terribly self-conscious about their bodies, which may seem alien.

Girls especially, as they begin to become conscious of boys, become self-critical of their bodies and their emerging sexual characteristics. Budding breasts are a source of wonder and joy, but also a source of concern. As a girl you may look at your changing body in the mirror and ask yourself questions about how you look. At this time, you examine all of your body intently, looking for flaws and comparing yourself to the perfect bodies and faces on TV and in movies. You sometimes are in anguish because you think your body isn't "good enough," or you agonize about whether boys will find you attractive. This is a sad mistake.

This body self-criticism affects boys as well as girls. If you are a boy, you may worry about being too tall or too short, survey yourself for muscle development, and examine your genitals carefully, wondering if they are "normal." Sometimes you may compare your genitals with those of other boys to try and determine what is the "correct" size and shape.

Dissatisfaction with your body cuts you off from your true self. Your body *is* you—there's no other body on Earth like your body. It's unique, just as your astrological chart is not like any other chart. But,

Like the Rosetta stone, for those who know how to read it, the body is a living record of life given, life taken, life hoped for, life healed. . . . To confine the beauty and value of the body to anything less than this magnificence is to force the body to live without its rightful spirit, its rightful form, its right to exultation. To be thought ugly or unacceptable because one's beauty is outside current fashion is deeply wounding to the natural joy that belongs to the wild nature.
Clarissa Pinkola Estes,
Women Who Run with the Wolves

and this is the important part, your body isn't *all of you*. You have a mind, a heart, a personality, character, abilities, and aims and goals as well.

You cannot change the fundamentals of who you are or what body you came into the world with. Therefore, it's vitally necessary for you to accept yourself as you *are* because you have little or no control over who you find yourself to be. You do not create who you are. At best, you discover it and use it well and wisely. Nothing can transform a fundamentally small, fine-boned person into a tall, husky person, just as it's impossible to turn a heavy-boned body into a fragile, thin body.

The human body is like a blank canvas upon which our imaginations create images. Too many of us suffer from bad body images. Failing to appreciate that the body is the representative of the soul and thinking ourselves unacceptable as we are, we try to become something we are not to comform to some outside standard of fitness or beauty. And when we do not—because we cannot—we feel inferior, and our self-esteem is damaged along with our soul. Though we may never resolve the debate about the precise moment in which the soul enters the body, what is clear is that the soul does inhabit the body, and when either soul or body is neglected or denigrated, both suffer.

Ideas about the body vary with the times. Standards of beauty, health, and appropriate size, weight, and appearance have fluctuated over the centuries, and even today different cultures have different standards and views of the body, its nature, and its use.

To watch a human body at rest or in movement is to glimpse the soul of a person. We see our souls articulated in our gestures, our movements, our shapes, our physiognomy, the color of our skin, the shine in our eyes. We see disturbances to the soul expressed in bodily functions gone awry—skin eruptions, impaired movement, disease, and malfunctioning organs are all symptoms of soul distress. The body is the visible expression of the soul, and just as every soul is beautiful, every body is beautiful in its own special way.

Your Moon Sign holds a wonderful secret about your body, how to take good care of it, and how to make friends with it. It's called your *self-nurturing highlight*. Since the Moon is intimately related to all our bodily functions, it makes sense that your Moon Sign will tell you a lot about your body, doesn't it?

Your Self-Nurturing Highlight through the Signs

Aries Moon Your self-nurturing highlight is *physical exercise,* especially if you are a Fire type. Sports that use a lot of energy, like running and tennis, help you to work off excess emotional tension and replenish your overall vitality. Make a definite plan and set aside time each day for this purpose. As you have little patience with any personal need that interferes with what you want to do, you tend to ignore physical symptoms until they worsen or become serious. Your tendency to rush is another problem as you don't take the time to eat properly. However, preventive health care would serve to keep the independence you value so highly, for when you are sick you become dependent on others.

Taurus Moon Your self-nurturing highlight is *green and growing things,* whether an outside garden or houseplants, especially if you are an Earth type. Taurus is the most representative of nature. Being around plants and soil and nurturing them will nurture *you.* Even if it's only a small window garden, make sure you have plants, especially flowering ones, in your environment. Go regularly to parks and nature spots, wilderness areas if you can reach them, to renew and refresh your lunar self. Food is important to you, but if weight is a problem establish a comfortable routine of light, healthy, tasty, regular meals to offset your tendency to overindulge.

Gemini Moon Your self-nurturing highlight is *talking with people you can trust.* This is a must for a Gemini Moon who needs to air troubles and grievances at length. Find friends who are good listeners and give them equal time. That way, you'll always have people to talk to who won't feel that you are taking advantage of them. Don't ever deprive yourself of this basic need to talk things out with a trusted friend. Action and thought are the twin pillars of Gemini, but it's easy to get stuck in the mental-only polarity. Offset this by sandwiching the necessary action in between discussing its pros and cons, before and after.

Cancer Moon   Your self-nurturing highlight is *proximity to water*. The Moon rules Cancer, and the Moon rules the ocean tides. Being near water, especially the sea, nourishes and refreshes you. The ceaseless movement of the ocean feeds your soul and reconnects you to your element, especially if you are a Water type. If you can't get to the ocean, find a stream to sit by or take frequent long soaks in the tub. Naturally nurturing, you may get so involved in the needs of others that you neglect your own important personal needs. If self-neglect is chronic, you tend to eat excess sweet and starchy foods to soothe your feelings of deprivation. Combat this by taking good care of yourself. Learn to cook so you can prepare good, comforting homemade meals. Frequent naps will serve to restore you to emotional balance.

Leo Moon   Your self-nurturing highlight is *getting out in the sun,* especially if you are a Fire type. The natural warmth of Leo Moon can run cold during winter months or from too much time indoors. Getting out in the sun (the Sun rules Leo) will rejuvenate you. Try to take a vacation in the sun each winter, even if it's only a weekend or a day trip. You need positive feedback from others, so ask for this, even though, since you don't like to show your needs or display "down" times, you may be reluctant to seek nurturing from others. Leo's pride gets in the way. Learn to stem your tendency toward excess giving. Save your money for some time in the sun.

Virgo Moon   Your self-nurturing highlight is *letting up on perfectionism*. Into every life some dirt must fall, and though you do need an orderly and neat environment, you don't have to drive yourself crazy to get it. Accept that nobody is perfect, not even you, and learn to let others help so you aren't doing all the work yourself. Suspend critical judgment and learn to relax and just "hang out." The ceiling won't cave in if you take time off and your room goes neglected for a day or two. Overcome your reluctance to self-nurture—it's not an indulgence, it's a necessity. Move "self-care" from the bottom of your list of priorities to the *top*.

Libra Moon Your self-nurturing highlight is *beauty in your environment*. Whether it is a vase of fresh flowers, a new quilt for your bed, or a beautifully arranged room, you respond to a calm and refined atmosphere. This is because Libra Moon is relational—you need a feeling of harmony in order to be in balance within. A natural diplomat, you need peaceful, artfully decorated surroundings. The food you eat should be visually appealing, and your life should be filled with music and beautiful things. This doesn't have to cost a fortune—wonderful treasures can be bought cheaply at flea markets and thrift shops. You need to do things with someone else, not alone, so find a buddy who enjoys out-of-the-way shopping and artistic activities.

Scorpio Moon Your self-nurturing highlight is *solitude,* especially around water, even if it's only in the bathtub. Time to be alone and regenerate yourself is of the utmost importance. Scorpio is the Sign of the physician, and you have great self-healing powers, but your intensity and determination often prevent you from using them. Because you are so strong, you tend to overdo. But if you neglect self-care, you could get sick with something difficult to diagnose and treat. Learning to forgive is a must. Brooding on hurts can make you sick.

Sagittarius Moon Your self-nurturing highlight is *traveling*. Perhaps you cannot go off on a jaunt around the world, but recognize that you need travel to restore and refresh yourself. Make an effort to take some trips, even if only short ones. Travel keeps you from becoming stale and resentful. If you absolutely cannot travel, spend time with travel books, magazines, TV programs, and videos, and begin a travel savings account. Put away a few dollars every time you can for a future trip. Don't deny yourself this necessity. Sagittarius is the Sign of optimism and cheerfulness. Use the power of positive thinking and daily affirmations.

Capricorn Moon Your self-nurturing highlight is *learn to live in the present*. Security-conscious Capricorn Moon is always thinking of the future rainy day and fails to enjoy today's sunshine. Neglecting yourself in favor of working all the time with your eye on future financial security isn't a good idea. Plus, you can make yourself sick if you overdo it. Learn to relax and enjoy what you already have. Remember that what you worry about rarely happens.

To reinforce your Moon self with the idea that you are financially secure, buy yourself as a present that is as elegant and expensive as you can afford but that is also practical.

Aquarius Moon Your self-nurturing highlight is *whatever is different and unusual*. Aquarius Moon thrives on being "far out"—the farther out, the better. A natural rebel, you will find it's best to satisfy your craving for the different rather than waiting until you build up to the point of running off with a punk-rock group! You thrive on going against the grain of society, but don't overdo this. Even though you may fight anything that seems to want to be in authority over you—like proper meals, sufficient rest, keeping clean and organized, and dressing for the weather—this is actually your key to the freedom you desire. Learn to take care of yourself. Do it your own way—but do it.

Body Attitude Test

- Are you at peace with your body and your animal qualities, or do you try to rise above them?
- Do you acknowledge and treat respectfully your physical needs—for food, elimination, rest, recuperation, and grooming—or do you try to hide from view the basic human reality of your animal self?
- Are you proud and joyful to have a body that displays your connection to nature, or are you riddled with shame and guilt about your body?
- Do you believe fundamentally that your body is a place where "sin" resides, that you must be constantly on the alert to stamp out all bodily desires and needs?
- Are you proud of your mental abilities but ashamed of your body and its functions?
- Do you feel that the sudden urges and uncontrollable functions of your body are disgusting or shameful?

Your answers to the above questions will indicate whether you see yourself as a totality or have a one-sided view of yourself. Until you bring your body fully into relationship with your mind and spirit, you will not experience yourself as the single, unified being you really are.

Pisces Moon Your self-nurturing highlight is *allowing the spiritual in your life*. Pisces Moon is naturally connected to the higher realm of Spirit, but when you fail to recognize this and provide for it, the results can be drug abuse, alcoholism, depression, even insanity. While you take care of others, you are likely to feel guilty about your own needs. Restore yourself through meditation, prayer, free-form dance, spontaneous art, and music, but *learn the basics of self-care*. Take refuge in your inspirational nature, but come back into the real world where your body lives and take care of its needs—feed and clothe yourself, take long baths, get regular checkups, and don't forget your vitamins. Then you can be a ministering angel to those in need whom you choose to serve.

The Sun/Moon Combinations:
How They Affect You *and* Your Relationships

You've learned about your Sun Sign and how your Moon Sign works and how to use Moon knowledge to take care of your emotional self and combat stress. Now we're going to take a look at the various Sun/Moon combinations. Understanding how your Sun and Moon interact is a big step toward understanding yourself *and* understanding how you relate to other people—your parents, brothers and sisters, and most especially your romantic interests.

First you need to understand how your own Sun/Moon combination works; then you can move on to figure out how your Sun/Moon works with somebody else's Sun/Moon. Clearly, there are many different relationships in your life, and the Moon is the primary guide to the emotional side of relationships.

From studying the Aspects, you already know how to compare your own Sun or Moon with the Sun or Moon of another person. For example, if you have an Aries Sun or Moon and another person has a Libra Sun or Moon, you know that this pairing forms an *Opposition*, or difficult Aspect. Same-Sign Suns and Moons can be compatible (and usually are), while those that form the Trine Aspect are always happy together.

Remember that you have an Aspect between *your own* Sun and

Practice Exercise: Your Moon Sign

My Moon Sign is _____

My Moon Sign characteristics are _____

_____

_____

The characteristics I most identify with are _____

_____

_____

The characteristics I least identify with are _____

_____

_____

The characteristics I would most like to develop are _____

_____

_____

What I like best about my Moon Sign is _____

_____

_____

What I like least about my Moon Sign is _____

_____

_____

Moon, and once you have grasped what that means you can easily read the same Aspect between you and another person.

If you are focused on a romantic partner, the Sun/Moon Aspects between you will tell you about some *basic* personality characteristics—but not about what attracts you or what makes you fall in love. Those are the department of Venus and Mars (which we will discuss in chapter 4). Right now, it's time to learn about your Sun and Moon combination.

Remember that the Sun represents the "I am" principle, and that you are slowly growing into your Sun Sign. It represents where you are going in life, what makes you feel important, your direction, and your purpose in life.

Often young people ask an astrologer, "I'm a Libra and he's a Saggitarius; will we get along?" The question cannot be answered except in general terms, because the Sun Sign isn't about relationships except in the long run, when a common or complementary purpose is important. During your teen years, the Sun isn't what's up-front in a romantic relationship.

The way your Sun/Moon pair interacts is vital overall, but right now you are more involved with your emotions and your body than with your long-term life purpose, so your Moon is likely to be more active.

Sun/Moon Combinations through the Signs

Keep in mind as you read the various Sun/Moon combos that they can apply not only to you but to anyone else you know, and they can be a great help in understanding other people.

Aries Sun/Aries Moon   This combo is a Conjunction, which means your outer and inner selves work together easily and well. Having them together, you express the Aries characteristics very strongly because you *feel* them inside yourself as well as express them in the world. Your courage and impulsiveness are emotional needs as well as your natural way of approaching life.

Aries Sun/Taurus Moon   This combo means you are at odds with yourself. Your Aries energy is slowed down by Taurus. Your get-up-and-go is held back by your need for security and being careful. Your impulsiveness combines with your need to be conservative, not an easy duo. You may switch back and forth between action and taking it easy.

Aries Sun/Gemini Moon Fire and Air activate each other, so this combo makes you excitable and nervous. It may be hard for you to get enough rest because your Moon needs a lot of diversity while your Sun likes action but runs down quickly. The characteristics of both will be exaggerated because Air increases Fire. You are likely to be extremely social and try to do too much.

Aries Sun/Cancer Moon This combo makes a Square Aspect, and there's a basic conflict between Aries's active nature and Cancer's need to stay home and be cozy. Stress results when you let your Sun energy override your Moon needs, but if you take care of them all will be well. You can go out and be active and then retreat into your inner world to recharge your batteries.

Aries Sun/Leo Moon This combo is a double whammy—a Trine in Fire. With both Sun and Moon in Fire Signs, you burn with a high flame and can accomplish much. What Cardinal Aries starts, Fixed Leo finishes. A natural leader with lots of stamina, your actions take form easily. You can be a dynamo in sports or theatrical activities.

Aries Sun/Virgo Moon This combo is an odd couple. Aries wants to rush ahead and forget the details, while Virgo needs to dot the *i*'s and cross the *t*'s, keeping everything neat and tidy. Virgo's earthy practicality irks action-oriented Aries, but you'll learn as you go along that it's best to let your Moon help with finishing your homework so you can be free to get out later.

Aries Sun/Libra Moon This combo makes a Square—not an easy Aspect. Your active nature is tempered by your Moon's need for quiet and peaceful surroundings. Your inner needs and outer expression require effort to work together smoothly. Don't short your Moon needs or you'll surely get sick, which will keep you from being active. Listen to your inner self.

Aries Sun/Scorpio Moon Water smothers Fire, so this combo is difficult. Your intense Moon needs and deep emotional nature can make you bossy. Hurt feelings can lead to rash action, even violence. By giving due respect to your Moon nature, you can avoid getting into trouble. Learning to handle your anger without using force or brooding excessively will keep things on an even keel.

Aries Sun/Sagittarius Moon This makes a happy Trine combination. Aries's active nature combines with Sagittarius's upbeat moods and urge to travel. You're a sunny person, full of energy and eager to be on the way to somewhere, and you're a fun companion. Doing and going are uppermost in your thoughts rather than being committed to one person. Outdoor activities are a learning experience for you.

Aries Sun/Capricorn Moon This is a Square—not an easy combo. Your Moon's need for financial security and hard work gets in the way of your basic active nature. By learning to harness the two in a harmonious way, you can get a lot done. Capricorn will work to finish what Aries starts and never complain about how much trouble it is. These two energies *can* work successfully.

Aries Sun/Aquarius Moon The only problem with this combo is that you may spend all of your time thinking up new projects, starting them, and then leaving them unfinished because you are on to something new and more exciting. Your active nature combined with your need to rebel and be different makes you an unusual and intriguing person.

Aries Sun/Pisces Moon This is not a comfortable combo. Your Moon's sensitivity throws cold water on your hot active nature, making you doubtful and insecure. Directing your activities toward spiritual pursuits or artistic achievements would create a balance. Your Aries courage combines with your Pisces caring to make you unafraid to combat injustice when and where you find it.

Taurus Sun/Aries Moon This combo makes you persistent in pursuing your aims. Your Moon's insistence on action pushes your naturally slow-going personality into get-up-and-go mode. Both a starter and a finisher, your emotional nature fires you to finish what you start. You make a powerful impression on others. Avoid attitude and arrogance; learn to see yourself objectively.

Taurus Sun/Taurus Moon Lucky you—you are one of the most stable people around. Your outer and inner self match perfectly and you exhibit Taurus's good nature and stamina strongly. Your problem is too much Taurus—you can turn stubborn if you are pushed too hard. But your sweet nature usually wins the day. Pal around with some high-energy types to get yourself moving.

Taurus Sun/Gemini Moon This combo mixes stability with instability, but Taurus has a calming effect on nervous Gemini. If you learn to use the positive sides of both Signs, this is a great mix. Your Moon's need for diversity is balanced by your Sun's demand for serene stability. You are a good learner with many interests and will carry through to the finish line.

Taurus Sun/Cancer Moon Earthy Taurus and watery Cancer are a good combo. Both like the domestic scene to be peaceful and quiet. Your Moon moods are centered by your basic stable nature. The problem is that hurt feelings will activate your protective tendency, turning from stubborn to sullen. Combat this by nurturing your Moon self, and don't ever be ashamed to cry!

Taurus Sun/Leo Moon This fixed Square needn't be a problem if you give your Moon what it needs—attention! Your Sun would be happy alone, but your Moon must hear the crowd clapping for its performance. Physically strong, you could choose sports that require endurance and generate approval. Artistically inclined, you would be a natural for drama class.

Taurus Sun/Virgo Moon This earthy Trine is an easy combo. Your Moon's need for perfection is complemented by your natural stamina. You will work for endless hours to create and complete your projects. Nothing is too much for you to take on, and your satisfaction comes from the work accomplished. You don't need a lot of praise or encouragement. Just remember to get some rest!

Taurus Sun/Libra Moon This combo can work well together. Your need for a calm, beautiful environment is echoed by your basic urge for peace and artistic experience. The danger is anger that you don't express. Holding in your feelings can tilt over to sulkiness, which eventually will explode powerfully. Your Moon can balance and lighten your resistance to change.

Taurus Sun/Scorpio Moon A powerful combo! Your intense Moon combines with your strong endurance to make you a power-house. Your need for privacy is reinforced by your Sun's placid nature. Keep in mind that your powerful emotional nature is backed by your endurance, and avoid carrying grudges. Try to be open about feelings. Discussing what's bothering you is a safety fuse.

Taurus Sun/Sagittarius Moon You may feel like two different people with this combo. Your Moon inspires you and helps get your stable self off its duff. Each has what the other lacks: your inner spontaneity needs your practicality to keep it in check. At the same time, it lightens up your materialistic inclinations. To avoid conflict, make sure your Moon isn't overridden by Sun.

Taurus Sun/Capricorn Moon This is an extremely stable combo. It gives you the ability to work hard for long periods of time and accomplish what you set out to do, but beware of overwork and insufficient rest. Your chilly Moon nature is warmed by your generous Sun nature. Being an earthy mix, your Earth characteristics are right up front and you take charge easily.

Taurus Sun/Aquarius Moon Not an easy combo, the Fixed Signs in this Square can be at odds with each other. However, your Moon needs tend to loosen up your Sun's conservative nature, and together they can put ideas into reality. This mixture makes you logical *and* practical, and you can be depended upon to be calm and reasonable when the waters around you get troubled.

Taurus Sun/Pisces Moon This combo works well. Your need to help is backed up with stability and stamina. Sun holds Moon's hand and calms her down when she is hurt by the big bad world. You can be a helper who rationally chooses whom should be helped. With your warm and solid nature, you can go off on flights of fancy without fear of getting lost in never-never land.

Gemini Sun/Aries Moon This talkative combo makes your mind sharp as a tack, and sometimes your tongue as well. Sarcasm and wounding witty remarks fly out of your mouth. Sharpen your wit on neutral targets, not your friends—or you'll soon have none. Your need to be independent combines with your lively personality and can make you impulsive. Curb this tendency.

Gemini Sun/Taurus Moon This combo makes you both flexible and dependable. Your stable inner emotional self calms down your natural nervous vibration, allowing you to understand complex situations. Because you go at a slow and steady pace emotionally, you can harness your busy mental nature and accomplish much. Self-expression through the arts helps to develop your sensitivity.

Gemini Sun/Gemini Moon This combo exaggerates Gemini characteristics, making you more Gemini than someone with a Gemini Sun only. You're forever flitting here and there, soaking up all the information you can lay your hands on. Your personality sparkles and you have many friendships involving much discussion. Make sure your mouth doesn't run your life! Get some quiet time.

Gemini Sun/Cancer Moon This combo tunes in to intuition. Your Moon understands the world of feeling, and your Sun thrives on ideas and words. Together, because of their differences, they make a fascinating pair. You react quickly and with much feeling, combining mental analysis with emotional sensitivity. Your problem is finding balance between mentality and emotionality.

Gemini Sun/Leo Moon This combo makes you a talker who wants attention, and you get it easily. You have a talent for public speaking and could join the debate team. You communicate well and want feedback on what you have to say. Brainstorming ideas is fun, and you have the determination to put them into action and get results. Your warm and witty personality makes you popular.

Gemini Sun/Virgo Moon This mental combo lets you put ideas into reality with ease. Your logical nature hooks up with your need to be of service and be precise about details. Your Moon nicely balances your tendency to be scattered mentally, so you don't waste your brainpower. Moon appreciates Sun's mental approach, but Sun may get frustrated by Moon's fussy attention to details.

Gemini Sun/Libra Moon This combo is a bit too rational and can get caught up in too much discussion. Moon's diplomacy and need for peace can hamper Sun's urge for constant diversity. You learn well and easily and like exploring new and different concepts, but this is not a practical mix. The danger is that you can get lost in your own mental gyrations and never get anything done.

Gemini Sun/Scorpio Moon   This combo is difficult. Moon's intense emotions interfere with Sun's lighthearted, flirty nature. Your need to be committed and intimate in relationships conflicts with your socializing, talkative nature. You may chatter on about superficial things while hiding your deepest feelings from others. Letting yourself discuss your feelings openly will help balance this team.

Gemini Sun/Sagittarius Moon   This is a happy combo because Air and Fire excite each other. With you there's plenty of give and take; you're full of ideas and love to build castles in the air. The difficulty is that you may never get them built on the ground! You tend to overdo the extroverted, fun-person role by running madly around collecting information and experiences to no purpose.

Gemini Sun/Capricorn Moon   This combo is a difficult one, for Moon's need for practical use of your time conflicts with Sun's urge for freedom to run around aimlessly. Moon grounds Sun, but this can feel uncomfortable and make you want to break away. Learn to put your ideas to practical ends to fulfill your Moon needs. Otherwise, you may be caught between Sun and Moon and feel alienated from yourself.

Gemini Sun/Aquarius Moon   This airy combination is fun and very mental. Your Moon doesn't like to fool with messy emotional scenes, and your Sun agrees that it's more pleasurable to spend time taking in information from as many sources as possible and then to think about it all in abstract terms. You may lack inspiration and run the danger of living in your head all the time.

Gemini Sun/Pisces Moon   This combo produces intuition and sensitivity but can scatter your resources. Your deep, compassionate, feeling nature conflicts with your basic urge not to commit to any one thing. Your Sun can support your Moon by gathering information on the causes that interest her need to help. The danger is a basic incompatibility that's frustrating.

Cancer Sun/Aries Moon This combo makes you a real starter, but you start fast and finish slow. You have a good memory and retain what you learn easily because you receive information through your feelings. Your natural urge to crawl inside yourself when hurt or disappointed is balanced by your emotional need to take action. A born rebel, you can go to extremes.

Cancer Sun/Taurus Moon This combo makes you charming and home-loving as well as practical and sometimes stubborn when you don't get your way. Your inner ability to stick to it when the going gets rough protects your tender, sensitive nature and will hit back if you are pushed. Watch out for broodiness and moodiness, and learn not to take things so personally.

Cancer Sun/Gemini Moon This combo is an odd mix. While you are sensitive to everything going on around you, emotionally you are lighthearted and don't take the heavy stuff too seriously. Luckily, your adaptable, versatile, emotional nature protects your tendency to be easily hurt. Decision making can be a problem, and you need to learn to curb worry over nothing.

Cancer Sun/Cancer Moon This combo reinforces all of Cancer's characteristics. In this case, because the Moon rules Cancer, the Sun takes on something of a lunar cast. Whatever house the two Planets occupy will be strongly oriented toward Moon qualities. You are extremely sensitive and easily hurt; family is ultra important and you want one of your own as soon as possible.

Cancer Sun/Leo Moon This combo may be difficult to reconcile because your basic nature is shy and retiring while your Moon needs to be in the limelight. Acting may be the solution because actors pretend to be someone else. In this mix, Moon is dominant—her needs make Sun uncomfortable. A firm home base helps.

Cancer Sun/Virgo Moon This combo can work well together. Your naturally kind nature combines with your need to be helpful and useful. You enjoy the domestic scene and like housekeeping and learning about food and nutrition. Studying the culinary arts or learning about health care would be good choices to combine your home-loving self with your heath-oriented emotional nature.

Cancer Sun/Libra Moon This combo creates the urge to merge. Your Sun wants a home of its own and your Moon needs a committed relationship, preferably marriage. Chances are you will want to marry early, but take care an unwanted pregnancy isn't the route you take! There's a strong urge that can't be denied, but don't let it send you off in the wrong life direction.

Cancer Sun/Scorpio Moon This Water combo can drown you in intense feelings. Your tendency to have hurt feelings activates Scorpio's sting. Your natural moodiness and sensitivity combined with Moon's intensity creates a personality with depth and compassion. Watch out for emotional excess, being clinging and dependent, and the tendency to obsess.

Cancer Sun/Sagittarius Moon This combo is like living with a moody, security-craving, home-loving person who also wants to be on the road all the time. Not easy! Sensitivity and insensitivity mix here, as do wanting to make a nest and waiting to leave the nest. Use your Moon's need for optimism and cheerfulness to lighten your Sun's heavy moods and cheer him up.

Cancer Sun/Capricorn Moon This combo is a happy one. Your home-loving, sensitive nature is helped out by your Moon's organizational and managerial needs. Your cold feelings are warmed up by your Sun's sentimental and protective nature, and this mixture can have a wonderful sense of humor combining looniness with irony. The danger is Moon's pessimism dragging Sun into depression.

Cancer Sun/Aquarius Moon This combo can be difficult to handle. In contrast to the usual emotional pattern, your Moon doesn't want to bother with emotions because they are messy, but your Sun is sensitive and sentimental. They are bound to quarrel, and you have to be the peacemaker who negotiates the treaty.

Cancer Sun/Pisces Moon This combo reinforces your sensitive nature with deep emotional sensitivity. It makes you a psychic sponge. You soak up everything of an emotional nature in the atmosphere and make it your own, even if it doesn't belong to you. You are able to "read" others' thoughts and feelings. You have difficulty separating yourself from emotional situations.

Leo Sun/Aries Moon With this combo you're a real fireball. You are courageous and have enthusiasm to spare. Both loyal and fiercely independent, you can always be counted on, and you stick by your friends unless they betray you. Self-reliance is your hallmark, but you have a tendency to overdramatize. Learn to see the big picture and get beyond the merely personal.

Leo Sun/Taurus Moon This combo makes you good-natured, warm, loyal, and firm of purpose. Your endurance is almost inexhaustible, and once you get going you are unstoppable. The danger is fear of change and getting stuck in a rut. Also, you can powerhouse your way through obstacles without first insuring that no one gets hurt. Learn diplomacy and recognize that compromise is often necessary.

Leo Sun/Gemini Moon This combo gives you ideas and the energy to put them into action. You have the ability to get your inner and outer self in sync, blending heart and head together. Be careful you don't gossip in order to get attention—you won't be appreciated if you do. Learn to be sociable without trying to impress people with your wit and charm.

Leo Sun/Cancer Moon This combo brings out your affectionate and nurturing inner nature and your strong protective instincts for anybody or anything smaller or weaker than you are. Although your inner nature is shy and retiring, you love the limelight and can use that bright spot to conceal your feelings. Getting overemotional is a danger. When hurt, you tend to withdraw.

Leo Sun/Leo Moon Congratulations! With this combo you are full of sunshine—one of the happiest persons around. That is, as long as you are the center of attention pretty much all of the time. You exude warmth and generosity and have more friends than you can count, as long as you curb your tendency to be self-centered to the point that others find you a boring pain.

Leo Sun/Virgo Moon This can be a touchy combo because your sunny nature is chilled by your emotional demand for practicality, which doesn't suit grandiose Leo. The upside is that you have staying power as well as the ability to handle details, and you can use this mix to lead as well as participate in the gritty details of any project. Your warmth and helpfulness make you popular.

Leo Sun/Libra Moon This is an easy combo, especially for the artistically inclined teen. Your inner sense of beauty and balance combine with your exuberant outer personality for good communication. Your need for calm and serenity tones down your boisterous demand for attention and gives a good balance.

Leo Sun/Scorpio Moon This is a powerful combo. Both are Fixed Signs giving you staying power plus intensity. You aren't easy to live with at times, even for yourself, because your deep emotional needs reinforce your craving for the limelight. You'll go to almost any length to get what you want. Be careful not to tread on others or use your power as a battering ram.

Leo Sun/Sagittarius Moon A happy Fire combo, your sunny nature is reinforced by your inner optimism and love of learning. A good student, you are popular and can get the crowd fired up easily. You are a leader and an idea producer who can make sparks fly. Temper can be a problem as you set off quickly, but you don't tend to sulk over things. Action quells your anger.

Leo Sun/Capricorn Moon This combo can work if you work it. Your stodgy inner self benefits from your extroversion and harnesses your tendency to grandstand. Still, your cool Moon and your hot Sun may sometimes be at odds with each other and require you to be a moderator. You may be rarin' to go shine on the world, but disappointment or failure can result in depression.

Leo Sun/Aquarius Moon This combo is a warm-cool mixture with fixity in common. You tend to be spontaneously warm one day and coolly rational the next. Too much extroversion can exhaust you; beware of filling your calendar too full. Give yourself time to wind down after a busy day, and take regular time alone to recharge both mentally and physically.

Leo Sun/Pisces Moon This combo makes you compassionate and your inner need to help others and engage in spiritual pursuits works well with your warmhearted personality. Your sensitive Moon tones down your tendency to self-centeredness. You are creative and could study art. You'd make a good camp counselor. Be careful your weepy Moon doesn't depress your sunny side.

Virgo Sun/Aries Moon　This combo gives you a keen wit, and you can express yourself with enthusiasm and precision. Your inner emotional nature burns with a high flame and ignites you mentally, making you witty and dynamic. Your ability to produce ideas from within through intuition combines with your ability to make things work on the practical level. Just don't oversell yourself.

Virgo Sun/Taurus Moon　This interesting earthy combo makes you a gentle and easygoing person who loves creature comforts. You aim to provide as much physical comfort for yourself as you can manage, and you'll work hard at the details because you love beautiful things. Underneath, you're a poet who is also practical. Guard against being an overcautious couch potato.

Virgo Sun/Gemini Moon　This flexible and interesting combo gives you a need to be mentally active and versatile with the staying power to sift through all your information sources and keep things orderly and neat. Although you love gossip, you are too honest to circulate false rumors. Your problem is keeping in touch with your feelings, which tend to skitter away from you.

Virgo Sun/Cancer Moon　A quiet combo, you are both sensitive and given to taking care of details. You love nurturing—people, pets, plants—and you do it with careful attention and loving care. Good at projects that let you utilize both your mental and emotional natures simultaneously, you may tend to get overinvolved and overburdened. Be careful not to take on more than you can handle and don't let others take advantage of your helpful, kind nature!

Virgo Sun/Leo Moon　Here's a combo that has a lot of potential for getting things done—and done right the first time. Your keen mental abilities are enhanced by your strong ethical sense. Your helpful nature and warm and sunny disposition make you a good friend. People appreciate both your generosity and your practical side. Letting people know you need praise and feedback may be a problem you'll have to overcome. You need to develop initiative and independence.

Virgo Sun/Virgo Moon　This Conjunction makes you more of a thinker than most people. You are a good student and can attend to the details of more than one project at a time. You are discriminating, precise, and accurate, and you like to work with details. The danger is in getting so caught up in counting the trees that you can't see the forest all around you.

Virgo Sun/Libra Moon　This combo can make you indecisive or too fussy about the details to decide on A over B. However, you are an independent thinker and enjoy learning. Your natural tact makes you do things tastefully and harmoniously. Standing up for yourself can be a problem, and you need to accept that some dirt and disorder can't be avoided.

Virgo Sun/Scorpio Moon　This combo can make for secrecy and a desire to be left alone to think and do your own thing. Interference in your projects makes you angry. You like to dig deep into your own inner self and sort things out without being bothered. You have great intuition and want to know what's really going on underneath appearances.

Virgo Sun/Sagittarius Moon　This flexible combo likes a lot of variety and can switch from one thought to another with lightning speed. Your inner optimism uplifts your tendency to depression and worry and lets you approach life philosophically and with warmth. Getting these twin sides of your nature together can be a challenge because caution curbs your need for freedom.

Virgo Sun/Capricorn Moon　This combo lets you think things out thoroughly and seriously before you take action. Your ability to get your work done is excellent. New ideas pop out like popcorn, and your emotional self takes them seriously and examines them for practicality, which means you don't waste time on useless projects. Use humor to lighten up and be less materialistic.

Virgo Sun/Aquarius Moon　This combo makes your mind ingenious and flexible, able to handle a variety of things simultaneously. You travel to strange and interesting places in your inner world without getting lost, bringing back inventions and great technological plans. Then you work though the details to get them from the abstract mental plane into the physical world. Develop warmth and restrain from being calculating.

Virgo Sun/Pisces Moon　This combo is extremely flexible; it may be difficult for you to settle down because your inner nature is always pulling you into never-never land. However, your sense of practical reality will always balance the situation. You have strong intuitions and a sympathetic nature, but you need to calm restlessness and deal more directly with others.

Libra Sun/Aries Moon With this Cardinal combo, you are both gentle and independent. Your natural good manners and refined ways are stimulated and contrasted by your inner need to take action and express yourself forcefully. At times, you will be in conflict between impatience and wanting to be polite. Take care you don't let your emotional enthusiasm derail you.

Libra Sun/Taurus Moon With this friendly combo, your nature is harmonious and affectionate. You appreciate all things beautiful and may have artistic talent. Your environment should be both lovely and very comfortable. The problem is your tendency to be influenced by others and fall into sentimentality. However, if you are pushed against your will, stubborness results.

Libra Sun/Gemini Moon This airy combo makes you a conversationalist. You express yourself with both wit and charm and are a popular person. Your natural good taste and refinement are enlivened by your quick mind, but you can be fickle in your emotions. Finding a stable center and getting grounded is a major challenge. Don't let fickle emotions keep you from solid learning.

Libra Sun/Cancer Moon With this Cardinal combo, you are sensitive to others' feelings and like to keep things peaceful and serene. Your moodiness is balanced by your need for harmony. Your perceptions of others are quick, and you have a marvelous capacity for making people feel comfortably at home. Don't let your amiability keep you from finding your own way.

Libra Sun/Leo Moon This romantic combo makes you an idealist with a good sense of aesthetics. A charmer, you can talk your way out of almost any scrape. Just don't overdo the charm or you'll be accused of insincerity. Indecision is a bore and you're prone to it, alternating between action and inaction. Watch your tendency to trust without proof of trustworthiness.

Libra Sun/Virgo Moon This mixed-match combo gives you lots of new ideas and flexibility along with a nature that is reasonable and charming. You have both analytical ability and a sense of proportion, but decision making is difficult and tedious. To make decisions more easily, learn to focus on the big picture instead of getting stuck in the details and endless options.

Libra Sun/Libra Moon   This gentle Conjunction puts your outer and inner nature in perfect harmony—just what you like best! Sensitive and romantic, you have great delicacy of feeling and are kind and considerate. Your problem is an inability to make decisions and fluctuating emotions, caused by your tendency to weigh the pros and cons to the *n*th degree. Work on standing your ground without worrying what others think.

Libra Sun/Scorpio Moon   This odd combo gives you an inner toughness and an outer gentleness. Your strong emotional nature makes you ambitious and powerful. You can put all your energy into your goals—if you can only decide what they are! Beware of using your deep emotional nature to take revenge secretly when you feel offended but can't come right out with your beef.

Libra Sun/Sagittarius Moon   With this lively combo you are never bored. As an initiator, you are also flexible. Sociable with a love of adventure, you have a strong sense of justice and will work to mediate disputes. Your problem is that you often flit from one thing to another, not resolving the first before taking up the second. You need to learn to focus and develop practicality.

Libra Sun/Capricorn Moon   This Cardinal combo makes a Square Aspect, which can have you at odds with yourself. Your gentle, polite nature can give in to your emotional need for control and management. You have good discipline and a strong sense of purpose, but you need to curb your opportunistic tendency and develop your sense of both individual needs and society's requirements.

Libra Sun/Aquarius Moon   This imaginative combo can get along well or quarrel, depending on the situation. You tend to flip back and forth between attachment and detachment. Your emotions run more to the mental than the feeling mode, and with a sensitive and romantic nature this can be a problem. You have good insight into human nature and can stand back and be objective.

Libra Sun/Pisces Moon   This gentle combo makes you extremely charming and sensitive, with excellent ability at observation. You have the ability to just *feel* what others are all about and be correct. Your twin problems are difficulty making decisions and a tendency to sacrifice your own needs in favor of the needs of others. Artistic pursuits will give you a much-needed outlet.

♏ ♈ **Scorpio Sun/Aries Moon** With this powerhouse combo, your character expresses itself passionately, courageously, and with resoluteness. Your inner need for action combines with your powerful outer drive, which means you can accomplish almost anything you set your mind to. You have the guts and the ability to identify problems and do something about them fast. Don't be bossy.

♏ ♉ **Scorpio Sun/Taurus Moon** This fixed combo is a powerful duo, practically unstoppable. You can plan on a large scale and follow through with inner determination as well as outer power. You combine artistic and practical qualities. You will stand up to the world and let the chips fall where they may. You know you are a winner, but learn to be graceful in in those occasional times when you lose.

♏ ♊ **Scorpio Sun/Gemini Moon** This oddball combo can be complementary if you work it right. You have a deep sense of honor, which offsets your somewhat fickle emotional nature. You may try using your emotional skills and versatility to change others, but that doesn't usually work, so be careful. The only person you can change is yourself! Cynicism can be a problem, as can getting in too deep. Learn to curb your extremism and your flighty nature.

♏ ♋ **Scorpio Sun/Cancer Moon** This watery combo gives you keen intuition and much emotional sensitivity—sometimes too much! Insecurity can be a problem, but this is a good duo if you can give up power struggles. Your outer strength protects your inner vulnerability, but don't use your Scorpio sting to get back at what hurts your feelings.

♏ ♌ **Scorpio Sun/Leo Moon** This magnetic combo's Fixed nature makes you someone to reckon with. Your sense of honor is deeply ingrained, and you'll hit back with force if anyone challenges you or it. Integrity is your hallmark. Your personality is charismatic—when you walk into a room, people know you're there! Overdramatizing is a problem, and you need to develop detachment.

♏ ♍ **Scorpio Sun/Virgo Moon** With this combo you can dig deeply to the bottom of things and make a precise plan for improvements or changes. Combining steadiness of purpose with flexibility of mind, you are gifted with much insight. A hard worker if you see the practical end of your efforts, you have patience and the stamina to see things through no matter what the obstacles.

Scorpio Sun/Libra Moon This combo gives you natural poise and the ability to smooth over disputes, along with a talent for developing unusually keen insights into others' motives. You can both initiate and finish what you start because you put a lot of emotional power behind what you want. Don't expect everyone to have your understanding or you'll suffer disappointment.

Scorpio Sun/Scorpio Moon With this extremely intense combo, you are self-reliant, magnetic, charismatic, passionate, and creative. Your matching outer and inner nature make you a powerhouse—for good or for evil. Be sure to keep your power drive in check and use it for positive ends. Don't try to dominate others or situations, and think before you use that Scorpio sting.

Scorpio Sun/Sagittarius Moon This combo makes an unlikely pair. Your lighthearted inner nature leavens your power-heavy driving outer nature. It's not a bad mixture, however, if you use it productively and positively. You are sincere about your principles and will defend them to the death. Curb impulsiveness, and don't be too blunt with the unsuspecting about what you are feeling!

Scorpio Sun/Capricorn Moon This combo is not one to take any guff from anyone. Strength and purpose combine here to make you a tough cookie with good insight, independence, intense drive, organizational ability, and the stamina to sustain your chosen direction. This duo makes you dynamic and practical. Your problems are lack of flexibility and a tendency to be overbearing.

Scorpio Sun/Aquarius Moon This Fixed combo can either get along or fight, and it's up to you to make it work. Your inner vision can get help from your outer power-in-the-world to make itself real rather than just imagined. Your independence is emotionally based and therefore strongly ingrained. You like to be different and are tolerant of others being different.

Scorpio Sun/Pisces Moon This watery combo is a good one. Your ultrasensitive inner nature is protected by the powerful guardian factor of your other personality. Take care, however, not to hit back hard enough to hurt someone, or your sensitive emotions will be guilt-ridden for years. You are extremely intuitive and can "tune in" automatically to people and situations around you.

Sagittarius Sun/Aries Moon With this dynamic Trine combo, you have enough energy for two people, and maybe three or four! Your enthusiasm and spirit of adventure are far-reaching. You love the outdoors and action sports. Caution: Take care you don't hurt yourself with your impulsive and fearless nature. This won't sit well with your dynamic duo, but please try to develop restraint.

Sagittarius Sun/Taurus Moon Lucky you—this combo gives you the best of both worlds. You are outgoing and adventurous and at the same time grounded and practical. You'll practically never set a foot wrong. Your noncommittal outer side is perfectly balanced by your affectionate inner nature. You love hugs! You may have artistic talent, so do explore it.

Sagittarius Sun/Gemini Moon This dynamic combo makes you an active person both physically and mentally. You're highly aware of what's going on all around you, and your spinning mind takes it all in. You express yourself well verbally but may have trouble settling down to the essay-writing part of your schooling. Maybe you could have your teacher let you give a speech instead!

Sagittarius Sun/Cancer Moon This Fire/Water combo can work, but you have to apply some extra effort to integrate your natural outgoing nature with your deeply sensitive and private emotional inner self. Don't despair—both Signs give you imaginative power, and you have the ability to blend intellectual understanding with feeling and intuition. Don't fall for the glamour pitch.

Sagittarius Sun/Leo Moon This dynamic, showboating Fire duo has all the energy of a jetliner. You are independent, outgoing, and principled, and you love to learn. Performance is in your veins, and acting is definitely a possibility. Warmth and loyalty run deep in you; your trouble spot comes with having to deal with so much impractical energy. Calm down with relaxation exercises.

Sagittarius Sun/Virgo Moon This versatile combo gives you an interesting personality—your mind can both grasp the broad principles and handle the picky details. Emotionally, you are quite grounded and not likely to fly off the handle when things go wrong. You're fun to be around—witty and full of humor. Just don't go too far, and watch out for a tendency to criticize.

Sagittarius Sun/Libra Moon This combo isn't really difficult, but it takes some doing to make it work harmoniously. Your rough-housing outer nature conflicts with your need for beauty, politeness, and refined surroundings. You may flip back and forth until you find the right balance. Your generous nature combines with a sense of proportion. Keep at least one foot on the ground.

Sagittarius Sun/Scorpio Moon This odd-couple combo isn't much of a problem as you know your own mind and can look at life from a broad perspective. You combine depth with humor and light-heartedness, but if your principles are challenged you'll defend them with all your considerable might. Outdoor activities, like active sports, can channel your intense emotional energy positively.

Sagittarius Sun/Sagittarius Moon This Fire Trine combo is almost all positive. Your inner and outer natures are in sync, making you able to see everything that happens in terms of its broader meaning. You love learning because your emotional nature craves it. You need travel and may take off on your own for a solitary backpacking adventure at an early age. Don't hurt yourself!

Sagittarius Sun/Capricorn Moon This dynamic combo makes you a different cup of tea from your fellows. Your somewhat cool, cautious emotional nature benefits from your hot outer nature, which is always in motion. You have the gift of seeing life in terms of both ethics and a sense of order. You express yourself with charm and humor when you're in the mood.

Sagittarius Sun/Aquarius Moon With this expressive combo, you're a good communicator who perceives the broad horizons of life easily. You will defend your point of view—verbally, not with your fists—when it is challenged. You may suffer from a touch of self-righteousness on occasion, and you need to learn that there's more to life than words and abstract thought—try to *feel* your emotions!

Sagittarius Sun/Pisces Moon With this flexible combo you are nothing if not interesting. Your inner sensitivity hooks up with your outer sense of justice and can make you a crusader for the under-privileged. Your natural awareness of influences from the world of spirit gives you a sympathic nature and produces charitable feelings for those in need. Don't overdo taking care of others to the point where you neglect your own needs.

Capricorn Sun/Aries Moon Not an easy combo, this Square pits your emotional need for action against your natural caution and concern for order and stability. Getting these two antagonists to work well together takes effort. You need to learn to channel your tendency to impulsiveness into your ability to organize and take charge so you can successfully chart your own course.

Capricorn Sun/Taurus Moon With this earthy combo you are one of the most stable teens imaginable. You naturally avoid the general group trends and exert your individuality. Your dependable, down-to-earth nature makes you a favorite with adults as well as peers. You are a leader who has stick-to-it practical qualities. Your problem is resisting the new and unusual. Lighten up!

Capricorn Sun/Gemini Moon This interesting combo makes you an idea person who can get the job done. You combine excitement and versatility with stability and practicality. Both ingenious and methodical, you have excellent imagination and the ability to realize your ideas. By learning to channel your active imagination into real projects, you'll come out a winner.

Capricorn Sun/Cancer Moon This combo lets you deal with practical matters in a sensitive manner. You can look deeply into yourself and others and use intuition to understand what's going on. A solid citizen with deep feelings, you are every parent's dream teen. Just don't crawl into your shell during rough times. Sleep on it. Tomorrow is always another day.

Capricorn Sun/Leo Moon This powerful combo gives you an air of authority. Your need for the limelight combines with immense stability and personal warmth. Each side of you has what the other lacks—your inner self is warm, spontaneous, generous, and inspiring, while your basic nature is solid and practical with an eye toward the end result. Avoid becoming too materialistic.

Capricorn Sun/Virgo Moon This earthy combo works extremely well. Virgo is the mental Earth Sign, and your emotional flexibility keeps your practical nature from getting stuck in a rut. New ideas come easily along with the concrete plans to make them work. Your problem is self-criticism and a yearning for impossible perfection. Learn to take time off for recreation.

Capricorn Sun/Libra Moon With this Cardinal combo, you have balance and foresight. You can envision the ideal direction you want to take and plan accordingly. Your high ideals combine with a pleasant personality and diplomatic ability. You appreciate beauty and demand quality and excellence. Your need for relationships lets you work well in twosomes. Your main problem is reconciling excess politeness with a strong personality.

Capricorn Sun/Scorpio Moon This powerful combo is practically unstoppable. Your intense emotional nature puts extra drive into your tendency to work hard and achieve. Goal oriented, you can plan in advance. You have a tendency to be a loner and need solitude often. Try to find a trusted friend as a listener who understands. Don't be judgmental, and work to develop some flexibility.

Capricorn Sun/Sagittarius Moon With this combo, you have a great sense of dry humor and can be the life of the party. A good student, you love learning and have the ability to organize your work well. Never short of energy, you see the large picture easily. You combine practicality with vision and spontaneity. Don't overwork, and exercise frequently to release your nervous energy. Relax!

Capricorn Sun/Capricorn Moon With this matching combo, you are more Capricorn than usual. Your emotional nature reinforces your basic drive, and you will work hard and long to achieve your considerable goals. Success is assured—your self-control is amazing. Problems result when you refuse to open yourself to relationships. Pessimism is a danger, as is a tendency to feel put upon.

Capricorn Sun/Aquarius Moon With this combo, you're never a boring person. Combining practicality with unusual ideas, you are an original. Go for the gold with your drive and ability to think big! Watch out for unrealistic, high-flown plans that defy reality, and find time to relax and play the intellectual games you love. Your problem is chilly emotions—practice learning to *feel*.

Capricorn Sun/Pisces Moon This combo gives you quietness and depth, with superior intuition. You understand people easily and are sympathetic to their problems. A doer and a feeler, you combine both and can make an impact. Don't flip-flop from one project to another; finish what you start and learn to focus. Be careful not to overdo on your urge to help others.

Aquarius Sun/Aries Moon   With this fun combo, you are a sparkler—full of energy and unusual ideas. You have a good mental understanding of how things work, and your emotional spontaneity fuels the flame of your far-reaching mind. An extrovert, you are likely to be involved in group activities and active solo sports. Your problem is emotional instability and detachment.

Aquarius Sun/Taurus Moon   With this sure and steady combo, you have real character. You are a loyal friend with tolerance for other people's differences. Physical comfort is important for you—if you are uncomfortable, your ability to think is hampered. Make sure you have a comfortable study environment. Your problem is stubborn refusal to change your mind.

Aquarius Sun/Gemini Moon   This combo gets along well but doesn't care much for the emotional side of life. Mentally you're ingenious, but emotionally you're fickle because you crave variety in relationships. A good student, you can express yourself well and with originality. Your problem is too many ideas for reality. Learn that the grass isn't always greener elsewhere.

Aquarius Sun/Cancer Moon   With this companionable combo, you have lots of friends who appreciate your unusual personality combined with your genuine warmth and caring nature. You have good insight into other people and can achieve balance between your sensitive inner self and your mental outer self. Don't let your strong attachment to your odd ideas take you out of this world!

Aquarius Sun/Leo Moon   With this sturdy combo, your inner and outer selves make a dynamic duo with imagination to spare. Your innovative ideas easily become reality. Romantic to the core and a good friend, you are popular, especially in groups—where you likely are a leading figure. Avoid hogging the center stage and let others have a chance for some attention. Practice quietness.

Aquarius Sun/Virgo Moon   This mentally oriented combo gives you logic, unusual ideas, and precision. You are extremely good at details and won't get lost in your abstract mental gyrations. You analyze objectively and can express yourself extremely well. Your problems are being a perfectionist, giving in to self-pity, and being too detached from the emotional sphere.

Aquarius Sun/Libra Moon   This sociable combo makes you a popular guy or gal. You attract others with your wit and kindness. You're a combination of the unusual and the traditional. Inside you love hearts and flowers, while outside you want high-tech to the max. You are intuitive and sensitive and like balance and harmony. Your problem is not getting enough time alone.

Aquarius Sun/Scorpio Moon   With this Fixed combo, you have the best and the worst of times. Your intense presence is magnetic and your self-confidence strong and firm. You have stamina, stability, and the ability to influence others—individually and in groups. Your problem is wanting to be in control and holding your feelings inside. Don't develop any grudges.

Aquarius Sun/Sagittarius Moon   This independent combo makes you forthright in expression and gives you a strong social consciousness. You like people—the more the merrier. A popular teen, you are admired for your spunk and different ways of seeing things. Your problem is lack of commitment and living too much in your head. Let your heart get into the act a little bit!

Aquarius Sun/Capricorn Moon   This responsible combo can make you overly serious with a touch of bossiness. You're imaginative, with the practical ability to execute your ideas into form. Group activities suit you well, and you are a good organizer for them. Your problem is *feelings*. Most of the time you consider them an irritant that you wish would go away. Let up a little!

Aquarius Sun/Aquarius Moon   This matched combo may make you seem—to others and yourself—as if you are from another planet. You are exceptionally different, and you express your unusual personality with pizzazz and flair. Parents may find your dress or makeup shocking, and peers may call you weird. Don't let it bother you. Learn to relate more on the person-to-person level.

Aquarius Sun/Pisces Moon   This fascinating combo gives you the inspiration to blend your thinking and feeling natures. A natural do-gooder, you love humanity both at large and individually, and you put your money where your mouth is by helping others less fortunate than yourself. You blend reason with sympathy and fantasy and can control your self-sacrificing tendency.

Pisces Sun/Aries Moon This neat combo combines energy and self-reliance with a kind heart and compassionate nature. You are energetic and sensitive. An expressive duo, this mix makes you exciting and inspirational. You like sharing your insights with others and will take up good causes with enthusiasm. Your problem is learning not to lose your sense of proportion.

Pisces Sun/Taurus Moon This likable combo makes you social and easygoing with both sensitivity and stability. Your stable, emotional nature balances your tendency to get lost in sentimentality and wishy-washy, overdone compassion. Self-pity can be a problem because when hurt you get sulky and stubborn. Develop a sense of self-worth, and use artistic ability as an outlet.

Pisces Sun/Gemini Moon This most flexible of all combos lets you learn easily as long as you are in sympathy with your environment. Boredom is the enemy and will quickly put you to sleep anywhere! Add diversity to your emotional life, but watch out for being fickle. Changeable as the winds, you are intuitive to the max and can "read" others easily. You're a charmer!

Pisces Sun/Cancer Moon This is the most sensitive combo imaginable. It makes you a softie for a sob story. You are sympathetic, compassionate, considerate, imaginative, and artistically inclined. You love being cuddled up at home where you can indulge your fantasy life privately. Being out in the world is hard, and you can counteract it by learning to detach emotionally.

Pisces Sun/Leo Moon Here's a combo that's perfect for a performer or actor. You are sensitive and dramatic with a generous nature and a powerful imagination you can project to the far horizons. Your inner stability helps steady your natural tendency to overreact to the cold, cruel world. Appearances count for you, but don't go overboard on the glam routine.

Pisces Sun/Virgo Moon This combo makes you flexible as a slender wand. You can waft from sitting on the clouds to hunkering down to the details of a school project with incredible ease. You are a wonderful combination of seriousness and sensitivity, and your sense of humor blends your intuition with logic. Lack of self-confidence is your problem. Use affirmations daily.

Pisces Sun/Libra Moon This artistic combo gives you an inborn sense of beauty and proportion. Everything you do is touched with fantasy, and your harmonious nature puts it all together beautifully. Imaginative and creative, you like everything to be pretty, sweet, kind, and gentle. Your problem is reality checks—do them often so that you don't lose touch with the real world.

Pisces Sun/Scorpio Moon This watery combo can't be beat for intuition and intense sensitivity. Your stable inner nature works well with your sense of whimsy and love of fantasy. There's a danger here, however, with getting involved in substance abuse due to depression. You may brood on death or suffer thoughts of suicide. If so, talk to your parents or another trusted adult.

Pisces Sun/Sagittarius Moon With this spiritual combo, you can see vast horizons and long-range directions. Sensitive and enthusiastic, you combine a love of learning with an intuitive nature. An explorer of both body and spirit, you love to travel both physically and in fantasy. Your problem is learning to focus on practicalities and not taking things too personally.

Pisces Sun/Capricorn Moon With this combo, your practical inner nature supports your soft-hearted core self. You have both vision and the means to realize it. Sensitive and compassionate, you also have a strong drive to accomplish. Your problem is self-pity and a tendency to depression and pessimism. Don't turn inward to the exclusion of cheerful social activities.

Pisces Sun/Aquarius Moon This friendly and helpful combo makes you a good activist for worthy causes. You make friends easily and your charm is infectious. People like your combination of sensitivity and a reasonable, detached point of view. Tolerant of other people's quirks, you have plenty of your own with your unusual ideas and fantasy life. Don't forget to get Scotty to beam you up!

Pisces Sun/Pisces Moon This matched combo is the most sensitive of all possible duos. You are a psychic sponge who soaks up everything in the atmosphere around you—other people's thoughts and feelings. You are deeply introspective and ultrasensitive. Your problem is identifying *your* feelings from the mix you absorb. You need much privacy, but beware of withdrawing totally.

Sun-Moon Practice Exercise

My Sun is in the Sign of _____

My Moon is in the Sign of _____

Using the example dialogue given below, write a "conversation" between your Sun and Moon, with lots of drama and detail.

Picture a teenager with an Aries Sun and a Taurus Moon in bed, sound asleep. Suddenly the alarm goes off with a shrill ring. He/she wakes up, runs a hand through tousled hair. Then follows an inner dialogue.

Aries: (Waking up hits "off" button.) Time to get going

Taurus: (Yawning, snuggling down in the bed sleepily.) Don't rush me. We got to bed awfully late last night. I'd like some snooze time.

Aries: (Impatient, irritated.) Hey, get moving! I haven't got all day. I've got things to do!

Taurus: (Yawning mightily, very reluctant to give up the warm, cozy comfort of bed.) Slow down. I need more sleep.

Aries: (Mentally stamping foot with impatience.) Will you just come on? There's no time for sleep now.

Taurus: (Grumblingly, forcing himself up.) What about breakfast? I don't seem to remember last night's dinner. Oh, ugh, that awful take-out stuff again. (Groans audibly at the memory.)

Aries: (In gear now, heading for the shower at a dead run.) I told you I've got an early practice. We'll grab a bite on the way to school.

Taurus: (Enjoying the warm shower but still thinking of his empty stomach.) Why are we always eating on the run? You know I hate fast food. I don't think I feel too good today.

Aries: (Triumphant, getting hastily dressed, grabbing backpack and dashing out the door.) Oh, stop being such a whiner. Hey, it's a great day to get things going!

Later that night . . .

Aries: (Holding head between hands mournfully.) What a headache! I'd better get some aspirin.

Taurus: (Sullen and self-righteous.) It comes from not eating all day, all this rushing around.

Aries: You're right. I'm famished. I'll ask Mom to order pizza. That's fast.

Taurus: I can't take any more junk food.

Aries: (Recognizing that he/she feels awful.) What a headache! This is terrible. I think I'm sick!

Taurus: (Secretly relishes the prospect of staying in bed and being fed and pampered.) Well, it's your own fault! I told you I needed more sleep and some decent food.

4. The Dance of Romance:
The Venus/Mars Pair

As we all know, science began with the stars, and mankind discovered in them the dominants of the ... "gods," as well as the curious psychological qualities of the Zodiac: a complete projected theory of human character.

Carl G. Jung

Venus: Your Love Nature

You've heard of her—Venus, the goddess of love. She was called Aphrodite in ancient Greece; the Romans renamed her. Although we tend to think of her as everything that is traditionally feminine—beauty, grace, charm, womanliness—*everybody* has Venus in their charts, males as well as females. As *the* romantic ideal, she has captured the imagination of artists and poets all over the world for centuries. There are literally hundreds of representations of Venus from all cultures. Ordinary people are also captivated by her mystery—that famous mystery of love. What is love? How does it happen? How do you know it's real? We all want to know.

Today we speak of "sex goddesses," meaning such charismatic beauties and sex symbols as Marilyn Monroe and all the other artificially blonde, perfectly shaped movie and TV stars. But Venus isn't to

The *Real* Love Goddess

As Aphrodite, Venus was a powerful goddess, definitely not someone to cross, as the following mythological tale clearly illustrates. Way back when, there was a king with three daughters. The third and youngest, named Psyche, was a great beauty and people came from far and wide to gaze upon her and admire her. When people began to compare this mere mortal slip of a girl to the great goddess of beauty, all hell broke loose.

The insulted Aphrodite put a blight on the land (jealousy is one of Venus's negative traits), and soon the starving populace was screaming at the king to do something. "Something" in those days was usually human sacrifice to appease an angry god. But the king couldn't bring himself to kill his beloved daughter, so she was put on top of a barren hill in the wilderness and left to her fate.

Poor girl! Alone, cold, hungry, feeling guilty for being beautiful and causing her people all this agony, she was in despair when she was suddenly magically transported by an invisible hand to an island palace of great beauty and luxury. Her every wish became a reality. Trays of food appeared out of nowhere, beautiful clothes hung in a huge closet. Nothing ever needed to be cleaned or washed. It was all perfect.

After a while Psyche became lonely and bored, but soon she was visited by an invisible lover and experienced divine rapture. He was Eros, great Aphrodite's son, who had fallen in love with this mortal. We know him as Cupid, the little baby with the arrows on valentines, but that's not the real story.

Eros told Psyche never to attempt to see him and continued to visit her nightly. She was quite happy with the arrangement, but when her sisters got wind of her situation they came along and nagged her to tears. "He's a monster," they said. Finally, they convinced her she had to check him out. So when he was sleeping she lit an oil lamp and held it up to have a look. Unfortunately, a drop of hot oil fell on him and woke him up.

Instantly, he and the palace were gone as if they had never existed and poor Psyche was right back where she started—alone in the world. What does one do in such a dire situation? Today we might pray or ask for an angel to guide us, but in ancient Greece, you looked for the nearest friendly goddess to ask for help. So Psyche sought out a temple to Demeter, a mother goddess, and finding it sorely neglected she began to sweep and dust and gathered fresh field flowers for an offering. Being a kindly mother, Demeter whispered into her mind that she had offended Aphrodite herself. Oh, dear! Psyche now knew she was in deep trouble and cursed her own beauty. After she had tidied up Demeter's shrine, she humbly went in search of Aphrodite to apologize and ask forgiveness, even though she wasn't at fault. Aphrodite gave her four impossible tasks to perform, each more difficult than the last.

Amazingly, as she went about her work, risking life and limb at every turn, she found helpers in the plant and animal kingdoms. She finished the tasks and reported back to the goddess, who turned into a charming mother-in-law! Eros appeared in person and they were wed.

By now, having been severely tested, Psyche was mature about what love is and what it is not, what is ideal and what is real.

Venus, then, isn't just a lady of leisure lying on a velvet couch eating chocolates—she's a powerful force within *you*. She's not one to fool around with unknowingly.

Therefore, learning about your own Venus and the Venus of any love interest will give you a vital window into the world of love— not the hearts-and-flowers sweetheart kind of love that's mere child's play, but the real thing with warts and all. If you think that love is the answer to all your problems and questions, trust me, it's more question than answer, more mystery than solution. Take heed! Don't play around with forces you don't yet understand. Go easy, because love comes in many disguises and can bring terrible pain in its wake, as Psyche discovered. What seems perfect can disappear in a flash of misunderstanding. Venus and her son, Eros (from whose name we derive the word *erotic),* are two sides of the same coin. Venus draws us to what we want, and through love we are changed, like it or not.

I am Venus,
Daughter of the Moon,
Sister of the Earth,
my true form clouded
by veils of illusion.
Handmaiden of the Great
   Mother,
I produce all life and nature
   on Earth.
I am Goddess of Love,
I am the eternally feminine.

be captured so easily on celluloid or projected via satellite! Your Venus nature, no matter if you are a girl or a boy, is something deep within. It has little to do with the manufactured, cosmetic-enhanced, face-lifted, worked-out media images of what is supposed to be beautiful or sexy.

Venus represents your *affections,* shows you what you *like and want,* describes your *social nature,* and tells you what you *value* or hold most dear. How many times do you say you "love" a piece of jewelry or clothing or hamburgers or pizza? Obviously that's not *love;* it's what you like or value or want. You love your parents and other relatives (maybe, maybe not), but when you think (or say) you love a person of the opposite (or same) sex, you are in very different territory. Venus is about *relating* to others in many different ways. Venus represents both whom you find attractive and whom you attract.

There are two ways Venus lets you know she is active. The first is that overwhelming, spontaneous attraction called love at first sight. It knocks you over. You didn't expect it, you didn't ask for it; now you have to cope with it. This is a dramatic introduction to the power of Venus.

The second is a gradual pull into a relationship. First you are drawn to someone as a pal or buddy, but the friendship needs time to ripen, like a peach on a tree. Trust must be built up and tested before a physical and emotional experience can happen.

However you experience the love goddess's energies, the more you know about them in your chart—and the other person's—the better you will handle this amazing life force, and the more likely you will be to establish happy romantic ties.

Venus through the Signs for Girls

Venus in Aries   You need constant excitement and new outlets for your love nature. Whatever is new and trendy turns you on—people as well as things. You like bright colors and lots of sound, and you have great energy for your many enthusiasms. You value people with active lives. You want a dynamic partner who can challenge you. When you're attracted to a guy, you go off like a rocket—you let him know you're interested.

Venus in Taurus   Your physical environment is important to you. It must be sensual, beautiful, and *comfortable.* You're loving and caring and crave intimacy. You like hugs and touching and want a partner who shows physical affection. You are attracted to a guy who is solid and dependable and who loves nature and good food. You can be possessive when attached, but you like to take it slow and easy before committing.

Venus in Gemini You are a social butterfly and love to flirt with as many guys as will gather around. Talking is your thing, and you do it with vivacity. You like gossip and miscellaneous information in detail. For you, love is a game to play and you don't want to be tied down. The way to your heart is through your active mind. You want a guy to sweep you off your feet, but he's got to be *interesting*. When bored, you take off.

Venus in Cancer You're an old-fashioned girl and not ashamed of it. You like hearts and flowers and want to be courted. You are supersensitive and easily hurt. Your romantic nature is powerful, but you wear your heart on your sleeve. You need most of all to feel secure with a guy and know he'll be there. Even as a teen you are on the lookout for a solid partner who can provide for you and a family.

Venus in Leo Your tastes are simple—you want only the best, grandest, most lavish! For you, love is a many-splendored thing. You want to be treated like a queen by a guy who acts like a king. You feel being adored is your right, and without constant praise you wilt. You're affectionate and want affection in return. Your life's a movie, and you're the star. You want a guy who can play the romantic lead opposite you.

Venus in Virgo You're a bit shy around boys because you are looking for someone who is exactly right. You're picky about who and what you like. Relationships aren't easy for you because you want everything *just right,* and when it's not you fret and become upset. You want a guy who likes to be helpful, and he must be honest and true. Being alone doesn't bother you because you know how to wait for what you truly want.

Venus in Libra Sharing is your middle name. You enjoy conversation about pleasant topics and are a good hostess. Your grace and lovely manners draw people to you. The guy who will get your attention is refined and mannerly, dresses well, and hangs around plenty.

Venus

The symbol, or glyph, for Venus is a cross topped with a circle. The cross represents the material world of matter, and the circle stands for spirit. Combined, these two elements making up the symbol for Venus indicate, in the language of astrology, that spirit and matter work together harmoniously. Venus *unites* those qualities within you. By extension, she attracts people to one another so that they can share both their physical and spiritual selves.

You like to swing back and forth between the hearts-and-flowers type of romance and an intellectual companionship. Whichever way, you *must* have a partner.

Venus in Scorpio You like to go to extremes in everything. Your taste is high-tech or all black. Sex is never far from your mind, even if you only think about it. It's your central core. Love and sex are bonded in your nature, so you aren't casual about whom you pick. You don't *need* physical sex, but you find the entire subject fascinating. You want a guy who is complex and sees you as a compelling puzzle, but you hate flattery.

Venus in Sagittarius Even if you keep it to yourself, you're very spiritually inclined. You love learning about other cultures. You can be simple and woodsy or dress up like a movie star. Adventure is your theme, and you want a guy who can take you camping or dancing at a fancy nightspot. Commitment can wait—you have too much to do, places to go, and things to learn before you'll be ready to settle down. You just like to have a good time.

Venus in Capricorn Inside you're deeply romantic, traditional, and very, very practical. Nothing flimsy, flighty, or flirty about serious you! The guy you pick must be *reliable* above all else. One missed appointment and he's history. You've got an eye toward the future and you want it financially secure. What gets your attention is competence and a guy, preferably college-bound, who has it together. Often you feel really lonely.

Venus in Aquarius You are a *personality*—always someone new to yourself and others. Some guys find this independence and flair threatening; you need a fellow who gives you space and isn't jealous of your many friends. Nonromantic, nonsexual relationships suit you fine. You don't like getting into heavy emotions, and commitment isn't a word you like.

Venus in Pisces Romantic is your middle name. You are a believer in true love and won't settle for less. Your idea of the perfect guy is someone sensitive who understands that there is spirit flowing through all life. Intimacy is important to you; you hate coldness and distance. You want to feel *close,* but you can be taken over by your sympathy for anyone needy. When you love, you give all. Guard your heart well!

Venus through the Signs for Boys

Venus in Aries   You are an impulsive romantic who fancies himself a dragon slayer rescuing the maiden held captive in the castle. To say you're idealistic in love is an understatement. You can't help being a bit macho with a lot of bravado, but no one minds because you're sincere. You like a girl with spunk who is competitive and playful and who can give as good as she takes. Conflict is a game you don't take seriously.

Venus in Taurus   You are nonaggressive about romance. You'd rather attract than pursue. You enjoy physical contact and have a highly developed sense of touch. Even though you are Mr. Practical, you can be highly romantic when inspired. You like a girl who is wholesome and curvacious, someone you can take home to meet your mother. If she can cook, so much the better! You are definitely possessive. If she's yours, she's *yours!*

Venus in Gemini   The way to your heart is through your brain. Mental stimulation keeps you going. Lots of variety is what you like; change is your life's blood. Your curiosity makes you want many different experiences. Flirting and gossiping are a pastime. You're a love 'em and leave 'em guy. The girl who attracts you must above all be interesting, witty, and fun. Going steady isn't for you—you keep your options open.

Venus in Cancer   You want closeness and sensitivity from others but find it hard to get. You're devoted and nurturing with easily hurt feelings that you hide by withdrawing. An old-fashioned gentleman, you want a girl who acts like a lady and enjoys staying home. If she gives you a sense of security, you'll stick to her like glue, especially if she's family oriented. Your idea of romance is taking care of each other's needs.

Venus in Leo   Whatever you do, it's on a grand scale, and that includes romance. You're generous to a fault as long as you get the respect you need. Your ideal girl is something of a showoff who makes a great entrance. You like to play and you love little kids. You express your emotions directly and with flair. Sometimes you are too openhearted and get hurt, and then you withdraw and sulk like a wounded lion in his den.

Venus in Virgo You are analytical even in love, and you tend to be critical of those you love. You want purity and perfection and can be overanalytical of emotions, but you're only trying to help. Somewhat shy, you're not aggressive about making dates and going out; you feel more comfortable in a group setting. The girl who attracts you is clean and neat, prim and proper. If you fall in love, you'll do anything for her that's useful.

Venus in Libra You are a gentleman—good manners, nice clothing, always polite and charming. A mainstream kind of guy, your style is old-fashioned, and you like a girl who minds her appearance. Relationships mean a lot to you, for you can't tolerate being alone. A ladylike personality attracts you. Your love nature is quiet and affectionate, and romance must include good conversation. Sharing is what you do best romantically.

Venus in Scorpio With you, sex is a major issue, and your thoughts are never far from it. You can find sexual undertones in everything. *Love* is a big word for you and you don't take it lightly. Naturally secretive, you can be intensely jealous and vindictive if betrayed. The girl who attracts you will have an air of mystery and something unusual about her—strong features or an intense manner. You don't love lightly.

Venus in Sagittarius Freedom is high on your priority list. "Don't fence me in" is your motto. The ideal is more attractive to you than the real. You want travel, adventure, good times, fun, and humor. The girl who wins your noncommittal heart will be outdoorsy and brainy, spiritually inclined with her feet on the ground. If you get the space you need and can share your adventures, you'll be true; otherwise, you'll split.

Venus in Capricorn Uppermost on your priority list is financial and emotional security. You work hard and contribute fully, and you want the rewards due you. A girl with money won't turn you off, but you also like class and high achievement. Failure and ridicule terrify you because they threaten your dignity. If you're with a girl who understands that, you react with loving kindness. You seem cool, but underneath lies a sexual furnace.

Venus in Aquarius You take pride in your special outlook on life—different to be sure! You're willing to experiment with all kinds of relationships and give others the freedom they need to be who they are. You understand that there's no one absolute way to have a romantic or sexual relationship. Emotional excess bores you, so intimacy doesn't come easily. You value *friendship* and want a girl*friend* who is independent and unusual.

Venus in Pisces For you, there is only one possible reason to have a romance and that's when it's real love, not the sentimental gooey kids' game all around you. A romantic at heart, you are also responsive to people's needs. You're drawn to sensitive, quiet girls with a spiritual or artistic bent. You *blend* with her. You don't care about size or color, class or race, so long as she touches your heartstrings and is sincere.

Mars: Your Sexual Self

What do you instantly think of when you hear the word *Mars?* **Men!** And war and aggressive behavior. Too bad that the concept "Men are from Mars, and women are from Venus" has been engraved on the public mind by a popular but misguided writer.

The true fact is that *both* women and men have Mars energy in them—and that applies just as well to girls and boys. Sure, it's easy to identify manliness and masculinity with Mars, but that's only *half* the story. The other half—ignored by most—is that every person alive has both masculine and feminine characteristics inside them. They may express these differently, but not necessarily according to their gender. The expression of Mars energy is an *individual* matter. There are men and boys whose basic makeup is more Venusian than Martian, and women and girls whose nature is more like Mars than like Venus. It is *not* a question of which sex you are. True enough, and most unfortunately, boys are taught from an early age to be macho—boys aren't supposed to cry or admit they are hurt. And it is equally true that girls are urged to hide their brains (around boys especially) and keep their natural aggressive tendencies well hidden lest they be thought nonfeminine or, worse still, masculine.

All of this is sheer nonsense. Mars, like all the rest of the Planets, has his good side and his bad side. What we think of as Mars is

Mars

Mars's symbol, or glyph, is a circle with an arrow extending outward from it. This represents the active male force. As Mars is a warrior, it also represents his sword and shield. Interpreted as an erect penis, it stands for virility and the ability to procreate, or beget children. As the desire principle, it indicates both sexual desire between males and females and what we desire to achieve in life. It is the energy that gets things done.

usually the negative masculine—the bully, the aggressive businessman, the authoritarian father, the bossy schoolboy.

There is no denying that these energies exist in the human psyche, but it's important to understand that they are in both males and females. The girl who goes for active or aggressive sports has likely got a strong Mars in her chart, while the boy who shuns such activities has a weak Mars placement. Remember, however: *both are okay*. You don't have to have a strong Mars to be a wonderful boy and a good man. And you don't need a strong Venus to be a feminine girl and a womanly adult.

Mars's special function is to create *separateness,* while Venus's is to create unity—two sides of the same coin. What happens is that Venus unites *love* with what to Mars is mere *lust*, or sheer physical sexual desire without any feeling of attachment to the sex object, be it male or female. That's why Venus and Mars are always considered as a pair in astrology.

Love without lust—or physical desire—is tame and tepid. Those suffering from it are usually merely in a dreamy state, yearning for an ideal love that is not a possibility in the real world. On the other hand, lust—or physical desire—without love leaves you feeling empty and drained, even if there was a temporary physical satisfaction. Anything that is totally physical without the addition of heart and spirit is bound to be unsatisfying, because human beings are made up of hearts and souls as well as physical bodies. And while bodies have their urgent needs (not all of them sexual!), hearts and souls have needs too. These needs can even be more important to some people than their sheer physical urges.

As you've probably figured out by now, Mars is the *energy principle*. Without Mars's energy, nothing would ever get done. His position by Sign indicates the channels into which energy will naturally flow and the uses to which energy will most easily be directed. Mars is the Planet through which the activities of the Sun and the needs of the Moon express themselves in action—through which your body and mind react to the impressions coming in through your senses and your emotions.

Mars is the action factor, and he also represents courage and forthrightness, characteristics that both boys and girls, men and women, can possess or not possess. When astrologers identify Mars with the

Mars Speaks

I am Mars,
Fire God,
Knight of the Sun,
Director of Spiritual Energy
into the matter of the
  material world.
I am the procreative power,
I am the inspiration for
  new ideas
and progressive projects.

"masculine principle," they don't mean human males but all of the traditional qualities that we admire in them—courage, energy, action, protectiveness, and valor. You can easily see that these words apply equally well to females. For example, there's nothing in this world more protective than a mother with a baby, be it a lion with a cub, a bird with nestlings, or a human mother with a child.

Though Mars is considered to be the primrary male energy, both males and females can have aggressive feelings, get angry, and feel passion. Women can be leaders, politicians, athletes, and soldiers. In fact, in ancient Greece there was a whole tribe of women warriors called Amazons. Whether you are a boy or a girl, Mars is where you find your heroic self.

In astrology, Mars tells how a person fights, what makes him or her angry, and where and what circumstances do this. In short, Mars tells how you *act*, not which sex you belong to. Of course, Mars also shows how you respond sexually in ways different from Venus. We'll get to that.

Mars in your chart is *how you act, what turns you on, what motivates you, how you handle your anger,* and *your natural level of aggression.*

Understanding your Mars energy is the key to using it properly, and realizing that there are many different ways to use Mars energy is the key to getting along with others.

Mars through the Signs for Boys

Mars in Aries   You act heroically and with self-motivation. You move quickly and are competitive. You know what you want when you want it, and you go after it. A warrior spirit lives in you, and you like a girl with get-up-and-go, someone who's always ready for a new adventure. Shyness and timidity turn you off immediately. You are attracted by a sporty girl who can match your outgoing nature while still being very feminine.

Mars in Taurus   You act peacefully, slowly, realistically, and kindly. You don't rush into a relationship. You are patient and can wait until you're sure. A caring guy with an affectionate and sensual nature, you want sex but are a gentleman. The girl who attracts you is traditional

and loves nature and physical comfort. You want a peaceful, calm relationship. Some mistake you for passive, but your feelings are strong.

Mars in Gemini You act logically, inconsistently, socially, and intelligently. Communication is your life's blood—you'd like your own TV, computer, and cell phone. The girl you like is a communicator, too. If she can stimulate your mind, you're hers so long as she gives you your freedom. Boredom is a horror you avoid. You'd rather *talk* about sex than bother doing it. The way to your heart is through your mind. You're a good catch—if she can catch you! Commitment is hard—you need to circulate.

Mars in Cancer You act sensitively, moodily, indirectly, and protectively. You are a survivor. Respectful of your mother, you give girls a feeling of security. Not a fighter, you hate confrontation. You like a girl who is home-loving, domestic, and ladylike, and you treat her gently. Emotional security means all to you, and when you feel threatened you retreat into your shell. A romantic, you want a girl who is old-fashioned and sweet.

Mars in Leo You act dramatically, grandly, playfully, and temperamentally. You like being male and are proud of it. Self-centered and attention-loving, you aren't cheap or petty; you give a lot. When you give your heart, it's to a girl who honors your integrity and makes an impressive appearance. You like her a bit flashy but never trashy. A king, you want a queen!

Mars in Virgo You act properly, helpfully, practically, and logically. You are rational and precise, a hands-on guy who doesn't mind getting dirty—for it's a pleasure to be clean again. Some think you are prudish, but underneath your prim exterior lies an earthy, sensual nature. You want a girl who is clean and neat, fit and intelligent. Classiness attracts you, and you're sensitive to what pleases the girl you choose.

Mars in Libra You are well-mannered, diplomatic, fair, and indecisive. You are a lover, not a fighter—except for justice. Standing up for yourself is difficult, and it's hard for you to show anger. Socially you're popular, and you like a girl who is graceful and charming with good taste—nothing flashy or trendy. Ideally, she is very feminine with a sharp brain. But you must be in a relationship or you suffer.

Mars in Scorpio You act passionately, seductively, intensely, and obsessively. You are a risk taker, but beware of taking risks with sex. It's a topic constantly on your mind, whether you have experienced it or not. For you, sex can be a spiritual experience or a physical one. You want both, and you look for a girl who is intense and can share your depths. Because you can discipline your desire, you can have sex or leave it alone.

Mars in Sagittarius You act positively, bluntly, humorously, spiritedly, and freely. You have an adventurous spirit and love to travel, even if only in imagination. The girl you like is an outdoorsy, intelligent type who loves learning. She has to have a good sense of humor. You want a relationship full of laughter and fun, or why bother? Sex isn't the main thing on your mind because you love your freedom and don't want a commitment.

Mars in Capricorn You act responsibly, seriously, ambitiously, and conservatively. You can be counted on for reliability and stability. Not a flashy guy, you're success oriented and serious about grades and getting ahead. The same holds true for relationships. You take your time and like a woman who is proper and knows how to behave socially. Your self-control hampers feelings, but when your inhibitions melt you can be passionate.

Mars in Aquarius You act objectively, coolly, rebelliously, and unconventionally. You are Mr. Cool. Male stuff like motorcycles and electronic gadgets interest you *mentally*. Macho isn't your style, and you steer clear of heavy emotional involvements. The type of girl you find sexy is intellectual, analytical, unusual, and exotic or far-out in some way. Sex isn't uppermost in your mind, though you're intrigued by it in the abstract.

Mars in Pisces You act sensitively, passively, kindly, and compassionately, and you have the soul of a poet. You may hide your sensitivity for fear of being ridiculed, and you are cautious about getting involved. A romantic at heart, you easily fall in love with the *idea* of love rather than a real girl who might not live up to your fantasy. Imagination fuels you sexually, and you respond to intimacy in a romantic atmosphere.

Mars through the Signs for Girls

Mars in Aries You are motivated by the desire for challenge, originality, and competition. Sometimes you're accused of not being feminine, but that's because you're a warrior woman who moves fast. You're not a romantic game-player—straight and to the point is your style. When you see the guy you want, you can make the first move if necessary. You have to be his one and only. You like a boy who is decisive and self-determined.

Mars in Taurus You are motivated by the desire for financial and emotional security. An earth-mother type, you are down-to-earth and practical. You want a steady, reliable, traditional boy who is potentially a good provider. A strong personality, you can intimidate or attract the boys. If your sensual needs are satisfied, you are a steadfast, affectionate partner.

Mars in Gemini You are motivated by the desire for communication, ideas, and information. Great conversation turns you on. You want a boy who is a talker—bright, witty, mentally stimulating. The most erotic part of you is your *mind,* and no boy who doesn't appeal to your brain will attract your sensuality. You are a natural flirt, a busy bee collecting different nectars. To avoid boredom, you play musical chairs with the boys.

Mars in Cancer You are motivated by the desire for sensitivity, nurturing, and being nurtured. Hurt feelings make you mad. You may show a crusty exterior, but underneath you're all hearts and flowers. A sentimental, romantic dreamer, you look for a boy who can understand your moods. Financial security is important because you want your own home one day. You seek a sense of security in a relationship with deep intimacy.

Mars in Leo You are motivated by the desire for love, loyalty, and power because you feel you were born to rule. You put honor above all and once you've formed an attachment, you give total trust. If betrayed, you are deeply hurt and withdraw into a massive sulk. The boy you like must be a romantic giver—you like the grand gesture. Your love life's an opera—soapy or classical. You want all the props plus a romantic lead.

Mars in Virgo You are motivated by the desire for perfection, a healthy lifestyle, and practicality. You do everything with great attention to detail. Efficient and helpful, you believe that skills are important. You want a boy who is good at doing useful things. What attracts you sexually is intelligence combined with neatness and cleanliness. Some think you are a prude, but it's just that you are most particular!

Mars in Libra You are motivated by the desire for approval, fairness, affection, and beauty. Polite and well-mannered, you seek a boy who is *nice,* even if that is an old-fashioned concept. A combination of brains and good looks is your ideal, but you will take one or the other because you cannot tolerate being alone for long. You *must* be in a relationship to be happy and often you choose wrongly because of this deep need.

Mars in Scorpio You are motivated by the desire for power, self-discipline, and depth of experience. You're not afraid to take romantic risks, for you like to test yourself. Naturally sexy, you are dynamic and attractive to the male sex, and you glory in it. You want a boy who is intense and devoted, who likes to dig deep into a relationship, and whom you don't intimidate. Sex is a big issue with you, but you can take it or leave it.

Mars in Sagittarius You are motivated by the desire for freedom above all else, and for knowledge and broader horizons. You like to be on the move, if only in your mind. You want a boy who is mental *and* spiritual, physical *and* emotional, and lots of fun, too. An independent thinker, you're hard to tie down. Your basic attitude is: If this one doesn't work, the next one will. A trip to the moon is your ideal vacation, you heartbreaker!

Mars in Capricorn You are motivated by the desire for financial and emotional security, success, and quality. You're a girl with definite plans about your life and where you are going. Mature at an early age, you value the bottom line. The boy who catches your eye will be practical and ethical, serious and devoted. If he proves himself, you'll slowly let down your guard and release a tremendous amount of powerful sexual energy.

Mars in Aquarius You are motivated by the desire for original-ity, world peace, and being regarded as unusual. Freedom is your thing, and you don't give it up easily. You get bored in a relationship quickly—if the guy isn't up to par mentally, you split without a backward look. Different sexual styles appeal to you—mentally if not in actuality. You like to be exploratory, if only in your mind. Commitment can wait.

Mars in Pisces You are motivated by the desire for compassion, creativity, spirituality, and union. An idealist and extreme romantic, you seek a guy who is poetic and kind, sensitive and sweet. The urge to merge is strong in you, but it must be veiled with perfumes and can-dlelight. Indirection is your mode of operation sexually. Take great care not to get involved with mind-altering drugs to hit that spiritual high you crave.

Taking a Chance on Sex: Should You?

Now that you know how the love goddess and the war god work in the charts of both girls and boys, you understand your own Venus and Mars energies and have a handle on the Venus and Mars ener-gies of other people. When you compare your Venus/Mars place-ments with someone else's, you will get an idea of how likely you are to hit it off.

Practice Exercise:
Doing a Comparison between Charts

Fill in the blanks below with the astrological *Signs* in which each Planet and the Ascendant appear. (You can make as many photocopies of this form as you like, as well as of the blank chart wheel, so you can compare yourself to any number of other people, including friends and your parents.)

Your Signs are:

Sun _____

Moon _____

Venus _____

Mars _____

ASC _____

Another person's Signs are:

Sun _____

Moon _____

Venus _____

Mars _____

ASC _____

When filled out the form will look like this sample.

Sun	Cancer		Sun	Scorpio
Moon	Sagittarius		Moon	Aries
Venus	Taurus		Venus	Leo
Mars	Libra		Mars	Virgo
ASC	Aquarius		ASC	Pisces

Love and War Themes

Venus Love Theme

This happens when both persons' Venuses are in the *same* Sign or when both Venuses occupy *compatible* Signs. The compatible Signs are the Trines.

This relationship will feel very good. When you are together, life is beautiful and harmonious. You enjoy being together and doing things together. With a Love Theme, you feel both attractive and attracted in the relationship. You are so in harmony that you may shut out the rest of the world and spend your time pampering each other and basking in what feels so good. Whether this relationship has any sexual passion or not will depend on your Mars placements. Same-Sign Moons will make this even more lovey-dovey.

Which Sign or Signs the two Venuses occupy in a Venus Love Theme will also make a difference in how the Venus energies play out.

Here's what to look for with same-Sign Venuses through the twelve Signs.

Aries　This will be a very charged-up relationship with lots of activity. The two of you will be on the go a lot, and it may start as a whirlwind romance that never lets up.

Taurus　This will be a calm and contained relationship with much affection between you. You'll enjoy taking it easy together in this lazy-daisy, comfort-loving Sign.

Gemini　This will be a talkative relationship that is mentally stimulating. You'll explore constantly to sate your mutual curiosity about everything, and you'll talk all the time.

Cancer　This will be a nurturing, domestic relationship with a lot of feeling. You'll enjoy being at home together and taking care of each other. Watch that you don't gain weight!

Leo　This will be a dramatic, high-flown, theatrical relationship with lots of flash and dash. Together you make an impressive couple. Don't compete for the limelight!

Virgo   This will be a calm, practical relationship. You both like doing useful things for each other and enjoy working on detailed projects together. You'll be health-conscious.

Libra   This will be a social relationship with many get-togethers with friends. Together you are a popular pair, and depending on your age marriage is a definite possibility.

Scorpio   This is a very intense relationship with much emphasis on sex, whether you are sexually active or not. As a couple, your involvement with each other is obvious.

Sagittarius   This is a lighthearted relationship with an emphasis on learning and sporty activities. You may have met on the tennis court, in the library, or on a field trip.

Capricorn   This is a serious relationship with emphasis on future financial security. Together you are a bit reserved and would rather work for good grades than go dancing.

Aquarius   This is a relationship less emotional than most, for you are both somewhat detached. You are friends first and enjoy each other's unusual personality.

Pisces   This is a relationship with a spiritual bent. You are both sensitive, artistic, and imaginative and can get into a private fantasy world. Don't ever do drugs together.

The Signs That Trine

In each group of the three Signs below, any Planet that falls in one of the Signs automatically trines to Planets in the other two.

♈ Aries	♌ Leo	♐ Sagittarius
♉ Taurus	♍ Virgo	♑ Capricorn
♊ Gemini	♎ Libra	♒ Aquarius
♋ Cancer	♏ Scorpio	♓ Pisces

Here's what to look for when both your Venuses are in the same Element—Fire, Earth, Air, or Water. (See chart page 147.)

Fire   Your relationship will be too hot to cool down. You'll both burn with a high flame, igniting each other's romantic ardor, constantly making the sparks fly freely.

Earth   Your relationship will be stable and steady. A solid couple, you'll enjoy quiet times and much affection. You both enjoy nature and practical, calm activities.

Air   Your relationship involves much discussion, for you love talking to each other and spinning daydreams about fantastic, unusual topics and adventures.

Water   Your relationship flows with much feeling. You like just being together without doing much of anything. You communicate without words as often as by talking.

Venus War Theme

This happens when the two Venuses occupy *opposite* Signs, or when they are in the *Square* Aspect. This isn't easy, but it's dynamic. You have lots of differences and may quarrel about what to do and when and with whom. Your love natures are different, which means that even though you are attracted you may not get along on a daily basis. You may fight over what movie to see, which restaurant to go to, or what friends to hang out with. With Venus, however, conflict is never too intense.

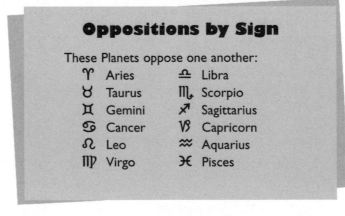

Oppositions by Sign

These Planets oppose one another:

♈	Aries	♎	Libra
♉	Taurus	♏	Scorpio
♊	Gemini	♐	Sagittarius
♋	Cancer	♑	Capricorn
♌	Leo	♒	Aquarius
♍	Virgo	♓	Pisces

Here's what to look for with your Venuses in Opposing Signs.

Aries/Libra   The Aries partner always wants to go first and can intimidate the Libra partner. If Aries is the boy, he'll be too brash for a Libra girl's refined nature. If it's the other way around, she will overwhelm him.

Taurus/Scorpio The Taurus partner wants calmness and comfort and finds Scorpio's intensity upsetting. If Taurus is the boy, his silent stubbornness will bring out the vamp in her. If it's the other way around, her firm practicality will make him try to get his way with sheer willpower.

Gemini/Sagittarius   The Gemini partner never wants to get heavy and can irritate Sagittarius's philosophical bent. If Gemini is the boy, he'll be too insubstantial for the girl. If it's the other way around, she will be a flirty gossip and frustrate his idealistic, romantic nature.

Cancer/Capricorn   The Cancer partner wants emotional security, which can irritate the materialistic Capricorn. If Cancer is the boy, the girl may scorn him as weak. If it's the other way around, she will cling to his stability.

Leo/Aquarius   The Leo partner wants excess emotional involvement with lots of drama, while the Aquarius partner likes to keep it cool. If Leo is the boy, his demand for attention will turn her off. If it's the other way around, her dramatizing will offend his cool rationality.

Virgo/Pisces   The Virgo partner is down-to-earth, while the Pisces partner lives in a romantic fantasyland. If the Virgo is the boy, he'll be too practical for her dreaminess. If it's the other way around, she will hate his spaciness.

Here's what to look for with the *Square* Aspect between your Venuses, or the Square's *Mode*—Cardinal, Fixed, and Mutable.

Cardinal Although you inspire each other to try new activities and think about things in new ways, you are prone to conflict when it comes to what you want personally. The danger is power struggles, in the open or hidden, when your personal enthusiasms conflict.

Fixed Although your relationship can have staying power, there is danger of mutual rigidity and fear of change. You may stay in the relationship out of insecurity or because you can't stand being alone. Control is an issue.

Mutable Although your relationship is flexible and you can both give and take, your tendency is to adjust too easily to the problems without thinking them through and getting to the solution. You may just drift apart because you don't really make a commitment or confront difficulties.

Squares by Sign

These Planets square one another:

♈ Aries	♋ Cancer and ♑ Capricorn
♉ Taurus	♌ Leo and ♒ Aquarius
♊ Gemini	♍ Virgo and ♐ Sagittarius
♋ Cancer	♈ Aries and ♎ Libra
♌ Leo	♉ Taurus and ♏ Scorpio
♍ Virgo	♊ Gemini and ♓ Pisces
♎ Libra	♋ Cancer and ♑ Capricorn
♏ Scorpio	♌ Leo and ♒ Aquarius
♐ Sagittarius	♍ Virgo and ♓ Pisces
♑ Capricorn	♋ Cancer and ♎ Libra
♒ Aquarius	♉ Taurus and ♏ Scorpio
♓ Pisces	♍ Virgo and ♐ Sagittarius

For more information on how the two Signs involved in a Square operate, go back and reread the description of Venus in the Signs for both of you, discussed at the beginning of this chapter.

It's important to remember that even when badly aspected—in an Opposition or a Square—Venus is never really difficult. She is always benevolent, and conflicts involving her can usually be solved with little effort. For example, Venus with Mars in an Opposition or Square Aspect usually means romantic and sexual attraction. Depending on the Signs involved, the dynamics may be softly sweet or generate heat.

You can easily figure out your Venus/Mars combos by looking at the Signs in which each appears. You already know which Signs are compatible and which conflict, and you know what the Signs mean individually. You can easily determine how your Venus operates with the other person's Mars, and how your Mars operates with his or her Venus. To make it easy for you, we'll review the Aspects focusing on Venus and Mars.

Venus in the *same Sign* (Conjunct) as **Mars** is lovingly mutual.
Venus in a *Trine* Aspect to **Mars** is easy and compatible.
Venus in the *opposite* Sign to **Mars** is sexually attractive.
Venus in a *Square* Aspect to **Mars** is a romantic challenge.

Mars Love Theme

This happens when Mars occupies the *same* Sign in both charts or when he is in *compatible* Signs, which are the *Trine* Aspects.

When Mars is your Love Theme, action and passion are combined. You two are a combustible pair and you like to do active things together, like sports, camping, and generally romping around. Depending on your age, sex will be a major issue. The temptation will be to dive in impulsively and take a chance on sex, maybe at an early age. *Don't*. This combo does not guarantee everyday compatibility or longevity, and it can tempt you into premature sexual activity. You are both eager to try sex and find the idea hot. Danger is attractive here, but common sense is definitely a must.

Which Sign or Signs your two Marses occupy in a Mars Love Theme will also make a difference in how the Mars energies affect your relationship. Review the signs for insights.

Here's what to look for with same-Sign Mars through the twelve Signs.

♈ **Aries** This will be a dynamic relationship with physical action. You will energize each other. Anger flares and then dies down.

♉ **Taurus** This will be a stable and easy relationship. You energize each other's affectionate natures. You're both slow to anger.

♊ **Gemini** This will be a communicative, talkative, lively relationship. You energize communications between you and others. Anger is mostly only on the surface and you can talk it out.

♋ **Cancer** This will be a sentimental, caring relationship that energizes feeling. The things you like to do together are homey and placid. Your anger comes from hurt feelings.

♌ **Leo** This will be a dynamic, outgoing relationship. You energize each other's dramatic flair and like to show off. Your anger is magnificent and noisy but usually harmless.

♍ **Virgo** This will be a mental, practical relationship. You energize each other's moderate, perfectionist nature. Your anger is quiet and you solve it analytically.

♎ **Libra** This will be a best-friends relationship. You energize sociability and diplomacy everywhere you go together. You both repress anger, though, and need to open it up.

♏ **Scorpio** This is a risk-taking, all-or-nothing relationship. You energize sex, passion, and intensity. You need maturity to handle this one. Your anger is deep and smoldering.

♐ **Sagittarius** This is a freedom-loving relationship. You energize philosophical thinking and uninhibited action. Your anger is short-lived, and you learn from your mistakes.

♑ **Capricorn** This is a disciplined, serious relationship. You energize organization and money-making together. Your anger is coldly rational, but hurt feelings can go deep.

 Aquarius This is a cerebral, detached relationship. You energize humanitarian urges and unconventional poses. Your anger is more ice than fire, and you analyze it away.

 Pisces This is a dreamy, inactive relationship. You energize idealism, sensitivity, and compassion. Both shy, your anger is passive-aggressive.

Here's what to look for with the Trine Aspect between your Mars and another person's Mars, or the Trine's *Element*—Fire, Earth, Air, or Water. (See the box on page 147 for Trines by Sign.)

Fire   Your relationship will be combustible—and you enjoy the possibility. Your mutual sense of independence keeps you both on your toes. Sexual sparks fly all over.

Earth   Your relationship will be grounded and calm. You make a solid couple with good common sense about sex and its consequences. Sensuality is what really matters.

Air   Your relationship will be cool, with sex often a topic of discussion, because you like to speculate mentally. Practicality is lacking, so take care of all precautions.

Water   Your relationship will be flowing and passive—you seem to become the same person. Intense and dreamy by turns, you often want to lock out the rest of the world.

Mars War Theme

This happens when Mars in one chart is *Opposite* or *Square* to the other person's Mars.

When Mars is your War Theme, look out! This is not a happy relationship, though some people do thrive on strife. You will fight constantly and always be having to "work through" your differences. You may even get physical about the fighting and hurt each other. Back away or back down, but don't let yourselves get caught up in enjoying the fire of adrenaline pumping through your veins. Sex is tempting, but it is not advised because it might become rough and get out of hand. You need maturity to handle this relationship, and you will be better off if you find someone else.

Which Sign or Signs the two Marses occupy in a Mars War Theme will also make a difference in how the Mars energies play out.

Here's what to look for with your Mars in *opposing* Signs. (See the box on page 148 for Oppositions by Sign.)

♈ ♎ **Aries/Libra** The Aries partner can overwhelm the Libra person. Aries shows anger immediately; Libra represses anger and blows up a year later. An Aries boy may offend a Libra girl's sense of harmony. If reversed, she may irritate his sense of refinement by not behaving in a ladylike manner.

♉ ♏ **Taurus/Scorpio** The Taurus partner prefers peace but if pushed will overpower Scorpio. If Taurus is the boy, he can be a real bull, and she will pull out all the stops to torment him. If reversed, she'll dig in her heels and rebuff his romantic and sexual overtures just to see him suffer.

♊ ♐ **Gemini/Sagittarius** The Gemini partner wants to flirt, and this offends Sagittarius's sense of ethics. If Gemini is the boy, she will soon find someone who acts honorably. If reversed, her flirtatious nature will get on his nerves and cause constant fighting over the issue of personal freedom.

♋ ♑ **Cancer/Capricorn** The Cancer partner hates to confront, which drives practical Capricorn crazy. If Cancer is the boy, his tendency to sulk when angry will cause many upsets. If reversed, her weepy moodiness will make him mad, and he'll try unsuccessfully to get her organized by using logic.

♌ ♒ **Leo/Aquarius** The Leo partner dramatizes emotion, and Aquarius hates emotional display. If Leo is the boy, he will be a showoff, which offends her. If reversed, her emoting all over the place will turn him off, and his detachment will wound her pride. This is a hard combo to live with.

♍ ♓ **Virgo/Pisces** The Virgo partner's practicality is an irritant to dreamy Pisces. If Virgo is the boy, he will try to help when she wants to be left in her dream state. If reversed, she will insist on his personal hygiene and make him withdraw into his fantasy world to get away from her.

Here's what to look for with the *Square* Aspect between your two Mars placements, or the Square's *Mode*—Cardinal, Fixed, and Mutable. (See the box on page 150 for Squares by Sign.)

Cardinal Although this relationship happens fast, it is prone to problems. Dynamic activity means different ways of doing things. You tend to go off in different directions, which causes conflict. Though you push each other to get what you each want, what you want is rarely the same thing.

Fixed Although your relationship can be a powerful combo, if things don't go well it's a major standoff. You each get your back up and refuse to budge from what you want, leaving no possibility of compromise. Your battles are huge, and constant power struggles can leave you drained.

Mutable Although your relationship is the easiest in this category, it's often too loose, like a two-person band playing different tunes simultaneously. Commitment comes hard here because of your mutual changeability. You are perpetually confused about who wants what, and when.

The Big Picture

With a Mars War Theme, your relationship is bound to be rocky and may blow apart or be less difficult depending on other factors, such as Venus and Moon placements, which influence the total picture. For example, if you have same-Sign Moons, you will be similar emotionally and get along well on an everyday basis. Sometimes when there is conflict with Mars placements, the same-Sign Moons will overcome it. At other times, they will make you realize that you are better off being just friends rather than trying to make it work romantically and sexually.

On the other hand, conflicting Moons will make the situation worse, because what makes you feel comfortable and at home with yourself will be at odds with the other person's basic needs. This is an important point when attempting to determine if a particular relationship will get past the starting gate. Getting involved in a romance isn't too difficult—but *staying* involved and making it work is a big job.

Mars Review

For more information on how the two Signs involved in a square operate, go back and reread the description of Mars in the Signs for both of you, discussed at the beginning of this chapter.

Love and War

In all of the Mars War Themes, if there is a Venus Love Theme between you the conflict will be lessened. Remember, Venus unites but Mars separates.

Interaction: The Opposite Attraction

You've already looked up your own Ascendant—and probably the Ascendant of anyone who interests you. Remember, the Ascendant is a *point,* not a Planet, and it *begins* the chart at the first House, your most personal area of life.

The other end of the horizontal line that divides the astrological chart in half, as the drawing on the facing page shows, is called the *Descendant,* and it lies directly opposite the Ascendant. The Descendant begins the *seventh House,* which governs one-on-one relationships, especially romantic ones. It is the traditional House of marriage.

Identify Your Ideal Love Partner

The seventh House also refers to *any* one-on-one partnership, whether it is romantic or not. Therefore, although we are going to discuss it in terms of romance and your ideal partner, it's also descriptive of any two-person partnership, such as co-captains of teams in school or business partners in the adult world.

As you see in the drawing, the ASC-DSC axis slices the chart in half horizontally. We call this the *relationship axis.* The Sign falling on the point of the Descendant, known as the *cusp* of the seventh House, is always in exact opposition to your Ascendant. Opposites do attract!

In fact, an article in a popular magazine entitled "Good Lasting-Love Match: A + B" said that research shows that "opposites often not only click but stick." What the magazine's researchers found was that couples with contrasting personality types were more committed and more optimistic about their long-term chances, including marriage. The expert who did the study reported, "As long as they are opposites, the relationship tends to function well."

That's certainly no news to astrologers, who for centuries have known that the Sign opposite your Ascendant reveals who you will attract and who will attract you!

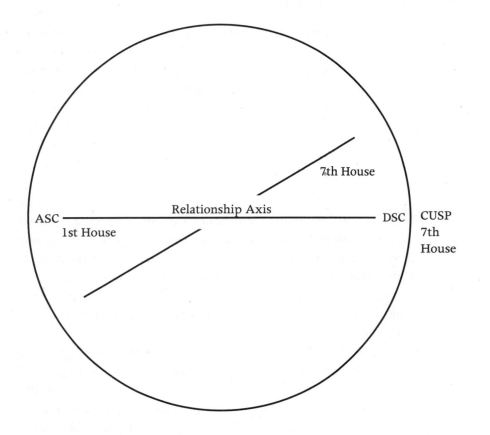

As you learned earlier, there are six pairs of opposite Signs. Here's a list showing the Ascendant first and its opposite Sign second.

Ascendant	Descendant
Aries	Libra
Taurus	Scorpio
Gemini	Sagittarius
Cancer	Capricorn
Leo	Aquarius
Virgo	Pisces
Libra	Aries
Scorpio	Taurus
Sagittarius	Gemini
Capricorn	Cancer
Aquarius	Leo
Pisces	Virgo

You are attracted to the *qualities* of the Descendant Sign. For example, if Scorpio is your Ascendant (often called the Rising Sign, or in this example, "Scorpio rising"), you will be attracted to the traits exhibited by the Sign Taurus. With Scorpio rising, you will want a steady and reliable love partner who is conscious of the value of money.

Reverse this to Taurus on the Ascendant, and you will have Scorpio on the Descendant. In this instance, the Taurus rising person will be attracted to someone with depth and mystery, passion and power, and a secretive nature.

By matching up your Ascendant with your Descendant from the list above, and then reading over the descriptions of the Signs involved, you can acquaint yourself with the qualities of the person who is most likely to attract you. You don't have to know his or her birthdate to do this (that can come later). You only have to be aware of the characteristics of the Sign on your *own* Descendant, and then watch for them in different girls and boys. A little awareness on your part will easily reveal these qualities.

Remember that it isn't usually the other person's *Sun Sign* that is involved. In other words, if you have Taurus on the Ascendant and you meet or know a boy or girl with Scorpio traits, it could mean that person has one or more planets other than the Sun placed in Scorpio. Or it could mean that the person has a Scorpio Ascendant, which would land on your Descendant by falling opposite your Taurus Ascendant.

A way to understand how your Descendant affects your attitude about relationships is by studying its Sign. As an example, a Capricorn Descendant opposite a Cancer Ascendant might indicate a person who seeks a powerful, protective, well-organized partner (Capricorn) because they feel helpless, insecure, unprotected, and lonely (Cancer).

Another case is the Libra Descendant. You will suffer if you are not in a relationship and will do everything you can to get into one. If one relationship breaks up, you will move as quickly as possible to get into another one, for the Libra cannot tolerate being alone.

To illustrate this point, take a woman with an Aries Ascendant and an Aquarius Sun and Venus. With our analysis of Aries and Aquarius, we'd call her very independent, and she is about some things. However, because she has a Libra Descendant she cannot go for long without being in a relationship and will make every effort to get into one, often going quickly from one relationship to another to avoid being alone for even a short time. Once securely in the relationship, she will again exhibit her natural Aries/Aquarius independence, but she will *always* need to be in a relationship to balance the independent side of her nature.

Naturally, if there are Planets located in the Sign opposite your Ascendant, it makes the situation more powerful. Any Planets placed in your seventh House will indicate important qualities you seek in a love partner or best friend. It's possible that these qualities are ones you feel you lack yourself, and you sense that the other person can fill in what's missing. (Planets in the sixth House in the same Sign as your Descendant will influence the seventh House, but less so than Planets actually in the seventh House.)

Let's have a look at the different Planets we have discussed so far—Sun, Moon, Venus, and Mars—to see what their effects are, as related to your romantic interest, when they are found in the seventh House of your chart.

Sun The Sun rules Leo, and with the Sun in your seventh House you are looking for an impressive partner to play a dominant role in the relationship. You also want to play a dominant role. Much personal pride is involved and you very much want the relationship to succeed in the eyes of others. There is a lot of dramatic flair here but you want mutual cooperation above all else. You want the relationship to improve your general social standing and popularity rating. Your ideal romantic partner is interested in expressing power and individuality through the relationship and will support you in your efforts to achieve the same goals.

Moon The Moon rules Cancer, the Sign of devotion, home, and nurturing. With the Moon placed in your seventh House, you want to be nurtured by a partner. You have a strong desire for emotional closeness and sharing, both giving and receiving intimacy. With this placement, it's possible your own mother isn't much of a nurturing person and you felt a lack of maternal closeness in your childhood. You crave affectionate gestures and a close emotional bond between you and your boyfriend or girlfriend, or with a best friend. You want to be able to be yourself in the relationship without being criticized or suffering makeover efforts. Your partner must be sympathetic to your sensitivity. He or she will need patience to deal with your moods, which can swing widely depending on whether you are happy or upset.

Venus Venus rules Libra, the Sign of marriage and the natural occupant of the seventh House. This is a happy placement, for Venus seeks harmony and balance and unites opposites. With Venus in your seventh House, you may be a "people pleaser" and feel that you need to be extra nice and polite to make people like you. Also, you may lack a sense of self-worth and have low self-esteem regarding your attractiveness or personality. If so, you will feel that the right partner will magically give you what you think you lack. Venus in the seventh House is an indicator that you tend to focus too much on outward appearances and work overtime to make yourself attractive to the opposite sex in order to get a partner. You may seek a steady relationship for the romantic fulfillment and emotional security it can give you; early marriage is often the case with Venus in the seventh House. Other Planets in the chart will affect how strong this influence is. For example, if you have any other Libra placements, the effect will be magnified. However, if you have strong and independent Planetary placements, such as Mars in Aries, it will be lessened.

Mars Energetic Mars rules the action Sign of Aries, making you quite aggressive about relationships—to the point of being competitive, even combative, depending on which Sign is involved. When you are attracted to someone, you feel it powerfully and go after the person immediately, whether obviously or subtly. You can be impulsive and get into relationships too quickly, without consideration of whether it's a good idea or the right person. You feel attracted and *bam*, you get involved right away if you can manage it. You need to prove yourself in all things, including love. Unfortunately, the old proverb "Marry in haste, repent in leisure" applies here, and disappointment in love is common with Mars in the seventh House. Sometimes you try to overpower the other person, indulging in loud bullying when you are frustrated or don't get what you want. You need someone who can stand up to your energy, and it's quite possible that both you and your partner will engage in impulsive and loud behavior with each other. This can cause a lot of conflict and unhappiness, especially if you have a Mars War Theme between you. Luckily, a Venus Love Theme will ease things up a bit, but Mars in the seventh House can be combustible, depending on which Sign he falls in. For instance, if Mars is also in Aries it will be World War III whenever either of you gets mad. But if Mars is in Libra you will stuff your anger inside until it finally explodes all over the place. Look to the Sign that Mars occupies for more information about how this fiery Planet will act. A Cancer or Pisces Mars won't blow up but will sulk or withdraw from the conflict, giving the partner the silent treatment, which is often worse than yelling or having a mutual shouting match that lets off the steam.

You can use the information in this chapter to compare all kinds of relationships—same-sex romances, nonromantic friendships, relationships with your parents and your siblings and other relatives. You can even compare yourself to your teachers, counselors, and any others with whom you have an interactive relationship. Just ask for their birthdates. Adjust the interpretation by eliminating the romantic/sexual themes and focus on the meaning of the Planets and the Signs they occupy.

For example, if your same-sex friend has Venus in the same Sign as you, the two of you will have much in common, like the same things, and flow together easily.

If the two of you have Venuses in an Opposition or a Square Aspect, you will disagree over your likes and dislikes and need to compromise to get along.

The same idea can be applied to Mars, and it can also be used with Venus/Mars combinations. Any combination in the same Sign or in a Trine Aspect will be easy, while any combination in an Opposition or a Square Aspect will be difficult and require adjusting to each other's points of view. Your energies will be different.

Practice Exercise:
Understanding the Descendant

My Ascendant is in_____

My Descendant is in_____

Planets I have in the Seventh House are:

_____

I am attracted to these qualities in other people:

_____

_____

Write a short statement about how you think your Descendant relates to the qualities you

find attractive in others.

_____

_____

_____

_____

List the Ascendant/Descendants of people who are important to you—romantic interests, friends,

parents, siblings, etc. See if you can relate their Descendants both to your own Descendant and also

to the people they find attractive, such as your parents or a sibling and his or her love interest.

THREE

The Astro-Wizards

5 Mercury— The Whiz Kid: Spinning on Air

*Mercury's function is to separate Man from the animal king-
dom through the use of the faculties of reason. It is this separation . . . and the development of the creative aspects of
mind which makes Man more widely conscious of himself
and his world. Mercury likes to improve things, to add to
Man's knowledge through inventions. He is the Planet of
progress through experimentation. Mercury is never satisfied
with what is established and is always seeking new avenues
for his inventive mind to explore.*

Alan Oken, As Above, So Below

The first Astro-Wizard we are going to investigate is Mercury. He is a
fascinating figure in both astrology and mythology.

Mercury rules communication, education, movement, and learning to think—all extremely important aspects of your teen years, when
your mind is forming concepts that will affect your thinking for years
ahead.

Throughout history, Mercury has been known as a god of many
talents, all of which deal with communication. As such, I see him as
the ideal god for the present age, the twenty-first century, with its rapidly expanding forms of e-communication. The mind-boggling speed

The Mythological Mercury

This multifaceted god was known in ancient Egypt as Thoth, the lord of divine books and scribe of the gods.

In India, he was the god of wisdom and was associated with Buddha, whose name means "enlightened by divine wisdom."

In ancient Greek mythology Mercury was known as Hermes, a great and wise teacher and speaker. Also known as the messenger of the gods, he is pictured with wings on his heels and his head to indicate the speed at which he travels . . . the speed of thought!

He is the patron of thought and its source, the human mind, and is represented as a slender, youthful figure. Thus, he is the ruler of youth, especially adolescents.

with which new technology is spinning out is typical of Mercury's fast-moving nature. And the bugs and boggles experienced with computers and the Internet are also typical of him, for one of his names is the Trickster God.

Mercury is a prankster and loves to play practical jokes on people—some harmless, some not so pleasant. We see this Mercurial trait reflected in stories of computer hackers (many of whom are talented teens) breaking into major systems just for the heck of it and not causing damage. However, we are also seeing serious threats caused by hackers intent on causing trouble, which is a negative use of Mercury's powers.

We need to take this god—whom most have considered to be a mere lightweight—much more seriously and give him due respect, because he is a powerhouse wearing the mask of innocence. Don't be fooled by this god—he is no one to play around with; he proves the proverb "Play with fire, and you'll get burned."

Astrologically, Mercury shows *how the mind works, how we learn,* and *how we communicate.* The *Aspects** to Mercury indicate *patterns of thinking*, but these are not carved in marble. They can be changed.

Who's in Charge of Your Mind?

Who's in charge of your mind? Your immediate response might be, "I am, of course!" But if you give it some thought, you may be surprised to discover that you aren't as much in charge of your mind—that is to say, what and how you think—as you might want to believe!

It was your parents who first told you what was and wasn't okay to think. The term "parent tapes" refers to the voices of our parents and other authority figures that most of us carry in our heads. "Eat your vegetables," "Get good grades," "No sex before marriage," "If you don't decide on a career before you go to college you'll be a failure" etc.—an unending inner stream of constraints and advice.

These parent tapes run nonstop—even if below conscious awareness. Many kids base their behavior on what Mom would think or what Dad would say or or how friends would react. Often the peer group

*Mercury can never be more than 28 degrees away from the Sun, so your Mercury will be in the same Sign as your Sun, in the Sign before your Sun, or in the Sign after your Sun. (To find your Mercury placement by Sign, see appendix 1.)

becomes a sort of dictator for what's okay and what's not acceptable. "They" become the trendsetters.

For example, a friend of mine was given an expensive wardrobe by a wealthy acquaintance who was a clothes freak. The clothes were expensive and in good taste, and my friend brought them all to my apartment to try them on. As she was trying on each garment, I complimented her on how good it looked. But each time her response was the same: "But what are *they* wearing this year?" No matter how nice the clothes might look on her, she couldn't be comfortable wearing them unless "they" were also wearing the same style this year! This was someone who was not in charge of what she thought.

Not being in charge of your mind produces an entire spectrum of difficulties—from minor ones, like not being able to decide what to wear based on your own needs and preferences, to major ones, like choosing a girl- or boyfriend or a college or course of study. If you base your decisions on someone else's qualifications as to who or what is right for you, you are not in charge of your mind.

You may have been raised being told what you should and should not do or think. If you accept this without self-examination, you are not in charge of your mind.

If you secretly believe something is what you truly want, and you allow yourself to be swayed by the opinions of others, you're letting someone else do your thinking.

Slavishly following the agenda of any group means that you are not in charge of your mind. And as long as you are not in charge of your mind, you are not in charge of your life!

We all have problems. To produce effective and workable solutions to the many problems confronting us, not only personally but worldwide, we need to learn to *see* in new ways. We must all become *seers*. The seer—one who sees—is the sage; he or she can see what others cannot see, and it is this capacity that we all need to develop in order to cope with the world around us—and with our own personal development.

Taking control of your own mind means making changes. The changes I am talking about have to do with being true to your mental self, which is unlike anyone else's mental self. Your mind is a power tool—you can learn to use it effectively by becoming aware of how the Planet *Mercury* operates in your chart.

Mercury

Mercury's symbol, or glyph, is a a circle sitting on a cross with a semicircle on top. It is a complex symbol open to many interpretations, as it combines the cross of matter, the circle of spirit, and the semicircle of the Moon. Taken altogether, this emblem stands for *active intelligence.*

Mercury in the Sky

Speed is only one of Mercury's astronomical characteristics. It's also the hottest, smallest, and closest to the Sun of the Planets in our solar system. Because he moves so quickly, Mercury takes only 88 of our days to go around the entire twelve Signs of the Zodiac. As Mercury lies so close to the Sun, he can be seen only at sunrise or sunset and is never visible in the night sky.

This is the key to getting unstuck from thinking patterns that don't represent the real you and to turning off those parent tapes forever. I'm not saying that parents can't or don't give good advice or that it's wrong to follow their advice. You should consider it to be just that: *advice*—to take or not take. Everybody has the right to make their own mistakes, to suffer and learn from them. That's what freedom is all about.

Naturally, the younger you are, the more you need your parents' counsel or your teachers' guidance. But in the end it is *your mind* and *your life*. If you don't use your mind well, you'll spoil your life.

Your Mercury placement tells you how your mind works. Are you a whiz kid or a slow but steady learner? Do you learn best in a structured or an unstructured environment? Is your mind stimulated by being outdoors, or do you prefer to study quietly in your room? These are Mercury functions.

Mercury plays an important role in the charts of young people—he was considered in ancient times to be the god of youth—especially those who are doing schoolwork at whatever level.

Mercury shows *how* you think (by Sign) and in what area your thinking is focused (by House placement).

Aspects to Mercury indicate ease of thought or difficulties with thinking. They can show if you are open-minded and mentally flexible or if you have rigid thought patterns, usually programmed in by parents, siblings, teachers, educational institutions, others' expectations, or just your own misperception of what you need to do in order to cope with life and its many trials and traumas.

Many people—teens especially—lack self-esteem, the sense of self-worth so necessary to feeling good about yourself and what you do, and therefore look for approval from their parents or others as a substitute. This results in a willingness to accept other people's thinking as being superior to their own. As a result, our society in general has become dependent on "experts"—those people with lots of letters after their names—to tell us what to do and how to think. Nowhere is it suggested that we might just learn to do that for ourselves, if we give it a bit of a try! And that is precisely what I am suggesting here—*you already have the power to think for yourself if you will simply tune in to your inner potential*.

If you've been led to believe that you're dumb or somehow not as smart as the next person, forget it! You're *not* stupid, no matter what anyone has told you in the past. Unlike the Scarecrow from *The Wizard of Oz*, you have a brain and you can learn to use it effectively. You can be a Power Thinker.

Every Mercury placement is distinctly different. As Mercury represents your mind and how it works, it follows that no two minds are alike.

The great American novelist Willa Cather once referred to "the furniture of the mind," comparing an unfurnished mind to an unfurnished house—bare and uncomfortable. However, and this is the good part, *learning*—and discarding what has been learned previously that either obstructs or clutters the mental atmosphere—is what furnishes the mind. And you can choose what furniture suits you, discarding what you don't want. You may have a perfectly good house (mind) that is filled with uncomfortable, ugly, depressing old furniture (habits and thought patterns), but with a bit of refurbishing—a new paint job, furniture that fits the needs and wants of the occupant—that same house can be made into the perfect space for whatever it is you want to do with your life.

The object is to change from what you are not to what you truly are, to return to your own state of being in which you existed before anyone got around to telling you what to think or how to behave, before you learned what was acceptable to others and what wasn't. Now, I won't pretend that making your own decisions is the easiest task in the world. For some, it will prove difficult. However, remember that every mind, including yours, has its own distinct characteristics, and that they are *all* valid and useful. The trick is not to try to jam a round peg into a square hole. If you're a creative, nonlogical type, then you must learn to use that characteristic to its best advantage. If you're a logical, linear type, that's information you can use. The point here is that there is no one best way to think or perceive or receive information from the environment. Each person is an individual with a mind that operates in its own particular way—and none is superior to any other.

It takes persistence, self-control, and self-knowledge to stick to your guns and find and hold to that inner reality that is your true self. But it is this path that makes you free—free to be who you are, free to think unfettered, free to "create your own reality." If you let him, Mercury will lead you to Power Thinking.

Burning the Rubbish in the Mind

After breathing quietly for a few minutes, imagine yourself gathering up all the unwanted material in your mind, just as you would gather up dead leaves and fallen tree limbs to make a bonfire. Now, take all of these old, unnecessary thoughts and pile them in a place where you can safely start a fire—a fireplace is good. As you collect them, say to yourself, "I now let go of worn-out thoughts, worn-out emotions, worn-out attitudes." After you have piled up your mental rubbish, strike an imaginary match to the pile, and as it goes up in flames say to yourself, "I now return this to the universe for cleansing. I don't need it anymore."

The Twelve Thinking Types:
Mercury through the Signs

Mercury shows how you learn and think. It's an important indication of your ability to communicate, with yourself as well as with others.

Mercury in Aries

Your mind works quickly, impulsively, originally, freshly, with inspiration, one-pointedly, and impractically.

Here, Mercury indicates a way of thinking that tends to be decisive and competitive. You are fond of debate and argument—sometimes for argument's sake. You make decisions impulsively and often have reason to regret not having thought the matter through. *Headstrong* describes you perfectly, and you are egotistic about your intelligence.

Patience is not your strong point, and you have little tolerance for delays or obstacles to action. Irritability and a quick temper are likely if your Sun is also in Aries.

You learn best in an active, action-oriented atmosphere when you are enthusiastic about your subject and you feel mentally challenged.

Your communication style is direct, outspoken, sudden, enthusiastic, aggressive, quick, impatient, and loud.

Mercury in Taurus

Your mind works slowly, steadily, practically, rigidly, thoroughly, retentively, and obsessively.

Mercury's quick-moving nature is slowed down by Taurus's concreteness and love of the practical. With Mercury here, you think in terms of common sense, not in flights of fancy. You make decisions deliberately after consideration of the practical effects, and you are interested in the financial factors involved.

You have great powers of concentration and can plod through your mental work without flagging from boredom or fatigue. The ability to ignore outside disturbances makes you a good student. People may think that your mind is slow, but it is only taking its time to thoroughly digest information.

You learn best in a calm and peaceful atmosphere that is physically comfortable and visually pleasing and when you can see a practical result of what you are learning and are allowed to go at your own pace.

Your communication style is clear, cautious, concrete, conservative, deliberate, slow-paced, and thorough.

Mercury in Gemini

Your mind works rapidly, changeably, flexibly, logically, with curiousity, and superficially.

Mercury rules Gemini and is very much at home here. You can reason with logic, and your curious nature makes you good at using your mind in a variety of ways. However, you become bored quickly and have a difficult time shutting out external distractions. It's often hard for you to concentrate. You want to know about everything, for no particular reason, just because it's interesting—for the moment. Nothing holds your mental attention for long.

Your mind is agile as a monkey and you register all speech and activity around you immediately, which can make for mental overload. You love a busy environment but can burn out from too much communication. It's hard for you to slow down mentally, but you can become irritable from fatigue, confusion, and overextension of your mental state.

You learn best in a socially oriented atmosphere that is varied, with lots going on at once, and when your curiosity is constantly aroused.

Your communication style is talkative, nervous, variable, easy, light, quick, stylish, and interesting.

Mercury in Cancer

Your mind works intuitively, emotionally, tenaciously, worriedly, illogically, unrationally, and psychically.

You have a difficult time separating your thinking from your feelings. Though you have an excellent memory, your emotional biases will cause you to take in some facts and ignore others because of how you feel about them. Much of what you like to think about centers around home and family.

You are highly susceptible to the opinions of others and are influenced mentally by emotional factors. Mental objectivity is difficult for you because emotion colors your thinking processes.

You learn best in a homey, nurturing atmosphere where you are allowed to be quiet and feel safe and when you have an emotional or personal interest in the subject and your imagination is engaged.

Your communication style is sensitive, personal, creative, nonverbal, emotional, clingy, whiny, and tenacious.

♌ Mercury in Leo

Your mind works dramatically, by seeing the big picture, clearly, vividly, dogmatically, and egocentrically.

You have a strong will and are capable of focused concentration. Your mind can fix on a goal and achieve it without giving up. You are aided by mental self-confidence.

A good problem solver, you like to deal with things in large, general terms. Details don't interest you, so often you leave things half-done. You form opinions slowly, but once you have done so your mind is difficult to change.

Leadership comes easily to you and you speak well and emphatically. You like to become well-versed in any subject that interests you so that you can speak like an authority.

You learn best in a dramatic atmosphere, where you can get lots of attention and feedback for your efforts, and when your heart is in what you are learning.

Your communication style is warm, opinionated, creative, dramatic, convincing, engaging, and loving.

♍ Mercury in Virgo

Your mind works practically, detailedly, critically, rationally, ingeniously, thoroughly, specifically, and sequentially.

Mercury rules Virgo, indicating an analytical mind with an impressive ability for practical reasoning. You think things through objectively without being emotionally involved. You insist on doing mental work correctly the first time, and you will work hard to make sure all details are taken care of.

People think you are overinvolved in trivial details, but you know the importance of the old proverb, "For want of a nail the shoe was lost; for want of a shoe, the horse was lost; for want of a horse, the king was lost; for want of a king, the kingdom was lost."

You learn best in an atmosphere that makes sense to you, that is clean and orderly, and where you can see the useful outcome of your learning.

Your communication style is logical, analytical, humble, factual, precise, detail-oriented, and measured.

Mercury in Libra

Your mind works cooperatively, judiciously, fairly, in a balanced manner, intellectually, and indecisively.

You are primarily concerned with using your mind to understand human relationships and their psychology. You have great interest in the thinking and behavioral patterns of other people, especially those with whom you have a close relationship. For you, good communications equal good relationships, and relationships are essential to your way of thinking.

You prefer to do your mental work with someone else or as part of a group. You like to be the one who acts as the mediator. Your mind is naturally diplomatic in its approach to social situations. Mentally you are refined, and you seek balance and justice in all dealings.

You learn best in an atmosphere where you have one-on-one contact with your teacher and fellow students, when you are working with a partner, and when your sense of harmony and beauty are stimulated.

Your communication style is graceful, gentle, persuasive, and classy.

Mercury in Scorpio

Your mind works perceptively, determinedly, deeply, sensitively, intensively, suspiciously.

You are intuitive and capable of profound insights. You have mental X-ray vision and can see right through the thoughts of others. You like to mentally examine human motivations. Perceptive mentality allows you to see things correctly, and you call it like you see it, no matter what. Tact is not your strong point, and you refuse to mince words when you choose to speak your mind.

You can be mentally secretive and withhold your thoughts from those whom you fear will misunderstand you. Your mind is resourceful and you can overcome mental obstacles that would floor lesser mental types. If offended, you can plot revenge nastily, even if you keep it mental.

Your determination can frighten others, so you sometimes make your plans internally, revealing them to no one. You carry a lot on your mind all the time and enjoy the process of deep thought.

You learn best in an atmosphere that allows you to explore the depth of the subject, when you can see the necessity for what you are learning, and when you feel fascinated by the topic.

Your communication style is intense, to the point, purposeful, definite, emotionally involved, and sarcastic.

Mercury in Sagittarius

Your mind works openly, adventurously, farsightedly, scatteredly, unrealistically, undisciplinedly, and optimistically.

You have a mind that is concerned with attitudes over facts, giving you much insight into the motivations of others. This Sign position gives Mercury the ability to foretell events and develop amazing insights.

You are direct in speech and say exactly what you think, no matter whom you offend. Blunt doesn't begin to describe it. Preoccupation with lofty ideas is part of your mental pattern, which makes you a good student and an avid learner.

You learn best in atmosphere where you feel free to come and go at will, when you are interested in the subject, and when travel is part of your learning experience.

Your communication style is blunt, truthful, philosophical, learned, lengthy, and exaggerated.

Mercury in Capricorn

Your mind works practically, organizedly, focusedly, ambitiously, slowly, rigidly, and managerially.

You are shrewd and mentally attracted to material accomplishments. A good organizer, you can get your life set up with routines to make everything you do more efficient.

You are methodical in your thoughts and how you express them, sometimes in a teacherlike manner. You are mentally goal oriented and you like to use your mind to make plans for the future, especially as it concerns making money.

Realism is your mental hallmark, and you have little to no patience for those who build mental castles in the air but don't have the practical ability to construct them on solid ground.

You learn best in an atmosphere where you are given a clear methodology to follow and when you can see the practical end result down the line.

Your communication style is dry, wry, serious, conscientious, ironic, boring, tedious, and teacherlike.

Mercury in Aquarius

Your mind works originally, impersonally, brilliantly, openly, intuitively, detachedly, and inventively.

First and foremost, your mind is open to new ideas and new experiences—the newer and farther out the better! You are able to see things in the light of a wonderful objectivity that allows you to detach emotionally from your thoughts. You can accept concepts that others find threatening, unnerving, or just plain incomprehensible.

Your mind is original and inventive, and you are always thinking up ideas that startle others, especially more traditional types like your parents and teachers. You might be called "weird" by schoolmates, but don't let that worry you. You are an original, not a copy.

Your mind naturally leans toward humanitarian concepts, and you seek mental stimulation through friendships and association with like-minded groups.

You learn best in an atmosphere that is unusual in some way with a highly mentally charged tone and when you are excited and interested by the subject.

Your communication style is intelligent, abstract, logical, interesting, shocking, and rebellious.

♓ Mercury in Pisces

Your mind works nonverbally, pictorially, whimsically, illogically, non-rationally, sensitively, intuitively, and psychically.

You have a vivid imagination and quite possibly a photographic memory. You are a natural telepath and may receive messages from non-visible sources. This is a gift and is nothing to be afraid of. Your hunches usually turn out to be correct even though you haven't a clue where they come from. You can mentally tune in to the minds of others around you and "read" their thoughts.

Your mind is a wonderful world of color and shapes, of artistic ideas and musical themes. You are poetic and find ordinary reality hard to live with. Decision making can be a problem, as you would rather day-dream than deal with practical reality. Your shyness keeps you from expressing your thoughts, so it's a good idea to draw, dance, or write them in a private journal.

You learn best in a creatively oriented atmosphere that stimulates your imagination and gives you the tools with which to express it and when you love what you are learning.

Your communication style is image-oriented, non-verbal, intuitive, creative, compassionate.

Mercury Practice Exercise

Review your Mercury Sign's attributes and then write a short description of how your mind works in different situations—when studying, when learning new things, when pursuing something that interests you. How do you approach mental tasks? What future work would you like to do?

_____

_____

Finding Your True Vocation or Career:
Mercury's House Position

The *House* position of your Mercury will tell you which area of life is most affected by this important Planet. As the ruler of your thinking process, Mercury's House position is the lens through which you focus your intelligence—in short, what kind of mind you have and how you use it.

The Sign position of your Mercury reveals much about your ability to make decisions, to organize mentally, and to communicate your thoughts to others. It also indicates your attitude toward sharing your thoughts with others.

Mercury's Sign in your chart will also tell you a great deal about what information and facts you notice and regard as important and what you choose to ignore or forget. Your attitude toward intellectual pursuits such as school, homework, independent learning, higher education, and your mind in general all belong to Mercury's sphere of influence.

The House position of your Mercury, as well as his Sign and various Aspects, tells much about what occupies your mind and in which areas of activity you are likely to be successful in terms of mental work and communications. And since we live in the Age of Communications—which is accelerating at an astonishing pace—Mercury and his House position can serve as a reliable guide to choosing a career or work path after high school or college.

As an example, Mercury in Gemini in the second House would indicate that the person would value information highly, would be able to communicate easily, and could work in almost any field of communications. Mercury in Cancer in the sixth House, on the other hand, that would indicate that the person would be successful performing service work related to home and family—perhaps as a family counselor or as a social worker specializing in children. (Refer to chapter 2 for the specific meaning of each House.)

Mercury On Your Mind:
The Monitoring Technique

Mercury can be as elusive as the silvery substance that bears his name. If you are having any problems focusing on what you want to study as a future job or career, the following technique will help. It's good practice for any time your mind feels cloudy or confused or if you need to make a decision.

As we go about our daily lives, we usually are in a blur of automatic, preprogrammed thoughts and activities. Most of the time our mental processes are like a slightly out-of-focus photograph. We ordinarily go into sharp focus only in times of crisis and emergency. As a result, we are often bored and qualitatively "not there." So much of our everyday life is such a blur of routine that we miss what is going on at the deeper levels of the self. To combat this tendency, I have developed and teach a technique I call *monitoring*, which is a way of consciously focusing on the day's input, either as it is happening or during brief periods of reflection.

If the idea of learning to monitor your thoughts and feelings seems daunting, do not let that prevent you from attempting it. Like learning to ride a bicycle, it at first seems clumsy and impossible, and then, suddenly—*bingo!*—you are off and away with astonishing ease.

Begin by *consciously* storing in your memory your thoughts, feelings, and reactions to the events of the day, especially those preceding or during a difficult or stressful time. For example, if you feel a cold coming on, go over the events leading up to the sensation of a congested head or a sore throat.

If you have trouble remembering, train yourself to take brief notes during the day at or following significant events, especially negative ones. Note the particulars of the situation along with your reactions. A few words will do—you will develop a kind of shorthand in time. The purpose is to give your memory a jog later and enable you to recall the entire event with its "feeling tone."

When thoughts and feelings arise from the inner self, do not ignore them or push them away; record them either mentally or physically so that they do not vanish into the well of forgetfulness. During the day, whenever you have a spot of unoccupied time—waiting for a bus, riding in a car, standing in line—review what you have noted to fix it firmly for later evaluation.

At the end of the day, set aside a few minutes to examine the entire day's input for insights about your inner workings, clues to your deepest thought. The more you are aware of these constantly ongoing processes, the better equipped you are to use your consciousness to its best advantage.

Keep a written record of your thoughts and feelings along with physical circumstances. Jot down whatever ideas occur to you, no matter how far out they seem. Refer to your notes frequently to remind yourself of what your mind is doing. You can keep a special notebook for this purpose.

In time, you will perceive patterns of meaning—your life is not an accidental or random event; it has meaning and purpose. Keeping watch over how your Mercury operates via a journal will provide important clues for your future life direction in terms of your career or work.

6 Cycles of Becoming an Adult

Jupiter: The Wizard of Win

The next Astro-Wizard we will examine is the giant among the Planets, Jupiter. The largest Planet in our solar system, Jupiter is composed mostly of gaseous material. Interestingly, he stands for the principle of *expansion* and *growth*. Used negatively, his energies cause overexpansion. The person misusing Jupiter becomes just a big gas ball!

Because Jupiter's influence is generally considered to be good—his placement in the chart is where prosperity, success, good luck, honor, and accomplishment happen—I call him the "Wizard of Win." Astrologers refer to him as the "greater benefic," meaning he brings benefits or good things. He's also called the "second sun" because of his connection with *Zeus,* his Greek name, meaning "bright heaven." In this sense, he brings us heaven's gifts of goodliness. He thus represents what might be called the *universal principle.*

Jupiter represents school and higher education, the law and the legal system, banking and the financial system, government, and whatever is institutional or organized for society's needs. The way you encounter the larger social order beyond your home and immediate neighborhood is through Jupiter's placement by Sign and House in your chart and the Aspects he makes to your personal Planets already discussed—Sun, Moon, Venus, Mars, and Mercury.

Jupiter Key Characteristics

Expansive	Overexpansive
Optimistic	Foolhardy
Abundant	Too much growth
Ethical	Judgmental
Enthusiastic	Unrealistic
Idealistic	Exaggerated
Principled	Dogmatic
Socially oriented	Hypocritical

Jupiter in the Signs

Jupiter takes twelve years to go through the twelve Signs of the Zodiac. It doesn't take a mathematical wizard to figure out that he stays one year in each Sign, so anyone born the same year you were born will have Jupiter in the same *Sign*—but not usually in the same House. (Remember that the houses are determined by your Ascendant, which is calculated from the date and *time* of your birth.) Jupiter's *Sign* position gives general information about your attitude toward ethics, religion, higher education, and spiritual development.

Here's an overview of how Jupiter's Sign position encourages you to grow beyond your small personal concerns and expand into an awareness of the larger world around you:

In **Aries**—by taking chances and trying new things.

In **Taurus**—by conserving your resources, loving nature, and deciding what you truly value.

In **Gemini**—by expanding your information sources and communicating information to others.

In **Cancer**—by being nurturing to others, caring about society, and showing empathy toward people different from you.

In **Leo**—by expressing your creativity in a public way and being a responsible leader when given the chance.

In **Virgo**—by paying attention to the details necessary to the success of group projects and doing volunteer work.

In **Libra**—by involving yourself in relationships beyond your personal interests and by showing a concern for justice.

In **Scorpio**—by using your ability to get to the bottom of social issues and by making changes in attitudes.

In **Sagittarius**—by attending college or another form of higher education and traveling in order to learn more.

In **Capricorn**—by setting goals for your future, dealing with necessities, and achieving practical results.

In **Aquarius**—by joining humanitarian groups and associations, developing many friendships, and learning ways of making your abstract concepts concrete.

In **Pisces**—by sharing your spiritual nature with others and using your creativity for the public good.

Jupiter

Jupiter's glyph is the semi-circle of the Moon (soul) above the cross of matter. Thus Jupiter indicates the point on the horoscope where the material world meets the spiritual world, where Universal Law is revealed. With Jupiter you move past the strictly *personal* into the larger sphere of social life, or into the world external to your intimate personal concerns and wishes. This first occurs when you enter grade school and becomes more evident when you go to high school, where you participate in many activities and are required to follow social rules and regulations.

According to esoteric tradition, the House where Jupiter is placed is where we have already earned karmic benefit and protection from the universe. For example, a person with Jupiter in the first House will never truly be down and out. He may have troubles, but rescue will always come, even if at the eleventh hour.

Jupiter in Aspect to the Personal Planets

You've already learned about the importance of the Aspects, their names, and how they are calculated. Here are some key words to show you how Jupiter's energy combines with the energy of your other Planets when he makes an Aspect to any of them. In all cases, Trines and Sextiles are considered happy or lucky, while Squares and Oppositions bring challenges and overexpansion.

Jupiter/Sun *Expansion combines with will.* Wider horizons. Urge to travel. Restlessness. Seeking. Squandering. Wandering. Luck. "The Cosmic Blessing."

Jupiter/Moon *Expansion combines with feeling.* All Aspects are basically harmonious. Travel, abundance, excess of feelings, much sensuality. Self-exploration. Wanderlust. Exaggeration of feeling. Laziness. Procrastination. "The Ray of Hope."

Jupiter/Venus *Expansion combines with personal magnetism.* Increases love experience. Many happy relationships over time. Material abundance. Extravagance. Socially ambitious. Popularity. Socially gracious. Sharing. "A Gift from Heaven."

Jupiter/Mars *Expansion combines with personal drive.* Enjoyment of life, very adventurous, self-indulgent, restless. Tendency to overextension and exaggerating one's importance. Practical interest in religious matters. "The True Believer."

Jupiter/Mercury *Expansion combines with communication.* Gives intellectual potential. Creates an abundance of ideas. Clear thinking. Focus on larger picture. Understanding of issues. Traveling to learn foreign languages. "The Translator."

Society and Civilization:
The Jupiter Cycle

As one of the "timer" Planets, Jupiter's twelve-year journey through the Signs of the Zodiac places him squarely between the personal, or faster-moving, Planets and those at a greater distance from our Sun, which move at increasingly slower speeds the farther out they are.

By approximately age twelve, you have already lived through your first Jupiter cycle. Around the time you reach puberty, you enter your *second* Jupiter cycle, which will last until you are about twenty-four.

The beginning of every Jupiter cycle indicates new growth and development. This is an important time because you are more in touch with Jupiter's energies than you were as a child. Since Jupiter is the connection with society at large, as a youngster you didn't have nearly as much contact outside your home and immediate environment as you do now that you are a teen. You most likely go to a larger school, meet more people on your own, travel independently, interact with strangers, and encounter social institutions more frequently as your life progresses toward adulthood.

This twelve-year cycle starts with what is known as your "Jupiter return," a phrase that means the Planet has reached the Sign it occupied when you were born. It has returned to the place where it began in your chart. At this time, you are in a position to move further out into the world. You are yearning for more independence from your parents and other authoritative figures and may exhibit much restlessness and rebelliousness. In a word, you want *freedom* to expand your life in all directions.

This is your first real opportunity to think about what you want out of your life and how you will go about getting it. Many teens are already beginning to consider college now, and you may experience opportunities for travel related to learning. For example, you could become a foreign-exchange student or host one in your home. During the first three years of the new cycle, you are in a period of conscious growth. You are aware of changes occurring both in your mental life and in your physical body and how you use it.

This period is the time to concentrate on school as preparation for going further with your education. It is also a time when you should engage in as much *informal* learning as possible—such as school-sponsored field trips; a summer camp that specializes in a subject such as music, foreign language, or sports like horseback riding and swimming; or local activities at a YMCA, YWCA, or other youth centers in your neighborhood.

In your mid-teens, you will experience Jupiter in Square Aspect to himself. At this time you have a strong desire to express yourself, and you have a tendency to go to excesses. This is normal for a teenager, but don't let it get out of hand. Don't take on more than you can handle in any area of your life or you'll suffer stress from spreading yourself too thin.

Now is the time to understand that you can't do everything you want when you want to do it, and to realize that you have to place some limitations on your urge to expand all over the place. Many teens during this period feel that they have to do it all—extracurricular school activities, sports, music and/or dance lessons, a busy social life, church involvements, part-time work, and a host of other possibilities. If you overcommit to projects and activities, you'll suffer anxiety and exhaustion.

A particular area where overextension is dangerous is money. You are likely to spend without thinking or make financial demands on your parents that are unrealistic. If you earn money yourself, you are likely to spend your entire paycheck frivolously instead of saving some of it for that proverbial rainy day or for some important purchase.

However, if you are careful with your money and make sure you really have the time and resources to accomplish your aims, your self-confidence and optimism will allow you to make great strides during this period. What this aspect of Jupiter does is test your sense of proportion.

As you enter your late teen years, you experience Jupiter in Trine Aspect to his natal position. Usually this is a time of optimism and positive thinking. You are looking forward to adulthood and have overcome many of the mid-teen-years crises, obstacles, and adjustments. You may be preparing for college or some advanced training in a trade.

This is when you should be making long-range plans for your future by examining your ideas and setting goals for yourself. There can be tensions during this period caused by the need to make decisions that will affect your future—whether to attend college, what col-

Jupiter Speaks

I am Jupiter,
largest and most majestic
   of Planets,
the Ruler called by a
   thousand names.
The Sun is my silent
   partner.
I am the Horn of Plenty,
Planet of Good Fortune.

lege to choose, writing college applications, concerns about financial matters, alternatives to college, and so forth.

However, this is also a good time to resolve these tensions, and you can trust in your ability to make the right decisions as long as you take the initiative and don't sit passively waiting for someone else to take care of things for you.

When you reach legal age—congratulations, you're twenty-one!—you are nearing the end of this Jupiter cycle, which ends when you are approximately twenty-three. Assuming you've done everything more or less right up to this point, it's all systems go! You'll feel good about yourself and confident that you can accomplish whatever you want. Moving out of your everyday world will be exciting, and you'll once again enlarge your scope of activity—this time with a real job and its challenges.

Saturn: The Wizard of Wisdom and Wit

In contrast to Jupiter, Saturn is the Planet of *restriction* and the necessary lessons of reality. Saturn is the bump you get when an overexpanded Jupiter balloon bursts! As the representative of the *reality principle,* Saturn brings tasks and trials from whatever area is indicated by the House he occupies and by the Aspects he forms to your personal Planets. The Planet of discipline and structure, he represents the testing process through which you achieve maturity.

Astrologers used to consider Saturn a real bad guy with no saving graces, but we've learned better. The lessons he teaches are hard, even harsh, but they are absolutely *necessary*. Without them, if there were only endless Jupiterian expansion, life on Earth would be impossible. Our Planet is now suffering from too much Jupiterlike growth and not enough Saturnlike restrictions. Everywhere we look there is overexpansion and overgrowth, from endless, ugly strip malls to overpopulation.

As teens in this new twenty-first century, you are the ones who, as adults, are going to have to solve this conflict between the excesses of the previous generations and the need to face practical reality, so it's a good idea to make friends with Saturn *now*. And a good friend he can be, if you understand him and use him well. He brings

Saturn

Interestingly, Saturn's glyph is made up of the same two symbols as Jupiter's, but the two are inverted. This shows him as the principle of *contraction*, or the limitations of a normal-sized, earthbound life.

Saturn Key Characteristics

Disciplined	Restricted
Practical	Limited
Structured	Rigid
Time-conscious	Fearful
Conservative	Confined
Mature	Cautious
Wise	Restrained

stability and permanence, dependability and endurance, responsibility and the capacity for self-sacrifice—all qualities you will need as you take up the tasks of adulthood and come to grips with the enormous challenges ahead of you in the future.

Saturn in the Signs

It takes approximately twenty-eight years for Saturn to visit all the Signs, so he stays in each one about two and a half years. See appendix 1 to find where Saturn was on your birth date. You can also look up Saturn's Sign position for your parents and older people as well as younger siblings and friends.

The Sign that Saturn occupies in your chart shows *how* you will learn the lessons life has for you, what you fear most, and how you can avoid using Saturn's energy negatively.

If in the year 2000 you are between twelve and eighteen, Saturn was visiting either Scorpio, Sagittarius, or Capricorn when you were born. Here's how he acts in those Signs and in Aquarius, which is his next placement.

Scorpio—Your greatest lessons will come through dealing with your sexual nature, coping with deep feelings, and sharing resources. You most fear having your inner secrets found out. You need to learn to admit being wrong.

Sagittarius—Saturn's lessons will come through education and new ideas, exploration of nature, and travel for learning. You most fear lack of knowledge. Avoid acting like a know-it-all.

Capricorn—Saturn's lessons will come from having duties, early responsibility, and learning about material reality. Being improper is what you fear. Learn to play and have more fun.

Aquarius—Saturn's lessons will come through associations with humanitarian aims, like-minded friends, and expressing your individuality. You fear not being accepted. Warm up emotionally.

Your first experience of Saturn's lessons was with your parents or others saying **NO**—you can't do that, or have that, or go there. Saturn represents authority and all authority figures—from your parents and teachers to law-enforcement officers and the national government. There are things you can and can't do and behaviors that are allowed, dis-

Saturn and Time

Saturn is related to time. He's often pictured as either the newborn baby signifying the New Year—which occurs when the Sun is in Capricorn, the Sign Saturn rules—or as an old man with a scythe who cuts down life. His connection with time comes from his ancient roots in Greek mythology; there he was called *Kronos*, which means time. Words like chronology and chronic derive from this Greek word.

It is interesting to note that Saturn is exalted in the marriage Sign of Libra, an indication that marriage, when seriously entered, is supposed to be a relationship that survives the tests of time and lasts "until death do us part." In past eras, marriage had little to do with love and romance; it was all about the stability of the family. Saturn is the bringer of stability.

couraged, or punished. How you learn to deal with authority figures in your life during your teens is one of the most important lessons you will ever learn.

Your goal should be to become your own authority figure, someone who can be trusted to make correct decisions, be on time, and do assigned tasks (such as homework and chores) without a parent or teacher standing over you. Once you learn to look to yourself for authority, you will be well on your way to becoming a responsible and fully functioning adult. If you don't learn this lesson in your teen years, you will always be looking for someone else to tell you what's right and wrong or what you should do or not do. The person without self-discipline is easily lost or led astray into trouble and disarray.

Saturn's is the stern, serious face of the planetary influences. By overcoming the obstacles he poses and passing his tests, you learn—sometimes with much effort and pain—what you need to know to best live your life. In the end this is the purpose of all of life's difficulties, no matter how hard it may be to accept this idea when you are in the throes of coping with life's trials!

It may not be fun to think about Saturn, but it is only through him and this process of growth—call it trial by fire—that you will eventually create an orderly life and an orderly Planet Earth with security for all. It's always better to learn his lessons early, when you are still young, for if you put them off until you are already grown-up they are that much harder—like learning to read and write at age forty-five!

Saturn Speaks

I am Saturn,
oldest of the gods.
Law-giver and Time-maker,
Cosmic Tester and Earthly
　　Teacher,
Old Father Time, Reaper,
Tempter, and Molder,
preserver of customs and
　　natural laws,
I solidify.

A hard worker, Saturn rules Capricorn, the natural executive of the Zodiac. Once his lessons are learned, he grants wisdom and an understanding of practical reality. And he's actually got a sense of humor—dry and wry but humor nonetheless. That's why I call him the Wizard of Wisdom and Wit.

The person using Saturn correctly can dream up castles in the air and then construct them on the ground so people can live in them. Saturn likes to produce something of long-lasting value, permanent if possible (the Egyptian pharoahs who had the pyramids built were probably a Saturnian lot!). The eyes of the world are important to Saturn, and he demands respect, even at the cost of love. Yet his love is sturdy, when it has been earned, and you can depend on him in a pinch. The road may be long and hard where he leads, but he carries his share and more along the way if you show him respect and allow him to warm up his chilly nature by your side.

Saturn can also play an important role in career choice and development, for his position can give vital clues about what type of profession will suit you. Whatever position he occupies, he indicates the kinds of responsibilities and tasks you must face in your journey through life.

Saturn in Aspect to the Personal Planets

The Aspects that Saturn makes to your personal Planets will provide you with more information about this important energy and how it operates in your life. Although Saturn represents restrictions and limitations, he is also about makings things happen in the real world. Here are some key words to indicate how Saturn's energy combines with the energy of your personal Planets.

Saturn/Sun *Consolidation combines with will.* You take life seriously, believe strongly in right and wrong, use structure, and experience limitation of freedom of will. Authority figures and personal discipline are issues. "The Architect."

Saturn/Moon *Consolidation combines with feelings.* There can be loneliness, inhibitions, depression, feelings of unworthiness. Developing self-confidence and honoring your feelings will help. You are gifted with patience. "The Call to Duty."

Saturn/Venus *Consolidation combines with personal magnetism.* You are loyal and make long-lasting relationships based on practical considerations. Emotional coldness and sexual repression are issues. This causes separations. "The Love Tester."

Saturn/Mars *Consolidation combines with personal drive.* This can inhibit action and anger, causing frustration. You work hard and can concentrate your energy on narrow objectives. You strive for success but have trouble with goals. "The Master Builder."

Saturn/Mercury *Consolidation combines with communication.* You are serious-minded, cautious, and conservative, with a methodical approach to problem solving. You want concrete results, not abstract theory. Anxiety is a problem. "The Worrier."

The Necessary Lessons of Reality: The Saturn Cycle

In a way, Jupiter and Saturn are "kissin' cousins." They are considered to be a pair, just like the Sun and Moon and Venus and Mars, but there's a big difference with this couple.

Jupiter, with his cycle of twelve years, is closest to the personal Planets, but Saturn, with his cycle of twenty-eight years, is closest to the *outer* Planets, those much farther away from our Earth and Sun. These outer Planets, which we will discuss a bit later on, are Uranus, Neptune, and Pluto. They are called the trans-Saturnian Planets. Because Saturn stands between them and Jupiter, Saturn is considered to be the bridge or gateway to the faraway planetary influences, which are less concerned with individuals and more concerned with generations.

Since Saturn's cycle covers the entire process of a person's development from birth to full maturity, he is the major timer of the Zodiac. This makes him a marker of predictable crises of development.

Each quarter of Saturn's cycle shows what is happening—the first quarter is from birth to age seven; the second, from seven to approximately fourteen. It's no surprise that a crisis period in Saturn's cycle occurs just as you are getting into your teens! What could be more of a life test than puberty? This quarter of his cycle is called "the

The Light of Egypt

But see, O immortal soul, the real Saturn as the Angel
of Life, having from time gathered the experiences
which crown him with light .... Behold the earthly miracle
of the caterpillar and the butterfly, of the toiling
mortal and the transcendent God!
—Zanoni, ancient poet

psychological level," and since it lasts until you are twenty-one, it's really important.

If your parents and teachers have helped you to weather the preteen years of your young life, you are now ready to take a giant step into your eventual maturity. It's a time of growth, but also a time of learning about the limitations of life on Earth. You want to rebel against authority and have unlimited freedom, but you find that's a bit scary. You still need your parents and other authority figures to set limits for you to observe.

You want and need to test yourself against these limits, which is why the teen years are famous for producing rebels—with or without a cause. If you don't have firm and consistent authority figures in your life, you may feel cast adrift and get into trouble, sometimes with the law—the ultimate authority figure. Your body is mature now, from a technical standpoint, but your emotional nature and your mental development are still in the process of growing.

You may appear very grown-up, and you may want to act more grown-up than you are or can really handle, and that's a danger. It's also where Saturn steps in to keep you in check so you don't hurt yourself or others. The more you prove to yourself and your parents and other adults that you can handle responsibility and make good decisions, the more freedom you will earn from Saturn.

At this time, most of your life is emotionally centered and self-oriented, and that's as it should be. You are learning about yourself and who you are and what you can do. It's an exciting time, but also a dangerous one. Before you hit your teens, you were pretty much under the control of adults, but now you are branching out and want to make your own rules.

The lesson Saturn has for you at this point is the central challenge of adolescence—to become aware of the *needs of others* in both intimate relationships and in larger, public ways. Saturn will be your guide in the process of learning to relate to others. As you form relationships—make best friends and look for or find a romantic partner—you must face two separate and sometimes conflicting inner urges.

The first, quite naturally—considering the biological changes occurring in your body—is for *love,* for a close, intimate relationship that will help you feel secure during this difficult and uncertain period of your development.

Saturn in the Sky

Although Saturn is twice as far from our Earth as Jupiter, he is so huge that he can be seen with the naked eye! His diameter is 75,000 miles, and he is second in size only to massive Jupiter. However, when we add in the many rings surrounding him, he becomes the most impressive of the Planets to see.

The second, a result of a different inner need—that of wanting to become a participant in the big world out there—is for *education.*

Depending on your entire chart, one or the other of these two urges will become primary, and the other will become secondary.

Look to your Venus and Mars positions to see if you will choose to concentrate on the romantic and sexual side, the *feeling and emotional* part of yourself, or on the intellectual and mental side, the *thinking and social awareness* part of life. If you fall into the first category—indicated by a Libra Descendant, Venus and/or Mars in Libra, emphasis on Planets in Water Signs, or Venus and Mars in the same Sign, especially in the first or seventh House—the "urge to merge" will be strong. You will be forever having "crushes" and mooning about for true love. *Love* may be the most important word in your vocabulary, and you will seek a steady relationship to balance your emotional insecurity and provide you with a sense of being complete.

As you search for this ideal love mate, you may find your grades dropping below acceptable levels, and you may obsess over the other person—like picking daisy petals, "He (or she) loves me, loves me not," or asking your friends endless questions such as, "Do you think he likes me?" and "Should I ask her out?" It's a time of anguish and emotional turmoil.

You may even be tempted to drop out of school to get married or have a live-together relationship because you feel that love is all—the most important thing that can ever happen to you. If you follow this course, Saturn's lessons will be extra hard, for almost no one gets to escape the reality of living life at the practical level of earning money and doing the laundry.

Unwise sexual involvement—in the name of love—may result in a pregnancy that could terminate your schooling at an early age. If this happens, your love may turn sour quickly. If a pregnancy is achieved purposefully—for any reason at all—you saddle your life with limitations before you have really begun to live it. If you experience an unwanted pregnancy, you will face some hard choices.

But if you can understand that this romantic search is basically a search for *yourself*—that you want to see yourself in another person's eyes because you aren't quite sure yet who you are—you will reach a higher level of emotional maturity, and you won't depend on having a partner to feel good about yourself.

An Amazing Fact

Despite his reputation as a heavy-duty Planet in the astrological chart, old Saturn has some surprises for the student. Consider this: his density is the *lowest* of all the Planets. Believe it or not, if an ocean could be found that was large enough to hold him—he would *float!*

The yearning for love is strong in the teen years, and it can remain strong for life. However, adulthood comes *after* these early Saturn lessons have been experienced, and with experience comes knowledge. In your teen years, love is just an *idea,* and often this idea is a product of what you see in the media—on TV, in movies, in magazines—especially those featuring celebrities.

Celebrity worship is common among teens, and you may be seeking a boyfriend or girlfriend who is some version of a celebrity you admire. Here's where our old friend Saturn steps in to shatter your illusions, because when you meet up with a *real* boy or girl and begin to get to know him or her—warts and all—you hit the wall of *reality,* of what *is,* not what you *think* it is. Teens call this "crushing," and the flip side of this particular coin is that you can indeed get painfully crushed when a cherished relationship breaks up. Assigning qualities to a boy or girl in the haze of romantic attraction can bring you down with a big bump of disillusionment that causes confusion and can result in bitterness.

At this point, one of two things can happen—either you go merrily down the same path looking for your ideal partner, or you stick it out and try to somehow make your love interest fit your idea of what love should be. Both of these paths lead nowhere.

The lesson of Saturn for you, as a teen seeking love, is to learn from your experiences of disappointment and disillusionment and to accept that real people just aren't what you have been dreaming about. The old saying that "the road to love is never smooth" applies especially to teen love. It's one of the bumpiest roads you'll ever travel, full of the potholes of mistaken identity (he or she turns out to be different from who you thought he or she was) and littered with broken hearts. One of them could be yours.

Even if you are a hopeless romantic, your astrological chart can be of help during this period of learning about what's real and what's only a dream. The important lesson for you in your teen years is to understand that mere romantic illusions are just that—*illusions*—and that a real person can never fulfill them. It's another way of becoming a grown-up. And here I must admit that the world is full of adults who never grew past their teenage ideas of what love should be. These are the ones who have married and divorced several times and who go on looking for a perfect love that exists nowhere but in their imaginations.

However, your internal vision of love is essential to your growth and development as a feeling person. You don't want to throw the baby out with the bathwater. Just understand that at your age love is a learning process—another kind of school where instead of reading and writing and computer skills you learn about your emotions and how to handle them. Pay attention and do your homework, by which I mean think about your relationships before, during, and after.

The term for this is *reflection*. As you reflect, or review, your love experiences, you learn. There's an old Chinese proverb that hits the spot here: "Life is pain. Pain makes you think. Thinking makes you wise. And wisdom makes life endurable." A word to the wise: *never, never, never, ever* stay in a relationship that isn't working just to avoid being alone. The same goes for a relationship that is abusive. Unfortunately, many teenagers, girls especially, confuse attention with love, even if the attention hurts. An absolute rule is:

If he or she hurts you, it isn't love.

Don't make the serious mistake of thinking differently, and don't ever let yourself believe that you are somehow going to make the other person change. Another absolute rule is:

The only person you can change is yourself.

I don't want to rain on anyone's love parade, but if you don't learn Saturn's lessons *now,* you'll have to go through it all again later, like being held back in school for failing to make your grades. And trust me, it's a lot worse the second or third time around. Youth is not a permanent state of being. No matter what you do, you will in a few years no longer be a teen. If you use these precious few years intelligently, you'll emerge a full-fledged adult, ready to lead a productive and happy life. But if you ignore Saturn's lessons, you will set yourself on a path of always looking for and never finding the love you seek.

If your inclination is toward the path of higher education and you think of school as a primary goal that will lead to a successful adult life, you are preparing yourself well to take the first major step into full adulthood. You are usually interested in social issues, politics, and the choosing of a profession as soon as you hit your teen years. By staying in school and following your desire to achieve the highest degree of education your finances will allow, you'll travel the

Gifts of Saturn

To those who resist Saturn's influence, his position in the horoscope will show restrictions, deprivations, and inhibitions. To those who learn to use his energy in a positive manner, and who are willing to listen to the sometimes stern voice of Kronos, Saturn will give strength of mind and purpose and help to balance one's temperament. He can calm unruly passions and he bestows a clear appreciation of material values.

high road exemplified by Capricorn, the Sign ruled by Saturn.

To do this you will need all the family support you can get, but if it is lacking, don't give up your cause. Do research to find out what help is available. There's a lot you can do to reach your goals even if your family isn't able or willing to help. Often a family can't help financially, but you can depend on them to cheer you on and give you *emotional* support, which can make all the difference. But if even emotional support is lacking, you can find teachers and friends who will serve as a support group. Never let yourself down by settling for less than you dream you can be. In this quest, Saturn will give you a helping hand, for he looks kindly on those who follow his lead and try to bring their life dreams into reality.

Now, it must be said that most people aren't all one way or the other, but some combination of the two types I have described. Even the most dedicated high-school student bound for college and graduate school wants love and sex to be a part of his or her life. But this type is able to put off romance until later so that school comes first.

And the most romantic dreamer can hardly remain unaware of the need to earn a living and deal with the practicalities of life's many ho-hum, everyday chores.

The secret is to find and maintain a balance between these two contradictory inner impulses. Both are valid; both are necessary. It's up to you to determine how much of your energy, both mental and emotional, to give to each side of yourself.

At the end of this phase of the Saturn cycle, you will be twenty-one and legally an adult. Congratulations!

7 Far Out— The Astro-Wizards beyond Saturn

n this chapter you are going to learn about *Uranus, Neptune,* and *Pluto,* called *trans-Saturnian* Planets because they are farther from our Sun than Saturn, the slowest moving of the closer Planets. The farther out they are, the slower the Planets move.

These Astro-Wizards are so far out that the first of them—Uranus, 1.7 billion miles from Earth—is nearly impossible to see with the naked eye, and then only if you know *exactly* where to look and have the long-distance vision of a hawk. It takes Uranus eighty-four years to visit all of the Signs of the Zodiac.

Neptune, a billion miles farther out, is invisible to the naked eye. Even when viewed through a telescope, he appears only as a greenish sphere circled by a dimly colored equatorial band. It takes him 164 years to visit all of the Signs of the Zodiac.

Pluto, the farthest out of the known Planets, is mysterious to us. Even the world's most powerful telescope reveals Pluto only as a small, yellowish disk with no surface markings visible. It takes him 242 years to visit all the Signs of the Zodiac. One of his secrets is that unlike the other Planets, which spend a regular amount of time in each Sign, Pluto can spend anywhere from thirteen to thirty-two years in just one Sign! There's a lot more to this wizard than meets the eye of the telescope.

Uranus: The Wizard of Odd

The Wizard of Odd is a bit like the Wizard of Oz in that he causes wonderful marvels to happen suddenly and unexpectedly. But he's no fake wizard; he's very real and most powerful. While Saturn shows where you experience restrictions and obstacles, Uranus tells about your urge for freedom from all restrictions, physical and mental. The action of Uranus, who rules electricity and electronics as well as invention and magic, is sudden and unexpected, so he is where you can expect the unexpected. Call him "the rule breaker."

Ruler of Aquarius, an Air Sign, Uranus is primarily *mental,* which is why astrologers call this wizard the "higher octave of Mercury." Where Uranus is placed in your chart by House is the area of your life where ideas are born—and where you express your individuality most strongly and kick up your heels (or at least want to).

This amazing wizard also gives you the opportunity to make direct contact with the Universal Mind through your intuition, or what is commonly called the sixth sense. He is the link between your mental efforts and the laws of the universe that bring things into being. With Uranus, you soar into the realms of originality and innovation, and there you find new ways to solve life's problems.

Uranus shows what you hope and dream and wish—he is the "what if" or "why not?" attitude, the inventor who says, "Let's see what happens if we do this or that," the experimenter who isn't afraid of putting two unknowns together just for the heck of it, just to see what will happen. The mind's pattern maker, he tries out everything mentally and then sets goals based on mental models.

Uranus in the Signs

As Uranus stays in each Sign approximately seven years, every person born during that seven-year period will have Uranus in the same Sign.

Uranus

Uranus's glyph represents the joining of the universal with the temporal, or the soul with the human (two semicircles). These are on either side of a cross, the symbol for matter and the world. Thus, through Uranus the human is linked to the divine. The small circle is the life energy force.

If you are a teen in the year 2000, you were born with Uranus in Sagittarius (1981–1988). Your generation is just now beginning to make itself felt as a social force. As you mature, you will be inspired by Uranus to devote your energies to the much-needed spiritual regeneration of humanity, which is represented by the Sign of Sagittarius.

You will question everything that previously has been accepted and overturn much that has been established in terms of religion and society, creating new and better forms. You will be attracted to new ideas and you won't put up with any restrictions on your right to think as you choose. Your generation is likely to produce a large number of freedom-loving, free-thinking inventors and innovators who will back up their ideas with action.

The generation born with Uranus in Capricorn (1988–1996) will also question all established authority and want to make far-reaching changes in social institutions. However, they will be extremely practical and down-to-earth about *how* changes are going to be made. They will build on what came before them. Previous innovative thinking will give them the tools for building a society with firm foundations in the world of practical reality, for in them Uranus combines with Saturn, the ruler of Capricorn.

Uranus in Aspect to the Personal Planets

Because Uranus spends so much time in each Sign, the major Aspects he makes to your personal Planets allow you to understand his energies and how they operate in your chart.

Aspects to Uranus indicate how you will tend to behave in a free-spirited way, be unconventional, knock over tradition, do the unusual thing, or produce the far-out idea.

Uranus/Sun *Intuition combines with will*. A life full of surprises and sudden flashes of insight. Strong independent streak. Can be erratic. Unusual experiences. Compulsive behavior. Inspirational and idealistic. "The Nonconformist."

Uranus/Moon *Intuition combines with feelings*. A deep understanding of human nature and compatibility with peoples of all kinds. Changing social groups frequently. Craving for excitement. Unconventional living habits. "Freedom Is Security."

Uranus Key Characteristics

Intuitive	Undisciplined
Innovative	Free-thinking
Unexpected	Surprising
Dynamic	Explosive
Electrifying	Destructive
Liberating	Rash
Humanitarian	Revolutionary
Technological	Gadget-obsessed

Uranus Rules the Net

The discovery of Uranus in 1781, just twenty-nine years after Benjamin Franklin made his famous kite experiment, coincided with the discovery of electricity and the development of electronics and telecommunications. Without Uranus, there wouldn't be an Internet!

Uranus Speaks

I am Uranus
the Awakener.
I am electric, I am the
   Atom Smasher,
revolutionary in nature,
unconventional, sudden,
   erratic.
I turn things over.

Uranus/Venus   *Intuition combines with personal magnetism.* Relationships are unconventional and usually not long-lasting. Art of an unusual nature is a strong interest and there may be talent. Every aspect of life is different from the norm. "The Different Drummer."

Uranus/Mars   *Intuition combines with personal drive.* Highly volatile and unstable. Erratic activity, sudden highs and lows of energy. Nervousness and irritability can cause danger of violence. Original ideas and methods. "A Lightning Bolt."

Uranus/Mercury   *Intuition combines with communication.* Some form of genius. Inventive, original, quick-minded. Flashes of ideas and concepts. Finds everyday world boring and irksome. May be mentally jumpy or dogmatic. "A Lightning Mind."

Uranus produces sudden change of all sorts and, like a thunderstorm, can often serve to clear the air. On occasion, Uranian energies take the form of violence. For example, someone who is accident-prone or who has a quick temper and gets into fights readily may have a Square Aspect between Mars and Uranus. The Mars-Uranus Opposition can indicate someone who is always against the system, wants to challenge all authority, and is in danger of breaking the law with serious consequences. Of course, these negative uses of Uranian energy can be avoided if you know they are there and where they are coming from. For instance, the person with the Square or Opposition might channel those explosive energies into political activism or unusual but peaceful methods of self-expression, such as inventing new electronic technology.

It is the opinion of the esoteric astrologers that Uranus has to do with the unique task of each person in this particular incarnation, that he is a clue to the soul's reason for making this journey. In a sense, where Uranus is the soul is most free of restrictions, where old karma has already been dissolved and where you can be truly yourself—unique and individual.

Neptune: The Wizard of Art

With this wonderful Astro-Wizard, you are in a world that is totally different from that of either Saturn or Uranus. Neptune is misty, dreamy, invisible, otherworldly, inspirational—in a word, *creative*. He is the Planet of poets and artists, mystics and musicians, dancers and dreamers, singers and storytellers—and of everyone who longs for a world where peace and love reign supreme. He is the Planet of impossible but tantalizing visions. An astrologer friend of mine once said of Neptune, "It's like trying to grab a handful of clouds and hold on to it."

Not surprisingly, the story of the discovery of Neptune is as mysterious as the Wizard himself. Here's how it came about: during the reign of Queen Victoria in England, two astronomers were trying to solve the puzzle of the then-unexplained and peculiar orbit of Uranus, which had the unsettling habit of arriving either before or after it was supposed to. (Typical of Uranus!)

Astronomically, each Planet in our solar system affects the others because of the forces of gravity, which hold the whole system together. Think about it—they all just hang there in space, going round and round forever, supported by absolutely nothing—except those mysterious forces of gravity, which even our most advanced physicists don't truly understand.

Anyway, this oddness of the Wizard of Odd made these smart astronomers suspect that there was *something* out there that was making Uranus behave in this distinctly irrational manner. The Victorians liked an orderly world, and so they wanted a sensible answer to this riddle.

Try as they might (and of course they didn't have any calculators to help them, let alone high-speed computers!), they couldn't figure it out until they decided that the culprit that was making Uranus behave so weirdly had to be *another Planet*. Finally, on September 23, 1846, they found him, and they named him after the great god of the oceans, which are still mostly unknown territory even today. Who knows what lies and lives in their darkest depths way beyond the reach of human technology? It's deep and pitch-black dark at the bottom of the sea, and it is full of creatures we can only imagine.

That's Neptune for you—a place you can reach only through

Neptune Key Characteristics

Spiritual	Escapist
Mystical	Unrealistic
Artistic	Dreamy
Creative	Disorganized
Compassionate	Self-pitying
Inspired	Deluded
Idealistic	Addictive

Neptune

Neptune's glyph—a trident such as that held by the Lord of the Oceans—is a semicircle (representing the soul) pierced by the cross of matter (Earthly manifestation). The resulting three-pronged fork suggests the physical body with its senses, the emotional "body," and the mind, or process of thinking. Together, these represent the *whole* person.

On another level, the glyph can be read as Spirit penetrating human consciousness, which produces the inspirations of poets and artists and the unselfish compassion of our humanitarian urges for worldwide love and peace. Neptune is thus considered the "higher octave" of Venus, representing not personal love but universal love of one's fellow human beings.

imagination. The English astronomers' imagination took them to the idea of another Planet, and finally they actually saw Neptune as a pale greenish globe floating way out beyond Uranus. At least now they had a logical explanation for Uranus's peculiar behavior, even if they didn't have a clue what Neptune was like. They knew he was there. Interesting, isn't it, that the Planet of the unseen was the mysterious force behind the Wizard of Odd's odd orbit?

With Neptune now in the futuristic Sign of Aquarius, it seems that telepathy may come to replace the telephone! Already our most reputable and advanced scientific laboratories are studying what is invisible—quantum physics and quarks—and proving their existence. Clearly, Neptune is a force to be reckoned with.

First Uranus's discovery pointed the way to electronics and our now extremely advanced technology, with satellite systems and the like. Then Neptune brought in interest in the psychic realm, which has spilled over into hard-core scientific investigation of what can't be seen with the naked eye, including serious study of telepathy and ESP, long-distance energy healing, and so on.

Isn't it curious that these undiscovered Planets present themselves to humanity's sight just at the same time that related earthly, human development is taking place? It looks suspciously like a master plan of some sort.

Neptune in the Signs

If you are a teen in 2000, you were born when Neptune was passing through either the Sign of Sagittarius (1970–1984) or the Sign of Capricorn (1984–2000).

The earliest of the Sagittarius generation is already reaching maturity, but many of you are still in your teen years. Generally speaking, this generation has produced young people who yearn to find positive expression for their spiritual needs, which they feel strongly. There are some clues to be had in the rise of fundamentalist religions all over the world, although by and large these are negative expressions of Neptune in Sagittarius. Another marker is the wide acceptance of psychic guidance through "readings" such as Tarot and astrology, subjects that are now of great interest to teens.

Neptune—
The Psychic Planet

Two years before Neptune was discovered, Mme. Helena Blavatsky, the founder of a movement called Theosophy, had journeyed to Tibet and India in search of spiritual enlightenment. Following Neptune's sighting, a wave of spiritualistic, psychic, mediumistic, and table-tapping mania swept over all of Britain and crossed the Atlantic Ocean to America. Everyone, it seems, was holding seances where lights went on and off while everyone around the table held hands. Misty figures floated about the room; unseen hands delivered papers supposedly written by disembodied entities. Objects flew across the empty space, tables leapt into the air, and sounds came out of nowhere.

Eventually, some of these mediums were proved to be fakes, but not all. Some psychic experiences were investigated and validated as genuine, with the result that today there are several groups that attempt to scientifically prove (or disprove) claims relating to the "paranormal," as such things are called.

If you belong to the budding Capricorn generation, you were born in the period that ushered in the collapse of the former Soviet Union and a great deal of chaos in economic and political structures worldwide. You are going to express Neptune's creative energies in a practical way. It's going to be your job to put back together what has been messed up, creating chaos all over the globe. You will be able to incorporate your spiritual values into the needs of practical reality as you begin to do adult work. You will be the adults who create a true and lasting world order, bringing peace to all.

Where Neptune is placed, you are filled with sympathy and compassion, learn universal love, and may be entirely too sensitive. You are inspired by ideals and your imagination knows no bounds. The visual arts and the ability to "see" also come from Neptune's creative region—higher states of consciousness, other worlds, spirit contacts, as well as the use or misuse of drugs and mind-altering substances fall under Neptune's veil. Alas, the poet may see marvelous worlds beyond

Neptune Rules the Deep

Neptune, a son of the cosmic Great Goddess and the brother of the sky-god Zeus, whom we call Jupiter, is aptly named. He represents the unfathomable in the human psyche . . . and beyond. Although ancient peoples couldn't actually know Neptune was out there, because they couldn't see him, they intuited his presence and personified him as a god. To the Greeks he was Poseidon, ruler of the waters of Earth; the Romans renamed him Neptune; and the Hindus called him Idapati, or "Master of the Waters." Taking 164 years to make a complete cycle of the Zodiacal circle, he spends approximately twelve years in each Sign, and no one will live out his entire round.

the world but drink or drug away the vision, for Neptune is the visionary but he doesn't particularly care whether the vision is made manifest. That's the job of Uranus and Saturn. Neptune is like a marvelous singer of songs and teller of stories who simply *flows out*—but he needs a manager and a secretary to get them down on paper and properly orchestrated for the general public to enjoy and appreciate.

Now is the time for you Neptune-in-Capricorn teens to begin thinking of your future, for you are the unfortunate inheritors of lax and irresponsible political policies. You need to learn early on how to actualize your ideas on an everyday basis. Don't wait until it's too late. Remember what the great German poet and philosopher Goethe said: "If you dream you can do it, *begin* and you will succeed."

Look to Neptune's Aspects in your chart to see how he affects you personally.

Neptune in Aspect to the Personal Planets

Neptune's Aspects show where you are stimulated by imaginative and creative impulses that come from the deep inner psyche. They show where you have "hunches" and dream of strange beings from out of your depths. When Neptune aspects the personal Planets, his influence is flowing from the transpersonal realm directly into the personal.

Neptune/Sun　*Illumination combines with will.* You are drawn to express your life purpose through a creative or helping profession. Astrologers often have this contact. You have an aura of mystery and glamour. Beware of self-deluding images of yourself or others. "The Inspirational Invisible."

Neptune/Moon　*Illumination combines with feelings.* You have a very imaginative and creative emotional life. You demand to be allowed to explore all avenues of self-expression. Moody and sensitive, you can be self-deceiving. Do not use drugs or alcohol. An extremely addictive placement. "The Visionary."

Neptune/Venus　*Illumination combines with personal magnetism.* Either you live a dreamlike, impractical life or you channel your inspiration into a beautiful creative outlet. You can be deceived in your relationships all too easily and sacrifice your personal interests for misguided love. "Artistic Imagination."

Neptune/Mars *Illumination combines with personal drive.* There is confusion about goals and a life purpose. You may try lots of different avenues. Consistency is a problem. Stay far away from all drugs and don't dabble in mysticism you don't understand. Your flexibility makes you creative. "Someday My Goal Will Come."

Neptune/Mercury *Illumination combines with communication.* You are either highly artistic and imaginatively communicative or prone to an excess of uncontrolled, undisciplined imagination. You have trouble distinguishing the real from the unreal. You fantasize obsessively. "The Inspirational Thinker."

Artists and mystics are Neptune's children—whether they are famous or whether what they do is personal and private, done for strictly spiritual or inner purposes. It's been said that the mystic is "an artist without a medium," and many mediums, psychics, and others who are tuned in to the "other world" have Neptune powerfully placed in their charts. These people have learned to love at large, as it were—they do not do their work for the love of a single person but for love of humankind as a whole. The true Neptunian personality loves for the sake of love itself, and many of the saintly and historically religious have belonged to this category.

Use this Wizard well, learn his ways, devote yourself to his aims, and he will reward you with amazing visions and insights. Always remember, however, that he is the Planet of *illusion*—a double-edged sword that cuts both ways. As the Great Illusionist, he performs amazing magical tricks that are great fun and can bring much joy. But as the Escape Artist, he can make you think you are contacting higher realms by using drugs and alcohol. *Don't be fooled.* Creativity is its own high; you don't need any chemical help to get "high." Learn to get high on yourself and your own imagination and spiritual potential. All you need to soar is Neptune and a glass of water; this wonderful Wizard, who will take you up, up, up, up, and away into the stratosphere of his multifaceted and magical realm—which is really *inside you.*

Neptune Speaks

I am the Master of the Sea.
I immerse the individual
in a greater purpose,
freeing the personality
from the subjective, the
  selfish;
teaching self-sacrificing
  love.

Pluto: The Wizard of Yon

Pluto Key Characteristics

Transforming	Obsessive
Powerful	Dictatorial
Revitalizing	Destroying
Renewing	Compulsive
Redeeming	Fanatical
Money-making	Ruthless
Regenerating	Eliminating

Our last Astro-Wizard is the newest of the known Planets. Pluto was discovered in 1930, just five years before Marie Curie's daughter Irene won (with her husband) the Nobel Prize for synthesis of the new radioactive elements, following up on her parents' work with radium.

Pluto symbolizes transformation of both psyche and form. It would not be too much to say that plutonium, the trigger of the atom bomb, transformed the entire world forever after. Neither the astronomers nor the astrologers know all that much about Pluto, but there is no question that power resides there, power of a most potent sort.

Deepest in space (nearly four billion miles from our Sun), Pluto is the only Planet with an irregular orbit, which sometimes brings it closer to the Sun than Neptune. His laws seem to be his own, and we don't actually know his true size. Some say he is the smallest and densest of the planetary bodies; others claim that what we see by telescope is only a bright core that is surrounded by a larger but dark and unseeable area. Whatever the case, astrologers associate this most compelling of Planets with the transformative process that goes on in the dark underworld of the psyche, sending up its aromas via dreams and, sometimes, compulsive behaviors. With Pluto we are in the realm of ancient Hades, as Pluto was named by the Greeks, who had great respect for the unfathomable power residing in the underworld.

Astronomers are now speculating about the existence of yet another Planet in our solar system even farther out than Pluto. But at the time of this writing, Pluto is still the farthest Planet from the Sun that we know about. As such, he describes the limits of our human consciousness.

Ruler of Scorpio, Pluto is known as the Great Transformer. Whatever he touches becomes something else and is stimulated to reveal its true nature, just as gold ore is often hidden under some valueless muck. He is the bottom-line fundamental in our lives, and he says a lot about how we deal with the hidden aspects of our own psyches and lives. He symbolizes death and rebirth on the spiritual plane, as well as power struggles of all sorts—those we have with others and those with ourselves.

Because of his long orbit, Pluto is the point where we connect, for good or for ill, with the rest of our society—not just our local environment but the totality of humanity, which, in some way, shares a world psyche. The forms of the psyche are the same everywhere—though they manifest differently in different cultures and at different times.

Pluto is also known as "Mr. Moneybags," because power begets money, and the great riches of the twentieth century came from deep within the earth—oil, gold, gems, and minerals. As ruler of the underworld, he is a dark force to be reckoned with.

Pluto takes some 244 years to circle the Zodiac, so none of us will experience more than a small slice of his influence. Since Pluto takes such a long time to visit all of the Signs of the Zodiac, his influence is not very noticable by Sign alone.

If you are sixteen or younger in 2000, you were born with Pluto in the Sign of Scorpio (1984–1995). Generally speaking, with Pluto in Scorpio, the Sign he rules, your generation will come into adulthood after a period of worldwide conflict. You will be the shepherds of the transformation of society in the wake of the dissolving old Age of Pisces. You will experience the breakdown of old forms of all sorts—political, educational, economic, social, scientific.

You are intense to the max, and your depth of perception may be frightening to your Pluto-in-Libra parents, whose main experiences of Pluto's unique ability to break down old forms and regenerate them came in the area of marriage. Probably only a few of you have your original two-parent families intact. Many of you are living with a single parent or are being shuttled back and forth between parents. Others of you who are now in the teen years may already be on your own—and not by choice. Pluto is a tough taskmaster, but you are strong by nature and unafraid of life's challenges. Your life isn't easy, but in a way you are lucky to have such a powerful Wizard in your corner to help you with the challenges that lie ahead in your young lives.

Look to the Aspects Pluto makes to your personal Planets (if any) for more information about how this powerful planetary Wizard operates in your life, because even a small fragment of his energy can be powerful indeed, especially if he is in close Aspect to a personal Planet.

Pluto

This glyph, although of recent origin, represents ancient symbolism. Here the semicircle of the soul is linked to the cross of matter, and over the two is the circle of Spirit. This symbol reveals the principle that the energy of the Spirit descends through the soul to man here on Earth.

Pluto in Aspect to the Personal Planets

As a generational Planet, Pluto doesn't operate much on the personal level unless he contacts you through your personal Planets—Sun, Moon, Venus, Mars, and Mercury. Here is an overview of how he operates when in Aspect to these:

Pluto/Sun *Regeneration combines with will.* Your potential creative ability is enormous, if you develop it. This can be a real challenge with much tension and anxiety, but you can do it if you try. You undergo many changes in the process. You possess great powers of self-renewal. "The Life Force."

Pluto/Moon *Regeneration combines with feelings.* You are subject to intense and volatile emotional outbursts or to panic attacks. Your self-expression comes from your emotional state. Try to overcome negative emotions such as hate, envy, and a desire for revenge, for they will hurt you. "The Purifier."

Pluto/Venus *Regeneration combines with personal magnetism.* Relationships go through many phases, or you have many relationships. You use them for self-transformation. Breakups are common due to jealousy and possessiveness, especially where sex is concerned. You can renew other people. "The Builder-Unbuilder."

Pluto/Mars *Regeneration combines with personal drive.* You seek to win at all costs. You tend to dominate, to want power, and to put an endless supply of energy into your desires. Learn that you don't need an atom bomb to kill an ant. Your sexual energies can serve your creative development. "The Nuclear Power Plant."

Pluto/Mercury *Regeneration combines with communication.* You are a deep thinker who likes to explore your many inner levels of perception. You may have disturbing thoughts that produce tension. Your extreme curiosity about other people's secrets may be troublesome and should be curbed. "The Detective" or "The Spy."

FOUR

The Parent Trap

8 You and Your Parents

The main purpose of astrology, especially for young people, is to help the individual learn who he or she really is and to accept it without being judgmental.

Robert Hand, *Planets in Youth*

There is a common saying that the only sure things in life are death and taxes. However, until the cloning of human beings becomes both possible and legal, there is one inescapable fact of life that everybody must deal with.

PARENTS!

Everybody on Earth (so far) has been born because of two parents, even if, as a result of our society's newly advanced birth technology, one of them is an unknown donor of male semen or female eggs.

You may live with your two birth parents, but today's teens are as likely to live with a single parent, a step-parent, grandparents or other relatives, or adoptive or foster parents as they are to live with both of their birth parents.

These multiple parent possibilities can make life confusing, especially for teens. It also creates a lot of confusion for the adults who have children and then divorce and remarry, or who give up children for adoption because they cannot care for them properly, or whose life circumstances cause authorities to step in and put at-risk children in foster care.

The Basic Facts of Parents

You can't change
Your parent as a person
    BUT
You can learn to accept
Your parent for who she or
    he is
You can't force your parents
To accept who you are
    BUT
You can learn to accept
    yourself
Remember also that
The only person in the
    world
You can change is
    YOURSELF

It's a mess. Unfortunately, it's one that many teens have to cope with as best they can. While I hope that *you* are living with your two birth parents, even that usually fortunate situation isn't always perfect.

Whether you have a relationship with both of your birth parents, only one of them, or neither of them, your life is influenced by them and their behavior both prior to your birth and later on. At the very least, for good or for ill, you carry their genes.

Astrology doesn't tell us about genes, but it does give good indications about parents, even absent ones. Whether your birth parents are in your life in a real way, are part-time parents, or are totally unknown to you, an influence exists.

If for some unhappy reason you are on your own without parental aid, if you know your parents' birthdates, this section may help you to understand them, which may in turn help you to help yourself.

Because there are now so many variables in the lives of teens regarding parents or parental figures, for the sake of simplicity and clarity this discussion assumes you have one or more parents—whether they are the birth parents or not. On a day-to-day basis, whoever is responsible for your welfare is, practically speaking, your parent(s).

We are going show you how to compare your chart with that of your parent(s). You can also use this technique to compare your chart with that of any adult who fills the role of your parent.

Later in this chapter, we will be more specific about your mother and father separately, and this discussion will apply to your birth parents. However, if you do not live with either your birth mother or your birth father, you may also find it useful regarding those whom you now consider to be your mother and father. I don't want to get too complicated about this, but I am trying to cover all the bases for you.

Parents Are People Too

Unfortunately, there is no simple solution to getting along with your parents. If you're lucky, sometimes you find it easy, but often a teen finds parental relationships extremely difficult. The purpose of this section is to help you understand that *your parents are people too.* And, like all people, they have their good points and their bad points. It's easy for a teen to see the bad up-front and let the good recede into the background. However, I don't deny that there can be lots of difficult adjustments necessary for you with your parents.

For a moment *accept* that your parents probably try their best for you. Sometimes they fail and sometimes they succeed; your personal situation will be different from anyone else's family interactions. We can choose our friends, but we are stuck with our family.

You have learned about comparing your chart with the charts of your love interests and your friends. Now we are going to have a look at how the teen-parent comparison works.

Because this is a complex issue with many parts, we are first going to explain the *Sign* comparisons. You know about the Signs and their general characteristics, but you might want to refresh your memory by rereading chapter 1. The Sign your parent(s) Planet(s) occupy and your own planetary line-up will color how you interpret the comparison.

For example, you already know that the Sun represents the ego and conscious will. If your parent's Sun and your Moon are involved in the comparison, it will be about your parent's ego and your emotions. You can judge the comparison according to *which* Planets occupy the Signs in the comparisons below. The Houses in which the Signs and Planets fall, in both your chart and your parent's chart, are also factors to consider in interpretation. For example, in the Sun/Moon combination given above, the House positions will show you which area of life is affected. If it's your Moon in the first House, it's about you personally. If your parent's Sun is in his or her third House, it will be about communication. If the Aspect is a difficult one (Square or Opposition), your tendency to take emotional issues very personally will interfere with your ability to communicate with your parent, and vice versa. On the other hand, if the Aspect between the two charts is an easy one (Trine or Sextile), emotion and communication will flow smoothly.

We have included charts going back to 1950 to make it easy for you to look up the Planets of older people. (See appendix 1.)

Parent-Teen Relationships through the Signs

Aries Parent

Aries Teen   You are both strong willed and want to dominate. Temper is a problem. If you have a parent who loses it frequently, the best path to take is avoidance. Learning to control your own temper—or finding safe outlets for it in active sports and vigorous games—will keep you out of harm's way.

Taurus Teen   Your parent may have a hard time realizing that you naturally move at a much slower pace than he or she does. Instead of balking and sulking, patiently explain to your parent that you don't like to be rushed or pushed, and ask to have your needs respected. Say you will do what is asked of you later on.

Gemini Teen   You make a lively pair, and you like to talk and communicate with each other. Your parent's fast pace excites you and usually there isn't much trouble here—except that neither of you is very good at completing things you start!

Cancer Teen   Your active parent needs help to understand your sensitive nature. Don't retreat into sulkiness or go off to your room and lock the door. Explain that you need privacy, and ask for your needs

Learning to Love YOU

Yes, romance is always in the air and it's fun, but you need to learn what it's all about—carefully. And sex is never far from a teenager's mind, no matter what adults might want to think. "Just say no!" is a great idea, and it does work for some teens. I hope it works for you, but I'm a realist and I know that early sexual activity isn't going to go away. Since that's one of the facts of life, the best thing for you to do is prepare yourself—with knowledge. Condoms can protect your health and sometimes prevent pregnancy, but all the contraception in the world can't keep you from getting badly hurt and carrying the scars of a broken heart around for years. Truly, an ounce of prevention is worth a pound of cure.

The last word on this subject is this: learn to love yourself *first,* and then you'll be able to safely experiment with loving someone else and all that goes with that leap into the unknown. Here's something to help you love yourself.

If a negative Venus is making you feel a lack of love, let me tell you a wonderful truth—when there is need for love we can supply it from within ourselves, to ourselves (as well as to others). Begin now to speak words of love to yourself, especially to any hurting or disliked part of yourself.

Wherever you are in your life, whatever problems you have now or have faced in the past, love is a powerhouse of spiritual energy. It connects you to all good in the universe, from which you can draw at will. When we love we feel transported, as if into another dimension, and we truly are in a higher place. You can climb to the stars on a beam of love. Self-love can be the secret weapon with which you vanquish the sorrows and ills of life. To practice generating love on a daily basis is powerful and effective, like pouring a healing balm over yourself. You will become quiet, peaceful, and filled with harmony. You will be in sync with your true self. By becoming a constantly radiating center of love, by filling yourself with the love you carry within you, you will heal what ails you and better your life in all ways.

Here are some affirmations you can use:

I generate love from the inexhaustible supply that fills the universe.

Love flows through me at all times in proportion to my needs and desires.

The love within me is mine to have and to use for all good purpose.

to be respected. Reward your parent by being sensitive to her or his needs. It's easy!

Leo Teen   This duo of Fire Signs can be enthusiastic or explosive. Your parent wants to be on the go and active, but you want more attention than you usually get. Explain to your parent that you need praise, encouragement, and feedback for your efforts and that you need to follow your own rhythm.

Virgo Teen   Your parent is an active person and not well organized. You try to help get him or her organized, but it's a losing proposition. Be satisifed with keeping your own room or space in an orderly condition, and ask other family members to respect your privacy and to leave your things alone.

Libra Teen   This is a Square Aspect, and can be difficult. You want things to be harmonious and quiet, and your parent may be too active for your comfort. Tell your parent that you will be more cooperative if you are given explanations and not commands.

Scorpio Teen   You go at a slower pace than your parent and want time to think. Explain to your active parent that you hate being yanked from one thing to another. Make an effort to share your feelings with your parent instead of clamming up.

Sagittarius Teen   Your active parent can help you to do lots of exploring, which you enjoy. You are a question box that never stops asking, so you may get some impatience as a reaction to your need to know. Ask for sources of information you can consult yourself, such as books and Internet access.

Capricorn Teen   Your parent is much too fast for your taste, and you have to ask him or her to slow down so you can catch up. Explain that it is easier for you to cooperate with family matters if you are given advance notice of events and of what is expected of you. Imitate your parent's spontaneity at times.

Aquarius Teen   Your parent can help you learn rather than just talking about your education. Take advantage of this, but explain that you have your own ideas about how to go about things, and ask that this need be respected. Give cooperation in return.

Pisces Teen   Your active parent may grate on your sensitive nerves with his or her abruptness. Explain that you need privacy and your own space, time alone to dream and be creative. Show your gentle side when there is conflict rather than retreating into your private, inaccessible inner world.

Taurus Parent

Aries Teen   You rush far ahead of your parent, and your overactive nature may irritate. Try to slow down and give your parent advance notice of what you need or have to do. Explain that you have a hard time with rules and regulations and need more freedom. Be responsible and affectionate.

Taurus Teen   This is usually a good combination unless there is an argument or conflict. You both tend to excess stubbornness. Instead of digging in your heels, look for some way out of a quarrel in other Planets. Extra effort to keep the lines of communication open will help.

Gemini Teen   Your parent can help you steady down and connect with the Earth plane, but you are likely to be impatient with what you consider stodgy and dull about your parent. Cut him or her some slack and explain that you need lots of activity and information, but don't bombard the parent with it all.

Cancer Teen   Your parent can help you with your moodiness, and you can enjoy quiet times together doing things around the house. When quarrels arise, don't crawl into your shell but show affection and do what you can to make your parent physically comfortable. Explain that you need private space and time.

Leo Teen   You share similar rhythms and can be fairly even-tempered together unless there is conflict, which will bring out stubbornness in your parent and dramatic scenes in you. Avoid useless contests of will—you will always lose. Instead, entertain your parent with your talents.

Libra Teen   You both appreciate beauty and calm surroundings and usually have a good relationship with lots of easy humor. Your parent will indulge your love of beauty with generosity. In return, give him or her lots of affection, and don't insist on rationalizing everything emotional.

Scorpio Teen   You are both extremely strong-minded, and this Opposition can cause a conflict of wills. Your parent has a hard time understanding your intensity, and you find him or her dull at times. However, your parent's calm nature can help you relax your intensity if you will share your feelings openly.

Sagittarius Teen   You need adventure and dream of far-off places you want to visit. Your materialistic parent thinks it will be too expensive or impractical, but you can learn from your parent how to make your dreams come true in a practical way. Give lots of affection when asking for money for travel!

Capricorn Teen   Together you are a practical and down-to-earth pair with not much conflict. Show emotional warmth toward your parent, even if you have to fake it. Affection is really important and will reassure you when you feel fearful or anxious.

Aquarius Teen   You are both Fixed Signs and want your own way. Your parent may not be tolerant of your rebellious nature and will seem too conservative to you. Explain your need to be experimental, and assure your parent you aren't going to go overboard. Go along with your parent's traditional ways.

Pisces Teen   Your parent can help you to get grounded in the real world, but you may have conflicts over what's practical. Ask for privacy and to be allowed to spend time alone. In return, do the practical chores asked of you and show affection.

Gemini Parent

Aries Teen   You are both quick moving and have similar inner rhythms, which make this combination fairly easy to live with. However, you get impatient with too much talking from your parent, who is forever explaining everything when you want to get going. Listen more and learn to look before you leap.

Taurus Teen   Your parent will often drive you nuts by shoving every new thing in your face at the same time or by changing activities every hour. You'll have to explain that you need to go at a slower pace, but don't just get balky and stubborn. The solution here is for you to *talk* to your parent more.

Gemini Teen   This is a talkative relationship, to say the least. You both jabber on incessantly and love doing it. Concentration is not natural to either of you, and you will probably have a good if not very productive relationship. You can learn a lot from your parent, but don't expect much follow-up.

Cancer Teen   You have difficulty with your parent interrupting you when you are not in the mood for talking or being disturbed. A natural talker, your parent can help you balance your moodiness with logic, but it's up to you not to throw your ever-changing moods around like stink bombs.

Leo Teen   Your parent is a pushover for you, and when you get an inch you take a mile. Your charm can backfire, however, if you overdo it. Let your parent teach you to look at many points of view, and reign in your tendency to be overbearing.

Virgo Teen   You and your parent will always have lots to talk about, but since you hate having your possessions disturbed you will have to stand up for your rights. Ask your parent for health and nutrition information, but don't fuss over every detail.

Libra Teen   You and your parent have a good basis for understanding each other intellectually. Unless there are other difficult Aspects, communications flow freely between you. However, your parent's disorganized manner can irritate you. Lend a hand to help her or him be neater.

Scorpio Teen   Your parent wants to know more than you want to tell. You have to explain that you can't share every thought with her or him, and ask for this to be respected. In return, try to be more open and avoid shutting yourself off emotionally.

Sagittarius Teen   You and your parent have a lot in common and share an ever-present curiosity about the world around you. However, you have to ask for deeper answers to your questions, and say you need more than surface information. You can learn a lot from your parent about different points of view.

Capricorn Teen   This is not an easy combination. You are very practical and down-to-earth, while your parent is sometimes impractical and can seem ditzy to you. You need to ask to be allowed to arrange your possessions and activities in your own organized way. In return, try to be more flexible.

Aquarius Teen   This is an easy relationship in which communications flow freely, but it's often not very emotional. You both like to talk, but expression of affection may not come easily. Luckily, your parent is receptive to your original thinking, but you may have to ask to be taken more seriously.

Pisces Teen   You and your parent share an imaginative world, and your parent can help you cope with the everyday world of life. You may have to ask to be allowed your own private time and space, and you don't like constant interruptions. Let your parent in on your dreams and fantasies occasionally.

Cancer Parent

Aries Teen   Your parent has the patience to deal with your strong will and active nature. Some of his or her patience may even rub off on you in time. Your parent likes a peaceful home, so try to curb your impulsiveness. You may have to remind your parent you aren't a baby anymore and ask for more freedom.

Taurus Teen   You are both affectionate and home-loving, and this can be an easy relationship. However, when conflict arises, the danger is that your parent may retreat into his or her shell, and you may dig in your heels and become stubborn and balky. Being openly affectionate will make things right soon.

Gemini Teen   Your parent can help calm down your fidgety nature. Let him or her teach you to be aware of your *feelings* as well as your mental gyrations. Your need for social activity can be accommodated by having friends come over to your house, but you may have to ask your parent not to fuss too much over you and them.

Cancer Teen   You and your parent have a close, often unspoken tie to each other, and you understand each other's frequent changes of moods. The danger is that your moods will clash. When that happens, concentrate on tuning in to your parent; let him or her know that you understand, and you'll be understood.

Leo Teen   You are like a ray of constant sunshine to your parent, who is likely to indulge your need for attention and make a great fuss over you, which you love. Just don't always hog the whole show, and return the affection and attention by respecting your parent's need for a calm home life.

Virgo Teen   You are both collectors, and you will enjoy each other's collections of things. Your parent likes sentimental and family mementos, and you can help organize them and keep them neat and clean. Don't criticize your parent's sentimental attachments. Absorb his or her emotional gifts.

Libra Teen   You are a people-pleaser and so rarely jar your parent's need for a calm atmosphere at home. Being mostly mental, you can learn about emotions from your parent. You may need to explain that you need outside friendships away from home.

Scorpio Teen   Your deeply sensitive moods will be understood by your parent, who can tune in to you. This may not always be what you want, because you like to keep your secrets. Confide in your parent when you have dark thoughts or moods, and let her or him guide you with reassurance and affection.

Sagittarius Teen   Your parent may have a hard time coping with your need for adventure and your constant curiosity about everything under the sun, but he or she can help you sort out which of your enthusiasms are real and which are just passing fancies.

Capricorn Teen   This Opposition can work if you work it. Your parent has the sympathetic, understanding nature needed to coax you to express your feelings by making you feel safe and loved. Curb your impatience with your parent's moods, and realize that you aren't the cause of them.

Aquarius Teen   You may be a trial to your conservative parent because of your unusual nature and zany ideas. Your choice of clothing may shock your sensitive, traditional parent and cause no end of bickering. Ask your parent to be open to your way of doing things, but don't push shocking behavior to the limit.

Pisces Teen   This is an easy and emotional relationship. Your parent can tune in to your extremely sensitive nature. The problem occurs when either one of you gets hurt feelings, as you both tend to withdraw. Cope with this by being affectionate and sharing your inner world. You'll get sympathy in return.

Leo Parent

Aries Teen   Your parent responds to your fiery, impulsive nature with enthusiasm and can help you steady your inner rhythms. You may offend your parent's sense of dignity and decorum with your brashness, and conflict can result. Affection and an effort to be more sedate will help smooth over matters.

Taurus Teen   This is a difficult combination because both are Fixed Signs. Depending on the Planets involved, your parent can help you develop generosity and you can lavish affection on him or her. Avoid conflict because it's hard for either of you to give in.

Gemini Teen   Your parent's loving and affectionate nature makes you feel safe and warm, but sometimes you hate so much self-centered behavior. You resist what you consider dominating authority by frittering away your energy on trivia and avoiding serious discussions. Ask for reasons behind the rules.

Cancer Teen   Your warmly affectionate parent can help you out of your tendency to sulky moodiness and coax you to be more outgoing. However, you may need to explain that sometimes you need to be alone and that this doesn't mean you are being antisocial. A little affection goes a long way here.

Leo Teen   A double Leo is a lot of sunshine all around, and usually this is a good relationship. However, there will always be a power struggle going on between you over who is getting the most attention. Giving attention and praise to your parent is the way to get attention and praise for yourself.

Virgo Teen   Your parent's warmth and centered nature can help you to find your own center. Naturally nervous and high-strung, you can lean on your parent for grounding. You don't mind your parent's self-centeredness, but you have to explain your need for order and let your parent know that your natural reserve isn't a way of detaching.

Libra Teen   You and your parent both like the happy side of life and will make an effort to be nice to each other. You like pleasing your parent, and he or she likes the praise and attention. But don't let any of your resentments build up into a festering sore. Let her or him know what you are feeling.

Scorpio Teen   Your parent's naturally open nature can help you deal with your inner intensity and tendency to have a suspicious temperament. However, you may have to ask your parent to allow you to keep your own secrets and not to pry unduly.

Sagittarius Teen   You and your parent generally get along well together, and his or her inventiveness and love of drama work well with your love of adventure and your open nature. Your restlessness, however, may bother your steady parent, and you may need to ask for clear and understandable answers to your questions.

Capricorn Teen   You may be overly serious for your fun-loving parent, but this can be overcome by openly discussing your concerns and your need for studiousness and practical knowledge. Your parent's natural warmth can make you feel loved and secure.

Aquarius Teen   You are both naturally outgoing people, but you are the one who is more active mentally, going into abstract spaces in your head. Your rebellious nature can cause trouble, but you can avoid this by respecting the house rules and not pushing your unusual ideas or form of dress to the max.

Pisces Teen   Your self-centered, attention-loving parent may try to push you into the public arena before you feel you can handle it. Tell your parent that too much public attention makes you uncomfortable, and ask for a private space where you can spend time alone.

Virgo Parent

Aries Teen   Your natural temperament is blunt, and neatness isn't your thing. Both characteristics will go against your parent's grain and may cause endless arguments. Learn to think before you speak. Avoid excess messiness, but explain that you just aren't temperamentally inclined to be a neatnik.

Taurus Teen   As mutual Earth Signs, you and your parent tend to get along well on the practical level. However, an overly orderly environment may not give you the sheer physical comfort you need. Explain that physical comfort is necessary for you, and ask for hugs and affection if it isn't given spontaneously.

Gemini Teen   You and your parent have a lot in common, and he or she will enjoy your sharp mind and quick perceptions. Your are both mental types who tend toward nervousness and fidgeting. Let your parent help you learn to concentrate and focus on tasks.

Cancer Teen   Your parent may drive you nuts with his or her intellectual approach to feelings. Explain that you learn through feeling and intuition better than through logical argument. Your parent's clear-mindedness can help you with mental skills.

Leo Teen   Your reserved parent will appreciate your natural warmth and affection, but your naturally slower pace may prove irksome to him or her. Explain that you need to be allowed to move in your own way. Ask for help with important decisions.

Virgo Teen   This can be a close relationship. You appreciate each other's qualities of neatness, order, cleanliness, and helpfulness. With little conflict, you get along well but your mutual reserve may inhibit expression of affection.

Libra Teen   Both of you have a tendency to be indecisive and thus can feed off each other's waffling around. Realize that you need to learn decision-making skills, and ask your parent to help you with this task. Always talk things over thoroughly.

Scorpio Teen   Your strong personality can overrun your somewhat timid parent, but don't take advantage of this and get into power struggles. Your parent's natural capacity for thoroughness can help you develop your own abilities in that area.

Sagittarius Teen   Your mutual flexibility can make this a fun relationship if you don't press too hard for big answers to your questions. Remember that your parent is detail-minded and isn't geared to the big picture that fascinates you. Ask for materials to satisfy your need for adventure and exploration.

Capricorn Teen   Since you both have a tendency to worry and look at the practical side of life, you need to seek balance between you. Your parent will appreciate your serious nature and help you with the details of your projects. Always express feelings of insecurity and ask for help coping with them.

Aquarius Teen   As you are a natural breaker of rules, you may upset your order-loving parent on a regular basis. However, since you are both mental types, you can talk about the situation. A little give-and-take goes a long way in this case.

Pisces Teen   Temperamentally you share a number of characteristics, but you are extremely sensitive and may resent your logical parent's input. You have to explain that sympathy works with you better than lectures, but you can allow your parent to help you bring order into your sometimes chaotic life.

Libra Parent

Aries Teen   It's natural for you to be a "Me first!" person, while your parent is very relationship oriented. This can cause problems, but you can learn the lesson of being fair from your parent. Work off excess energy positively.

Taurus Teen   Your parent will be responsive to your love of beauty and can help you develop it. You are naturally possessive of your things, but your parent can help you learn to share. If you don't receive affection, ask for it openly.

Gemini Teen   As mutual mental types who both like to discuss everything, your verbal communication will be great. However, your parent's need for a well-ordered, peaceful home and your need to have a million things going at once can cause trouble. Learn to slow down and focus more.

Cancer Teen   Your moody, broody nature is hard for your parent to understand, and he or she may irritate you by wanting to discuss your feelings endlessly and often. Explain that you need to have time and private space to work out your feelings in your own way.

Leo Teen   Your big smile and warm, affectionate nature delight your parent, but you need to curb your tendency to hog the limelight. Learn to respect other people's opinions, and don't interrupt adults' conversations to show off.

Virgo Teen   This combination is a good basis for mutual understanding. Your parent can help you develop your appreciation of the arts, and you can return the favor by helping him or her in practical ways and by being helpful around the house.

Libra Teen   This is a pleasant and easy combination. Both of you like the same things and agree on almost everything, but there is a danger of your not learning how to make decisions on your own. Find someone who is decisive to teach you this skill.

Scorpio Teen   Your intensity may baffle your placid and harmony-loving parent, even frightening him or her at times. However, your parent can teach you about justice and fairness, and you can give assurance of your honesty and strength.

Sagittarius Teen   Both of you are basically happy-natured and socially oriented. You love people and enjoy company; however, your natural tendency to have a big mouth and say exactly what you think can offend your polite parent's sensibilities. Work out your energy outdoors, where you can make a mess.

Capricorn Teen   Your parent will appreciate your natural neatness and organizational abilities, as he or she enjoys a calm and orderly home. You may have to explain that you need to have time alone, and that this doesn't mean you are antisocial.

Aquarius Teen   Your parent will find your tendency to be rebellious hard to handle. Being nice all the time and being forced into a politeness you don't feel makes you want to kick over the fence and run. It's always best to talk these things out.

Pisces Teen   Your parent will appreciate your sensitive nature and love of beauty and art. As you can charm easily with your pleasant ways, you two ordinarily get along well. However, you may have to ask for your own private space and time alone, so tell your more social parent that you need this.

Scorpio Parent

Aries Teen   This can be a combative combination. Your impulsive nature combined with your parent's intensity can be explosive. You need to learn to control your need for activity and develop sensitivity to your parent's moods. Work off excess energy in active sports whenever there is danger of a conflict.

Taurus Teen   This is sometimes a tough combination. Both of you are strong willed and don't like to be pushed around. There can be clashes of wills. Give affection, try to understand your parent's intensity, and ask for help and advice when you have problems to solve.

Gemini Teen   Your parent can help you learn to concentrate and go into things more deeply. Your fidgety nature and need for lots of information can irritate your sometimes stolid parent. Explain that you need to know about lots of things, and in return respect your parent's need for privacy.

Cancer Teen   You are both quite sensitive of each other's feelings. Your parent can help you develop some of the emotional toughness you lack, which you need to overcome your insecurities. Neither of you tends to be open and frank, so in times of stress try not to crawl into your shell. Make an effort to communicate.

Leo Teen   Since both of you are Fixed Signs in this combination, there is danger of stonewalling during times of stress, with neither one of you willing to compromise. Your natural warmth and charm can help defuse a bad situation, especially if you don't insist on hogging the center of attention.

Virgo Teen   Your parent can set high standards that you will take seriously, and you enjoy the challenge of improving your performance. Your tendency to worry and fuss over details may irritate your parent, and his or her moods can make you feel weighed down. Both of you need to try for lightness.

Libra Teen   Your parent can help you develop drive and good work habits, traits that aren't natural to your makeup. Your desire to examine both sides of all questions can upset your parent's tendency to strong and unchanging opinions. Your diplomatic nature will come in handy when disputes arise.

Scorpio Teen   You are birds of a feather, but your combined intensity can make for heavy going at times. You appreciate each other's depths and are sensitive to your mutual moods and needs. When you are angry or depressed, confide in your parent.

Sagittarius Teen   Your outgoing nature and demand for freedom is likely to make life difficult at times for your intense parent. Try to exercise your adventuresome nature in a positive way, and ask for permission to go on excursions. If you develop self-discipline, parental discipline won't be needed.

Capricorn Teen   The natural intensity of your parent can help you develop your own potential for being organized and thorough. Don't take your parent's emotional intensity personally—it's just the way he or she is. And try not to worry so much about it.

Aquarius Teen   You and your parent have a natural tendency to see the world differently. You may feel he or she is too demanding and respond with a rebellious attitude. This isn't necessary. Making an effort at communication will help matters. Tone down the visible signs of expressing your individuality.

Pisces Teen   You and your parent can flow together well some of the time, but at other times your extreme sensitivity and his or her intensity will clash, and you will feel hurt and restricted. Explain that routine goes against your nature and ask for private time and space, but don't throw emotional fits.

Sagittarius Parent

Aries Teen   You both love adventure, the outdoors, and action sports. Your parent will enjoy introducing you to many exciting things, and you generally enjoy being together. However, you will need to find someone more stable to teach you the skills of self-discipline and self-control.

Taurus Teen   Your parent moves too fast for your comfort, and you often feel you are being pushed and shoved about against your will. It's necessary for you to explain to him or her that you have a slower-paced nature and need that respected. Ask for advance notice of any change of plans.

Gemini Teen   Both of you are inquisitive and into a lot of activities, and you usually get along well together. You parent will be happy to provide you with lots of information, but you will have to ask for guidance at times or you'll become overloaded.

Cancer Teen   Your outgoing parent has a hard time understanding your sensitive nature and your need for "nesting" and privacy. You can learn how to be more open from her or him, but you will have to ask for private space and time to be alone.

Leo Teen   Both of you have playful natures, so this combination is usually enjoyable. Your parent's natural optimism feeds your need for encouragement and praise. Conflicts are rare, but you may need to learn to curb your egotism.

Virgo Teen   This is a pleasant combination, because your parent can help you stay out of a rut and encourage you to be open to trying new things. You can help her or him be more orderly and organized. Ask for sufficient undisturbed time to finish your projects.

Libra Teen   As you are both inclined to be friendly and optimistic, you usually enjoy each other's company. You may at times feel embarrassed by his or her bluntness, but take advantage of his or her independent nature to overcome your indecision.

Scorpio Teen   Your intensity and need for privacy and secrets may baffle your open and outgoing parent and cause some distress if you are pressed to open up when you don't feel like doing so. Explain to your parent that you and he or she have different natures, and ask him or her to respect your need for privacy.

Sagittarius Teen   You are two peas in a pod, and being so much alike has its advantages and disadvantages. However, you usually get along well, especially when you are doing outdoorsy things together, like sports or camping. You'll have to develop your own ways of curbing restlessness and achieving perseverance.

Capricorn Teen   Your sports-loving parent can encourage you to avoid being a couch potato or a bookworm by exercising with you and encouraging your participation in sports. Your seriousness can be fed by your parent's broad knowledge of the world.

Aquarius Teen   This is a sociable combination, and you both have a lot of interest in ideas and mental activity. You will likely go beyond him or her with your offbeat notions, but this should not cause much conflict if you respect family traditions.

Pisces Teen   Your outgoing, optimistic parent can help you overcome your tendency to live in your private dream-and-fantasy world, but don't expect her or him to totally understand your sensitive nature. Ask for your privacy and time alone.

Capricorn Parent

Aries Teen   Your conservative parent can help you learn to curb your impulsive, leap-before-you-look nature, but you will at times find his or her restrictions hard to live with. Explain that you need to venture out on your own, and give assurances that you won't take unnecessary chances.

Taurus Teen   You both can enjoy a variety of down-to-earth activities and do things together that have a practical end or goal. Your nature is less serious and more easygoing than his or hers, but problems usually arise only when you procrastinate.

Gemini Teen   Your parent can help you organize your many interests and learn to think—once in a while!—before you speak. You may have to ask for reasonable explanations of rules and regulations. Don't start activities you can't finish.

Cancer Teen   Your parent's rigid and strict scheduling will always be difficult for you to handle. You will have to explain that you do your best when left to follow your own inclinations and moods, but do follow up with performance of duties. Showing affection will warm up your naturally chilly parent.

Leo Teen   Your naturally affectionate nature will warm the somewhat distant emotional nature of your parent, and you can use your charm to get your way, but don't overdo the dramatics or you'll get a cold shoulder. Remember to share the limelight.

Virgo Teen   This earthy combination is usually quite pleasant. Your parent can help you avoid excess self-criticism and curb your fussiness and need for perfection. You both have trouble expressing affection and must make an effort.

Libra Teen   This combination can go either way—pleasant or disruptive. Your nature is more easygoing and less serious than your parent's. Ask to be allowed to develop your artistic tendencies even if they aren't practical.

Scorpio Teen   Your intensity and your parent's seriousness can work well together, but you both need to learn to lighten up. Your parent can help you channel your intense energy into practical and worthwhile activities. Expressing emotions openly is difficult for you both. Practice communicating.

Sagittarius Teen   Your outgoing and optimistic nature can help your serious parent lighten up, but he or she may think you are a lightweight because you yearn for adventure and knowledge. Don't take off without permission, and act responsibly.

Capricorn Teen   You are both serious in nature and inclined to ambition, so you usually get along well. The problem for both of you is learning to lighten up, play, and relax more. Find ways to show feeling and discover activities you can enjoy together.

Aquarius Teen   Your rebellious nature and insistence on your individuality may upset your conservative parent considerably. Explain that you need to be experimental, but don't shove bizarre behavior or dress in your parent's face unnecessarily.

Pisces Teen   Your serious-minded parent may seem a drag to your dreamy and unstructured nature. However, he or she can help you cope with the real world of practical reality. Ask for your own private space and time to be alone with your fantasies.

Aquarius Parent

Aries Teen   Your parent can handle your adventurous nature and help you learn to disagree with others without getting angry. You can stimulate her or his interest in unusual ideas, and usually this works well. Avoid being impulsive and blunt.

Taurus Teen   This is a potentially difficult combination. You like to go at your own leisurely pace and not to be pushed before you are ready to move. Your parent is always presenting you with new ideas and activities, and this can cause you distress. Explain that you need time to get used to new things.

Gemini Teen   Your parent will encourage you to develop your many and various interests and will help you learn social skills. However, don't bother trying to change his or her mind once it's made up. You are the one with a changeable mind!

Cancer Teen   Your parent has too many newfangled ideas for your old-fashioned nature, and there might be conflicts in the home over decor and privacy. Explain that you need quiet time and that your moods aren't meant to annoy her or him.

Leo Teen   Your parent can help you learn to share and cooperate and not to always to hog the center stage, but you may balk against this lesson and get into a contest of wills. It's better to avoid this, as he or she is very strong-minded.

Virgo Teen   Your parent's ability to constantly come up with new ideas may either stimulate or irritate you, or both. You have a fear of trying new things and don't want them forced on you. Learn to express your feelings and ask for privacy.

Libra Teen   You have a people-pleasing nature and can accept the odd new ideas your parent comes up with because you want to keep the peace and not argue. But you need to develop your own set of beliefs and not become merely a mouthpiece for your parent.

Scorpio Teen   This combination is a Square and can be difficult because of your intense need for privacy and keeping your own counsel. You parent wants to discuss everything endlessly and you feel he or she is prying. Try to share some of your feelings.

Sagittarius Teen   The two of you can communicate easily and readily. Your parent will encourage your participation in active sports and outdoor activities. He or she can help you control your restless nature if you will follow a few rules.

Capricorn Teen   You and your parent will likely disagree about a number of things, including your need to be organized and to establish routines that make you comfortable. His or her attraction to whatever is new and trendy isn't your style.

Aquarius Teen   As you both are mental, like what's new and different, and have unusual personalities, you are unlikely to clash seriously over how you act and dress and the friends you choose. Learning to be alone is a challenge for you.

Pisces Teen   Your mentally active parent's new ideas and expressiveness may get on your sensitive nerves. Explain that you need some solitude and privacy and don't appreciate being interrupted. He or she can teach you to be independent and less fearful.

Pisces Parent

Aries Teen   Your impulsive and imprudent nature may upset your gentle parent, who is timid and careful. He or she will enjoy your fun nature but may have difficulty handling your headstrong impulsiveness. Try to be sensitive to parental concerns.

Taurus Teen   Your love of beauty and art matches well with your sensitive parent's nature, and you can enjoy these things together. Your practical nature can help him or her function better in the real world. Lots of affection can be had here.

Gemini Teen   Your parent loves fantasy, and your natural wit and whimsy will delight him or her. Misunderstandings can be caused by your being more mental and less emotionally sensitive than her or him, but some effort on your part will pay dividends.

Cancer Teen   This is a lovely combination. Both of you will enjoy spinning dreams and fantasies together, and you are both likely to be sensitive to each other's moods. Both of you are tuned in to the flow of feelings.

Leo Teen   Your sensitive, mild-mannered parent will enjoy your warmth and affectionate nature. Unfortunately, your stronger personality can take over the entire household, so you have to learn to share the spotlight and respect others' rights.

Virgo Teen   Although you are basically compatible, your parent can help you tune in to the magical realm of dreams and fantasy instead of getting caught up in so much thinking and fiddling about with details. You can help him or her organize.

Libra Teen   Your gentle-natured parent easily tunes in to your love of beauty and art, and generally you get along well together. You need to learn decision-making skills elsewhere, though, and may make an effort to help her or him be more balanced.

Scorpio Teen   This watery combination makes it easy for both of you to tune in to each other's feelings, and you have unspoken communications. However, your stronger personality may tempt you to become a young tyrant and manipulate him or her. Don't take advantage of your parent's good nature this way.

Sagittarius Teen   Your bursting-with-energy nature may be difficult for your sensitive, quiet-natured parent to endure. He or she will enjoy your warm nature and outgoing personality, but you need to turn down the volume for his or her comfort level.

Capricorn Teen   Your down-to-earth seriousness can be lightened up a lot by your fantasy-prone parent, who can put you in touch with the magical realm of the imagination. Your practical abilities can help him or her to cope with everyday life situations.

Aquarius Teen   This is an interesting combination. You both love flights of fancy, but you are mentally creative and your parent is artistically imaginative. He or she can help you stay in touch with your feeling nature, and you provide stability.

Pisces Teen   You are so much alike that you may not know where you start and your parent ends. This can make for an easy relationship with lots of empathy between you, but it also makes it hard to separate yourself from your parent. You have to work to develop your own separate identity.

The Moon, Your Mother, and You

Astrologically speaking, the Moon unquestionably represents the Universal Mother and, by implication, your own mother. The Moon in *your* chart describes how you experience, "see," or feel about her. It might not be an accurate description of who she actually *is*, but it will tell what you believe her to be in terms of your interaction with her.

Naturally, this is not a foolproof system, but as a rule of thumb it works amazingly well across the board. Following are the Moon Signs and how they relate to your view of mother. Your *mother's* Moon Sign will describe *her* perception of her own mother, your maternal grandmother, and through examination of both your and her Moon Signs you can get a sense of how her mother influenced her.

Your Mother in Your Moon by Sign

When YOUR moon is in:

Aries   You see your mother as a courageous, lively, and assertive woman with a fighting spirit. She's always on the go, active, sporty—not your traditional cookie-baking mom. She passes on to you these action-oriented qualities.

Taurus   You are likely to have a traditional mother who either is a stay-at-home mom or would like to be. She's a real Earth Mother type, nurturing and grounded. She enjoys mothering and keeping house. She's a practical rock you can always lean on.

Gemini   Your mother has many and varied interests and is always on the go. She's always glad to answer your questions and be your friend, and she may seem more a big sister than a mother. There's always a lot of friendly communication between you.

Cancer   You have a tight bond with your mother that will last a lifetime. A good homemaker, she shows you love and is sensitive to your needs but may be a "smother mother" who hinders your developing independence. You may cling to her.

Moon Key Characteristics

Feelings	Moods
Sensitivity	Femininity
The Mother	Dependency
Nurturing	Neediness
Changeability	Emotion
Food and cravings	Self-indulgence
Home and family	Attachment
Subconsciousness	Intuition

Leo   Your mother is dramatic and self-centered. She loves attention and will hog the center stage, sometimes depriving you of the attention you want for yourself, or she may long to be a stage mother and push you to fulfill her dreams.

Virgo   Your mother is likely a working mom, perhaps a nurse or social worker who has a full-time job away from home. She inspires you to do your best but may demand too much from you in terms of neatness and cleanliness because she hates mess.

Libra   Your mother is a hearts-and-flowers, sentimental valentine who appreciates nice things and a lovely home environment. She wants you to be polite and nice and teaches you that pleasing others is important. She hates confrontation.

Scorpio   Your mother has fought many battles in her life, and she is strong because of it. Her emotions are intense, but she may hide them away from prying eyes. You can sense her moods and feel her suffering, and you are deeply affected by her personality.

Sagittarius   Your mother loves knowledge, and she is a lifelong learner herself who is interested in your education. She puts an emotional value, not a purely intellectual one, on learning. She is always ready to discuss your profound questions.

Capricorn   Your mother may suffer from recurring bouts of depression and may withdraw emotionally. This can hurt you or make you feel down about yourself. It's important for you to develop a positive attitude toward your own life and future.

Aquarius   Your mother is unusual in some way. She may be interested in liberal politics or social reform, and her ideas may be very different. Or she could be a kooky artistic type who seems spaced out. Not the standard-issue parent, she's a friend.

Pisces   Your mother may spend her time rescuing the world's strays, both human and animal, and may seem saintly to you and others. Or perhaps she is emotionally immature and can't cope with reality. She may neglect her family, be an alcoholic, or take drugs.

The Aspects that your Moon makes to your mother's Moon will color the above interpretations. If your Moon Signs are in Square or Opposition, you will have emotional conflicts. If they are in Trine or Sextile, you will be emotionally compatible. Also, the Houses of your two Moons play a part. Whether you are a girl or a boy also influences your experience of your mother. Girls naturally tend to identify with their mothers but may not want to be like them. Boys often seek girlfriends who are either like their mothers or as different from them as possible. Whether positive or negative, your relationship with your mother has a lasting effect. How you feel about her will color your ideas of future parenthood.

Aspects to your Moon in your own chart will also affect how you see your mother. Read your Moon Aspects for more information in specific areas shown by the Planet in Aspect to your Moon.

A True Story about One Mother and Three Moon Signs

It may seem odd that your Moon Sign could describe your relationship to your mother—or your *perception* of her. Let me give you an example from real life of how this works:

This true story is about a mother with three children.

Her first child was a boy with his Moon in Cancer, indicating he would experience his mother as very nurturing and home-loving.

He was much wanted and eagerly awaited by his young mother, whose primary goal since her early teens had been marriage and children. Although she finished college, she married almost immediately after graduation, eager to have a family.

After the birth of her first child, she stayed at her parent's home for a few weeks so that *her* mother could help to mother the new infant. After returning to her own house, she became a stay-at-home mother totally devoted to her child.

This boy, now a man, is deeply attached to both his mother and his maternal grandmother, and, true to Moon in Cancer, he is a nurturing and family-oriented person with several children of his own to whom he is totally devoted.

This mother's second son, the result of an unplanned and unwanted pregnancy that occurred when the first baby was less than a year old, arrived with his Moon in Scorpio, the Sign of early childhood trauma. His perception of their mother—the same woman who had joyfully nurtured her firstborn—was totally different from his older brother's.

It's also important to note that the Moon in a girl's chart and the Moon in a boy's chart operate somewhat differently in terms of the Moon-as-mother. For a girl, there is *identification* with her own ability to bear children. For the boy, there is the *experience of being mothered,* which will relate to how he feels about girls in their future maternal role as opposed to a romantic role.

Another factor in the Moon-as-mother astrological interpretation is that the mother is the child's first experience of a human relationship, the basis upon which all else is founded. The *internal* perception of this mother energy is more important than your actual mother because it will deeply affect how you will function as an adult when you are married and have children.

The second preganancy overwhelmed the mother, and she resented having another baby when she had one still in diapers. Her plan had been to wait two or three years between children. And since she already had a boy, she had wanted a girl and was disappointed to get another son.

This second son perceived his mother as rejecting and withdrew deeply inside himself, hiding his feelings from her for fear of being hurt. He became wary of females and something of a loner. Now a grown man, he is a bachelor who keeps emotional distance between himself and his mother.

The third child, a girl, came along several years after the two boys, arriving when the Moon was in Pisces. After her birth, the woman suffered a series of difficult-to-diagnose illnesses and was in and out of the hospital frequently, with little energy to take care of her baby girl.

Although she loved and pampered her daughter when she was well enough to do so, from the child's point of view the mother was unreliable, fading in and out of the home like a ghostly figure—now she saw her, now she didn't.

The daughter saw her mother as a vague and shadowy figure whom she loved but who wasn't quite there. Eventually she began to take care of her mother, and as an adult she became a nurse for mentally ill people.

In this example, we observe three children from the same two parents whose perceptions of their mother were all entirely different from one another. Their adult relationships with their mother are reflected in their Moon Signs.

Your Father Experience

Astrologers can say for certain that the Moon and the mother are directly connected, but the father connection is harder to pin down.

This is because the relationship with the mother (if it is not broken) is basic. The child shares the mother's body—in the most intimate of all relationships—for nine months and through the nursing stage. A baby is literally part of her or his mother during pregnancy and nursing.

But your father is *external* to this process, no matter how much he tries to participate in his wife's pregnancy, the birth experience, and helping to raise the child. The mother simply *is,* while the father relationship must be built through a different process of relating.

This is a crucial difference. When defining the father through the birth chart, there are two primary things astrologers look at: the placement of the Sun and Saturn in your chart, and Aspects to all the outer Planets, are indicators of the father energy.

Here is a brief look at how your Sun relates to your perception of your father through the Signs.

When YOUR Sun is in:

Aries   You experience your father as manly and robust, full of energy and a go-getter in the outside world.

Taurus   You experience your father as a solid citizen, financially stable, reliable, and able to handle practical necessities.

Gemini   You experience your father as a good communicator, more of an interesting friend or pal than an authority figure.

Cancer   You experience your father as nurturing and almost motherly, sensitive, and moody. As a man, he may seem weak and passive.

Leo   You experience your father as strong and generous but also dominant and demanding as an authority figure.

Virgo   You experience your father as practical and down-to-earth, but you may find him a fusspot who is easily irritated.

Libra   You experience your father as polite and pleasant, kind and diplomatic—a rational and even-handed authority figure.

Scorpio   You experience your father as somewhat dogmatic, intense, and secretive, with the capacity to be mean or violent.

Sagittarius   You experience your father as a teacher who is interested in your education and helps you relate to learning and nature.

Capricorn   You experience your father as the ultimate authority figure, someone whose word is law but who can be counted on.

Aquarius   You experience your father as detached from your life, nonemotional, but interesting for his ideas and mental life.

Pisces   You experience your father as a vague authority figure who has problems coping with the practical world and may have a problem with substance abuse.

Sun Key Characteristics

Individuality	Egotism
The Father	Authority
Consciousness	Logic
Physical vitality	Left brain
Will	Lack of sensitivity
Ambition and drive	Pride
Creative potential	Self-consciousness

Aspects from the Planets Jupiter, Saturn, Uranus, Neptune, and Pluto to your Sun will color how you perceive your father:

Sun/Jupiter contacts will give you the sense that your father is expansive and generous, giving material support.

Sun/Saturn contacts will give you the sense of being restricted and limited by your father in a negative way, or there may be separation from him or lack of emotional help.

Sun/Uranus contacts will give you the sense that your father is unreliable, unconventional, aloof, or quirky.

Sun/Neptune contacts will give you the sense that your father is an illusion—he may be absent from home frequently, be mentally preoccupied, or have substance-abuse problems.

Sun/Pluto contacts will give you the sense that your father is powerful and may indicate a violent disposition. Power struggles are usual and child abuse can occur.

As with the Moon, whether you are a boy or a girl will color your perception of your father as shown by your Sun Sign. Boys will tend to identify with or rebel against their sense of who their father is. Girls will choose or reject boys as romantic interests based on their father perceptions of how a man behaves.

Stormy Weather

When a relationship between a teen and her or his parent or parents is difficult, astrologers often find people with elemental makeups that don't get along with each other.

This is just part of the parent-teen relationship picture, but it's an important part and one where solutions are available.

First, however, let's look at the Elements in terms of your relationship with your parents. You learned about your own elemental makeup in chapter 2, and you discovered your Element type by doing the exercise there.

Now you need to know your parent's Element type. To make life easier for you, there's a simple way to determine your parent's Element type using the method given at the end of the exercise on page 61. To do this, you only need your parent's birthdate and the planetary tables in appendix 1.

Look up all of your parent's planetary placements and list them in the format given in the Element exercise. The *time* of your parent's birth will provide the Ascendant Sign, but if you don't know the time, it's okay. The Planets will give you sufficient information to determine your parent's Element type.

Once you know your parent's Element type, you can compare it with *your* Element type and find out where the elemental conflict or disharmony is coming from. Here's an overview of the Signs in the Elements to help you scope out your parent's elemental relationship to your elemental self.

Fire

Aries is the hottest of the *Fire* Signs. It is quick, impulsive, impatient, and driven to take action immediately. Its energy burns hot and high but goes out quickly.

Leo stabilizes the energy of *Fire*. It is creative, dramatic, and bold and tends to grand gestures. It burns slowly and steadily and smolders for a long time.

Sagittarius makes *Fire* energy mental and objective. It seeks to learn and is eager to tell the world what it knows. It burns rapidly at a high rate of speed and then sputters out.

Earth

Taurus is the most earthy of the *Earth* Signs. It is strong but materialistic, possessive, stolid, stubborn, and immovable. It takes hold with deep roots and holds on for dear life.

Virgo is the most mental of the *Earth* Signs and is less oppressively solid. It is still practical and no dreamer; its energy, however, is that of a thinker.

Capricorn is where the *Earth* Signs reach a peak. It is a leader, a military commander, the boss, the CEO. The ultimate authority figure of the Zodiac, it wants to rule.

Air

Gemini is naturally the airiest of the *Air* Signs. It floats about like a cloud, gathering information like a bee gathers nectar. It goes up like a balloon and stays up forever.

Libra is where the energy of *Air* is used to balance all kinds of relationships. It ponders, weighs, and rationalizes. Think of the symbol of the scales of justice.

Aquarius is an oddball *Air* Sign because it is stable, a quality rare to air. For this reason it is intellectual, but once its mind is made up, forget about changing it.

Water

Cancer is the Water Mother. It is all-nurturing, family-oriented to the max, caring, and guarding. It can be a "smother mother" or father. It protects and holds on tight: the Crab.

Scorpio is where *Water* runs deep and fathomless like a submarine stalking its prey. It's full of unknown depths and hard to understand. This water is still, not flowing.

Pisces is the *Water* Sign that is the most watery of all. It is at home in the misty regions of the constantly moving sea of life's energies. Its feelings are like the ocean tides.

When two people are elementally different, they may love each other but not like each other on a daily basis. You may have that experience with a parent. At times you may find him or her interesting and exciting but at the same time irritating and difficult. The result is constant quarreling. When this is the case, there are always things to be worked out between you, and often you may feel you are doing all the compromising. You may feel your parent is insensitive to your needs or simply doesn't understand them.

Knowing the characteristics of the Signs in their Elements will help you better understand your relationship with your parent, especially if it isn't easy. Sometimes you can understand only *why you can't understand,* but even that can be of help. When you know that your elemental energy is different from your parent's, and you grasp that the difference between you isn't your fault—or even your parent's fault—but a simple matter of elemental differences, it's easier to work things out.

You and your parent may be the *same* elemental type, *compatible* types, or *incompatible* types.

Here's how Element compatibilities work out:

If you are both Fire types you enjoy many activities together and are able to be independent of each other, but you both need space to breathe. When conflict arises, sparks fly high because you both have spirit and quick tempers. If you have a fight, it's a good idea to do something physical while you work it out—run, go for a brisk walk together, or play an active game, like tennis or basketball. Action will help to dissolve the bad feelings.

If you are both Earth types you are both stable and solid characters with a tendency to be conservative. Usually you are useful to each other, helping each other by doing chores and practical things, but when a problem arises, you can both dig in your heels and refuse to compromise. Doing what is the most practical thing is the best solution for both.

If you are both Air types your relationship is talkative and you both enjoy discussing everything endlessly. However, when feelings are at issue, the talking doesn't get anywhere. You both use your ability to rationalize to mask your feelings. When bad feelings cloud your relationship, make an effort to be more open about what you are feeling and ask your parent to do the same.

If you are both Water types your relationship is full of feeling and you enjoy just being together. You feel naturally intimate and close. In this situation, finding your own identity can be a challenge because you and your parent flow into each other easily without many boundaries. You even have the same moods. You are both sensitive and easily hurt, so you need to exercise mutual care, and *you* must learn that your feelings belong to you and that you aren't responsible for anyone else's feelings or moods.

If one of you is a Fire type and one is an Air type you two communicate well and there is a lot of give and take. The Fire person inspires the Air person's sense of logic, and the Air person feeds the Fire person's flames of ideas. You easily support each other's projects and ideas. The Air person understands the Fire person's spontaneity. You have fun together and enjoy brainstorming ideas and putting them into action. When problems arise, the solution is to withdraw temporarily until matters cool down and settle.

If one of you is a Fire type and one is an Earth type you are different but compatible. The Fire person activates the Earth person and gets him or her going. Each of you has what the other lacks. The Fire person is full of hope, spontaneity, and vision, while the Earth person has the practical nature to make things real. When problems occur, the Fire person's speed and brashness can burn the Earth person, and the Earth person's resistance can smother the Fire person's joy and optimism.

If one of you is a Fire type and one is a Water type you make an emotional combination. Together you can be creative and expressive. You produce a lot of feeling and inspiration that you can share. This combination can make for steam heat when things aren't going well, and there is danger of overreacting and getting emotionally out of control. The Water person can put out the Fire person's heat, and the Fire person can make the Water person's feelings dry up. When things go wrong between you, don't just keep on emoting and acting out. Take a breather to regain control.

If one of you is an Air type and one is an Earth type you may have difficulty achieving a meeting of the minds but if you succeed, your combination draws on both logic and practicality. The Air person finds the Earth person dull and dry, and the Earth person is irritated by the Air person's excessive rationalizing and mental approach to practical problems. Sometimes it can seem as if you two come from different planets. There's not much to be done about this except for you to develop tolerance for your parent's way of doing things and to go your own way when you can.

If one of you is an Air type and one is a Water type you share intuition and sensitivity. The Water person understands feelings and has compassion, and the Air person understands ideas and mental concepts. Your differences can fascinate you, but there is danger of overreacting when disputes occur. The Water person becomes frustrated with the Air person's distance and control over feelings. The Air person can feel trapped by the Water person's never-ending demands for emotional connection.

If one of you is an Earth type and one is a Water type your relationship has a comfortable, homey quality to it. Usually you and your parent feel warmth toward each other, and you appreciate your parent as a parent. Together you can deal with practical matters in a feeling way. The Water person can moisten and refresh the Earth person's dryness, while the Earth person offers the Water person a sense of stability and security. When problems arise, you can rely on mutual affection to see you through a crisis.

Immovable Object/Irresistible Force

In chapter 2 you learned about the *Modes* of the Signs of the Zodiac. You discovered your own Mode type. Now we are going to look at how your Mode type and your parent's Mode type get along together—or don't get along, as the case may be.

When considering the Mode types, remember that the Modes are *always* in either Opposition or Square Aspect to each other, and that these are difficult positions.

You're Both in the Same Mode

If you are both Cardinal types your relationship is one of action, and when you are getting on well together, you inspire each other to try new activities and to think about things in a new way or see the world in a new light. With this combination, there is danger of battles of will and power struggles when your enthusiasms are mismatched. This is the "irresistible force" combination. Learning to compromise is your best defense.

Cardinals tend to fight over who goes first, who makes the decisions, who initiates projects or activities, and in general who runs the show.

If you are both Fixed types your relationship is deep and meaningful, though not always easy. When you are getting along well, you share a lot of power and can stand up to the world as a unified pair. When problems arise—as they must—you must work hard to resolve them because you are both good at stonewalling. This is the "immovable object" combination. Developing emotional and mental flexibility will help you deal with any bad situation.

Fixed Mode types can have titanic conflict because of mutual immobility, stubborness, and refusal to yield or compromise. The Fixed Mode hates to be the one to give in and has the tendency to dig in for a long sustained battle.

If you are both Mutable types you have a relationship that is both flexible and interesting. However, it can be like a two-person band playing different tunes at the same time. Sometimes it works in harmony and sometimes it clashes. Since both of you adjust easily to different situations, conflict isn't usually too severe. The biggest problem you face is mutual avoidance of conflict when it does arise. If you can learn to confront rather than fade out, you will be able to keep things on an even keel.

Mutable Mode types have less of a tendency to be in conflict, because mutual flexibility and a willingness to change leaves both room to maneuver when problems arise.

You Are in Different Modes

If one of you is Cardinal and the other is Fixed you have a combination of will and power, or will *versus* power if conflict arises. If your parent is the Fixed type, your best defense is not an offense but to take the initiative to make things better and present a plan. If you are the Fixed type, you will have to learn give-and-take and to let go.

If one of you is Cardinal and the other is Mutable you are never bored with each other. You enjoy having new ideas and being creative together. A problem can arise when you go from one thing to another without finishing what has already been started. If your parent is the Cardinal type, he or she can help you focus. If you are the Cardinal type, you can rely on your parent's flexibility to help work out disagreements or difficulties.

If one of you is Fixed and the other is Mutable you have a complementary relationship. The Mutable person uses his or her flexibility to get around the Fixed person's immobility. If your parent is the Fixed type, you can use your ability to bend with the wind to cope with his or her stubborness and refusal to change a position. If you are the Fixed type, your parent can teach you how to relax, let go, and be more adept at identifying problems and finding solutions. You can learn to take risks and try new things.

Tools for Tough Times

Astrology is neither a perfected science nor solely an art form created by the intuitive faculties of the various people who practice it. Astrology combines certain elements of sceince, art, and intuition and as such it is a unique field of study.

—Alan Leo, *As Above, So Below*

Having made it into your teens, you already know that life isn't fair and that bad things happen to good people. You've had your share of unpleasant or downright awful experiences. This chapter is going to talk about the downside of life, for the simple reason that it can't be avoided by anyone, and I, for one, don't think it's fair to pretend that everything's rosy when in fact it can be some very dark shades, including black.

We all know hard stuff happens. When you're a teenager, emotions tend to run higher and it can be hard to keep perspective. You may not be in a position to control events or people outside yourself, but there are things you *can* do to give yourself strength and clarity and personal resilience in the face of hard situations.

During tough times, astrology can be your best friend, a real helper. Humans are extremely complex beings and each one of has an *unconscious*. Dr. Barbara Brown, the author of a wonderful book called

Star Sense

The natal horoscope isn't to be considered the final answer to all the questions life presents us. However, once you learn the language of your Planets, you have a handy, useful guide to your life as it unfolds. If you work with the planetary cycles, you can learn from your hang-ups and ease any difficulties along the way. Learning the cosmic connections can make your protential talents and joys multiply to fulfill your dreams.

"We will, by conscious command, evolve cerebral centers which will permit us to use powers that we now are not even capable of imagining."

—Dr. Frederic Tilney

Supermind, says: "Our highest, most elegant intellectual capacities lie untapped and unrecognized in what we call the unconscious."

Astrology provides a direct route into your unconscious patterns and processes. It's quicker and more accurate than psychology. For one thing, it's about *you,* not about a general theory of human behavior, which might or might not fit.

This is because you came into the world with all your Planets' energies already inside you, waiting to be developed and used. With knowledge of them, you are in a position to be *aware* of your inborn unconscious patterns, a great advantage! Some people go all through life unaware of what is motivating them or causing unwanted or pain-producing behavior and reactions. The more aware you are, the more you can be in control of how you behave and react.

Astrology can let you pinpoint your weaknesses and show you how to marshal your strengths to bolster them, letting you deal more effectively with what's hurting and make it better. And, since being forewarned is to be forearmed, astrology proves the old adage that an ounce of prevention is worth a pound of cure.

Another word often used interchangeably with unconscious is *subconscious,* but we won't split hairs over the two definitions. Let me tell you about your unconscious. It knows everything about your life from the moment of conception to this very day. It has a complete record of everything you have ever experienced, thought, felt, dreamed, and wished.

There is no computer system on Earth that matches the capacity of a single brain's vast reservoir of data. In fact, it would take dozens, maybe thousands, of huge computers even to begin to approach the capabilities of your unconscious mind.

Not only does this part of the mind have a complete record of your past, it is also already forming your future, which it contains like an acorn contains an oak tree. Your *conscious* mind has the power to reach out beyond your physical self—both in time and in space—and let you travel far and wide—to the past, to the future, to places you have never visited, to places not yet possible to visit (such as other Planets).

Think about it: if your *conscious* mind, which has many limitations, can do all of these marvelous things, what your unconscious mind, which has absolutely no limitations, can do is positively mind-boggling.

The prefix *un-* or *sub-* conjures up the image of a basement in the mind, and that's unfortunate. The unconscious is actually all around us, like the air we breathe. And just like air, we can't actually see it.

My term for this magical and mysterious part of us humans is the *nonconscious;* it includes both the past and the future and at every moment is in a state of arriving. When you went to bed last night, your dreams were in your future. When you woke up this morning, they were in your past. So looked at in this way, past, present, and future are one continuous flow.

Just as dreams are often full of images and tell a story, the unconscious utilizes the mind's amazing ability to create *images.* So far as we know, humans are the only species with this marvelous ability. We call it the *imagination,* which you already know is a function of Neptune in your chart. (My Neptune is in the tenth House, so I use his energies in my profession.)

As an example of how this process works, when I sit at my keyboard and tap-tap away, pages get written, but often I have the feeling that it isn't really *me* in charge. I often have the sense of something else at work, rather than my conscious mind. After a lot of thought and quite a few books, I tried to get a handle on what was actually happening deep inside of me, and my imagination furnished me with an image of a troop of elves who represent my unconscious process, kind of like the seven dwarves who saved Snow White and took care of her.

When a project (or my life) is going well, I say the elves are happy. When I'm having a difficult time, I say that the elves are unhappy because they don't like what I'm doing.

As I worked with this image over time, I found the elf idea helped me in all sorts of situations, not just with work. Once, when I got hung-up while writing another book, I even had a dream of the elves busily dashing around and bringing in information to the central office (my conscious mind).

Personalizing "my" elves along astrological lines—one for each sign of the Zodiac—was a natural extension, and I found that thinking of "them" as distinct individuals made it easier for me to get in touch with what was bothering me or causing me anguish or emotional pain and to come up with solutions to problems.

Now, as a rational being, I know there aren't any elves living inside my head, but it's been a great help to me to act *as if* I have these helpers.

"We will eventually discover that all persons have the full range of psychic phenomena as potentialities, all unconsciously understood."
—Willis Harmon, Stanford Research Institute

"Most of you can think of at least once when you consciously felt you just couldn't do it—write a paper, pass a test, keep going in an athletic event. But then your grit and determination kep you going past the obstacle, whether it was fear or fatigue. You got what runners call a 'second wind.' Suddenly you felt a great welling up of energy you didn't know you had, and you finished your task with ease, even exhilaration. You were tapping into your unconscious reserves, which are always available upon demand."
—M. J. Abadie, *Your Psychic Potential*

Personalizing the murky and little understood unconscious processes gives me a sense of clarity about what's happening down deep.

By using imagination, I have conversations with the elves, who I realize are at some level different facets of myself—you might call them my elf-selves. Lots of people would laugh at this concept and find it ridiculous. That's because most people think anything that isn't verifiable through the five physical senses can't be real, but this isn't true. Mental and emotional pain is every bit as real as physical pain, and often much more intense. And the mind's unconscious processes, which never stop even though we are unaware of them—your dreams are proof of this—are as real as anything you can see, hear, touch, smell, or taste.

I'm not trying to oversimplify what is a complex and extremely mysterious process, but perhaps if I tell you what happened to me while I was writing this chapter you'll be able to understand how your own unconscious works and how it can help to solve your problems.

When I started to write about the bad things that can happen to teens, I felt that I couldn't do it at all—because my own teen years were dark and difficult. I got really depressed. I remembered all too clearly how it felt, which was horrible. For a couple of years during high school the idea of suicide was very attractive and I thought about it a lot. If you've ever had really bad thoughts—and I know that many teens have them—you know what I'm talking about.

So I telephoned my editor, Laura, who is a wonderful lady with two teenage kids, and told her I was having problems. I asked her if we could just leave the discussion about the bad stuff out of the book. I told her my elves wouldn't cooperate and I couldn't help you deal with the bad things because they refused to do their part. Though most of the book had gone well, now I was stuck.

We talked about how much teens need to know that they aren't alone when they are dealing with feeling sad, lonely, depressed, angry, or isolated or when there are family problems like alcoholism, drug use, and child abuse. We know these things happen to teens, and we know how hard it is to keep steady when you're going through a storm. So we both felt something helpful ought to be included in the book.

After talking to Laura, I sat down and tried to get in touch with the elves to ask them for their help, and I "saw" them all sitting around in a sad huddle, with long faces. Their caps drooped and the bells on

"Discoveries in brain research, consciousness research, physics, parapsychology, and molecular biology are converging toward a radical, new world-view . . . but the politics of science is frustrating the most exciting adventure of this century or any other: the search for what it means to be human."
—Marilyn Ferguson,
The Aquarian Revolution

their pointy-toed shoes didn't jingle. I knew they didn't want to write about the bad things because doing so made *them* feel bad and sad and depressed, and they weren't having any fun.

"Hey, guys," I said, "I really need your help on this."

But the only response I got was glum faces that almost made me cry, caps that drooped almost to the floor, and silent toe bells. Still, they'd helped me to do some really hard work before; we'd written about sickness and serious emotional problems and gotten through it, but it always for adults, never for teens. Everything that hurts seems to hurt worse when you are a teen because you haven't had the chance or the time to develop defenses or learn how to cope.

Since Laura and I had decided this material needed to be in the book, I had to get the elves to cooperate so I could finish writing the chapter. Finally, I asked them for some ideas about how to handle talking about the bad stuff in a way that would be understandable to teens without going into a lot of deep psychological theory.

Then, all of a sudden, the littlest elf—she's a Pisces—jumped up and cried out, "Stories! Let's tell them stories! I love stories!" And she began to jump up and down in excitement.

"Stories?" I said. "What kind of stories?"

"Oh, you know," the Gemini elf said, "those stories you like to write about how you can make pictures with your mind to make things work better."

"Yeah," chimed in the Sagittarius elf. "Those are good stories. They teach how to see life from a philosophical angle and help you to get the big picture."

"And they teach you to detach from painful emotions," added the Aquarius elf from his perch at a distance.

Then Big Elf, a Taurus who is kind of the daddy elf, said, "That's a good idea. Those stories aren't just mental exercises . . ."

"What do you call those stories?" interrupted the Gemini elf.

". . . they work and have very practical results," finished the Taurus elf slowly and calmly.

"Do you mean the special techniques for using your mind's power of imagination?" I asked.

"Tell us what you call them," said the Virgo elf, settling his glasses on his nose. "I'll put them in the proper order for the teens," he added, as always trying to help.

"I believe that the human mind has reached a point in evolution where it is about to develop new powers—powers that would once have been considered magical. Indeed, it has always possessed greater powers than we now realize: of telepathy, premonition of danger, second sight, healing power . . . magical power rises from the subconscious. . . ."
—Colin Wilson, *The Occult*

"Images the mind makes work into life."
—Euripedes, *Medea*

"They're called *visualizations*," I answered, "or mind movies."

"I like the visualization stories because you get to be the writer, director, and producer and play the leading role," said the Leo elf importantly. "They can be really dramatic and interesting."

"Sometimes I call them meditations," I told them.

"Meditations are nice," the Libra elf said quietly. "They help to harmonize a person when life gets out of balance."

"They also penetrate into the inner self," the Scorpio elf spoke in a deep voice. "That's where real changes take place."

"Yes," shouted the Aries elf. "Let's get started on them right now. I'm sure the teens will like them."

"They are serious business," cautioned the Capricorn elf. "They require work."

"That won't matter," the Cancer elf, who tends to be a bit of a mother hen, responded. "If the stories will help the teens deal with the bad things, then we have to let them know about how to create their own visualizations."

"Okay," I said. "We'll do the visualizations for the teens."

At that point, all the elves' faces brightened and their caps perked up. Soon they were all jumping around and the bells on their pointy-toed shoes jingled merrily.

And so it was that I found the solution to my problem. The great Albert Einstein wrote, "The intellect has little to do on the road to discovery. There comes a leap in consciousness, call it intuition . . . the solution comes to you and you don't know how or why."

Visualization stories have the ability to hook up with *your* own non-conscious mind and resonate there. They can make it easier to deal with

The Power of Imagination

Visualization techniques work because your mind doesn't know the difference between what is real and what you tell it is real. There's an old saying, "Be careful what you wish for, you may get it!" The mind is so powerful that we can literally make what we want happen. Because the mind responds most readily to pictures and images (*imagination* = image-making), when you use the visualization technique you are in possession of a powerful tool. Always use it wisely and well, and never try to do any harm or it will backfire on you.

any bad stuff. You have already seen some examples earlier in the book. By using them, you will learn to trust your own nonconscious self to come up with solutions to problems, even very difficult ones.

You can tie in your Planets to the visualizations. For example, if you are having an emotional problem, look to your Moon for help. Read the section referring to your Moon and think about the strengths and positive attributes it has. Find these positive qualities in yourself and focus on them.

If it's communications problems you're suffering, go to Mercury and review your Mercury's qualities. If you find you are using his negative side, switch to the positive.

With love problems, contact the goddess Venus. Read the description for your Venus and discover how you are using her energies. It will be apparent to you if your Venus is in a bad mood and acting negatively!

Anger and resentment feelings are usually a result of Mars on the warpath. Look for other ways you can use your Mars energy to avoid getting trapped by angry feelings.

As you read through the various visualizations, choose the ones that seem most appropriate to your particular situation at the time. This isn't a one-size-fits-all method, but you can tailor the visualizations to suit your own purposes and needs.

Not everything will work for everyone. And what works for you one time may not fit the bill another time. Play around with the "stories"—rewrite them if you like—or write your own! Consider these stories to be guidelines and examples of what you can do with your own imagination. You'll find paths into your unconscious that will surprise and amaze you.

Be an explorer of the unknown you—get in touch with the magical realm that lies within you, for it contains unlimited riches, and as a problem-solver it's unbeatable.

Don't ask too much of yourself too soon. Using visualization techniques is a *process,* not a pill. It takes some time to get used to them and how they work. Remember, you are learning a new skill. Like playing a musical instrument, you learn by steps and in stages. As you practice, you'll discover what works best for *you,* and that's all that matters.

As you limber up your imagination and begin to flex your expectation muscles, you'll start to feel awfully good about yourself and your potentials. You'll *feel* smarter—because you'll *be* smarter. Someone remarked that violins are useful instruments—you can use them for doorstops or you can learn to play exquisite music on them. Think of your unconscious as a violin. It is there waiting for you to learn to make beautiful music with your life. Of course, you will need to overcome skepticism. You are being asked to believe in something you have been told is not "real." But you can disprove that with your own experience using visualizations.

Resentment-Neutralizing Exercise

One form of Mars energy is *anger*. Mars shows how you become angry. If you are using his energy negatively, how you handle anger will be an issue for you.

Here's how Mars becomes angry in each of the Signs:

In **Aries**—Mars angers instantly, with action, impulsively.

In **Taurus**—Mars angers slowly, totally, physically, with force.

In **Gemini**—Mars angers unpredictably, logically, mentally.

In **Cancer**—Mars angers emotionally, sullenly, in private, sulkily.

In **Leo**—Mars angers loudly, dramatically, totally.

In **Virgo**—Mars angers analytically, critically, coldly, logically.

In **Libra**—Mars angers inconsistently, with difficulty, verbally.

In **Scorpio**—Mars angers intensely, destructively, with deep emotion.

In **Sagittarius**—Mars angers in a big way, explosively, with much energy.

In **Capricorn**—Mars angers sarcastically, coldly, emphatically.

In **Aquarius**—Mars angers with detachment, analytically, originally.

In **Pisces**—Mars angers passively, emotionally, overwhelmingly.

If you have been using your Mars energy negatively when you become angry, chances are you have built up a load of resentments on top of your anger. Here's how to get rid of both your negative anger and your resentments:

Affirmations for Releasing Resentment (Use daily♦)

I now reclaim my own power in this situation.
I release all that is not positive for my life.
What happened in the past is now over and done with.
My love for myself overcomes all resentment.
I now release and let go of all resentful feelings.
The divine in me now releases me from all resentment.

Also do this meditation. First breathe deeply until you feel relaxed. Tell yourself you are now ready to let go of all anger and resentments.

Then imagine a bubble of beautiful royal purple, like a magical carriage, drawing up in front of you. Step inside. There you will find an altar, upon which is a flame of purple fire. Speak your anger and resentment to the flame, which will consume it.

Next you see a pool of purple-tinted water. Allow all anger and resentments to come to its surface. Transfer them one by one to the purple flame, and watch them go up in lavender smoke.

Finally, when the water in the pool is clear of all your anger and resentments, wash your hands in it and proclaim, "I am now free of all anger and resentment. I am cleansed and purified. I now release all anger and resentment forever."

Let the purple flame flare up, burning higher and higher until it has reached a peak. See all of your anger and resentment consumed in the flame.

The visualization techniques presented here can let you reprogram your inner mind so that astrological energies that you may have been using negatively are rechanneled into *self-fulfilling powers*. There are no *bad* energies—just energy that is badly used.

The power of visualization is proved by experiments in hospitals with young cancer patients who were taught to imagine their white blood cells as powerful and hungry sharks eating up their cancer cells or as Superman destroying the bad cells. After practicing the visualizations twice daily for a week, the children's blood count was taken again. The results were startling. They showed amazing improvement in the white blood cell count. The images created in the minds of the children had actually affected their physical tissues! Many other experiments have shown this stunning power of the mind's image-making capability. It will work for you, too.

The Uncanny Power of Visualizations

How to Make Mind Movies

The key to the power of images is:

Envision yourself as already being in the desired state.

Next, you fill in the movie with rich sensory details. Your subconscious mind responds to information about the realm of the senses. Imagine *being* the person you really want to be—and already are in your inner self. *See, hear,* and *feel* what that would be like. "Put on" that person, so to speak, like you would put on a beautiful coat. Walk around in your ideal self, feeling down to your toes and bones what that experience would be like. How does it feel?

Remember, this is *your* movie. You are the writer, producer, director, *and* the star. You don't need to worry about the *how* of it; that will take care of itself. You need only to richly imagine the end result and see yourself as having attained it.

A clear mental picture of the goal and the circumstances that will surround it is the path to success. Vague wishes or unspecific thoughts won't work. Don't say, "I wish I felt better," and try to turn that thought into a mind movie. Instead, think "I want to be fit, energetic, and happy." Then see yourself as you would be in that desired state. The specific images are up to you. It's essential that the images you choose have *meaning* for you.

When you have created the perfect picture of yourself and your

Personalize Your Planets!

You can give your Planets names and characteristics by envisioning them as characters in a play you are writing and allowing them to have a dialogue. Here's an example:

Venus in Aries: "Action is what I like. I want the newest, the latest. I thrive on new experiences. Just give me something I haven't experienced already."

Moon in Libra: "Strife and discord upset me. I like traditional things and I want peace more than anything. I'm a sensitive person who hates crudeness or bad manners."

Mars in Leo: "I was born to rule. I like to run things. I'll admit I can be self-centered, but I'm never mean-spirited. Just pay attention to me."

Virgo Ascendant: "I'm a cautious person and I don't like disorder or people rushing around to no purpose. I'm rational and careful and don't like to draw attention to myself."

Write your own dialogue for *your* Planets, letting them have a conversation with each other. Here, Venus might complain about Ascendant's wimpy caution, which keeps her from flirting as much as she'd like. Mars might tell Moon that she's a prissy pain who keeps her from dressing extravagantly because of what people will think.

Have fun making up your own plot lines and stories to personify your Planets for yourself. We call this *Astrodrama*, and it's a really good technique.

---

life, run your mind movie on a screen that you have set up for it. If you like, stage it as a play. You are going to watch your mind movie three times, in progressive sequences. The first time, just run it through and watch closely to see what you can refine or improve, like a rehearsal or trying on clothes to see if they fit. At this point, you are critiquing, not participating. The second time is a full dress rehearsal with all of the details in exact place, just as it will be opening night. There's even an audience—you—to applaud your efforts. On the third viewing, *you see yourself actually stepping into the role you have designed for yourself.* This is the real thing and you are in it, not just observing or critiquing.

AstroTeen Tip

How to dialogue with your Planets:

Either orally or in writing, create a dialogue with your individual Planets. Express how you feel about each one and its characteristics and how they affect your life. Tell each about the problems or benefits it creates for you. Ask what it wants and what it needs or why it is not satisfied. Allow your Planets to respond and to enlighten you about the role each plays in your life.

Sample AstroVision Exercise

To help you harmonize your various planetary selves, I created a series of special visualizations using astrological themes called *AstroVision*. Here is the one for balancing any two Planets' energies. Just choose the two you want to work with.

Prepare for this exercise by first walking about and taking a good long stretch to loosen your muscles and ready yourself for an inner experience. Then sit or recline in a comfortable position you can hold for ten to fifteen minutes. Loosen or remove any tight clothing and close your eyes. First, pay total attention to your breath, without making any changes; simply observe the breath coming in and going out for several minutes until you feel a sense of relaxation and unwinding as you proceed to your inner self.

Now, imagine yourself holding one Planet in each hand. You may want to do this with your hands outstretched, in your lap, or wherever feels comfortable. Allow yourself to feel the weight of each Planet, as if you were trying to discover the differences between them. Choose one and put the other down. Then, with both hands, turn your chosen Planet about in your hands as you would an object that is new to you. Feel the size, texture, and weight of it. See if it has any other characteristics, such as smell or sound or color.

Spend at least a few minutes with the first planetary energy, making friends with it as you might with a new puppy or kitten. Then put it down and take up the second in your hands, repeating the procedure.

After familiarizing yourself with the two on an individual basis, feel intuitively how they relate to each other. See if you want to say anything to either or both. You may want to ask questions, find out the best way to use the energies, or see what each needs of you. Ask each if it feels fulfilled or if you can bring more of its energy into focus in your life. Ask how to do this.

Then take them up together, one in each hand, and see what happens. You may feel that they want to dialogue or that they have something to give each other or to work out together. Give them equal time.

Do this exercise whenever you want to get in touch with your inner Planets and their relationship to each other within you.

You have an invisible dimension within yourself. You can create places where you can go in times of stress and pain, especially emotional pain. The feeling you get is like being so wealthy that you know you can never run out of money, no matter how much you spend. Once you have made contact with any part of your deep inner self, it will always be available to you.

One of the major blocks each of us must overcome is *fear*. Fear holds us back from living fully, from experiencing fully, from a healthy ability to confront the inevitable challenges in our lives. When you emerged into this world from your mother's womb, you did not fear life or anything in it. Soon, however, the adults around you began to instill fear in you. "Don't do that, you'll get hurt," "Be careful," "Watch out," "Don't go there," "Don't do that, it's dangerous," became words you heard practically every day. Naturally, what was once a healthy ability to face life's challenges became fear—of coming to harm, of failure, of rejection, of not being liked or loved, of loss, and so on.

As a newborn, you came fearlessly into a world you did not yet know. Deep within everyone is a place of no fear. Use this inner sanctuary. When you're feeling lonely and blue, discouraged or distressed, unloved or unwanted, don't despair. You *are* a wonderful person with a purpose in life and reason for being on this Earth, even if your days seem dark at the moment. You can also use the visualization exercises that follow to help you in troubled times.

In his book *Recovering the Soul*, Larry Dossey, M.D., discusses the evidence for the mind as a force "ultimately independent of the physical brain and body."

Keep a Visualization Journal

It's really helpful to keep a record of your experience with visualizations. A small notebook is excellent. Make a note of the date, the time of day, how you were feeling, and the details of any problem you wanted to solve. Write down how you felt before you did the visualization and what the results were—how you felt afterward, what you did to make things better, anything you changed such as an attitude or actual behavior. Go back and review your journal each time you experiment with a new visualization or dialogue with your Planets. As you get more practice with these techniques, you'll find it fascinating to see how far you have progressed when you re-read earlier experiences.

Creating Your Sanctuary

Find a time when you can be alone and undisturbed for half an hour. Spend a few minutes breathing slowly and rhythmically, and allow your body to relax completely.

Now, create in your mind a picture of a lovely place—it might be a secluded spot in a woods or a cove on a beach. It can be outdoors or indoors. Letting yourself feel relaxed and free, think leisurely about what a sanctuary would mean to you. As this picture emerges (you don't actually have to *see* it, you only have to *know* it), let yourself be absorbed into its quiet, beauty, silence, and sense of comforting solitude.

When you have an image in your mind or a feeling about what your sanctuary is like, continue to fill in all the details. Imagine what a perfect room of your own would look and feel like. What would you put there? A comfortable chair, a bowl of fresh flowers, pictures on the wall? Make this picture as complete as you possibly can, with colors, smells, and textures. Walk about the environment you are creating and claim it for your own personal place of inner solitude.

When you feel that you have taken complete possession of your special place, perform a symbolic gesture—such as writing your name or placing a favorite object there—that will enable you to return to your sanctuary at will. The purpose is to make it easy for you to recall this experience. After you have done this, breathe slowly and quietly for a few minutes before returning to your everyday state of mind.

You have now created your sanctuary. You can return anytime you want, whenever you choose.

AstroTeen Tip

Whenever you're feeling blue, out of sorts, or sick or when you just want off the planet, review your Moon Sign's *self-nurturing highlight* in chapter 3.

How to Generate Love

You have the ability to generate love at will. To experience this, sit, recline, or lie down in a comfortable position and close your eyes. Begin with a few deep breaths to relax. Now picture your dominant hand in your mind. Find your hand mentally and begin sending it love. Radiate love out of your heart center to your hand. Soon it will begin to respond to the love you are generating by feeling warm and alive. Next, send love to other parts of your body at will. Concentrate on sending the love out and feeling it being received.

Continue sending yourself love until you feel filled with a glowing warmth coming from your heart center. Picture this love as a beautiful, pure, white light cascading through your entire body, loosening tension, soothing emotional hurt, and healing pain or discomfort. Say, "I give this total pure love to myself. I honor myself with love now." Feel this love energy pulsating through your entire being while you imagine it as a beam of light streaming out of your heart center and filling every cell in your body, every crevice in your emotions, every thought in your mind. See this beam of powerful light leave your body and flow out to the universe, filling it with radiance. Now see the radiance returning to you, entering your heart center, and filling you with the power of self-generated love.

Treasure-Map Technique

All you need to make a treasure map is a large piece of poster board, glue or tape, and cutouts of pictures. You can, for example, cut pictures from magazines of people doing things you would like to be able to do. When you have collected a sufficient number of pictures representing your wishes, paste them on the poster board in any manner that appeals to you, using an image of particular significance at the center. Some like to use a religious symbol; some use a photograph of themselves. Once you have made your treasure map, put it where you can view it often. Spend a few minutes viewing it in a relaxed state just before sleep and again just after waking. You can also make a portable treasure map by using a small notebook, which you can flip through during free moments away from home.

Finding Your Authentic Self

You will need half an hour of quiet time to do this meditation. It can take you very deeply into yourself, so be prepared for some surprises. Above all, do not be frightened or repulsed should you encounter anything you don't expect. We all have dark corners, and the only way to light them is to inhabit them. On the other hand, you may be quite pleasantly surprised to discover your authentic self is quite to your liking and is simply waiting for you to uncover it and be your friend.

Find a time when you can be alone and undisturbed. If possible, take a leisurely warm bath or shower using scented soap or bath salts. Dry yourself gently and dress in something soft, loose, and clean.

Now, breathe deeply several times and allow yourself to drift into a state of deep meditation. You are going to find a lovely spot somewhere outdoors—it could be in a woods, in a park, in a garden, on the beach, by a lakeshore, or anywhere else you fancy.

After you have envisioned this place, take a walk and look around. You are going to find a small, secret door someplace. It might be in the ground, under the water, in a tree, hidden under fallen leaves, or under a hedge.

When you find the secret door, open it carefully. It isn't locked, but the hinges might be rusty from lack of use. When you open the secret door, you will find a spiral staircase leading downward in a clockwise direction. Descend the staircase. As you spiral clockwise down the staircase, count down from ten to one; at ten allow your body to relax further; at nine, your awareness sharpens and anticipates; at eight, you are enveloped in silence; at seven, you feel safe and comfortable; at six, five, and four you are in a state of complete relaxation and begin to sense there is magic here. At three and two your senses tingle with expectation as you prepare to meet your true self. At one, as you step from the last rung of the spiral staircase, you have left the upper world behind and find yourself in a beautiful room that houses your authentic self.

Look around this room. You have seen it before. It was there the day you were born. Before you came to this Earth plane you knew who you were, and you still know, but you have forgotten. This experience is like meeting someone you knew as a child, someone you loved very much but have lost touch with over the years. Now you will meet yourself again and for the first time.

Take a comfortable seat in this lovely room and ask your true self to come forth. Imagine this self standing in front of you and observe its form, figure, posture, and pose. Tell yourself you will recall this experience completely and that all the observations will remain as vivid memories that you can call to mind at any time in the future. When you see an image of your authentic self, observe details—clothing, facial expression, age, style. Allow this image to move and change and stay with it for a few moments.

Acknowledge this self and take some time to get to know him or her. Ask your authentic self if it has anything to say to you at this time. Express your love for your authentic self, and affirm your determination to live by and for it. If at first you feel uncomfortable, be patient until you become accustomed to this person, who is you at your best, the *you* you truly are, the person you came to this Earth to be.

Before beginning your ascent back to the ordinary world, make a symbolic gesture to your authentic self. You can hug him or her and promise to return often. You might want to place a vase of fresh flowers on a table there as an indication you have visited. Do whatever comes to your mind at the time that expresses how you feel about the meeting.

After making your symbolic gesture, slowly ascend the spiral staircase, counting from one to ten while going upward, breathing evenly as you do, and return to the secret door, which is a sacred portal to the *self*. Follow your footsteps back to where you started and gradually bring yourself back to normal waking consciousness. Write down what you experienced and read it over frequently.

You can do this meditation as often as you like. As you become better acquainted with your authentic self, you will learn more and more and develop a relationship. You can always go through the secret door and down the spiral staircase when you want to commune with your deepest, truest self, which will provide you with comfort and guidance.

Mind-Calming Visualization

Let your mind take you to a beautiful natural setting. It can be a place you love to visit, a place you have seen in a magazine or on TV, or an imaginary place.

You might take a walk through snowy woods, hike up a mountain pass, have a leisurely sit-down by the side of a cool lake, or go to the beach at whatever time of year you like best. The idea is to pick something you find calming and soothing.

For example, try imagining sitting by a lake in spring when the wildflowers are just beginning to bloom. Visualize yourself walking down a country road to the shore of the lake, enjoying the cool yet warm spring air with its breeze that hints of nature's renewal. Allow yourself to feel invigorated yet relaxed. Feel the warmth of the spring sun on your shoulders. You might take off your jacket and turn up your face to its gentle warmth, which foretells the summer to come.

When you reach the lake's shore, find a comfortable spot to sit and relax—enjoy the feel of the grass beneath you, smell the scent of the wildflowers, watch the gentle swell of the lake waters, listen to the birds chirping, see the myriad forms of life all about you exhibiting nature's annual renewal of herself.

Take off your shoes and dabble your feet in the water, feeling its refreshing coolness. Perhaps a small fish nibbles at your bare toes and tickles you. Watch a pair of ducks land on the lake and see the waterbirds soaring overhead in the clear blue sky. Feel at one with the scene. Notice how the water catches the sun's light and see the reflection of a passing cloud on its placid surface.

Take your time to enjoy this place, letting all your worries and tensions slip away until you feel utterly calm.

Once you have done this meditation, you can return here whenever you like. You can change or vary the scene at will. For example, I have a special place I go that is perched on a mountainside. It is the retreat of a Buddhist monk I call Genji. I have been going there for several years, at all seasons, in all weathers, at all times of the day and night. The place changes with the hour, the month, and the season. In winter, I enjoy the mountain's stark beauty, softened by snow at times, and I watch the play of moonlight on the glistening white snow, which enhances the silence. In spring, I thrill at all the little new shoots and buds coming out and eagerly look for the emerging growth. Summer brings things to full bloom and produces brilliant colors in the garden. In autumn, when things are beginning to withdraw into their dormant state, comes the harvest, and the sunsets are of a particularly spectacular beauty. I never tire of this ever-changing place, which always puts me into a state of deep and serene calm.

Self-blessing is another way of restoring the soul to wholeness. When we bless the totality of ourselves, we acknowledge the soul and its needs. When we bless, we invoke the sacred and connect to it. In so doing, we reconnect to our whole selves—and this acts as a healing balm. This is especially useful when we are in psychic or emotional

Self-Blessing Technique

To do this, you need only assemble some common household items: salt (symbolizing wisdom, the "salt of the earth"); water, preferably pure (symbolizing life itself, for without water there would be no life on Earth); a white candle (representing the element of fire and symbolizing the ongoing, everchanging creativity of the divine nature); a flower or small bunch of grasses or fresh herbs (symbolizing Nature); a clean white cloth (to cover the table or space upon which you will set the items); and an attractive cup or glass (to serve as your chalice).

After you have assembled your items and chosen a place to serve as your altar (this can be a small table or a dresser top cleared for the purpose), take a bath or shower (representing purification) and, if weather and privacy permit, remain naked. Otherwise, clad yourself in something loose and comfortable, preferably white. Arrange the items on the cloth on the table to suit your taste, with the flower or herbs and the candle in the center, the cup containing the water in front, and the salt on the floor in front of you. Stand barefoot on the salt in front of the altar for a moment and center yourself to give the blessing. Then step forward and light the candle. Holding your index finger and middle finger to your thumb (a boon-bestowing position known as a *mudra*), dip your fingers into the water and touch your forehead, saying, "Blessed be my mind and its ability to form thought, which forms my reality."

Continue to bless yourself with the blessings given below, each time dipping your fingers into the water and touching the part of your body mentioned.

• Blessed be my nose, which breathes Spirit.
• Blessed be my ears, which hear the sound of Spirit.

pain, a condition the Jungian psychologist James Hillman describes as ". . . the soul in neurosis trying to make itself heard." Soul wounds cannot be treated with superficial means: we must go deeply and clean the wounds so they can heal completely. Blessing the self helps do that. It is a form of self-absolution.

- Blessed be my eyes, which see Spirit everywhere.
- Blessed be my lips, which speak Spirit's truth.
- Blessed be my heart, which gives and receives divine love.
- Blessed be my body [touching your abdomen], which is the temple where Spirit dwells.
- Blessed be my genitals, which have the power to bring forth life as I was brought forth into life.
- Blessed be my legs, which give me the ability to stand up to all challenges I face.
- Blessed be my feet, which walk the path of Spirit.

Remain standing quietly for a few moments to let the blessing penetrate deeply, and then say, "I give myself absolution. I am one with Life. I am one with Spirit."

After finishing this blessing, remain standing on the salt and feel the Earth power flowing through you. Bless the Earth on which you stand, and of which you are a part. Reflect that whatever your mind thinks, your feet will follow. The aim is to empower yourself to create a life orientation toward yourself and your world that will allow you to be who you truly are in Spirit every day. You *are* divine—you have the power.

You can use these words or words you choose yourself, but remember that words have enormous power, so choose your blessing words carefully. Thoughts are things, and the conscious manifestation of thought is words. So when you speak words, do so with the knowledge that you have a responsibility to choose them wisely and well. Many cultures believe that words—or any sounds, whether speech or music—once uttered, continue forever: the vibration released never stops.

Avoid Put-downs

Avoid using any negative words in relation to yourself. *Never* call yourself stupid, or any other negative word, and never use such words about others. Always find a positive way to frame your emotional response verbally. It's always okay to *feel* what you feel—but it's never okay to express your feelings in a way that will hurt you or anyone else. If you remember and practice that one simple rule, you will be surprised how much happier and more fulfilled you will be, and problems won't seem as bad if you put them into the right perspective by reframing.

Making Lemons into Lemonade

"When life hands you a lemon, make lemonade" is an old saying that has a lot of helpful truth in it. There's a recently developed technique called *reframing* that is a neat way to put the sweetener in the sour stuff.

A *frame* is an opening through which we perceive our experience. It's a sort of personal map that we use to guide our journey through life. However, it's important to understand that the map isn't the territory. A map of Kansas isn't the state of Kansas, just like the menu in a restaurant isn't the food itself.

All of us have our personal framework through which we experience what happens to us, good or bad. It's the old question about whether the glass is half full or half empty. If you see it as half full, you feel you have some left to enjoy, but if you consider it to be half empty, then you are anxious about not having enough.

What reframing does is allow you to change the picture you have of the world, or of any specific experience—like, say, a quarrel with your parent, a death in the family, and bad feelings such as fear, anxiety, loneliness, and sadness.

When such feelings arise, you place a frame around them or you stick them into a frame you made years and years ago that you use for everything that comes along. Your frame is nothing but a *concept*—it's not a reality. For example, if you live in the United States and you are out walking on a country road at night and hear hoofbeats—do you think it's a *zebra*? Not likely. Your mental framework doesn't include zebras running around your countryside. If every time you have a fight with a parent it's about the same old thing—how you dress, what you want to do, how much freedom you can have, your allowance, or any of a dozen other common topics of confrontation between teens and their parents—you probably pop it into the same frame you've been using since you were a little kid. You deliver the same old message to yourself, "She's so uncool," or "He's a jerk," or [fill in the blank]. *Question:* What to do about it? *Answer:* Reframe.

Tips to Help You Reframe Bad Experiences

Believe in your ability to be in good relationships with all the people in your life.
Go to your sanctuary and ask for guidance or review your authentic self.

Trust your inner self, which is your intuition.
When you get a message from your inner self do not attempt to ignore, change, or deny it. Don't pretend everything is all right when it isn't.

Recognize that as a spiritual being you are unlimited.
Do not accept others' evaluations of you as limited. Know that you are potentially unlimited, and that what you can imagine, you can do.

Understand that all relationships, even difficult ones, serve a purpose in your life.
Painful experience is a great teacher, if it is put into the proper perspective. When bad things happen, ask yourself, "What is the lesson for me in this experience?"

Understand that your relationships are inner structures that you create.
Your thoughts, feelings, needs, desires, hopes, wishes, and reactions are the bricks and mortar of your relationships, and they are every bit as real as buildings made from steel and concrete. This Inner structure you have created needs energy to sustain it, just as you need food. When you withdraw energy from it, it will cease to have power over you.

Use visualization techniques frequently.
You can visualize all your relationships—with your parents, siblings, relatives, teachers, friends, and boy- or girlfriends—just the way you want them to be.

In closing what has been a long work dedicated to the idea that teens are very special people who deserve the best adults can offer them, I want to leave you with what I consider a most special visualization. It was inspired in me by my many years of working with a wise and

Experiencing the Divine in the Ordinary

First, choose an object upon which to focus. It can be anything out of your usual environment—something of which you are particularly fond or to which you have a sentimental connection. I find that beginners do well working with plants or flowers, because these are obviously alive. Items from nature, such as a seashell or a crystal, also work well, but any object will do.

Next, pick a place where you can be comfortable and remain undisturbed for about twenty minutes. It can be indoors or outside—in a garden or on the beach. Wear loose clothes and eliminate distractions.

Place the object in front of you, on a table or the floor or the ground. Allow yourself a few minutes to relax and form a one-on-one relationship with the object you have chosen.

Now, take several deep breaths, exhaling slowly while clearing your mind of random thoughts. Begin to focus closely on the object and concentrate on it to the exclusion of all else, as if you were looking through a microscope that can reveal the smallest intimate details of the object. Through this concentration and attention, you are going to penetrate its essence and become one with it, coming to understand that you and it are of the same essential stuff.

As you view the object, try to sense what it would say to you if it could speak. Imagine the hidden knowledge it contains, which it has learned on its journey through life and time. If it is a plant, imagine the thousands of ancestor plants that grew and spread their seeds so that your plant could have life and be here with you now. If it's a rock, consider the eons spent building it and where it might have been originally in the geological strata.

Continuing to focus, really *look* at the object. If it is a plant or flower, examine each leaf or petal, noticing the delicate veins or shadings of color. Really look, as if you have never before seen anything like it. Make experiencing the object's reality something entirely new, as if it were transported

wonderful man, Joseph Campbell, who understood the importance of the spiritual dimension of life better than anyone else I have ever known or come across.

to your hand from another Planet. Imagine how you would consider a moon rock!

You might want to ask the object a question or try to communicate with it in some way. A name might occur to you. Remember that it was the task of Adam and Eve to name all the plants and animals. *Naming* is a powerful spiritual link with what is other-than-ourselves. In the story of Rumplestiltskin, for example, the lovely queen saves herself and her child, who was promised as the price of turning the flax into gold, by discovering the name of the little gnome. Everything has a secret name. See if you can discover your object's secret name.

Take notice of its unique shape and other characteristics. Examine its construction for small details that set it apart from similar objects. Acknowledge its uniqueness. Like you, it is one of a kind.

Whatever it is, realize that it is made up of the same electrons whirling around the nuclei of atoms as are you, and envision these in both the object and in yourself as coming from the same universal source of pure energy that has been transformed into matter. Recognize that you and the object are one and interrelated. Credit yourself with having the power to experience this unified life field. Reject the notion of being a separate being in a fragmented world and accept the reality that you are connected to everything in the universe, that your sense of apartness is merely the result of perceptual limitations that you can transcend.

Now, see yourself as able to perceive the true nature of the universe, in which everything is connected to everything else. Imagine what it would be like to live in a world where everyone realized this as the ultimate Truth. Envision peace and plenty for all as a result of the world being recognized as a unified whole, rather than merely a collection of separate and unrelated parts. Finish by sending love and harmony to the object and thanking it for existing and gracing your environment.

After you finish, do something very ordinary—like eating a piece of fruit or taking a walk. Focus on the experience to the exclusion of everything else, noticing all the fine details.

If eating a fruit, first examine the piece with care, noticing any tiny details. For example, if it is an orange, look closely at the pores in the skin. Feel the shape in your hands, imagine the tree upon which it grew, and picture the people who planted the tree, tended its growth, and harvested the crop.

Imagine the entire chain that brought the piece of fruit to you, from the person who picked it to the checker at the supermarket where you bought it and everyone in between. Maybe it came from a foreign country and traveled thousands of miles across an ocean to get to you. How might it have felt about its journey? How many hands did it pass through? Literally hundreds of people were involved in the process.

Imagine the fruit as a small seed, and think about the entire life process that transformed that seed into a fruit-bearing tree. Eat the fruit slowly, in tiny bites, savoring each, noticing how you react to the experience of taking in life-sustaining nourishment from the life source. Imagine all the fruit trees in the world as emanating from the same energy, and understand that you are incorporating that universal energy into your own body by eating the fruit.

Mentally celebrate the joys and benefits of the everyday reality in which you live and have your being. Consider that the flavor of the entire ocean is contained in but a single drop, that the entire mystery of life lies within a seed or the tiniest egg.

Think about these words, written by Joseph Campbell in *The Hero with a Thousand Faces,* his book about the amazing journey life can be:

. . . the ideals and temporal institutions of no tribe, race, continent, social class, or century, can be the measure of the inexhaustible and multifariously wonderful divine existence that is the life in all of us.

Appendix I

Planetary Tables

How to Find the Moon Sign

Find the year of birth in the tables provided. Then find the birth month at the top of the appropriate table. Find date of birth in the column below it. If it is not listed, then the Sign given for the listed date that is closest to and preceding the birthdate is the Moon Sign. For instance, if you were born on February 3, 1950, you would see that for February 2, the Sign listed is Leo, meaning the Moon is in the Sign Leo. For February 5, Virgo is listed. This means that the Moon is in the Sign Leo until February 5 and your Moon is in the Sign Leo.

If birth occurred on a day that starts a new Sign (February 5 in this example), the Moon may be in the preceding Sign. The only way to be absolutely sure is to have a chart done professionally or by a computer service. (See appendix 2 for resources.) In lieu of this, read the text for both Signs, and see which seems more like the person.

1950

JAN	FEB	MAR	APR	MAY	JUN	JUL	AUG	SEP	OCT	NOV	DEC
1 GEM	1 CAN	1 CAN	1 VIR	1 LIB	1 SAG	1 CAP	1 PIS	1 ARI	1 GEM	1 CAN	1 LEO
4 CAN	2 LEO	3 LIB	3 LIB	2 SCO	2 CAP	4 PIS	5 TAU	4 CAN	4 CAN	3 LEO	3 LEO
6 LEO	5 VIR	4 VIR	5 SCO	4 SAG	4 AQU	6 ARI	7 GEM	7 CAN	6 LEO	5 VIR	5 LIB
8 VIR	7 LIB	6 LIB	7 SAG	6 CAP	7 PIS	9 TAU	10 CAN	9 LEO	9 VIR	7 LIB	7 SCO
10 LIB	9 SCO	8 SCO	9 CAP	8 AQU	9 ARI	11 GEM	11 LEO	11 VIR	11 LIB	9 SCO	9 SAG
13 SCO	11 SAG	11 SAG	11 AQU	10 PIS	12 TAU	14 CAN	13 VIR	13 LIB	13 SCO	11 SAG	11 CAP
15 SAG	13 CAP	12 CAP	13 PIS	12 ARI	14 GEM	16 LEO	15 LIB	16 SCO	15 SAG	13 CAP	13 AQU
17 CAP	15 AQU	15 AQU	16 ARI	15 TAU	17 CAN	19 VIR	17 LIB	18 SAG	17 CAP	15 AQU	15 PIS
19 AQU	17 PIS	17 PIS	18 TAU	17 CAN	19 LEO	21 LIB	20 SCO	20 CAP	19 AQU	18 PIS	17 ARI
21 PIS	20 ARI	19 ARI	21 GEM	20 CAN	21 VIR	23 SCO	22 SAG	21 PIS	21 PIS	20 ARI	20 TAU
24 TAU	22 TAU	22 TAU	23 GAN	21 VIR	24 LIB	25 SAG	24 CAP	24 PIS	24 TAU	22 TAU	22 GEM
26 TAU	25 GEM	24 GEM	26 LEO	26 SCO	26 SCO	27 CAP	26 AQU	26 ARI	26 TAU	25 GEM	25 CAN
29 GEM	28 CAN	27 CAN	28 VIR	27 LIB	28 SAG	29 AQU	28 PIS	29 TAU	29 GEM	28 LEO	27 LEO
31 CAN		29 LEO	30 LIB	29 SCO	30 CAP	31 PIS	30 ARI	30 TAU	31 CAN	30 LEO	30 VIR
		31 VIR		31 SAG			31 ARI				31 VIR

1951

JAN	FEB	MAR	APR	MAY	JUN	JUL	AUG	SEP	OCT	NOV	DEC
1 LIB	1 SCO	1 SAG	1 AQU	1 ARI	1 ARI	1 GEM	1 CAN	1 VIR	1 LIB	1 SCO	1 CAP
3 SCO	2 SAG	3 CAP	3 PIS	3 ARI	2 TAU	4 CAN	3 LEO	4 LIB	3 SCO	2 SAG	3 AQU
5 SAG	4 CAP	5 AQU	6 ARI	5 TAU	4 GEM	6 LEO	5 VIR	6 SCO	5 SAG	4 CAP	5 PIS
7 CAP	6 AQU	7 PIS	8 TAU	8 GEM	7 CAN	9 VIR	8 LIB	8 CAP	8 CAP	6 AQU	7 ARI
9 AQU	8 PIS	9 ARI	11 GEM	10 CAN	9 LEO	11 LIB	10 SCO	10 CAP	10 AQU	8 PIS	10 TAU
11 PIS	10 ARI	12 TAU	13 CAN	13 LEO	12 VIR	14 SCO	12 SAG	12 PIS	12 PIS	10 ARI	12 GEM
14 ARI	12 TAU	14 GEM	16 LEO	15 VIR	14 LIB	16 SAG	14 CAP	14 PIS	14 ARI	13 TAU	15 CAN
16 TAU	15 GEM	17 CAN	18 VIR	18 LIB	16 SCO	18 CAP	16 AQU	17 ARI	16 TAU	15 GEM	17 LEO
19 GEM	17 CAN	19 LEO	20 LIB	20 SCO	18 SAG	20 AQU	18 PIS	19 GEM	19 GEM	17 CAN	20 VIR
21 CAN	20 LEO	22 VIR	22 SCO	22 SAG	20 CAP	22 PIS	20 ARI	21 GEM	21 CAN	20 LEO	22 LIB
24 LEO	22 VIR	24 LIB	24 CAP	24 PIS	22 AQU	24 ARI	22 TAU	24 CAN	24 LEO	22 VIR	24 SCO
26 VIR	24 LIB	26 SCO	26 CAP	26 AQU	24 PIS	26 TAU	25 GEM	26 LEO	26 VIR	25 LIB	27 SAG
28 LIB	27 SCO	28 SAG	28 AQU	28 PIS	26 ARI	29 GEM	27 CAN	29 VIR	28 LIB	27 SCO	29 CAP
30 SCO	28 SCO	30 CAP	30 AQU	30 ARI	28 PIS	31 CAN	30 LEO	30 VIR	31 SCO	29 SAG	31 AQU
31 SCO		31 CAP		31 ARI	30 TAU		31 LEO			30 SAG	

1952

JAN	FEB	MAR	APR	MAY	JUN	JUL	AUG	SEP	OCT	NOV	DEC
1 AQU	1 ARI	1 TAU	1 GEM	1 CAN	1 VIR	1 LIB	1 SAG	1 CAP	1 PIS	1 ARI	1 GEM
2 PIS	2 TAU	3 GEM	2 CAN	2 LEO	3 LIB	3 SCO	3 CAP	2 AQU	3 ARI	2 TAU	4 CAN
4 ARI	5 GEM	5 CAN	4 LEO	4 VIR	5 SCO	5 SAG	5 AQU	4 PIS	5 TAU	4 GEM	6 LEO
6 TAU	7 CAN	8 LEO	7 VIR	9 SCO	8 SAG	7 CAP	6 ARI	6 ARI	8 GEM	6 CAN	8 GEM
8 GEM	10 LEO	11 VIR	9 LIB	9 SCO	10 CAP	9 AQU	8 TAU	8 TAU	10 CAN	8 GEM	11 LIB
11 CAN	12 VIR	13 LIB	12 SCO	12 AQU	12 AQU	11 PIS	11 GEM	10 GEM	12 LEO	11 LIB	14 SCO
13 LEO	15 LIB	15 SCO	14 SAG	15 AQU	14 PIS	13 ARI	14 GEM	13 CAN	15 VIR	14 SCO	16 SAG
16 VIR	17 SCO	18 SAG	16 CAP	16 ARI	16 ARI	15 TAU	16 CAN	15 LEO	17 LIB	16 SAG	18 CAP
18 LIB	19 SAG	20 CAP	18 AQU	17 PIS	18 TAU	18 GEM	18 VIR	18 VIR	20 SCO	18 CAP	20 AQU
21 SCO	21 CAP	22 AQU	20 PIS	20 ARI	20 GEM	20 CAN	21 VIR	20 LIB	22 SAG	21 CAP	22 PIS
23 SAG	23 AQU	24 PIS	22 ARI	22 TAU	23 CAN	23 LEO	23 SCO	22 SAG	24 CAP	23 AQU	24 ARI
25 CAP	26 PIS	26 ARI	25 TAU	24 GEM	25 LEO	25 VIR	26 SCO	25 PIS	26 AQU	25 PIS	26 TAU
27 AQU	28 ARI	28 TAU	27 GEM	28 VIR	27 VIR	28 LIB	29 SAG	27 CAP	29 PIS	27 ARI	29 GEM
29 PIS	29 ARI	30 GEM	29 CAN	29 LEO	30 LIB	30 SCO	31 CAP	29 AQU	31 ARI	30 TAU	31 CAN
31 ARI		31 GEM	30 CAN	31 LEO		31 SCO		30 AQU			

1953

JAN	FEB	MAR	APR	MAY	JUN	JUL	AUG	SEP	OCT	NOV	DEC
1 CAN	1 VIR	1 VIR	1 LIB	1 SAG	1 CAP	1 AQU	1 ARI	1 GEM	1 CAN	1 VIR	1 LIB
2 LEO	4 LIB	3 LIB	2 SCO	4 CAP	2 AQU	2 PIS	2 TAU	3 CAN	2 LEO	4 LIB	3 SCO
5 VIR	6 SCO	5 SCO	4 SAG	6 AQU	4 PIS	4 ARI	4 GEM	5 LEO	5 VIR	6 SCO	6 SAG
7 LIB	9 SAG	8 SAG	6 CAP	8 PIS	6 ARI	6 TAU	6 CAN	8 VIR	7 LIB	9 SAG	8 CAP
10 SCO	11 CAP	10 CAP	9 AQU	10 ARI	8 TAU	3 GEM	9 LEO	10 LIB	10 SCO	11 CAP	10 AQU
12 SAG	13 AQU	12 AQU	11 PIS	12 TAU	11 GEM	10 CAN	11 VIR	13 SCO	12 SAG	13 AQU	13 PIS
14 CAP	15 PIS	14 PIS	13 ARI	14 GEM	13 CAN	13 LEO	14 LIB	15 SAG	15 CAP	15 PIS	15 ARI
15 AQU	17 ARI	16 ARI	15 TAU	16 CAN	15 LEO	15 VIR	16 SCO	17 CAP	17 AQU	18 ARI	17 TAU
18 PIS	19 TAU	18 TAU	17 GEM	18 LEO	18 VIR	18 LIB	19 SAG	20 AQU	19 PIS	20 TAU	19 GEM
20 ARI	21 GEM	20 GEM	19 CAN	21 VIR	20 LIB	20 SCO	21 CAP	22 PIS	21 ARI	22 GEM	21 CAN
23 TAU	23 CAN	23 CAN	21 LEO	23 LIB	23 SCO	22 SAG	23 AQU	24 ARI	23 TAU	24 CAN	23 LEO
25 GEM	26 LEO	25 LEO	24 VIR	26 SCO	25 SAG	25 CAP	25 PIS	26 TAU	25 GEM	26 LEO	26 VIR
27 CAN	28 VIR	28 VIR	27 LIB	29 SAG	27 CAP	27 AQU	27 ARI	28 GEM	27 CAN	28 VIR	28 LIB
30 LEO		30 LIB	29 SCO	31 CAP	29 AQU	29 PIS	29 TAU	30 CAN	30 LEO	30 VIR	31 SCO
31 LEO		31 LIB	30 SCO		30 AQU	31 ARI	31 GEM		31 LEO		

1954

JAN	FEB	MAR	APR	MAY	JUN	JUL	AUG	SEP	OCT	NOV	DEC
1 SCO	1 CAP	1 CAP	1 PIS	1 ARI	1 GEM	1 CAN	1 LIB	1 VIR	1 SCO	1 CAP	1 AQU
2 SAG	3 AQU	3 AQU	3 ARI	3 TAU	3 CAN	3 LEO	4 LIB	2 SCO	2 SAG	4 AQU	3 PIS
5 CAP	5 PIS	5 PIS	5 TAU	5 GEM	5 LEO	5 VIR	6 SCO	5 SAG	5 CAP	6 PIS	5 ARI
7 AQU	7 ARI	7 ARI	7 GEM	7 CAN	8 VIR	7 LIB	8 SAG	7 CAP	7 AQU	8 ARI	7 TAU
9 PIS	9 TAU	9 TAU	9 CAN	9 LEO	10 LIB	10 SCO	11 CAP	10 AQU	9 PIS	10 TAU	9 GEM
11 ARI	11 GEM	11 GEM	12 LEO	11 VIR	12 SCO	12 SAG	13 AQU	12 PIS	11 ARI	12 GEM	11 CAN
13 TAU	14 CAN	13 CAN	14 VIR	14 LIB	15 SAG	15 CAP	16 PIS	14 ARI	13 TAU	14 CAN	13 LEO
15 GEM	15 LEO	15 LEO	16 LIB	16 SCO	18 CAP	17 AQU	18 ARI	16 TAU	15 GEM	16 LEO	16 VIR
17 CAN	18 VIR	18 VIR	19 SCO	19 SAG	20 AQU	19 PIS	20 TAU	18 GEM	18 CAN	19 VIR	18 LIB
20 LEO	21 LIB	20 LIB	21 SAG	21 CAP	22 PIS	21 ARI	22 GEM	20 LEO	20 LEO	21 LIB	21 SCO
22 VIR	23 SCO	23 SCO	24 CAP	23 AQU	24 ARI	24 TAU	24 CAN	23 VIR	22 VIR	24 SCO	23 SAG
25 LIB	26 SAG	25 SAG	26 AQU	26 PIS	26 TAU	26 GEM	26 LEO	25 LIB	25 LIB	26 SAG	26 CAP
27 SCO	28 CAP	28 CAP	29 PIS	28 ARI	28 GEM	28 CAN	29 VIR	27 SCO	27 SCO	28 CAP	28 AQU
30 SAG		30 AQU	30 PIS	30 TAU	30 CAN	30 LEO	31 LIB	30 SAG	30 SAG	30 CAP	30 PIS
31 SAG				31 TAU		31 LEO			31 SAG		31 PIS

1955

JAN	FEB	MAR	APR	MAY	JUN	JUL	AUG	SEP	OCT	NOV	DEC
1 PIS	1 TAU	1 GEM	1 CAN	1 VIR	1 LIB	1 SCO	1 CAP	1 AQU	1 PIS	1 TAU	1 GEM
2 ARI	2 GEM	3 CAN	2 LEO	4 LIB	2 SCO	2 SAG	3 AQU	2 PIS	2 ARI	2 GEM	2 CAN
4 TAU	4 CAN	6 LEO	4 VIR	6 SCO	5 SAG	5 CAP	6 PIS	4 ARI	4 TAU	4 CAN	4 LEO
6 GEM	6 LEO	8 VIR	6 LIB	9 SAG	7 CAP	7 AQU	8 ARI	7 TAU	6 GEM	6 LEO	6 VIR
8 CAN	8 VIR	10 LIB	9 SCO	11 CAP	10 AQU	10 PIS	10 TAU	9 GEM	8 CAN	9 VIR	8 LIB
10 LEO	11 LIB	13 SCO	11 SAG	14 AQU	12 PIS	12 ARI	12 GEM	11 CAN	10 LEO	11 LIB	10 SCO
12 VIR	13 SCO	15 SAG	14 CAP	16 PIS	15 ARI	14 TAU	14 CAN	13 LEO	12 VIR	13 SCO	13 SAG
14 LIB	15 SAG	18 CAP	16 AQU	18 ARI	17 TAU	16 GEM	17 LEO	15 VIR	15 LIB	16 SAG	16 CAP
17 SCO	18 CAP	20 AQU	19 PIS	20 TAU	19 GEM	18 CAN	19 VIR	17 LIB	17 SCO	18 CAP	18 AQU
19 SAG	20 AQU	22 PIS	21 ARI	22 GEM	21 CAN	20 LEO	21 LIB	20 SCO	19 SAG	21 AQU	21 PIS
22 CAP	23 PIS	24 ARI	23 TAU	24 CAN	23 LEO	22 VIR	23 SCO	22 SAG	22 CAP	23 PIS	23 ARI
24 AQU	25 ARI	27 TAU	25 GEM	26 LEO	25 VIR	25 LIB	26 SAG	25 CAP	24 AQU	26 ARI	25 TAU
27 PIS	27 TAU	29 GEM	27 CAN	29 V1R	27 LIB	27 SCO	28 CAP	27 AQU	27 PIS	28 TAU	27 GEM
29 ARI	28 TAU	31 CAN	29 LEO	31 LIB	30 SCO	29 SAG	31 AQU	30 PIS	29 ARI	30 GEM	29 CAN
31 TAU			30 LEO			31 SAG			31 TAU		31 LEO

1956

JAN	FEB	MAR	APR	MAY	JUN	JUL	AUG	SEP	OCT	NOV	DEC
1 LEO	1 LIB	1 SCO	1 SAG	1 CAP	1 PIS	1 ARI	1 TAU	1 CAN	1 LEO	1 LIB	1 SCO
2 VIR	3 SCO	3 SAG	3 CAP	3 AQU	4 ARI	3 TAU	2 GEM	2 LEO	2 VIR	2 SCO	2 SAG
4 LIB	6 SAG	6 CAP	5 AQU	5 PIS	6 TAU	6 GEM	4 CAN	4 VIR	4 LIB	5 SAG	4 CAP
7 SCO	8 CAP	9 AQU	8 PIS	7 ARI	8 GEM	8 CAN	6 LEO	6 LIB	6 SCO	7 CAP	7 AQU
9 SAG	11 AQU	11 PIS	10 ARI	9 TAU	10 CAN	10 LEO	8 VIR	9 SCO	8 SAG	10 AQU	9 PIS
12 CAP	13 PIS	14 ARI	12 TAU	12 GEM	12 LEO	12 VIR	10 LIB	11 SAG	11 CAP	12 PIS	12 ARI
14 AQU	15 ARI	16 TAU	14 GEM	14 CAN	14 VIR	14 LIB	12 SCO	13 CAP	13 AQU	15 ARI	14 TAU
17 PIS	18 TAU	18 GEM	17 CAN	16 LEO	16 LIB	16 SCO	15 SAG	16 AQU	16 PIS	17 TAU	17 GEM
19 ARI	20 GEM	20 CAN	19 LEO	18 VIR	19 SCO	19 SAG	17 CAP	18 PIS	18 ARI	19 GEM	19 CAN
21 TAU	22 CAN	22 LEO	21 VIR	20 LIB	21 SAG	21 CAP	20 AQU	21 ARI	21 TAU	21 CAN	21 LEO
24 GEM	24 LEO	24 VIR	23 LIB	22 SCO	24 CAP	23 AQU	22 PIS	23 TAU	23 GEM	23 LEO	23 VIR
26 CAN	26 VIR	27 LIB	25 SCO	25 SAG	26 AQU	26 PIS	25 ARI	25 GEM	25 CAN	25 VIR	25 LIB
28 LEO	28 LIB	29 SCO	28 SAG	27 CAP	29 PIS	28 ARI	27 TAU	28 CAN	27 LEO	28 LIB	27 SCO
30 VIR	29 LIB	31 SAG	30 CAP	30 AQU	30 PIS	31 TAU	29 GEM	30 LEO	29 VIR	30 SCO	29 SAG
31 VIR				31 AQU			31 CAN		31 LIB		31 SAG

1957

JAN	FEB	MAR	APR	MAY	JUN	JUL	AUG	SEP	OCT	NOV	DEC
1 CAP	1 AQU	1 PIS	1 ARI	1 TAU	1 CAN	1 LEO	1 LIB	1 SAG	1 CAP	1 AQU	1 PIS
3 AQU	2 PIS	4 ARI	2 TAU	2 GEM	3 LEO	2 VIR	3 SCO	3 CAP	3 AQU	2 PIS	2 ARI
6 PIS	5 ARI	6 TAU	5 GEM	4 CAN	5 VIR	4 LIB	5 SAG	6 AQU	6 PIS	4 ARI	4 TAU
8 ARI	7 TAU	9 GEM	7 CAN	6 LEO	7 LIB	6 SCO	8 CAP	8 PIS	8 ARI	7 TAU	7 GEM
11 TAU	9 GEM	11 CAN	9 LEO	9 VIR	9 SCO	9 SAG	10 AQU	11 ARI	11 TAU	9 GEM	9 CAN
13 GEM	11 CAN	13 LEO	11 VIR	11 LIB	11 SAG	11 CAP	12 PIS	13 TAU	13 GEM	12 CAN	11 LEO
15 CAN	14 LEO	15 VIR	13 LIB	13 SCO	14 CAP	13 AQU	15 ARI	16 GEM	15 CAN	14 LEO	13 VIR
17 LEO	15 VIR	17 LIB	15 SCO	15 SAG	16 AQU	16 PIS	17 TAU	18 CAN	18 LEO	16 VIR	15 LIB
19 VIR	17 LIB	19 SCO	18 SAG	18 CAP	19 PIS	18 ARI	20 GEM	20 LEO	20 VIR	18 LIB	17 SCO
21 LIB	19 SCO	21 SAG	20 CAP	20 AQU	21 ARI	21 TAU	22 CAN	22 VIR	22 LIB	20 SCO	20 SAG
23 SCO	22 SAG	24 CAP	22 AQU	22 PIS	23 TAU	23 GEM	24 LEO	24 LIB	24 SCO	22 SAG	22 CAP
26 SAG	24 CAP	26 ACU	25 PIS	25 ARI	26 GEM	25 CAN	26 VIR	26 SCO	26 SAG	24 CAP	24 AQU
28 CAP	27 AQU	29 PIS	27 ARI	27 TAU	28 CAN	27 LEO	28 LIB	28 SAG	28 CAP	27 AQU	27 PIS
30 AQU	28 ACU	31 ARI	30 TAU	29 GEM	30 LEO	29 VIR	30 SCO	30 SAG	30 AQU	29 PIS	29 ARI
31 AQU				31 GEM		31 LIB	31 SCO		31 AQU	30 PIS	31 ARI

1958

JAN	FEB	MAR	APR	MAY	JUN	JUL	AUG	SEP	OCT	NOV	DEC
1 TAU	1 GEM	1 CAN	1 LEO	1 LIB	1 SCO	1 CAP	1 AQU	1 ARI	1 TAU	1 GEM	1 LEO
3 GEM	2 CAN	3 LEO	2 VIR	3 SCO	2 SAG	3 AQU	2 PIS	3 TAU	3 GEM	2 CAN	4 VIR
5 CAN	4 LEO	5 VIR	4 LIB	5 SAG	4 CAP	6 PIS	4 ARI	6 GEM	6 CAN	4 LEO	6 LIB
7 LEO	6 VIR	7 LIB	6 SCO	7 CAP	6 AQU	8 ARI	7 TAU	8 CAN	8 LEO	6 VIR	8 SCO
9 VIR	8 LIB	9 SCO	8 SAG	10 AQU	8 PIS	11 TAU	10 GEM	11 LEO	10 VIR	9 LIB	10 SAG
12 LIB	10 SCO	11 SAG	10 CAP	12 PIS	11 ARI	13 GEM	12 CAN	13 VIR	12 LIB	11 SCO	12 CAP
14 SCO	12 SAG	14 CAP	12 AQU	14 ARI	13 TAU	16 CAN	14 LEO	15 LIB	14 SCO	13 SAG	14 AQU
16 SAG	14 CAP	16 AQU	15 PIS	17 TAU	16 GEM	18 LEO	16 VIR	17 SCO	16 SAG	15 CAP	16 PIS
18 CAP	17 AQU	18 PIS	17 ARI	20 GEM	18 CAN	20 VIR	18 LIB	19 SAG	18 CAP	17 AQU	19 ARI
20 AQU	19 PIS	21 ARI	20 TAU	22 CAN	20 LEO	22 LIB	20 SCO	21 CAP	20 AQU	19 PIS	21 TAU
23 PIS	22 ARI	24 TAU	22 GEM	24 LEO	23 VIR	23 SCO	23 SAG	23 AQU	23 PIS	22 ARI	24 GEM
25 ARI	24 TAU	26 GEM	25 CAN	26 VIR	25 LIB	26 SAG	25 CAP	26 PIS	25 ARI	24 TAU	26 CAN
28 TAU	27 GEM	28 CAN	27 LEO	28 LIB	27 SCO	28 CAP	27 AQU	28 ARI	28 TAU	27 GEM	29 LEO
30 GEM	28 GEM	31 LEO	29 VIR	31 SCO	29 SAG	31 AQU	29 PIS	30 ARI	30 GEM	29 CAN	31 VIR
31 GEM			30 VIR		30 SAG		31 PIS		31 GEM	30 CAN

1959

JAN	FEB	MAR	APR	MAY	JUN	JUL	AUG	SEP	OCT	NOV	DEC
1 VIR	1 SCO	1 SCO	1 CAP	1 AQU	1 ARI	1 TAU	1 GEM	1 LEO	1 VIR	1 SCO	1 SAG
2 LIB	3 SAG	2 SAG	2 AQU	2 PIS	3 TAU	3 GEM	2 CAN	3 VIR	2 UB	3 SAG	2 CAP
4 SCO	5 CAP	4 CAP	5 PIS	4 ARI	6 GEM	6 CAN	4 LEO	5 LIB	4 SCO	5 CAP	4 AQU
6 SAG	7 AQU	6 AQU	7 ARI	7 TAU	8 CAN	8 LEO	7 VIR	7 SCO	7 SAG	7 AQU	7 PIS
8 CAP	9 PIS	9 PIS	10 TAU	9 GEM	11 LEO	10 VIR	9 LIB	9 SAG	9 CAP	9 PIS	9 ARI
11 AQU	12 ARI	11 ARI	12 GEM	12 CAN	13 VIR	13 LIB	11 SCO	11 CAP	11 AQU	12 ARI	11 TAU
13 PIS	14 TAU	13 TAU	15 CAN	14 LEO	15 LIB	15 SCO	13 SAG	13 AQU	13 PIS	14 TAU	14 GEM
15 ARI	17 GEM	16 GEM	17 LEO	17 VIR	17 SCO	17 SAG	15 CAP	16 PIS	15 ARI	17 GEM	16 CAN
18 TAU	19 CAN	18 CAN	19 VIR	19 LIB	19 SAG	19 CAP	17 AQU	18 ARI	18 TAU	19 CAN	19 LEO
20 GEM	21 LEO	21 LEO	22 LIB	21 SCO	22 CAP	21 AQU	19 PIS	20 TAU	20 GEM	22 LEO	21 VIR
23 CAN	23 VIR	23 VIR	24 SCO	23 SAG	24 AQU	23 PIS	21 ARI	23 GEM	23 CAN	24 VIR	24 LIB
25 LEO	26 LIB	25 LIB	26 SAG	25 CAP	26 P15	25 ARI	24 TAU	25 CAN	25 LEO	26 LIB	26 SCO
27 VIR	28 SCO	27 SCO	28 CAP	27 AQU	28 ARI	28 TAU	27 GEM	28 LEO	28 VIR	28 SCO	28 SAG
29 LIB		29 SAG	30 AQU	29 PIS	30 TAU	30 GEM	29 CAN	30 VIR	30 LIB	30 SAG	30 CAP
31 LIB		31 CAP		31 PIS		31 GEM	31 CAN		31 LIB		31 CAP

1960

JAN	FEB	MAR	APR	MAY	JUN	JUL	AUG	SEP	OCT	NOV	DEC
1 AQU	1 PIS	1 ARI	1 GEM	1 CAN	1 LEO	1 VIR	1 SCO	1 CAP	1 AQU	1 ARI	1 TAU
3 PIS	2 ARI	2 TAU	4 CAN	3 LEO	2 VIR	4 SCO	3 SAG	3 AQU	2 PIS	3 TAU	3 GEM
5 ARI	4 TAU	5 GEM	6 LEO	6 VIR	4 LIB	6 SAG	5 CAP	5 PIS	5 ARI	5 GEM	5 CAN
8 TAU	6 GEM	7 CAN	9 VIR	8 LIB	7 SCO	8 CAP	8 AQU	7 ARI	7 TAU	8 CAN	8 LEO
10 GEM	9 CAN	9 LEO	11 LIB	10 SCO	9 SAG	10 AQU	9 PIS	9 TAU	9 GEM	10 LEO	10 VIR
13 CAN	11 LEO	12 VIR	13 SCO	12 SAG	11 CAP	12 PIS	11 ARI	12 GEM	12 CAN	13 VIR	13 LIB
15 LEO	14 VIR	14 LIB	15 SAG	14 CAP	13 AQU	14 ARI	14 TAU	14 CAN	14 LEO	15 LIB	15 SCO
18 VIR	16 LIB	17 SCO	17 CAP	16 AQU	15 PIS	17 TAU	17 GEM	17 LEO	17 VIR	18 SCO	17 SAG
20 LIB	18 SCO	19 SAG	19 AQU	18 PIS	17 ARI	19 GEM	19 CAN	19 VIR	19 LIB	20 SAG	19 CAP
22 SCO	20 SAG	21 CAP	21 PIS	21 ARI	19 TAU	22 CAN	22 LEO	22 LIB	21 SCO	22 CAP	21 AQU
24 SAG	23 CAP	23 AQU	24 ARI	23 TAU	22 GEM	24 LEO	24 VIR	24 SCO	23 SAG	24 AQU	23 PIS
26 CAP	25 AQU	25 PIS	26 TAU	26 GEM	24 CAN	27 VIR	25 LIB	26 SAG	25 CAP	26 PIS	25 ARI
28 AQU	27 PIS	27 ARI	28 GEM	28 CAN	27 LEO	29 LIB	28 SCO	28 CAP	28 AQU	28 ARI	28 TAU
30 PIS	29 ARI	30 TAU	30 GEM	31 LEO	29 VIR	31 SCO	30 SAG	30 AQU	30 PIS	30 TAU	30 GEM
31 PIS		31 TAU			30 VIR				31 PIS		31 GEM

1961

JAN	FEB	MAR	APR	MAY	JUN	JUL	AUG	SEP	OCT	NOV	DEC
1 GEM	1 LEO	1 LEO	1 LIB	1 SCO	1 CAP	1 AQU	1 AQI	1 TAU	1 CAN	I LEO	1 VIR
2 CAN	3 VIR	2 VIR	3 SCO	3 SAG	3 AQU	3 P15	3 TAU	2 GEM	4 LEO	3 VIR	3 LIB
4 LEO	5 LIB	5 LIB	5 SAG	5 CAP	5 PIS	5 ARI	5 GEM	4 CAN	6 VIR	5 LIB	5 SCO
7 VIR	8 SCO	7 SCO	8 CAP	7 AQU	7 ARI	7 TAU	8 CAN	7 LEO	9 LIB	8 SCO	7 SAG
9 LIB	10 SAG	10 SAG	10 AQU	9 PIS	10 TAU	9 GEM	10 LEO	9 VIR	11 SCO	10 SAG	10 CAP
11 SCO	12 CAP	11 CAP	12 PIS	11 ARI	12 GEM	12 CAN	13 VIR	12 LIB	14 SAG	12 CAP	12 AQU
14 SAG	14 AQU	13 AQU	14 ARI	13 TAU	14 CAN	14 LEO	15 LIB	14 SCO	16 CAP	14 AQU	14 PIS
16 CAP	16 PIS	16 PIS	16 TAU	16 GEM	17 LEO	17 VIR	18 SCO	16 SAG	18 AQU	17 PIS	16 ARI
18 AQU	18 ARI	18 ARI	18 GEM	18 CAN	19 VIR	19 LIB	20 SAG	19 CAP	20 PIS	19 ARI	18 TAU
20 PIS	20 TAU	20 TAU	21 CAN	21 LEO	22 LIB	22 SCO	22 CAP	21 AQU	22 ARI	21 TAU	20 GEM
22 ARI	23 GEM	22 GEM	23 LEO	23 VIR	24 SCO	24 SAG	24 AQU	23 PIS	24 TAU	23 GEM	23 CAN
24 TAU	25 CAN	25 CAN	26 VIR	26 LIB	26 SAG	26 CAP	25 PIS	25 ARI	27 GEM	25 CAN	25 LEO
26 GEM	28 LEO	27 LEO	28 LIB	28 SCO	29 CAP	28 AQU	28 ARI	27 TAU	29 CAN	28 LEO	27 VIR
29 CAN		29 VIR	30 LIB	30 SAG	30 CAP	30 PIS	31 TAU	29 GEM	31 LEO	30 VIR	30 LIB
31 LEO		31 VIR		31 SAG		31 PIS		30 GEM			31 LIB

1962

JAN	FEB	MAR	APR	MAY	JUN	JUL	AUG	SEP	OCT	NOV	DEC
1 SCO	1 SAG	1 SAG	1 AQU	1 PIS	1 TAU	1 GEM	1 LEO	1 VIR	1 SCO	1 SAG	1 CAP
4 SAG	2 CAP	2 CAP	2 PIS	2 AQU	2 GEM	2 CAN	3 VIR	2 LIB	4 SAG	3 CAP	2 AQU
6 CAP	4 AQU	4 AQU	4 ARI	4 TAU	4 CAN	4 LEO	5 LIB	4 SCO	6 CAP	5 AQU	4 PIS
8 AQU	6 PIS	6 PIS	6 TAU	6 GEM	7 LEO	7 VIR	8 SCO	7 SAG	9 AQU	7 PIS	6 AQU
10 PIS	8 ARI	8 ARI	8 GEM	8 CAN	9 VIR	9 LIB	10 SAG	9 CAP	11 PIS	9 ARI	9 ARI
12 ARI	11 TAU	10 TAU	11 CAN	10 LEO	12 LIB	12 SCO	13 CAP	11 AQU	13 ARI	11 TAU	11 GEM
14 TAU	12 GEM	13 GEM	13 LEO	13 VIR	14 SCO	14 SAG	15 AQU	13 PIS	15 TAU	13 GEM	13 CAN
16 GEM	15 CAN	14 CAN	16 VIQ	15 LIB	17 SAG	16 CAP	17 PIS	15 ARI	17 GEM	15 CAN	15 LEO
19 CAN	18 LEO	17 LEO	18 LIB	18 SCO	19 CAP	19 AQU	19 ARI	17 TAU	19 CAN	17 LEO	17 VIR
21 LEO	20 VIR	19 VIR	21 SCO	20 SAG	21 AQU	20 PIS	21 TAU	19 GEM	21 LEO	20 VIR	20 LIB
24 VIR	23 LIB	22 LIB	23 SAG	23 CAP	23 PIS	23 ARI	23 GEM	22 CAN	24 VIR	22 LIB	22 SCO
26 LIB	25 SCO	24 SCO	25 CAP	25 AQU	25 ARI	25 TAU	25 CAN	24 LEO	26 LIB	25 SCO	25 SAG
29 SCO	27 SAG	27 SAG	28 AQU	27 PIS	27 TAU	27 GEM	28 LEO	26 VIR	29 SCO	27 SAG	27 CAP
31 SAG	28 SAG	29 CAP	30 PIS	29 ARI	30 GEM	29 CAN	30 VIR	29 LIB	31 SAG	30 CAP	29 AQU
		31 AQU		31 TAU		31 LEO	31 VIR	30 LIB			31 AQU

1963

JAN	FEB	MAR	APR	MAY	JUN	JUL	AUG	SEP	OCT	NOV	DEC
1 PIS	1 TAU	1 TAU	1 CAN	1 LEO	1 VIR	1 SCO	1 SAG	1 AQU	1 PIS	1 ARI	1 GEM
2 ARI	3 GEM	2 GEM	3 VIR	3 VIR	2 LIB	4 SCO	4 SAG	3 AQU	2 ARI	2 TAU	3 CAN
5 TAU	5 CAN	5 CAN	6 VIR	5 LIB	4 SCO	6 CAP	6 AQU	6 ARI	5 TAU	3 GEM	5 LEO
7 GEM	8 LEO	7 LEO	8 LIB	8 SCO	7 SAG	9 AQU	7 PIS	7 PIS	7 GEM	6 CAN	7 VIR
9 CAN	10 VIR	9 VIR	11 SCO	10 SAG	9 CAP	11 PIS	9 ARI	10 GEM	9 CAN	8 LEO	10 LIB
11 LEO	12 LIB	12 LIB	13 SAG	13 CAP	11 AQU	13 ARI	11 TAU	12 CAN	11 LEO	10 VIR	12 SCO
14 VIR	15 SCO	14 SCO	16 CAP	15 AQU	14 PIS	15 TAU	14 GEM	14 LEO	14 VIR	13 LIB	15 SAG
16 LIB	17 SAG	17 SAG	18 AQU	17 PIS	16 ARI	17 GEM	16 CAN	16 VIR	16 LIB	15 SCO	17 CAP
19 SCO	20 CAP	19 CAP	20 PIS	20 ARI	18 TAU	19 CAN	18 LEO	19 LIB	19 SCO	17 SAG	20 AQU
21 SAG	22 AQU	22 AQU	22 ARI	22 TAU	20 GEM	22 LEO	20 VIR	21 SCO	21 SAG	20 CAP	22 PIS
23 CAP	24 PIS	24 PIS	24 TAU	24 GEM	24 CAN	24 VIR	23 LIB	24 SAG	24 CAP	22 AQU	24 ARI
26 AQU	26 ARI	26 ARI	26 GEM	26 CAN	26 LEO	26 LIB	25 SCO	26 CAP	26 AQU	25 PIS	26 TAU
28 PIS	28 TAU	28 TAU	28 CAN	28 LEO	29 VIR	29 SCO	28 SAG	29 AQU	28 PIS	27 ARI	28 GEM
30 ARI		30 GEM	30 LEO	30 VIR	29 LIB	31 SAG	30 CAP	30 AQU	31 ARI	29 TAU	30 CAN
31 ARI		31 GEM		31 VIR	30 LIB		31 CAP			30 TAU	31 CAN

1964

JAN	FEB	MAR	APR	MAY	JUN	JUL	AUG	SEP	OCT	NOV	DEC
1 LEO	1 VIR	1 LIB	1 SCO	1 SAG	1 AQU	1 PIS	1 TAU	1 GEM	1 LEO	1 VIR	1 SCO
4 VIR	2 LIB	3 SCO	2 CAP	2 CAP	3 PIS	3 ARI	3 GEM	2 CAN	3 VIR	2 LIB	4 SAG
6 LIB	5 SCO	6 SAG	4 CAP	4 AQU	5 ARI	5 TAU	5 CAN	4 LEO	5 LIB	4 SCO	6 CAP
8 SCO	7 SAG	7 AQU	7 AQU	7 PIS	7 TAU	7 GEM	7 LEO	5 LIB	8 SCO	6 SAG	9 AQU
11 SAG	10 CAP	11 AQU	9 PIS	9 ARI	9 GEM	9 CAN	9 VIR	8 LIB	10 SAG	9 CAP	11 PIS
13 CAP	12 AQU	13 PIS	11 ARI	11 TAU	11 CAN	11 LIB	11 LIB	10 SCO	12 CAP	11 AQU	14 ARI
16 AQU	15 PIS	13 ARI	14 TAU	13 GEM	13 LEO	13 VIR	14 SCO	12 CAP	15 AQU	14 PIS	16 TAU
18 PIS	17 ARI	17 TAU	16 GEM	15 CAN	16 VIR	15 LIB	16 SAG	15 CAP	17 PIS	16 ARI	18 GEM
20 ARI	19 TAU	21 CAN	18 CAN	16 VIR	18 LIB	17 SCO	19 CAP	17 PIS	20 ARI	18 TAU	20 CAN
23 TAU	21 GEM	24 LEO	20 LEO	19 VIR	20 SCO	20 SAG	21 AQU	20 PIS	22 TAU	20 GEM	22 LEO
25 GEM	23 CAN	26 VIR	22 VIR	22 LIB	23 SAG	23 CAP	24 PIS	22 TAU	24 GEM	22 CAN	24 VIR
27 CAN	25 LEO	28 LIB	24 LIB	24 SCO	25 CAP	25 AQU	26 ARI	24 GEM	26 CAN	24 LEO	26 LIB
29 LEO	27 VIR	30 SCO	27 SCO	26 SAG	28 AQU	27 PIS	28 TAU	27 GEM	28 LEO	27 VIR	28 SCO
31 VIR	29 VIR	31 SCO	29 SAG	28 AQU	30 PIS	30 ARI	30 GEM	29 CAN	30 VIR	29 LIB	31 SAG
			30 SAG	29 CAP		31 ARI	31 GEM	30 CAN	31 VIR	30 LIB	30 LIB
				31 CAP							

JAN	FEB	MAR	APR	MAY	JUN	JUL	AUG	SEP	OCT	NOV	DEC
1 SAG	1 AQU	1 AQU	1 PIS	1 TAU	1 GEM	1 LEO	1 VIR	1 LEO	1 SAG	1 AQU	1 PIS
2 CAP	4 PIS	3 PIS	2 ARI	3 GEM	2 CAN	3 VIR	2 LIB	2 SAG	2 CAP	4 PIS	3 ARI
5 AQU	6 ARI	5 ARI	4 TAU	5 CAN	4 LEO	5 LIB	4 SCO	5 CAP	5 AQU	6 ARI	6 TAU
7 PIS	8 TAU	8 TAU	6 GEM	8 LEO	6 VIR	8 SCO	6 SAG	7 AQU	7 PIS	8 TAU	8 GEM
10 ARI	11 GEM	10 GEM	8 CAN	10 VIR	8 LIB	10 SAG	9 CAP	10 PIS	10 ARI	11 GEM	10 CAN
12 TAU	13 CAN	12 CAN	10 LEO	12 LIB	10 SCO	12 CAP	11 AQU	12 ARI	12 TAU	13 CAN	12 LEO
14 GEM	15 LEO	14 LEO	12 VIR	14 SCO	13 SAG	15 AQU	14 PIS	15 TAU	14 GEM	15 LEO	14 VIR
16 CAN	17 VIR	16 VIR	15 LIB	16 SAG	15 CAP	17 PIS	16 ARI	17 GEM	16 CAN	17 VIR	16 LIB
18 LEO	19 LIB	18 LIB	17 SCO	19 CAP	18 AQU	20 ARI	19 TAU	19 CAN	19 LEO	19 LIB	19 SCO
20 VIR	21 SCO	20 SCO	19 SAG	21 AQU	20 PIS	22 TAU	21 GEM	21 LEO	21 VIR	21 SCO	21 SAG
22 LIB	23 SAG	23 SAG	22 CAP	24 PIS	23 ARI	25 GEM	23 CAN	23 VIR	23 LIB	24 SAG	23 CAP
25 SCO	25 CAP	25 CAP	24 AQU	26 ARI	25 TAU	27 CAN	25 LEO	26 LIB	25 SCO	26 CAP	26 AQU
27 SAG	28 AQU	28 AQU	27 PIS	29 TAU	27 GEM	29 LEO	27 VIR	28 SCO	27 SAG	28 AQU	28 PIS
30 CAP		30 PIS	29 ARI	31 GEM	29 CAN	31 VIR	29 LIB	30 SAG	30 CAP	30 AQU	31 ARI
31 CAP		31 PIS	30 ARI		30 CAN		31 SCO		31 CAP		

JAN	FEB	MAR	APR	MAY	JUN	JUL	AUG	SEP	OCT	NOV	DEC
1 ARI	1 GEM	1 GEM	1 LEO	1 VIR	1 SCO	1 SAG	1 AQU	1 PIS	1 ARI	1 GEM	1 CAN
2 TAU	3 CAN	2 CAN	3 VIR	2 LIB	3 SAG	2 CAP	4 PIS	2 ARI	2 TAU	3 CAN	3 LEO
5 GEM	5 LEO	5 LEO	5 LIB	4 SCO	5 CAP	5 AQU	6 ARI	5 TAU	5 GEM	5 LEO	5 VIR
7 CAN	7 VIR	7 VIR	7 SCO	7 SAG	8 AQU	7 PIS	9 TAU	7 GEM	7 CAN	8 VIR	7 LIB
9 LEO	9 LIB	8 LIB	9 SAG	9 CAP	10 PIS	10 ARI	11 GEM	9 CAN	9 LEO	10 LIB	9 SCO
11 VIR	11 SCO	11 SCO	11 CAP	11 AQU	13 ARI	12 TAU	13 CAN	12 LEO	11 VIR	12 SCO	11 SAG
13 LIB	13 SAG	13 SAG	14 AQU	14 PIS	15 TAU	15 GEM	15 LEO	14 VIR	13 LIB	14 SAG	13 CAP
15 SCO	16 CAP	15 CAP	16 PIS	16 ARI	17 GEM	17 CAN	17 VIR	16 LIB	15 SCO	16 CAP	16 AQU
17 SAG	18 AQU	18 AQU	19 ARI	19 TAU	20 CAN	19 LEO	19 LIB	18 SCO	17 SAG	18 AQU	18 PIS
20 CAP	20 PIS	20 PIS	21 TAU	21 GEM	22 LEO	21 VIR	21 SCO	20 SAG	20 CAP	21 PIS	21 ARI
22 AQU	23 ARI	23 ARI	24 GEM	23 CAN	24 VIR	23 LIB	24 SAG	22 CAP	22 AQU	23 ARI	23 TAU
25 PIS	26 TAU	25 TAU	26 CAN	25 LEO	26 LIB	25 SCO	26 CAP	25 AQU	24 PIS	26 TAU	26 GEM
27 ARI	28 GEM	27 GEM	28 LEO	27 VIR	28 SCO	27 SAG	28 AQU	27 PIS	27 ARI	28 GEM	28 CAN
30 TAU		30 CAN	30 VIR	30 LIB	30 SAG	30 CAP	31 PIS	30 ARI	29 TAU	30 CAN	30 LEO
31 TAU		31 CAN		31 LIB		31 CAP			31 TAU		31 LEO

JAN	FEB	MAR	APR	MAY	JUN	JUL	AUG	SEP	OCT	NOV	DEC
1 VIR	1 LIB	1 SCO	1 SAG	1 AQU	1 PIS	1 ARI	1 GEM	1 CAN	1 LEO	1 LIB	1 SCO
3 LIB	2 SCO	3 SAG	2 CAP	4 PIS	2 ARI	2 TAU	3 CAN	2 LEO	2 VIR	2 SCO	2 SAG
5 SCO	4 SAG	5 CAP	4 AQU	6 ARI	5 TAU	5 GEM	6 LEO	4 VIR	4 LIB	4 SAG	4 CAP
8 SAG	6 CAP	8 AQU	6 PIS	9 TAU	7 GEM	7 CAN	8 VIR	6 LIB	6 SCO	6 CAP	6 AQU
10 CAP	9 AQU	10 PIS	9 ARI	11 GEM	10 CAN	9 LEO	10 LIB	8 SCO	8 SAG	8 AQU	8 PIS
12 AQU	11 PIS	13 ARI	11 TAU	14 CAN	12 LEO	12 VIR	12 SCO	10 SAG	10 CAP	11 PIS	10 ARI
14 PIS	13 ARI	15 TAU	14 GEM	16 LEO	14 VIR	14 LIB	14 SAG	13 CAP	12 AQU	13 ARI	13 TAU
17 ARI	15 TAU	18 GEM	16 CAN	18 VIR	16 LIB	16 SCO	16 CAP	15 AQU	14 PIS	16 TAU	15 GEM
19 TAU	18 GEM	20 CAN	19 LEO	20 LIB	19 SCO	18 SAG	19 AQU	17 PIS	17 ARI	18 GEM	18 CAN
22 GEM	21 CAN	22 LEO	21 VIR	22 SCO	21 SAG	20 CAP	21 PIS	20 ARI	19 TAU	21 CAN	20 LEO
24 CAN	23 LEO	24 VIR	23 LIB	24 SAG	23 CAP	22 AQU	23 ARI	22 TAU	22 GEM	23 LEO	23 VIR
26 LEO	25 VIR	26 LIB	25 SCO	26 CAP	25 AQU	25 PIS	26 TAU	25 GEM	24 CAN	25 VIR	25 LIB
28 VIR	27 LIB	28 SCO	27 SAG	28 AQU	27 PIS	27 ARI	28 GEM	27 CAN	27 LEO	28 LIB	27 SCO
30 LIB	28 LIB	30 SAG	29 CAP	31 PIS	30 ARI	30 TAU	31 CAN	29 LEO	29 VIR	30 SCO	29 SAG
31 LIB		31 SAG	30 CAP			31 TAU		30 LEO	31 LIB		31 CAP

JAN	FEB	MAR	APR	MAY	JUN	JUL	AUG	SEP	OCT	NOV	DEC
1 CAP	1 PIS	1 ARI	1 TAU	1 GEM	1 LEO	1 VIR	1 LIB	1 SAG	1 AQU	1 PIS	1 ARI
2 AQU	3 ARI	4 TAU	3 GEM	3 CAN	4 VIR	3 LIB	2 SCO	2 CAP	4 PIS	2 ARI	2 TAU
4 PIS	6 TAU	6 GEM	5 CAN	5 LEO	6 LIB	5 SCO	4 SAG	4 AQU	6 ARI	5 TAU	4 GEM
7 ARI	8 GEM	9 CAN	8 LEO	7 VIR	8 SCO	7 SAG	6 CAP	6 PIS	8 TAU	7 GEM	7 CAN
9 TAU	11 CAN	11 LEO	10 VIR	9 LIB	10 SAG	9 CAP	9 AQU	9 ARI	11 GEM	10 CAN	9 LEO
12 GEM	13 LEO	14 VIR	12 LIB	12 SCO	12 CAP	11 AQU	10 PIS	11 TAU	13 CAN	12 LEO	12 VIR
14 CAN	15 VIR	16 LIB	14 SCO	14 SAG	14 AQU	14 PIS	13 ARI	13 GEM	16 LEO	15 VIR	14 LIB
17 LEO	17 LIB	18 SCO	16 SAG	16 CAP	16 PIS	16 AQI	15 TAU	16 CAN	18 VIR	17 LIB	16 SCO
19 VIR	19 SCO	20 SAG	18 SCO	18 AQU	19 ARI	18 TAU	17 GEM	18 LEO	20 LIB	19 SCO	18 SAG
21 LIB	22 SAG	22 CAP	20 AQU	20 PIS	21 TAU	21 GEM	20 CAN	21 VIR	23 SCO	21 SAG	20 CAP
23 SCO	24 CAP	24 AQU	23 PIS	23 ARI	24 GEM	23 CAN	22 LEO	23 LIB	25 SAG	23 CAP	22 AQU
25 SAG	26 AQU	26 PIS	25 ARI	25 TAU	26 CAN	26 LEO	25 VIR	25 SCO	27 CAP	25 AQU	24 PIS
27 CAP	28 PIS	29 ARI	28 TAU	27 GEM	29 LEO	28 VIR	27 LIB	27 SAG	29 AQU	27 PIS	27 ARI
30 AQU	29 PIS	31 TAU	30 GEM	30 CAN	30 LEO	30 LIB	29 SCO	29 CAP	31 PIS	29 ARI	29 TAU
31 AQU				31 CAN		31 LIB	31 SAG	30 CAP		30 ARI	31 TAU

JAN	FEB	MAR	APR	MAY	JUN	JUL	AUG	SEP	OCT	NOV	DEC
1 GEM	1 CAN	1 LEO	1 VIR	1 LIB	1 SAG	1 CAP	1 PIS	1 TAU	1 GEM	1 CAN	1 LEO
3 CAN	2 LEO	4 VIR	2 LIB	2 SCO	2 CAP	2 AQU	2 ARI	3 GEM	2 LEO	2 LEO	2 VIR
6 LEO	4 VIR	6 LIB	5 SCO	4 AQU	4 AQU	4 PIS	6 GEM	6 CAN	6 VIR	4 VIR	4 LIB
8 VIR	7 LIB	8 SCO	7 SAG	6 CAP	6 PIS	6 ARI	6 GEM	8 LEO	8 VIR	7 LIB	7 SCO
10 LIB	9 SCO	10 SAG	9 CAP	8 AQU	9 ARI	9 ARI	8 LEO	11 VIR	11 LIB	9 SCO	9 SAG
13 SCO	11 SAG	12 CAP	11 AQU	10 PIS	11 TAU	11 GEM	12 LEO	13 LIB	13 SCO	11 SAG	11 CAP
15 SAG	13 CAP	15 AQU	13 PIS	12 ARI	13 GEM	13 CAN	13 LIB	16 SCO	15 SAG	14 CAP	13 AQU
17 CAP	15 AQU	17 PIS	15 ARI	15 TAU	16 CAN	16 LEO	17 LIB	18 SAG	18 SAG	16 AQU	15 PIS
19 AQU	17 PIS	19 ARI	18 TAU	17 GEM	19 LEO	18 VIR	18 LIB	20 CAP	19 AQU	18 PIS	17 ARI
21 PIS	19 ARI	21 TAU	20 GEM	20 CAN	21 VIR	20 LIB	20 SCO	22 AQU	21 PIS	20 ARI	19 TAU
23 ARI	22 TAU	24 GEM	22 CAN	22 LEO	23 LIB	23 SCO	24 CAP	24 PIS	24 ARI	22 TAU	22 GEM
25 TAU	24 GEM	26 CAN	25 LEO	25 VIR	26 SCO	25 SAG	25 SAG	26 ARI	26 TAU	24 GEM	24 CAN
28 GEM	27 CAN	29 LEO	27 VIR	27 LIB	28 SAG	27 CAP	28 PIS	28 TAU	28 GEM	27 CAN	27 LEO
30 CAN	28 CAN	31 VIR	30 LIB	29 SCO	30 CAP	29 AQU	30 ARI	30 GEM	30 CAN	29 LEO	29 VIR
31 CAN				31 SAG		31 PIS	31 ARI		31 CAN	30 LEO	31 VIR

1970

JAN	FEB	MAR	APR	MAY	JUN	JUL	AUG	SEP	OCT	NOV	DEC
1 LIB	1 SAG	1 SAG	1 AQU	1 PIS	1 TAU	1 GEM	1 CAN	1 VIR	1 LIB	1 SCO	1 CAP
3 SCO	2 SAG	3 CAP	4 PIS	3 ARI	4 GEM	3 CAN	2 LEO	3 LIB	3 SCO	2 SAG	3 AQU
5 SAG	4 CAP	5 AQU	6 ARI	5 TAU	6 CAN	6 LEO	4 VIR	6 SCO	5 SAG	4 CAP	5 PIS
7 CAP	6 AQU	7 PIS	8 TAU	7 GEM	8 LEO	8 VIR	7 LIB	8 SAG	8 CAP	6 AQU	8 ARI
9 AQU	8 PIS	9 ARI	10 GEM	10 CAN	11 VIR	11 LIB	9 SCO	10 CAP	10 AQU	8 PIS	10 TAU
11 PIS	10 ARI	11 TAU	12 CAN	12 LEO	13 LIB	13 SCO	12 SAG	12 AQU	12 PIS	10 ARI	12 GEM
13 ARI	12 TAU	13 GEM	15 LEO	15 VIR	16 SCO	15 SAG	14 CAP	14 PIS	14 ARI	12 TAU	14 CAN
16 TAU	14 GEM	16 CAN	17 VIR	17 LIB	18 SAG	18 CAP	16 AQU	16 ARI	16 TAU	14 GEM	16 LEO
18 GEM	17 CAN	18 LEO	20 LIB	19 SCO	20 CAP	20 AQU	18 PIS	19 TAU	18 GEM	16 CAN	19 VIR
20 CAN	19 LEO	21 VIR	22 SCO	22 SAG	22 AQU	22 PIS	20 ARI	21 GEM	20 CAN	19 LEO	22 LIB
23 LEO	22 VIR	23 LIB	24 SAG	24 CAP	24 PIS	24 ARI	22 TAU	23 CAN	23 LEO	21 VIR	24 SCO
25 VIR	24 LIB	26 SCO	27 CAP	26 AQU	26 ARI	26 TAU	24 GEM	25 LEO	25 VIR	24 LIB	26 SAG
28 LIB	27 SCO	28 SAG	29 AQU	28 PIS	28 TAU	28 GEM	26 CAN	28 VIR	28 LIB	27 SCO	29 CAP
30 SCO	28 SCO	30 CAP	31 AQU	30 ARI	30 TAU	30 CAN	29 LEO	30 VIR	30 SCO	29 SAG	31 AQU
31 SCO		31 CAP		31 ARI		31 CAN	31 LEO		31 SCO	30 SAG	

1971

JAN	FEB	MAR	APR	MAY	JUN	JUL	AUG	SEP	OCT	NOV	DEC
1 AQU	1 ARI	1 TAU	1 GEM	1 CAN	1 VIR	1 LIB	1 SCO	1 CAP	1 AQU	1 ARI	1 TAU
2 PIS	2 TAU	4 GEM	2 CAN	2 LEO	3 LIB	3 SCO	2 SAG	3 AQU	2 PIS	3 TAU	2 GEM
4 ARI	4 GEM	6 CAN	5 LEO	4 VIR	6 SCO	5 SAG	5 CAP	5 PIS	4 ARI	5 GEM	4 CAN
6 TAU	7 CAN	8 LEO	7 VIR	6 LIB	8 SAG	8 CAP	6 AQU	7 ARI	6 TAU	7 CAN	6 LEO
8 GEM	9 LEO	11 VIR	10 LIB	9 SCO	11 CAP	10 AQU	9 PIS	9 TAU	8 GEM	9 LEO	9 VIR
10 CAN	12 VIR	13 LIB	12 SCO	12 SAG	13 AQU	12 PIS	11 ARI	11 GEM	10 CAN	11 VIR	11 LIB
13 LEO	14 LIB	16 SCO	15 SAG	14 CAP	15 PIS	14 ARI	13 TAU	13 CAN	13 LEO	14 LIB	14 SCO
VIR	17 SCO	18 SAG	17 CAP	16 AQU	17 ARI	16 TAU	15 GEM	15 LEO	15 VIR	16 SCO	16 SAG
18 LIB	19 SAG	21 CAP	19 AQU	18 PIS	19 TAU	18 GEM	17 CAN	18 VIR	18 LIB	19 SAG	19 CAP
20 SCO	21 CAP	23 AQU	21 PIS	21 ARI	21 GEM	21 CAN	19 LEO	20 LIB	20 SCO	21 CAP	21 PIS
23 SAG	23 AQU	25 PIS	23 ARI	23 TAU	23 CAN	23 LEO	22 VIR	23 SCO	23 SAG	24 AQU	23 ARI
25 CAP	26 PIS	27 ARI	25 TAU	25 GEM	26 LEO	25 VIR	24 LIB	25 SAG	25 CAP	26 PIS	25 ARI
27 AQU	27 ARI	29 TAU	27 GEM	27 CAN	28 VIR	28 LIB	27 SCO	28 CAP	28 AQU	28 ARI	27 TAU
29 PIS	28 ARI	31 GEM	29 CAN	29 LEO	30 VIR	30 SCO	29 SAG	30 AQU	30 PIS	30 TAU	30 GEM
31 ARI			30 CAN	31 LEO		31 SCO	31 SAG		31 PIS		31 GEM

1972

JAN	FEB	MAR	APR	MAY	JUN	JUL	AUG	SEP	OCT	NOV	DEC
1 CAN	1 LEO	1 VIR	1 SCO	1 SAG	1 CAP	1 AQU	1 ARI	1 GEM	1 CAN	1 VIR	1 LIB
3 LEO	2 VIR	2 LIB	4 SAG	3 CAP	2 AQU	2 PIS	2 TAU	3 CAN	2 LEO	3 LIB	3 SCO
5 VIR	4 LIB	5 SCO	6 CAP	6 AQU	4 PIS	4 ARI	4 GEM	5 LEO	4 VIR	5 SCO	5 SAG
8 LIB	6 SCO	7 SAG	8 AQU	8 PIS	6 ARI	6 TAU	6 CAN	7 VIR	7 LIB	8 SAG	8 CAP
10 SCO	9 SAG	10 CAP	11 PIS	10 ARI	8 TAU	8 GEM	8 LEO	9 LIB	9 SCO	10 CAP	10 AQU
13 SAG	11 CAP	12 AQU	13 ARI	12 TAU	10 GEM	10 CAN	11 VIR	12 SCO	12 SAG	13 AQU	13 PIS
15 CAP	14 AQU	14 PIS	15 TAU	14 GEM	13 CAN	12 LEO	13 LIB	14 SAG	14 CAP	15 PIS	15 ARI
17 AQU	16 PIS	16 ARI	17 GEM	16 CAN	15 LEO	14 VIR	16 SCO	17 CAP	16 AQU	18 ARI	17 TAU
19 PIS	18 ARI	18 TAU	19 CAN	18 LEO	17 VIR	16 LIB	18 SAG	19 AQU	19 PIS	20 TAU	19 GEM
22 ARI	20 TAU	20 GEM	21 LEO	21 VIR	19 LIB	19 SCO	21 CAP	21 PIS	21 ARI	22 GEM	21 CAN
24 TAU	22 GEM	22 CAN	23 VIR	23 LIB	22 SCO	22 SAG	23 AQU	24 ARI	23 TAU	24 CAN	23 LEO
26 GEM	24 CAN	25 LEO	26 LIB	26 SCO	24 SAG	24 CAP	25 PIS	26 TAU	25 GEM	26 LEO	25 VIR
28 CAN	27 LEO	27 VIR	28 SCO	28 SAG	27 CAP	27 AQU	27 ARI	28 GEM	27 CAN	28 VIR	27 LIB
30 LEO	29 VIR	30 LIB	30 SCO	31 CAP	29 AQU	29 PIS	29 TAU	30 CAN	29 LEO	30 LIB	30 SCO
31 LEO		31 LIB			30 AQU	31 ARI	31 GEM		31 LEO		31 SCO

1973

JAN	FEB	MAR	APR	MAY	JUN	JUL	AUG	SEP	OCT	NOV	DEC
1 SAG	1 CAP	1 CAP	1 PIS	1 ARI	1 GEM	1 CAN	1 VIR	1 LIB	1 SAG	1 CAP	1 AQU
4 CAP	3 AQU	2 AQU	3 ARI	3 TAU	3 CAN	2 LEO	3 LIB	2 SCO	4 CAP	3 AQU	3 PIS
6 AQU	5 PIS	4 PIS	5 TAU	5 GEM	5 LEO	4 VIR	5 SCO	4 SAG	7 AQU	5 PIS	5 ARI
9 PIS	7 ARI	7 ARI	7 GEM	7 CAN	7 VIR	7 LIB	8 SAG	7 CAP	9 PIS	8 ARI	7 TAU
11 ARI	10 TAU	9 TAU	9 CAN	9 LEO	9 LIB	9 SCO	10 CAP	9 AQU	11 ARI	10 TAU	9 GEM
13 TAU	12 GEM	11 GEM	11 LEO	11 VIR	12 SCO	12 SAG	13 AQU	12 PIS	13 TAU	12 GEM	11 CAN
15 GEM	14 CAN	13 CAN	14 VIR	13 LIB	14 SAG	15 CAP	15 PIS	14 ARI	16 GEM	14 CAN	13 LEO
17 CAN	16 LEO	15 LEO	16 LIB	16 SCO	17 CAP	17 AQU	18 ARI	16 TAU	18 CAN	16 LEO	15 VIR
19 LEO	18 VIR	17 VIR	18 SCO	18 SAG	19 AQU	19 PIS	20 TAU	18 GEM	20 LEO	18 VIR	18 LIB
22 VIR	20 LIB	20 LIB	21 SAG	21 CAP	21 W	21 ARI	22 GEM	20 CAN	22 VIR	20 LIB	20 SCO
24 LIB	23 SCO	22 SCO	23 CAP	23 AQU	23 ARI	24 TAU	24 CAN	23 LEO	24 LIB	23 SCO	22 SAG
26 SCO	25 SAG	24 SAG	26 AQU	26 PIS	26 TAU	26 GEM	26 LEO	25 VIR	26 SCO	25 SAG	25 CAP
29 SAG	28 CAP	27 CAP	28 PIS	28 ARI	28 GEM	28 CAN	28 VIR	27 LIB	29 SAG	28 CAP	27 AQU
31 CAP		29 AQU	30 ARI	30 TAU	30 CAN	30 LEO	30 LIB	29 SCO	31 CAP	30 AQU	30 PIS
		31 AQU		31 TAU		31 LEO	31 LIB	30 SCO			31 PIS

1974

JAN	FEB	MAR	APR	MAY	JUN	JUL	AUG	SEP	OCT	NOV	DEC
1 ARI	1 TAU	1 GEM	1 CAN	1 VIR	1 LIB	1 CAP	1 CAP	1 AQU	1 ARI	1 TAU	1 GEM
4 TAU	2 GEM	4 CAN	2 LEO	3 LIB	3 SCO	2 SAG	3 AQU	2 PIS	4 TAU	2 GEM	2 CAN
6 GEM	4 CAN	6 LEO	4 VIR	6 SCO	5 SAG	4 CAP	5 PIS	4 ARI	6 GEM	4 CAN	4 LEO
8 CAN	6 LEO	8 VIR	6 LIB	8 SAG	7 CAP	7 AQU	8 ARI	6 TAU	8 CAN	7 LEO	6 VIR
10 LEO	8 VIR	10 LIB	8 SCO	10 CAP	9 AQU	9 PIS	10 TAU	9 GEM	10 LEO	9 VIR	8 LIB
12 VIR	10 LIB	12 SCO	11 SAG	13 AQU	12 PIS	12 ARI	13 GEM	11 CAN	12 VIR	11 LIB	10 SCO
14 LIB	13 SCO	14 SAG	13 CAP	15 PIS	14 ARI	14 TAU	15 CAN	13 LEO	15 LIB	13 SCO	13 SAG
16 SCO	15 SAG	16 CAP	16 AQU	18 ARI	17 TAU	16 GEM	17 LEO	15 VIR	17 SCO	15 SAG	15 CAP
19 SAG	17 CAP	19 AQU	18 PIS	20 TAU	19 GEM	18 CAN	19 VIR	17 LIB	19 SAG	18 CAP	17 AQU
21 CAP	20 AQU	22 PIS	21 ARI	22 GEM	21 CAN	20 LEO	21 LIB	19 SCO	21 CAP	20 AQU	20 PIS
24 AQU	22 PIS	24 ARI	23 TAU	24 CAN	23 LEO	22 VIR	23 SCO	21 SAG	24 AQU	23 PIS	22 ARI
26 PIS	25 ARI	26 TAU	25 GEM	26 LEO	25 VIR	24 LIB	25 SAG	24 CAP	26 PIS	25 ARI	25 TAU
29 ARI	27 TAU	29 GEM	27 CAN	29 VIR	27 LIB	26 SCO	28 CAP	26 AQU	29 ARI	27 TAU	27 GEM
31 TAU	28 TAU	31 CAN	29 LEO	31 LIB	29 SCO	29 SAG	30 AQU	29 PIS	31 TAU	30 GEM	29 CAN
			30 LEO		30 SCO	31 CAP	31 AQU	30 PIS			30 LEO

1975

JAN	FEB	MAR	APR	MAY	JUN	JUL	AUG	SEP	OCT	NOV	DEC
1 LEO	1 LIB	1 LIB	1 SAG	1 CAP	1 AQU	1 ARI	1 TAU	1 CAN	1 LEO	1 LIB	1 SCO
2 VIR	3 SCO	2 SCO	3 CAP	3 AQU	2 PIS	4 TAU	3 GEM	3 LEO	3 VIR	3 SCO	3 SAG
4 LIB	5 SAG	4 SAG	5 AQU	5 PIS	4 ARI	6 GEM	5 CAN	5 VIR	5 LIB	5 SAG	5 CAP
6 SCO	7 CAP	7 CAP	8 PIS	8 ARI	7 TAU	9 CAN	7 LEO	7 LIB	7 SCO	8 CAP	7 AQU
9 SAG	10 AQU	9 AQU	10 ARI	10 GEM	9 GEM	11 LEO	9 VIR	9 SCO	9 SAG	10 AQU	10 PIS
11 CAP	12 PIS	13 TAU	13 TAU	13 CAN	11 CAN	13 VIR	11 LIB	11 SAG	11 CAP	12 PIS	12 ARI
14 AQU	15 ARI	14 ARI	15 GEM	15 LEO	13 LEO	15 LIB	13 SCO	14 CAP	14 AQU	15 ARI	15 TAU
16 PIS	17 TAU	17 TAU	18 CAN	17 VIR	15 VIR	17 SCO	15 SAG	16 AQU	16 PIS	17 TAU	17 GEM
19 ARI	20 GEM	19 GEM	20 LEO	19 LIB	17 LIB	19 SAG	18 CAP	19 PIS	19 ARI	20 GEM	19 CAN
21 TAU	22 CAN	21 CAN	22 VIR	21 SCO	20 SCO	21 CAP	20 AQU	21 ARI	21 TAU	22 CAN	22 LEO
23 GEM	24 LEO	24 LEO	24 LIB	23 SAG	22 SAG	24 AQU	22 PIS	24 TAU	23 GEM	24 LEO	24 VIR
26 CAN	26 VIR	26 VIR	26 SCO	25 CAP	24 CAP	26 PIS	25 ARI	26 GEM	26 CAN	27 VIR	26 LIB
28 LEO	28 LIB	28 LIB	28 SAG	28 AQU	26 AQU	29 ARI	28 TAU	29 CAN	28 LEO	29 LIB	28 SCO
30 VIR		30 SCO	30 CAP	30 AQU	29 PIS	31 TAU	30 GEM	30 CAN	30 VIR	30 LIB	30 SAG
31 VIR		31 SCO		31 AQU	30 PIS		31 GEM		31 VIR		31 SAG

1976

JAN	FEB	MAR	APR	MAY	JUN	JUL	AUG	SEP	OCT	NOV	DEC
1 CAP	1 AQU	1 PIS	1 ARI	1 TAU	1 CAN	1 LEO	1 LIB	1 SAG	1 CAP	1 PIS	1 ARI
4 AQU	2 PIS	3 ARI	2 TAU	2 GEM	3 LEO	2 VIR	3 SCO	3 CAP	3 AQU	4 ARI	3 TAU
6 PIS	5 ARI	6 TAU	4 GEM	4 CAN	5 VIR	4 LIB	5 SAG	5 PIS	5 PIS	6 TAU	6 GEM
8 ARI	7 TAU	8 GEM	7 CAN	6 LEO	7 LIB	6 SCO	7 CAP	8 PIS	7 ARI	9 GEM	8 CAN
11 TAU	10 GEM	11 CAN	9 LEO	9 VIR	9 SCO	9 SAG	9 AQU	10 ARI	10 TAU	11 CAN	11 LEO
13 GEM	12 CAN	13 LEO	11 VIR	11 LIB	11 SAG	11 CAP	11 PIS	13 TAU	13 GEM	13 LEO	13 VIR
16 CAN	14 LEO	15 VIR	13 LIB	13 SCO	13 CAP	13 AQU	14 ARI	15 GEM	15 CAN	16 VIR	15 LIB
18 LEO	17 VIR	17 LIB	15 SCO	15 SAG	15 AQU	15 PIS	16 TAU	17 CAN	17 LEO	18 LIB	18 SCO
20 VIR	19 LIB	19 SCO	17 SAG	17 CAP	18 PIS	18 ARI	19 GEM	20 LEO	20 VIR	20 SCO	20 SAG
22 LIB	21 SCO	21 SAG	19 CAP	19 AQU	20 ARI	20 TAU	21 CAN	22 VIR	22 LIB	22 SAG	22 CAP
24 SCO	23 SAG	23 CAP	22 AQU	21 PIS	23 TAU	23 GEM	24 LEO	24 LIB	24 SCO	24 CAP	24 AQU
26 SAG	25 CAP	25 AQU	24 PIS	24 ARI	25 GEM	25 CAN	26 VIR	26 SCO	26 SAG	26 AQU	26 PIS
29 CAP	27 AQU	28 PIS	27 ARI	26 TAU	28 CAN	27 LEO	28 LIB	28 SAG	28 CAP	29 PIS	28 ARI
31 AQU	29 AQU	30 ARI	29 TAU	29 GEM	30 LEO	29 VIR	30 SCO	30 CAP	30 AQU	30 PIS	31 TAU
		31 ARI	30 TAU	31 CAN		31 VIR	31 SCO		31 AQU		

1977

JAN	FEB	MAR	APR	MAY	JUN	JUL	AUG	SEP	OCT	NOV	DEC
1 TAU	1 CAN	1 CAN	1 LEO	1 LIB	1 SCO	1 CAP	1 AQU	1 ARI	1 TAU	1 CAN	1 LEO
2 GEM	4 LEO	3 LEO	2 VIR	3 SCO	2 SAG	3 AQU	2 PIS	3 TAU	2 GEM	4 LEO	3 VIR
5 CAN	6 VIR	5 VIR	4 LIB	5 SAG	4 CAP	5 PIS	4 ARI	5 GEM	5 CAN	6 VIR	6 LIB
7 LEO	8 LIB	7 LIB	6 SCO	7 CAP	6 AQU	7 ARI	6 TAU	7 CAN	7 LEO	8 LIB	8 SCO
9 VIR	10 SCO	9 SCO	8 SAG	9 AQU	8 PIS	10 TAU	9 GEM	10 LEO	10 VIR	11 SCO	10 SAG
12 LIB	12 SAG	11 SAG	10 CAP	11 PIS	10 ARI	12 GEM	11 CAN	12 VIR	12 LIB	13 SAG	12 CAP
14 SCO	14 CAP	14 CAP	12 AQU	14 ARI	13 TAU	15 CAN	14 LEO	15 LIB	14 SCO	15 CAP	14 AQU
16 SAG	16 AQU	16 AQU	14 PIS	16 TAU	15 GEM	17 LEO	16 VIR	17 SCO	16 SAG	17 AQU	16 PIS
18 CAP	19 PIS	18 PIS	17 ARI	19 GEM	18 CAN	20 VIR	18 LIB	19 SAG	18 CAP	19 PIS	18 ARI
20 AQU	21 ARI	20 ARI	19 TAU	21 CAN	20 LEO	22 LIB	20 SCO	21 CAP	20 AQU	21 ARI	21 TAU
22 PIS	23 TAU	23 TAU	21 GEM	24 LEO	23 VIR	24 SCO	22 SAG	23 AQU	23 PIS	23 TAU	23 GEM
25 ARI	26 GEM	25 GEM	24 CAN	26 VIR	25 LIB	26 SAG	25 CAP	25 PIS	25 ARI	25 GEM	26 CAN
27 TAU	28 GEM	28 CAN	27 LEO	29 LIB	27 SCO	28 CAP	27 AQU	27 ARI	27 TAU	28 CAN	28 LEO
30 GEM		30 LEO	29 VIR	31 SCO	29 SAG	30 AQU	29 PIS	30 TAU	30 GEM	30 CAN	31 VIR
31 GEM		31 LEO	30 VIR		30 SAG	31 AQU	31 ARI		31 GEM		

1978

JAN	FEB	MAR	APR	MAY	JUN	JUL	AUG	SEP	OCT	NOV	DEC
1 VIR	1 SCO	1 SCO	1 CAP	1 AQU	1 ARI	1 TAU	1 CAN	1 LEO	1 VIR	1 SCO	1 SAG
2 LIB	2 SAG	2 SAG	3 AQU	2 PIS	3 TAU	2 GEM	3 LEO	2 VIR	2 LIB	3 SAG	2 CAP
4 SCO	5 CAP	4 CAP	5 PIS	4 ARI	5 GEM	5 CAN	6 VIR	5 LIB	4 SCO	5 CAP	4 AQU
6 SAG	7 AQU	6 AQU	7 ARI	6 TAU	7 CAN	7 LEO	9 LIB	7 SCO	7 SAG	7 AQU	6 PIS
8 CAP	9 PIS	8 PIS	9 TAU	9 GEM	10 LEO	10 VIR	11 SCO	9 SAG	9 CAP	9 PIS	9 ARI
10 AQU	11 ARI	10 ARI	11 GEM	11 CAN	13 VIR	12 LIB	13 SAG	11 CAP	11 AQU	11 ARI	11 TAU
12 PIS	13 TAU	13 TAU	14 CAN	14 LEO	15 LIB	15 SCO	15 CAP	14 AQU	13 PIS	14 TAU	13 GEM
15 ARI	16 GEM	15 GEM	16 LEO	16 VIR	18 SCO	17 SAG	17 AQU	16 PIS	15 ARI	16 GEM	16 CAN
17 TAU	18 CAN	18 CAN	19 VIR	19 LIB	20 SAG	19 CAP	19 PIS	18 ARI	17 TAU	18 CAN	18 LEO
19 GEM	21 LEO	20 LEO	21 LIB	21 SCO	22 CAP	21 AQU	21 ARI	20 TAU	20 GEM	21 LEO	21 VIR
22 CAN	23 VIR	23 VIR	23 SCO	23 SAG	24 AQU	23 PIS	24 TAU	22 GEM	22 CAN	23 VIR	23 LIB
25 LEO	26 LIB	25 LIB	26 SAG	25 CAP	26 PIS	25 ARI	26 GEM	25 CAN	25 LEO	26 LIB	26 SCO
27 VIR	28 SCO	27 SCO	28 CAP	27 AQU	28 ARI	28 TAU	28 CAN	27 LEO	27 VIR	28 SCO	28 SAG
29 LIB		29 SAG	30 AQU	29 PIS	30 TAU	30 GEM	31 LEO	30 VIR	29 LIB	30 SAG	30 CAP
31 LIB		31 CAP				31 GEM			31 LIB		31 CAP

1979

JAN	FEB	MAR	APR	MAY	JUN	JUL	AUG	SEP	OCT	NOV	DEC
1 AQU	1 ARI	1 ARI	1 GEM	1 CAN	1 LEO	1 VIR	1 SCO	1 SAG	1 AQU	1 PIS	1 TAU
3 PIS	3 TAU	4 CAN	4 LEO	2 LIB	2 LIB	3 SAG	2 CAP	2 CAP	4 PIS	2 ARI	3 GEM
5 ARI	6 GEM	5 GEM	6 LEO	5 LIB	5 SCO	5 SCO	6 CAP	4 AQU	6 ARI	4 TAU	6 CAN
7 TAU	8 CAN	7 CAN	9 VIR	6 VIR	7 SCO	7 SAG	6 PIS	6 PIS	8 TAU	6 GEM	8 LEO
9 GEM	11 LEO	10 LEO	11 LIB	11 SCO	9 SAG	9 CAP	10 PIS	8 ARI	10 GEM	8 CAN	10 VIR
12 CAN	13 VIR	12 VIR	14 SCO	13 SAG	12 CAP	11 AQU	12 ARI	11 TAU	12 CAN	11 LEO	13 LIB
14 LEO	16 LIB	15 LIB	16 SAG	14 CAP	14 AQU	13 PIS	14 TAU	12 GEM	14 LEO	13 VIR	16 SCO
17 VIR	18 SCO	17 SCO	13 CAP	18 AQU	16 PIS	15 ARI	16 GEM	15 CAN	17 VIR	16 LIB	18 SAG
19 LIB	20 SAG	20 SAG	20 AQU	20 PIS	18 ARI	17 TAU	18 CAN	17 VIR	19 LIB	18 SCO	20 CAP
22 SCO	23 CAP	22 CAP	22 PIS	22 ARI	20 TAU	20 GEM	21 LEO	20 VIR	22 SCO	20 SAG	22 AQU
24 SAG	25 AQU	24 AQU	24 ARI	24 TAU	22 GEM	22 CAN	23 VIR	22 LIB	24 SAG	23 CAP	24 PIS
26 CAP	27 PIS	26 PIS	27 TAU	26 GEM	25 CAN	25 LEO	26 LIB	25 SCO	27 CAP	25 AQU	26 ARI
28 AQU	28 PIS	28 ARI	29 GEM	28 CAN	27 VIR	27 VIR	28 SCO	27 CAP	29 AQU	27 PIS	29 TAU
30 PIS		30 TAU		31 LEO		30 LIB	30 SAG	29 CAP	31 PIS	29 ARI	31 GEM
31 PIS		31 TAU				31 LIB		30 CAP		30 ARI	

1980

JAN 1 GEM, 2 CAN, 4 LEO, 7 VIR, 9 LIB, 12 SCO, 14 SAG, 16 CAP, 19 AQU, 21 PIS, 23 ARI, 25 TAU, 27 GEM, 29 CAN, 31 CAN
FEB 1 LEO, 3 VIR, 6 LIB, 8 SCO, 11 SAG, 13 CAP, 15 AQU, 17 PIS, 19 ARI, 21 TAU, 23 GEM, 26 CAN, 28 LEO, 29 LEO
MAR 1 VIR, 3 LIB, 6 SCO, 9 SAG, 11 CAP, 13 AQU, 16 PIS, 18 ARI, 20 TAU, 22 GEM, 24 CAN, 26 LEO, 29 VIR, 31 LIB
APR 1 LIB, 3 SCO, 5 SAG, 8 CAP, 10 AQU, 12 PIS, 14 ARI, 16 TAU, 18 GEM, 20 CAN, 22 LEO, 25 VIR, 27 LIB, 30 SCO
MAY 1 SCO, 2 SAG, 5 CAP, 7 AQU, 9 PIS, 11 ARI, 13 TAU, 15 GEM, 18 CAN, 20 LEO, 22 VIR, 25 LIB, 28 SCO, 30 SAG, 31 SAG
JUN 1 CAP, 3 AQU, 5 PIS, 8 ARI, 10 TAU, 12 GEM, 14 CAN, 16 LEO, 18 VIR, 21 LIB, 24 SCO, 26 CAP, 28 AQU, 30 CAP
JUL 1 AQU, 3 PIS, 5 ARI, 7 TAU, 9 GEM, 11 CAN, 14 LEO, 16 VIR, 18 LIB, 21 SCO, 23 SAG, 25 CAP, 28 AQU, 30 PIS, 31 PIS
AUG 1 ARI, 3 TAU, 5 GEM, 8 CAN, 10 LEO, 12 VIR, 14 LIB, 17 SCO, 20 SAG, 22 CAP, 24 AQU, 27 TAU, 28 ARI, 30 TAU, 31 TAU
SEP 1 TAU, 2 GEM, 4 CAN, 6 LEO, 8 VIR, 11 LIB, 13 SCO, 16 SAG, 18 CAP, 21 AQU, 23 PIS, 25 ARI, 27 TAU, 29 GEM, 30 GEM
OCT 1 CAN, 3 LEO, 6 VIR, 8 LIB, 11 SCO, 13 SAG, 16 CAP, 18 AQU, 20 PIS, 22 ARI, 24 TAU, 26 GEM, 28 CAN, 29 GEM
NOV 1 LEO, 2 VIR, 6 LIB, 7 SCO, 10 SAG, 12 CAP, 14 AQU, 17 PIS, 19 ARI, 21 TAU, 23 GEM, 25 CAN, 27 LEO, 29 VIR, 30 VIR
DEC 1 LIB, 2 LIB, 4 SCO, 7 SAG, 9 CAP, 12 AQU, 14 PIS, 16 ARI, 18 TAU, 20 GEM, 22 CAN, 24 LEO, 27 VIR, 29 LIB, 31 LIB

1981

JAN 1 SCO, 3 SAG, 6 CAP, 8 AQU, 10 PIS, 12 ARI, 14 TAU, 17 GEM, 19 CAN, 21 LEO, 23 VIR, 25 LIB, 28 SCO, 31 SAG
FEB 1 SAG, 2 CAP, 4 AQU, 6 PIS, 9 ARI, 11 TAU, 13 GEM, 15 CAN, 17 LEO, 19 VIR, 22 LIB, 24 SCO, 27 SAG, 28 SAG
MAR 1 CAP, 2 AQU, 6 PIS, 8 ARI, 10 TAU, 12 GEM, 14 CAN, 16 LEO, 19 VIR, 21 LIB, 24 SCO, 26 SAG, 29 CAP, 31 AQU
APR 1 AQU, 2 PIS, 4 ARI, 6 TAU, 9 GEM, 11 CAN, 13 LEO, 15 VIR, 17 LIB, 20 SCO, 22 SAG, 25 CAP, 27 AQU, 30 PIS
MAY 1 PIS, 2 ARI, 4 TAU, 6 GEM, 8 CAN, 10 LEO, 13 VIR, 15 LIB, 17 SCO, 20 SAG, 22 CAP, 25 AQU, 27 PIS, 29 ARI, 31 TAU
JUN 1 TAU, 2 CAN, 4 CAN, 6 LEO, 8 VIR, 11 LIB, 13 SCO, 16 SAG, 18 CAP, 21 AQU, 23 PIS, 25 ARI, 27 TAU, 30 GEM
JUL 1 GEM, 2 CAN, 4 LEO, 6 VIR, 8 LIB, 11 SCO, 13 SAG, 16 CAP, 18 AQU, 20 PIS, 23 ARI, 25 TAU, 27 GEM, 29 CAN, 31 LEO
AUG 1 LEO, 2 VIR, 5 LIB, 7 SCO, 10 SAG, 12 CAP, 15 AQU, 17 PIS, 19 ARI, 21 TAU, 23 GEM, 25 CAN, 27 LEO, 30 VIR, 31 VIR
SEP 1 LIB, 3 SCO, 6 SAG, 8 CAP, 11 AQU, 13 PIS, 15 ARI, 17 TAU, 19 GEM, 21 CAN, 24 LEO, 26 VIR, 28 LIB, 30 LIB
OCT 1 SCO, 3 SAG, 6 CAP, 8 AQU, 11 PIS, 13 ARI, 15 TAU, 17 GEM, 19 CAN, 21 LEO, 23 VIR, 26 LIB, 28 SCO, 30 SAG, 31 SAG
NOV 1 SAG, 2 CAP, 5 AQU, 7 PIS, 9 ARI, 11 TAU, 13 GEM, 15 CAN, 17 LEO, 19 VIR, 22 LIB, 24 SCO, 27 SAG, 29 CAP, 30 CAP
DEC 1 AQU, 4 PIS, 6 ARI, 9 TAU, 11 GEM, 13 CAN, 15 LEO, 17 VIR, 19 LIB, 21 SCO, 24 SAG, 26 CAP, 29 AQU, 31 PIS

1982

JAN 1 PIS, 3 ARI, 5 TAU, 7 GEM, 9 CAN, 11 LEO, 13 VIR, 15 LIB, 18 SCO, 20 SAG, 23 CAP, 25 AQU, 28 PIS, 30 ARI, 31 ARI
FEB 1 TAU, 3 GEM, 5 CAN, 7 LEO, 10 VIR, 12 LIB, 14 SCO, 17 SAG, 19 CAP, 22 AQU, 24 PIS, 26 ARI, 28 TAU
MAR 1 TAU, 3 GEM, 5 CAN, 7 LEO, 9 VIR, 11 LIB, 14 SCO, 16 SAG, 19 CAP, 21 AQU, 23 PIS, 26 ARI, 28 TAU, 30 GEM, 31 GEM
APR 1 CAN, 3 LEO, 5 VIR, 8 LIB, 10 SCO, 12 SAG, 15 CAP, 17 AQU, 20 PIS, 22 ARI, 24 TAU, 26 GEM, 28 CAN, 30 LEO
MAY 1 LEO, 2 VIR, 5 LIB, 7 SCO, 10 SAG, 12 CAP, 15 AQU, 17 PIS, 19 ARI, 22 TAU, 24 GEM, 26 CAN, 28 LEO, 30 VIR, 31 VIR
JUN 1 LIB, 3 SCO, 6 SAG, 8 CAP, 11 AQU, 13 PIS, 16 ARI, 18 TAU, 20 GEM, 22 CAN, 24 LEO, 26 VIR, 28 LIB, 30 LIB
JUL 1 SCO, 3 SAG, 6 CAP, 8 AQU, 11 PIS, 13 ARI, 15 TAU, 17 GEM, 19 CAN, 21 LEO, 23 VIR, 26 LIB, 28 SCO, 30 SAG, 31 SAG
AUG 1 SAG, 2 CAP, 4 AQU, 6 PIS, 7 PIS, 9 ARI, 12 TAU, 14 GEM, 16 CAN, 18 LEO, 20 VIR, 22 LIB, 24 SCO, 27 SAG, 29 CAP, 31 CAP
SEP 1 AQU, 3 PIS, 5 ARI, 6 ARI, 8 TAU, 10 GEM, 12 CAN, 14 LEO, 16 VIR, 18 LIB, 21 SCO, 23 SAG, 26 CAP, 28 AQU, 30 AQU
OCT 1 PIS, 3 ARI, 5 TAU, 7 GEM, 9 CAN, 11 LEO, 14 VIR, 16 LIB, 18 SCO, 20 SAG, 23 CAP, 25 AQU, 28 PIS, 30 ARI, 31 ARI
NOV 1 TAU, 4 GEM, 6 CAN, 8 LEO, 10 VIR, 12 LIB, 14 SCO, 17 SAG, 19 CAP, 22 AQU, 24 PIS, 27 ARI, 29 TAU, 30 TAU
DEC 1 GEM, 3 CAN, 5 LEO, 7 VIR, 9 LIB, 12 SCO, 14 SAG, 17 CAP, 19 AQU, 22 PIS, 24 ARI, 26 TAU, 28 GEM, 30 CAN, 31 CAN

1983

JAN 2 VIR, 4 LIB, 7 SCO, 9 SAG, 12 CAP, 14 AQU, 17 PIS, 19 ARI, 21 TAU, 24 GEM, 26 CAN, 28 LEO, 30 VIR
FEB 1 LIB, 3 SCO, 5 SAG, 8 CAP, 10 AQU, 13 PIS, 15 ARI, 18 TAU, 20 GEM, 22 CAN, 24 LEO, 26 VIR, 28 LIB
MAR 2 SCO, 5 SAG, 7 CAP, 10 AQU, 12 PIS, 15 ARI, 17 TAU, 19 GEM, 21 CAN, 23 LEO, 26 VIR, 28 LIB, 30 SCO
APR 1 SAG, 3 CAP, 6 AQU, 8 PIS, 11 ARI, 13 TAU, 15 GEM, 18 CAN, 20 LEO, 22 VIR, 24 LIB, 26 SCO, 28 SAG
MAY 1 CAP, 3 AQU, 6 PIS, 8 ARI, 11 TAU, 13 GEM, 15 CAN, 17 LEO, 19 VIR, 21 LIB, 23 SCO, 26 SAG, 28 CAP, 31 AQU
JUN 2 PIS, 5 ARI, 7 TAU, 9 GEM, 11 CAN, 13 LEO, 15 VIR, 17 LIB, 20 SCO, 22 SAG, 24 CAP, 27 AQU, 29 PIS
JUL 2 ARI, 4 TAU, 7 GEM, 9 CAN, 11 LEO, 13 VIR, 15 LIB, 17 SCO, 19 SAG, 22 CAP, 24 AQU, 27 PIS, 29 ARI
AUG 1 TAU, 3 GEM, 5 CAN, 7 LEO, 9 VIR, 11 LIB, 13 SCO, 15 SAG, 18 CAP, 20 AQU, 23 PIS, 25 ARI, 28 TAU, 30 GEM
SEP 1 CAN, 3 LEO, 5 VIR, 7 LIB, 10 SCO, 12 SAG, 14 CAP, 17 AQU, 19 PIS, 22 ARI, 24 TAU, 26 GEM, 29 CAN
OCT 1 LEO, 3 VIR, 5 LIB, 7 SCO, 9 SAG, 12 CAP, 14 AQU, 16 PIS, 19 ARI, 21 TAU, 24 GEM, 26 CAN, 28 LEO, 30 VIR
NOV 1 LIB, 3 SCO, 6 SAG, 8 CAP, 10 AQU, 13 PIS, 15 ARI, 18 TAU, 20 GEM, 22 CAN, 24 LEO, 26 VIR, 29 LIB
DEC 1 SCO, 3 SAG, 5 CAP, 8 AQU, 10 PIS, 13 ARI, 15 TAU, 17 GEM, 20 CAN, 22 LEO, 24 VIR, 26 LIB, 28 SCO, 30 SAG

1984

JAN 2 CAP, 4 AQU, 6 PIS, 9 ARI, 11 TAU, 14 GEM, 16 CAN, 18 LEO, 20 VIR, 22 LIB, 24 SCO, 26 SAG, 29 CAP, 31 AQU
FEB 3 PIS, 5 ARI, 8 TAU, 10 GEM, 12 CAN, 15 LEO, 17 VIR, 19 LIB, 21 SCO, 23 SAG, 25 CAP, 28 AQU
MAR 1 PIS, 4 ARI, 6 TAU, 8 GEM, 11 CAN, 13 LEO, 15 VIR, 17 LIB, 19 SCO, 21 SAG, 23 CAP, 26 AQU, 28 PIS, 31 ARI
APR 2 TAU, 5 GEM, 7 CAN, 9 VIR, 11 VIR, 13 LIB, 15 SCO, 17 SAG, 20 CAP, 22 AQU, 25 PIS, 27 ARI, 30 TAU
MAY 2 GEM, 4 CAN, 6 LEO, 8 VIR, 11 LIB, 13 SCO, 15 SAG, 17 CAP, 19 AQU, 22 PIS, 24 ARI, 27 TAU, 29 GEM
JUN 1 CAN, 3 LEO, 5 VIR, 7 LIB, 9 SCO, 11 SAG, 13 CAP, 16 AQU, 18 PIS, 21 ARI, 23 TAU, 26 GEM, 28 CAN, 30 LEO
JUL 2 VIR, 4 LIB, 6 SCO, 9 SAG, 11 CAP, 13 AQU, 16 PIS, 18 ARI, 21 TAU, 23 GEM, 25 CAN, 27 LEO, 29 VIR, 31 LIB
AUG 3 SCO, 5 SAG, 7 CAP, 9 AQU, 12 PIS, 14 ARI, 17 TAU, 19 GEM, 22 CAN, 24 LEO, 26 VIR, 28 LIB, 30 SCO
SEP 1 SAG, 3 CAP, 5 AQU, 8 PIS, 11 ARI, 13 TAU, 16 GEM, 18 CAN, 20 LEO, 22 VIR, 24 LIB, 26 SCO, 28 SAG, 30 CAP
OCT 1 CAP, 3 AQU, 5 PIS, 8 ARI, 10 TAU, 13 GEM, 15 CAN, 18 LEO, 20 VIR, 22 LIB, 24 SCO, 26 SAG, 28 CAP, 30 AQU
NOV 2 PIS, 4 ARI, 7 TAU, 9 GEM, 12 CAN, 14 LEO, 16 VIR, 18 LIB, 20 SCO, 22 SAG, 24 CAP, 27 AQU, 29 PIS
DEC 1 ARI, 4 TAU, 6 GEM, 9 CAN, 11 LEO, 13 VIR, 15 LIB, 17 SCO, 20 SAG, 22 CAP, 24 AQU, 26 PIS, 29 ARI, 31 TAU

1985

JAN	FEB	MAR	APR	MAY	JUN	JUL	AUG	SEP	OCT	NOV	DEC
3 GEM	2 CAN	1 CAN	2 VIR	1 LIB	2 SAG	1 CAP	2 PIS	1 ARI	3 GEM	2 CAN	1 LEO
5 CAN	4 LEO	3 LEO	4 LIB	3 SCO	4 CAP	3 AQU	4 ARI	3 TAU	5 CAN	4 LEO	4 VIR
7 LEO	6 VIR	5 VIR	6 SCO	5 SAG	6 AQU	5 PIS	7 TAU	6 GEM	8 LEO	6 VIR	6 LIB
9 VIR	8 LIB	7 LIB	8 SAG	7 CAP	8 PIS	7 ARI	9 GEM	8 CAN	10 VIR	9 LIB	8 SCO
12 LIB	10 SCO	9 SCO	10 CAP	9 AQU	11 ARI	10 TAU	11 CAN	10 LEO	12 LIB	11 SCO	10 SAG
14 SCO	12 SAG	11 SAG	12 AQU	12 PIS	13 TAU	13 GEM	14 LEO	13 VIR	14 SCO	13 SAG	12 CAP
16 SAG	14 CAP	14 CAP	14 PIS	14 ARI	16 GEM	15 CAN	16 VIR	15 LIB	16 SAG	15 CAP	14 AQU
18 CAP	17 AQU	16 AQU	17 ARI	17 TAU	18 CAN	18 LEO	18 LIB	17 SCO	18 CAP	17 AQU	16 PIS
20 AQU	19 PIS	19 PIS	20 TAU	19 GEM	20 LEO	20 VIR	20 SCO	19 SAG	20 AQU	19 PIS	19 ARI
23 PIS	21 ARI	21 ARI	22 GEM	22 CAN	23 VIR	22 LIB	22 SAG	21 CAP	23 PIS	21 ARI	21 TAU
25 ARI	24 TAU	23 TAU	25 CAN	24 LEO	25 LIB	24 SCO	25 CAP	23 AQU	25 ARI	24 TAU	24 GEM
28 TAU	27 GEM	26 GEM	27 LEO	26 VIR	27 SCO	26 SAG	27 AQU	25 PIS	28 TAU	26 GEM	26 CAN
30 GEM		28 CAN	29 VIR	29 LIB	29 SAG	28 CAP	29 PIS	28 ARI	30 TAU	29 CAN	29 LEO
		31 LEO		31 SCO		31 AQU		30 TAU			31 VIR

1986

JAN	FEB	MAR	APR	MAY	JUN	JUL	AUG	SEP	OCT	NOV	DEC
2 LIB	1 SCO	2 SAG	2 AQU	2 PIS	3 TAU	3 GEM	2 CAN	3 VIR	2 LIB	1 SCO	2 CAP
4 SCO	3 SAG	4 CAP	5 PIS	4 ARI	5 GEM	5 CAN	4 LEO	5 LIB	5 SCO	3 SAG	4 AQU
6 SAG	5 CAP	6 AQU	7 ARI	6 TAU	8 CAN	8 LEO	6 VIR	7 SCO	7 SAG	5 CAP	6 PIS
8 CAP	7 AQU	8 PIS	9 TAU	9 GEM	10 LEO	10 VIR	9 LIB	9 SAG	9 CAP	7 AQU	9 ARI
11 AQU	9 PIS	11 ARI	12 GEM	12 CAN	13 VIR	12 LIB	11 SCO	11 CAP	11 AQU	9 PIS	11 TAU
13 PIS	11 ARI	13 TAU	14 CAN	14 LEO	15 LIB	15 SCO	13 SAG	13 AQU	13 PIS	11 ARI	14 GEM
15 ARI	13 TAU	16 GEM	17 LEO	17 VIR	17 SCO	17 SAG	15 CAP	16 PIS	15 ARI	14 TAU	16 CAN
17 TAU	16 GEM	18 CAN	19 VIR	19 LIB	19 SAG	19 CAP	17 AQU	18 ARI	18 TAU	16 GEM	19 LEO
20 GEM	18 CAN	21 LEO	21 LIB	21 SCO	21 CAP	21 AQU	19 PIS	20 TAU	20 GEM	19 CAN	21 VIR
22 CAN	21 LEO	23 VIR	24 SCO	23 SAG	23 AQU	23 PIS	22 ARI	23 GEM	23 CAN	21 LEO	24 LIB
25 LEO	23 VIR	25 LIB	26 SAG	25 CAP	26 PIS	25 ARI	24 TAU	25 CAN	25 LEO	24 VIR	26 SCO
27 VIR	26 LIB	27 SCO	28 CAP	27 AQU	28 ARI	28 TAU	26 GEM	28 LEO	27 VIR	26 LIB	28 SAG
29 LIB	28 SCO	29 SAG	30 AQU	29 PIS	30 TAU	30 GEM	29 CAN	30 VIR	30 LIB	28 SCO	30 CAP
		31 CAP		31 ARI			31 LEO			30 SAG	

1987

JAN	FEB	MAR	APR	MAY	JUN	JUL	AUG	SEP	OCT	NOV	DEC
1 AQU	1 ARI	1 ARI	2 GEM	2 CAN	3 VIR	3 LIB	1 SCO	2 CAP	1 AQU	2 ARI	1 TAU
3 PIS	4 TAU	3 TAU	4 CAN	4 LEO	5 LIB	5 SCO	3 SAG	4 AQU	3 PIS	4 TAU	4 GEM
5 ARI	6 GEM	5 GEM	7 LEO	7 VIR	8 SCO	7 SAG	6 CAP	6 PIS	6 ARI	6 GEM	6 CAN
7 TAU	9 CAN	8 CAN	9 VIR	9 LIB	10 SAG	9 CAP	8 AQU	8 ARI	8 TAU	9 CAN	8 LEO
10 GEM	11 LEO	10 LEO	12 LIB	11 SCO	12 CAP	11 AQU	10 PIS	10 TAU	10 GEM	11 LEO	11 VIR
12 CAN	14 VIR	13 VIR	14 SCO	13 SAG	14 AQU	13 PIS	12 ARI	13 GEM	12 CAN	14 VIR	14 LIB
15 LEO	16 LIB	15 LIB	16 SAG	15 CAP	16 PIS	15 ARI	14 TAU	15 CAN	15 LEO	16 LIB	16 SCO
17 VIR	18 SCO	18 SCO	18 CAP	17 AQU	18 ARI	18 TAU	16 GEM	17 LEO	17 VIR	18 SCO	18 SAG
20 LIB	21 SAG	20 SAG	20 AQU	20 PIS	20 TAU	20 GEM	19 CAN	20 VIR	20 LIB	21 SAG	20 CAP
22 SCO	23 CAP	22 CAP	22 PIS	22 ARI	23 GEM	22 CAN	21 LEO	22 LIB	22 SCO	23 CAP	22 AQU
24 SAG	25 AQU	24 AQU	25 ARI	24 TAU	25 CAN	25 LEO	24 VIR	25 SCO	24 SAG	25 AQU	24 PIS
26 CAP	27 PIS	26 PIS	27 TAU	26 GEM	28 LEO	27 VIR	26 LIB	27 SAG	26 CAP	27 PIS	26 ARI
28 AQU		28 ARI	29 GEM	29 CAN	30 VIR	30 LIB	29 SCO	29 CAP	29 AQU	29 ARI	29 TAU
30 PIS		30 TAU		31 LEO			31 SAG		31 PIS		31 GEM

1988

JAN	FEB	MAR	APR	MAY	JUN	JUL	AUG	SEP	OCT	NOV	DEC
2 CAN	1 LEO	2 VIR	1 LIB	3 SAG	1 CAP	1 AQU	1 ARI	2 GEM	1 CAN	2 VIR	2 LIB
5 LEO	4 VIR	4 LIB	3 SCO	5 CAP	3 AQU	3 PIS	3 TAU	4 CAN	4 LEO	5 LIB	5 SCO
7 VIR	6 LIB	7 SCO	5 SAG	7 AQU	5 PIS	5 ARI	5 GEM	6 LEO	6 VIR	7 SCO	7 SAG
10 LIB	9 SCO	9 SAG	8 CAP	9 PIS	8 ARI	7 TAU	8 CAN	9 VIR	9 LIB	10 SAG	9 CAP
12 SCO	11 SAG	11 CAP	10 AQU	11 ARI	10 TAU	9 GEM	10 LEO	11 LIB	11 SCO	12 CAP	12 AQU
15 SAG	13 CAP	14 AQU	12 PIS	13 TAU	12 GEM	11 CAN	12 VIR	14 SCO	14 SAG	14 AQU	14 PIS
17 CAP	15 AQU	16 PIS	14 ARI	16 GEM	14 CAN	14 LEO	15 LIB	16 SAG	16 CAP	17 PIS	16 ARI
19 AQU	17 PIS	18 ARI	16 TAU	18 CAN	17 LEO	16 VIR	18 SCO	19 CAP	18 AQU	19 ARI	18 TAU
21 PIS	19 ARI	20 TAU	18 GEM	20 LEO	19 VIR	19 LIB	20 SAG	21 AQU	20 PIS	21 TAU	20 GEM
23 ARI	21 TAU	22 GEM	20 CAN	23 VIR	22 LIB	21 SCO	22 CAP	23 PIS	22 ARI	23 GEM	22 CAN
25 TAU	23 GEM	24 CAN	23 LEO	25 LIB	24 SCO	24 SAG	24 AQU	25 ARI	25 TAU	25 CAN	25 LEO
27 GEM	26 CAN	27 LEO	25 VIR	28 SCO	26 SAG	26 CAP	26 PIS	27 TAU	27 GEM	27 LEO	27 VIR
30 CAN	28 LEO	29 VIR	28 LIB	30 SAG	29 CAP	28 AQU	28 ARI	29 GEM	29 CAN	30 VIR	30 LIB
			30 SCO			30 PIS	30 TAU		31 LEO		

1989

JAN	FEB	MAR	APR	MAY	JUN	JUL	AUG	SEP	OCT	NOV	DEC
1 SCO	2 CAP	2 CAP	2 PIS	2 ARI	2 GEM	2 CAN	3 VIR	1 LIB	1 SCO	2 CAP	2 AQU
4 SAG	4 AQU	4 AQU	4 ARI	4 TAU	4 CAN	4 LEO	5 LIB	4 SCO	4 SAG	5 AQU	4 PIS
6 CAP	6 PIS	6 PIS	6 TAU	6 GEM	7 LEO	6 VIR	8 SCO	6 SAG	6 CAP	7 PIS	7 ARI
8 AQU	8 ARI	8 ARI	8 GEM	8 CAN	9 VIR	8 LIB	10 SAG	9 CAP	9 AQU	9 ARI	9 TAU
10 PIS	11 TAU	10 TAU	11 CAN	10 LEO	11 LIB	11 SCO	12 CAP	11 AQU	11 PIS	11 TAU	11 GEM
12 ARI	13 GEM	12 GEM	13 LEO	13 VIR	14 SCO	14 SAG	15 AQU	13 PIS	13 ARI	13 GEM	13 CAN
14 TAU	15 CAN	14 CAN	15 VIR	15 LIB	16 SAG	16 CAP	17 PIS	15 ARI	15 TAU	15 CAN	15 LEO
16 GEM	17 LEO	17 LEO	18 LIB	18 SCO	19 CAP	18 AQU	19 ARI	17 TAU	17 GEM	17 LEO	17 VIR
19 CAN	20 VIR	19 VIR	20 SCO	20 SAG	21 AQU	20 PIS	21 TAU	19 GEM	19 CAN	19 VIR	19 LIB
21 LEO	22 LIB	22 LIB	23 SAG	22 CAP	23 PIS	23 ARI	23 GEM	21 CAN	22 LEO	22 LIB	22 SCO
23 VIR	25 SCO	24 SCO	25 CAP	25 AQU	25 ARI	25 TAU	25 CAN	24 LEO	24 VIR	25 SCO	24 SAG
26 LIB	27 SAG	27 SAG	28 AQU	27 PIS	27 TAU	28 GEM	28 LEO	26 VIR	26 LIB	27 SAG	27 CAP
29 SCO		29 CAP	30 PIS	29 ARI	30 GEM	30 CAN	30 VIR	29 LIB	28 SCO	30 CAP	29 AQU
31 SAG		31 AQU		31 TAU					31 SAG		

1990

JAN	FEB	MAR	APR	MAY	JUN	JUL	AUG	SEP	OCT	NOV	DEC
1 PIS 3 ARI 5 TAU 7 GEM 9 CAN 11 LEO 13 VIR 16 LIB 18 SCO 21 SAG 23 CAP 26 AQU 28 PIS 30 ARI	1 TAU 3 GEM 5 CAN 8 LEO 10 VIR 12 LIB 15 SCO 17 SAG 20 CAP 22 AQU 24 PIS 26 ARI 28 TAU	2 GEM 5 CAN 7 LEO 9 VIR 12 LIB 14 SCO 16 SAG 19 CAP 21 AQU 24 PIS 26 ARI 28 TAU 30 GEM	1 CAN 3 LEO 5 VIR 8 LIB 10 SCO 13 SAG 15 CAP 18 AQU 20 PIS 22 ARI 24 TAU 26 GEM 28 CAN 30 LEO	3 VIR 5 LIB 8 SCO 10 SAG 13 CAP 15 AQU 17 PIS 20 ARI 22 TAU 24 GEM 26 CAN 28 LEO 30 VIR	1 LIB 4 SCO 6 SAG 9 CAP 11 AQU 14 PIS 16 ARI 18 TAU 20 GEM 22 CAN 24 LEO 26 VIR 29 LIB	1 SCO 4 SAG 6 CAP 9 AQU 11 PIS 13 ARI 15 TAU 17 GEM 19 CAN 21 LEO 24 VIR 26 LIB 28 SCO 31 SAG	2 CAP 5 AQU 7 PIS 9 ARI 12 TAU 14 GEM 16 CAN 18 LEO 20 VIR 22 LIB 25 SCO 27 SAG 30 CAP	1 AQU 3 PIS 6 ARI 8 TAU 10 GEM 12 CAN 14 LEO 16 VIR 19 LIB 21 SCO 24 SAG 26 CAP 29 AQU	1 PIS 3 ARI 5 TAU 7 GEM 9 CAN 11 LEO 14 VIR 16 LIB 18 SCO 21 SAG 23 CAP 26 AQU 28 PIS 30 ARI	2 TAU 4 GEM 6 CAN 8 LEO 10 VIR 12 LIB 15 SCO 17 SAG 20 CAP 22 AQU 25 PIS 27 ARI 29 TAU	1 GEM 3 CAN 5 LEO 7 VIR 9 LIB 12 SCO 14 SAG 17 CAP 19 AQU 22 PIS 24 ARI 26 TAU 28 GEM 30 CAN

1991

JAN	FEB	MAR	APR	MAY	JUN	JUL	AUG	SEP	OCT	NOV	DEC
1 LEO 4 VIR 6 LIB 8 SCO 11 SAG 13 CAP 16 AQU 18 PIS 20 ARI 23 TAU 25 GEM 27 CAN 29 LEO 31 VIR	2 LIB 4 SCO 7 SAG 9 CAP 12 AQU 14 PIS 17 ARI 19 TAU 21 GEM 23 CAN 25 LEO 27 VIR	2 LIB 4 SCO 6 SAG 9 CAP 11 AQU 14 PIS 16 ARI 18 TAU 20 GEM 22 CAN 25 LEO 27 VIR 29 LIB 31 SCO	3 SAG 5 CAP 8 AQU 10 PIS 12 ARI 15 TAU 17 GEM 19 CAN 21 LEO 23 VIR 25 LIB 28 SCO 30 SAG	2 CAP 5 AQU 7 PIS 10 ARI 12 TAU 14 GEM 16 CAN 18 LEO 20 VIR 22 LIB 25 SCO 27 SAG 30 CAP	1 AQU 4 PIS 6 ARI 8 TAU 10 GEM 12 CAN 14 LEO 16 VIR 19 LIB 21 SCO 23 SAG 26 CAP 29 AQU	1 PIS 3 ARI 6 TAU 8 GEM 10 CAN 12 LEO 14 VIR 16 LIB 18 SCO 21 SAG 23 CAP 26 AQU 28 PIS 31 ARI	2 TAU 4 GEM 6 CAN 8 LEO 10 VIR 12 LIB 15 SCO 17 SAG 20 CAP 22 AQU 25 PIS 27 ARI 29 TAU 31 GEM	3 CAN 5 LEO 7 VIR 9 LIB 11 SCO 13 SAG 16 CAP 18 AQU 21 PIS 23 ARI 25 TAU 28 GEM 30 CAN	2 LEO 4 VIR 6 LIB 8 SCO 11 SAG 13 CAP 16 AQU 18 PIS 21 ARI 23 TAU 25 GEM 27 CAN 29 LEO 31 VIR	2 LIB 5 SCO 7 SAG 9 CAP 12 AQU 15 PIS 17 ARI 19 TAU 21 GEM 23 CAN 25 LEO 28 VIR 30 LIB	2 SCO 4 SAG 7 CAP 9 AQU 12 PIS 14 ARI 17 TAU 19 GEM 21 CAN 23 LEO 25 VIR 27 LIB 29 SCO

1992

JAN	FEB	MAR	APR	MAY	JUN	JUL	AUG	SEP	OCT	NOV	DEC
1 SAG 3 CAP 6 AQU 8 PIS 11 ARI 13 TAU 15 GEM 17 CAN 19 LEO 21 VIR 23 LIB 25 SCO 28 SAG 30 CAP	2 AQU 4 PIS 7 ARI 9 TAU 12 GEM 14 CAN 16 LEO 18 VIR 20 LIB 23 SCO 25 SAG 27 CAP 29 AQU	3 PIS 5 ARI 8 TAU 10 GEM 12 CAN 14 LEO 16 VIR 18 LIB 20 SCO 23 SAG 25 CAP 27 AQU 30 PIS	1 ARI 4 TAU 6 GEM 8 CAN 10 LEO 12 VIR 15 LIB 17 SCO 19 SAG 21 CAP 24 AQU 26 PIS 29 ARI	1 TAU 3 GEM 5 CAN 8 LEO 10 VIR 12 LIB 14 SCO 16 SAG 19 CAP 21 AQU 24 PIS 26 ARI 28 TAU 31 GEM	2 CAN 4 LEO 6 VIR 8 LIB 10 SCO 13 SAG 15 CAP 17 AQU 20 PIS 22 ARI 25 TAU 27 GEM 29 CAN	1 LEO 3 VIR 5 LIB 7 SCO 10 SAG 12 CAP 15 AQU 17 PIS 20 ARI 22 TAU 24 GEM 27 CAN 29 LEO 31 VIR	2 LIB 4 SCO 6 SAG 8 CAP 11 AQU 13 PIS 16 ARI 18 TAU 21 GEM 23 CAN 25 LEO 27 VIR 29 LIB 31 SCO	2 SAG 5 CAP 7 AQU 10 PIS 12 ARI 15 TAU 17 GEM 19 CAN 21 LEO 24 VIR 26 LIB 28 SCO 30 SAG	2 CAP 5 AQU 7 PIS 10 ARI 12 TAU 14 GEM 17 CAN 19 LEO 21 VIR 23 LIB 25 SCO 27 SAG 29 CAP	1 AQU 3 PIS 6 ARI 8 TAU 11 GEM 13 CAN 15 LEO 17 VIR 19 LIB 21 SCO 24 SAG 26 CAP 28 AQU	1 PIS 3 ARI 6 TAU 8 GEM 10 CAN 12 LEO 14 VIR 16 LIB 19 SCO 21 SAG 23 CAP 26 AQU 28 PIS 31 ARI

1993

JAN	FEB	MAR	APR	MAY	JUN	JUL	AUG	SEP	OCT	NOV	DEC
2 TAU 4 GEM 7 CAN 9 LEO 11 VIR 13 LIB 15 SCO 17 SAG 19 CAP 22 AQU 24 PIS 27 ARI 29 TAU	1 GEM 3 CAN 5 LEO 7 VIR 9 LIB 11 SCO 13 SAG 16 CAP 18 AQU 21 PIS 23 ARI 26 TAU 28 GEM	2 CAN 5 LEO 7 VIR 9 LIB 11 SCO 13 SAG 15 CAP 17 AQU 20 PIS 22 ARI 25 TAU 27 GEM 30 CAN	1 LEO 3 VIR 5 LIB 7 SCO 9 SAG 11 CAP 14 AQU 16 PIS 18 ARI 21 TAU 23 GEM 26 CAN 28 LEO 30 VIR	2 LIB 4 SCO 6 SAG 9 CAP 11 AQU 13 PIS 16 ARI 18 TAU 21 GEM 23 CAN 25 LEO 28 VIR 30 LIB	1 SCO 3 SAG 5 CAP 7 AQU 10 PIS 12 ARI 15 TAU 17 GEM 19 CAN 21 LEO 23 VIR 25 LIB 28 SCO 30 SAG	2 CAP 5 AQU 7 PIS 10 ARI 12 TAU 15 GEM 17 CAN 19 LEO 21 VIR 23 LIB 25 SCO 27 SAG 30 CAP	1 AQU 3 PIS 6 ARI 8 TAU 11 GEM 13 CAN 15 LEO 17 VIR 19 LIB 21 SCO 24 SAG 26 CAP 28 AQU 31 PIS	2 ARI 5 TAU 7 GEM 10 CAN 12 LEO 14 VIR 16 LIB 18 SCO 20 SAG 22 CAP 24 AQU 27 PIS 29 ARI	2 TAU 4 GEM 7 CAN 9 LEO 11 VIR 13 LIB 15 SCO 17 SAG 20 CAP 22 AQU 24 PIS 27 ARI 29 TAU	1 GEM 3 CAN 5 LEO 7 VIR 9 LIB 11 SCO 14 SAG 16 CAP 18 AQU 20 PIS 23 ARI 26 TAU 28 GEM 30 CAN	3 LEO 5 VIR 7 LIB 9 SCO 11 SAG 13 CAP 15 AQU 18 PIS 20 ARI 23 TAU 25 GEM 28 CAN 30 LEO

1994

JAN	FEB	MAR	APR	MAY	JUN	JUL	AUG	SEP	OCT	NOV	DEC
1 VIR 3 LIB 5 SCO 8 SAG 10 CAP 12 AQU 14 PIS 17 ARI 19 TAU 22 GEM 24 CAN 26 LEO 28 VIR 31 LIB	2 SCO 4 SAG 6 CAP 8 AQU 11 PIS 13 ARI 16 TAU 18 GEM 20 CAN 23 LEO 25 VIR 27 LIB	1 SCO 3 SAG 5 CAP 7 AQU 10 PIS 12 ARI 15 TAU 17 GEM 20 CAN 22 LEO 24 VIR 26 LIB 28 SCO 30 SAG	1 CAP 4 AQU 6 PIS 9 ARI 11 TAU 14 GEM 16 CAN 18 LEO 21 VIR 23 LIB 25 SCO 27 SAG 29 CAP	1 AQU 3 PIS 6 ARI 8 TAU 11 GEM 13 CAN 16 LEO 18 VIR 20 LIB 22 SCO 24 SAG 26 CAP 28 AQU 31 PIS	2 ARI 4 TAU 7 GEM 9 CAN 12 LEO 14 VIR 16 LIB 18 SCO 21 SAG 23 CAP 25 AQU 27 PIS 29 ARI	2 TAU 4 GEM 7 CAN 9 LEO 11 VIR 14 LIB 16 SCO 18 SAG 20 CAP 22 AQU 24 PIS 27 ARI 29 TAU	1 GEM 4 CAN 6 LEO 9 VIR 11 LIB 13 SCO 16 SAG 18 CAP 20 AQU 22 PIS 24 ARI 26 TAU 28 GEM 31 CAN	2 LEO 4 VIR 6 LIB 8 SCO 10 SAG 13 CAP 15 AQU 17 PIS 19 ARI 22 TAU 24 GEM 27 CAN 29 LEO	2 VIR 4 LIB 6 SCO 8 SAG 10 CAP 12 AQU 14 PIS 17 ARI 19 TAU 22 GEM 24 CAN 27 LEO 29 VIR 31 LIB	2 SCO 4 SAG 6 CAP 8 AQU 11 PIS 13 ARI 15 TAU 18 GEM 20 CAN 23 LEO 25 VIR 28 LIB 30 SCO	2 SAG 4 CAP 6 AQU 8 PIS 10 ARI 13 TAU 15 GEM 18 CAN 20 LEO 23 VIR 25 LIB 27 SCO 29 SAG 31 CAP

1995

JAN	FEB	MAR	APR	MAY	JUN	JUL	AUG	SEP	OCT	NOV	DEC
2 AQU	1 PIS	2 ARI	1 TAU	1 GEM	2 LEO	2 VIR	3 SCO	1 SAG	2 AQU	1 PIS	3 TAU
4 PIS	3 ARI	5 TAU	3 GEM	3 CAN	5 VIR	4 LIB	5 SAG	3 CAP	5 PIS	3 ARI	5 GEM
7 ARI	5 TAU	7 GEM	6 CAN	6 LEO	7 LIB	6 SCO	7 CAP	5 AQU	7 ARI	5 TAU	8 CAN
9 TAU	8 GEM	10 CAN	9 LEO	8 VIR	9 SCO	8 SAG	9 AQU	7 PIS	9 TAU	8 GEM	10 LEO
12 GEM	10 CAN	12 LEO	11 VIR	10 LIB	11 SAG	10 CAP	11 PIS	9 ARI	12 GEM	10 CAN	13 VIR
14 CAN	13 LEO	14 VIR	13 LIB	13 SCO	13 CAP	12 AQU	13 ARI	12 TAU	14 CAN	13 LEO	15 L1B
16 LEO	15 VIR	16 LIB	15 SCO	15 SAG	15 AQU	14 PIS	15 TAU	14 CAN	16 LEO	15 VIR	17 SCO
19 VIR	17 LIB	19 SCO	17 SAG	17 CAP	17 PIS	17 ARI	18 GEM	17 CAN	19 VIR	18 LIB	19 SAG
21 LIB	19 SCO	21 SAG	19 CAP	19 AQU	19 ARI	19 TAU	20 CAN	19 LEO	21 LIB	20 SCO	21 CAP
23 SCO	22 SAG	23 CAP	21 AQU	21 PIS	22 TAU	22 GEM	23 LEO	22 VIR	23 SCO	22 SAG	23 AQU
25 SAG	24 CAP	25 AQU	24 PIS	23 ARI	24 GEM	24 CAN	25 VIR	24 LIB	26 SAG	24 CAP	25 PIS
27 CAP	26 AQU	27 PIS	26 ARI	26 TAU	27 CAN	27 LEO	28 LIB	26 SCO	28 CAP	26 AQU	28 ARI
30 AQU	28 PIS	30 ARI	28 TAU	28 GEM	29 LEO	29 VIR	30 SCO	28 SAG	30 AQU	28 PIS	30 TAU
				31 CAN		31 LIB		30 CAP		30 ARI	

1996

JAN	FEB	MAR	APR	MAY	JUN	JUL	AUG	SEP	OCT	NOV	DEC
1 GEM	3 LEO	1 LEO	2 LIB	2 SCO	2 CAP	2 AQU	2 ARI	1 TAU	3 CAN	2 LEO	2 VIR
4 CAN	5 VIR	3 VIR	4 SCO	4 SAG	4 AQU	4 PIS	4 TAU	3 GEM	5 LEO	4 VIR	4 LIB
6 LEO	8 LIB	6 LIB	7 SAG	6 CAP	6 PIS	6 ARI	6 GEM	5 CAN	8 VIR	7 LIB	6 SCO
9 VIR	10 SCO	8 SCO	9 CAP	8 AQU	9 ARI	8 TAU	9 CAN	8 LEO	10 LIB	9 SCO	9 SAG
11 LIB	12 SAG	10 SAG	11 AQU	10 PIS	11 TAU	11 GEM	11 LEO	11 VIR	13 SCO	11 SAG	11 CAP
14 SCO	14 CAP	13 CAP	13 PIS	12 ARI	13 GEM	13 CAN	14 VIR	13 LIB	15 SAG	13 CAP	13 AQU
16 SAG	16 AQU	15 AQU	15 ARI	15 TAU	16 CAN	16 LEO	17 LIB	15 SCO	17 CAP	16 AQU	15 PIS
18 CAP	18 PIS	17 PIS	17 TAU	17 GEM	18 LEO	18 VIR	19 SCO	18 SAG	19 AQU	18 PIS	17 ARI
20 AQU	20 ARI	19 ARI	20 GEM	19 CAN	21 VIR	21 LIB	21 SAG	20 CAP	21 PIS	20 ARI	19 TAU
22 PIS	22 TAU	21 TAU	22 CAN	22 LEO	23 LIB	23 SCO	23 CAP	21 AQU	23 ARI	22 TAU	22 GEM
24 ARI	25 GEM	23 GEM	25 LEO	25 VIR	26 SCO	25 SAG	26 AQU	24 PIS	26 TAU	24 GEM	24 CAN
26 TAU	27 CAN	26 CAN	27 VIR	27 LIB	28 SAG	27 CAP	28 PIS	26 ARI	28 GEM	27 CAN	26 LEO
29 GEM		28 LEO	30 LIB	29 SCO	30 CAP	29 AQU	30 ARI	28 TAU	30 CAN	29 LEO	29 VIR
31 CAN		31 VIR		31 SAG		31 PIS		30 GEM			31 LIB

1997

JAN	FEB	MAR	APR	MAY	JUN	JUL	AUG	SEP	OCT	NOV	DEC
3 SCO	1 SAG	1 SAG	1 AQU	1 PIS	1 TAU	1 GEM	2 LEO	3 LIB	3 SCO	1 SAG	1 CAP
5 SAG	4 CAP	3 CAP	4 PIS	3 ARI	4 GEM	4 CAN	4 VIR	6 SCO	5 SAG	4 CAP	3 AQU
7 CAP	6 AQU	5 AQU	6 ARI	5 TAU	6 CAN	5 LEO	7 LIB	8 SAG	8 CAP	6 AQU	5 PIS
9 AQU	8 PIS	7 PIS	8 TAU	7 GEM	8 LEO	8 VIR	9 SCO	10 CAP	10 AQU	8 PIS	8 ARI
11 PIS	10 ARI	9 ARI	10 GEM	9 CAN	11 VIR	10 LIB	12 SAG	12 AQU	12 PIS	10 ARI	10 TAU
13 ARI	12 TAU	11 TAU	12 CAN	12 LEO	13 LIB	13 SCO	14 CAP	14 PIS	14 ARI	12 TAU	12 GEM
15 TAU	14 GEM	13 GEM	14 LEO	14 VIR	16 SCO	15 SAG	16 AQU	17 ARI	16 TAU	14 GEM	14 CAN
18 GEM	16 CAN	16 CAN	17 VIR	17 LIB	18 SAG	18 CAP	18 PIS	19 TAU	18 GEM	17 CAN	16 LEO
20 CAN	19 LEO	18 LEO	19 LIB	19 SCO	20 CAP	20 AQU	20 ARI	21 GEM	20 CAN	19 LEO	19 VIR
23 LEO	21 VIR	21 VIR	22 SCO	22 SAG	22 AQU	22 PIS	22 TAU	23 CAN	23 LEO	21 VIR	21 LIB
25 VIR	24 LIB	23 LIB	24 SAG	24 CAP	24 PIS	24 ARI	24 GEM	25 LEO	25 VIR	24 LIB	24 SCO
28 LIB	26 SCO	26 SCO	27 CAP	26 AQU	26 ARI	26 TAU	27 CAN	28 VIR	28 LIB	26 SCO	26 SAG
30 SCO		28 SAG	29 AQU	28 PIS	29 TAU	28 GEM	29 LEO	30 LIB	30 SCO	29 SAG	28 CAP
		30 CAP		30 ARI		30 CAN	31 VIR				31 AQU

1998

JAN	FEB	MAR	APR	MAY	JUN	JUL	AUG	SEP	OCT	NOV	DEC
2 PIS	2 TAU	2 TAU	2 CAN	2 LEO	3 LIB	3 SCO	2 SAG	3 AQU	2 PIS	1 ARI	2 GEM
4 ARI	4 GEM	4 GEM	4 LEO	4 VIR	5 SCO	5 SAG	4 CAP	5 PIS	4 ARI	3 TAU	4 CAN
6 TAU	7 CAN	6 CAN	7 VIR	7 LIB	8 SAG	8 CAP	6 AQU	7 ARI	6 TAU	5 GEM	6 LEO
8 GEM	9 LEO	8 LEO	9 LIB	9 SCO	10 CAP	10 AQU	8 PIS	9 TAU	8 GEM	7 CAN	9 VIR
10 CAN	11 VIR	11 VIR	12 SCO	12 SAG	13 AQU	12 PIS	11 ARI	11 GEM	10 CAN	9 LEO	11 LIB
13 LEO	14 LIB	13 LIB	14 SAG	14 CAP	15 PIS	14 ARI	13 TAU	13 CAN	13 LEO	11 VIR	14 SCO
15 VIR	16 SCO	16 SCO	17 CAP	16 AQU	17 ARI	16 TAU	15 GEM	15 LEO	15 VIR	14 LIB	16 SAG
18 LIB	19 SAG	18 SAG	19 AQU	19 PIS	19 TAU	18 GEM	17 CAN	18 VIR	17 LIB	16 SCO	19 CAP
20 SCO	21 CAP	21 CAP	21 PIS	21 ARI	21 GEM	21 CAN	19 LEO	20 LIB	20 SCO	19 SAG	21 AQU
23 SAG	23 AQU	23 AQU	23 ARI	23 TAU	23 CAN	23 LEO	22 VIR	23 SCO	23 SAG	21 CAP	23 PIS
25 CAP	25 PIS	25 PIS	25 TAU	25 GEM	25 LEO	25 VIR	24 LIB	25 SAG	25 CAP	24 AQU	25 ARI
27 AQU	27 ARI	27 ARI	27 GEM	27 CAN	28 VIR	28 LIB	26 SCO	28 CAP	27 AQU	26 PIS	28 TAU
29 PIS		29 TAU	29 CAN	29 LEO	30 LIB	30 SCO	29 SAG	30 AQU	30 PIS	28 ARI	30 GEM
31 ARI		31 GEM		31 VIR			31 CAP			30 TAU	

1999

JAN	FEB	MAR	APR	MAY	JUN	JUL	AUG	SEP	OCT	NOV	DEC
1 CAN	1 VIR	1 VIR	2 SCO	2 SAG	3 AQU	2 PIS	1 ARI	2 GEM	1 CAN	1 VIR	1 LIB
3 LEO	4 LIB	3 LIB	4 SAG	4 CAP	5 PIS	5 ARI	3 TAU	4 CAN	3 LEO	4 LIB	3 SCO
5 VIR	6 SCO	6 SCO	7 CAP	7 AQU	8 ARI	7 TAU	5 GEM	6 LEO	5 VIR	6 SCO	6 SAG
7 LIB	9 SAG	8 SAG	9 AQU	9 PIS	10 TAU	9 GEM	7 CAN	8 VIR	7 LIB	9 SAG	8 CAP
10 SCO	11 CAP	11 CAP	12 PIS	11 ARI	12 GEM	11 CAN	9 LEO	10 LIB	10 SCO	11 CAP	11 AQU
12 SAG	14 AQU	13 AQU	14 ARI	13 TAU	14 CAN	13 LEO	12 VIR	13 SCO	12 SAG	14 AQU	13 PIS
15 CAP	16 PIS	15 PIS	16 TAU	15 GEM	16 LEO	15 VIR	14 LIB	15 SAG	15 CAP	16 PIS	16 ARI
17 AQU	18 ARI	17 ARI	18 GEM	17 CAN	18 VIR	17 LIB	16 SCO	18 CAP	17 AQU	18 ARI	18 TAU
19 PIS	20 TAU	19 TAU	20 CAN	19 LEO	20 LIB	20 SCO	19 SAG	20 AQU	20 PIS	20 TAU	20 GEM
22 ARI	22 GEM	21 GEM	22 LEO	21 VIR	23 SCO	22 SAG	21 CAP	22 PIS	22 ARI	23 GEM	22 CAN
24 TAU	24 CAN	23 CAN	24 VIR	24 LIB	25 SAG	25 CAP	24 AQU	25 ARI	24 TAU	25 CAN	24 LEO
26 GEM	26 LEO	26 LEO	27 LIB	26 SCO	28 CAP	27 AQU	26 PIS	27 TAU	26 GEM	27 LEO	26 VIR
28 CAN		28 VIR	29 SCO	29 SAG	30 AQU	30 PIS	28 ARI	29 GEM	28 CAN	29 VIR	28 LIB
30 LEO		30 LIB		31 CAP			30 TAU		30 LEO		31 SCO

2000

JAN	FEB	MAR	APR	MAY	JUN	JUL	AUG	SEP	OCT	NOV	DEC
3 SAG	1 CAP	2 AQU	1 PIS	3 TAU	1 GEM	2 LEO	1 VIR	2 SCO	1 SAG	3 AQU	2 PIS
5 CAP	4 AQU	4 PIS	3 ARI	5 GEM	3 CAN	4 VIR	3 LIB	4 SAG	4 CAP	5 PIS	5 ARI
7 AQU	6 PIS	7 ARI	5 TAU	7 CAN	5 LEO	7 LIB	5 SCO	6 CAP	6 AQU	8 ARI	7 TAU
10 PIS	8 ARI	9 TAU	7 GEM	9 LEO	7 VIR	9 SCO	8 SAG	9 AQU	9 PIS	10 TAU	9 GEM
12 ARI	11 TAU	11 GEM	9 CAN	11 VIR	9 LIB	11 SAG	10 CAP	11 PIS	11 ARI	12 GEM	11 CAN
14 TAU	13 GEM	13 CAN	11 LEO	13 LIB	12 SCO	14 CAP	13 AQU	14 ARI	13 TAU	14 CAN	13 LEO
16 GEM	15 CAN	14 LEO	13 VIR	15 SCO	14 SAG	16 AQU	15 PIS	16 TAU	16 GEM	16 LEO	15 VIR
18 CAN	17 LEO	17 VIR	15 LIB	18 SAG	16 AQU	19 PIS	18 ARI	18 GEM	18 CAN	18 VIR	18 LIB
20 LEO	19 VIR	19 LIB	18 SCO	20 CAP	19 PIS	21 ARI	20 TAU	20 CAN	20 LEO	20 LIB	20 SCO
23 VIR	21 LIB	22 SCO	20 SAG	23 AQU	21 ARI	24 TAU	22 GEM	23 LEO	22 VIR	23 SCO	22 SAG
25 LIB	23 SCO	24 SAG	23 CAP	25 PIS	24 TAU	26 GEM	24 CAN	25 VIR	24 LIB	25 SAG	25 CAP
27 SCO	26 SAG	27 CAP	25 AQU	28 ARI	26 GEM	28 CAN	26 LEO	27 LIB	26 SCO	27 CAP	27 AQU
29 SAG	28 CAP	29 AQU	28 PIS	30 TAU	28 CAN	30 LEO	28 VIR	29 SCO	29 SAG	30 AQU	30 PIS
			30 ARI		30 CAN		30 LIB		31 CAP		

2001

JAN	FEB	MAR	APR	MAY	JUN	JUL	AUG	SEP	OCT	NOV	DEC
1 ARI	2 GEM	1 GEM	2 LEO	1 VIR	2 SCO	1 SAG	3 AQU	1 PIS	1 ARI	2 GEM	2 CAN
4 TAU	4 CAN	4 CAN	4 VIR	3 LIB	4 SAG	4 CAP	5 PIS	4 ARI	4 TAU	4 CAN	4 LEO
6 GEM	6 LEO	6 LEO	6 LIB	6 SCO	6 CAP	6 AQU	8 ARI	6 TAU	6 GEM	7 LEO	6 VIR
8 CAN	8 VIR	8 VIR	8 SCO	8 SAG	9 AQU	9 PIS	10 TAU	9 GEM	8 CAN	9 VIR	8 LIB
10 LEO	10 LIB	10 LIB	10 SAG	11 CAP	11 PIS	11 ARI	12 GEM	11 CAN	10 LEO	11 LIB	10 SCO
12 VIR	12 SCO	12 SCO	13 CAP	13 AQU	14 ARI	14 TAU	15 CAN	13 LEO	13 VIR	13 SCO	12 SAG
14 LIB	15 SAG	14 SAG	15 AQU	15 PIS	16 TAU	16 GEM	17 LEO	15 VIR	15 LIB	15 SAG	15 CAP
16 SCO	17 CAP	16 CAP	18 PIS	18 ARI	18 GEM	18 CAN	19 VIR	17 LIB	17 SCO	17 CAP	17 AQU
18 SAG	20 AQU	19 AQU	20 ARI	20 TAU	21 CAN	20 LEO	21 LIB	19 SCO	19 SAG	20 AQU	20 PIS
21 CAP	22 PIS	21 PIS	23 TAU	22 GEM	23 LEO	22 VIR	23 SCO	21 SAG	21 CAP	22 PIS	22 ARI
23 AQU	25 ARI	24 ARI	25 GEM	25 CAN	25 VIR	24 LIB	25 SAG	24 CAP	23 AQU	25 ARI	25 TAU
26 PIS	27 TAU	26 TAU	27 CAN	27 LEO	27 LIB	26 SCO	27 CAP	26 AQU	26 PIS	27 TAU	27 GEM
28 ARI		29 GEM	29 LEO	29 VIR	29 SCO	29 SAG	30 AQU	29 PIS	28 ARI	30 GEM	29 CAN
31 TAU		31 CAN		31 LIB		31 CAP			31 TAU		31 LEO

2002

JAN	FEB	MAR	APR	MAY	JUN	JUL	AUG	SEP	OCT	NOV	DEC
2 VIR	1 LIB	2 SCO	1 SAG	2 AQU	1 PIS	1 ARI	2 GEM	1 CAN	1 LEO	1 LIB	1 SCO
4 LIB	3 SCO	4 SAG	3 CAP	5 PIS	4 ARI	4 TAU	5 CAN	3 LEO	3 VIR	3 SCO	3 SAG
6 SCO	5 SAG	6 CAP	5 AQU	7 ARI	6 TAU	6 GEM	7 LEO	5 VIR	5 LIB	5 SAG	5 CAP
9 SAG	7 CAP	9 AQU	8 PIS	10 TAU	9 GEM	8 CAN	9 VIR	7 LIB	7 SCO	7 CAP	7 AQU
11 CAP	10 AQU	11 PIS	10 ARI	12 GEM	11 CAN	11 LEO	11 LIB	9 SCO	9 SAG	10 AQU	9 PIS
13 AQU	12 PIS	14 ARI	13 TAU	15 CAN	13 LEO	13 VIR	13 SCO	11 SAG	11 CAP	12 PIS	12 ARI
16 PIS	15 ARI	16 TAU	15 GEM	17 LEO	15 VIR	15 LIB	15 SAG	14 CAP	13 AQU	15 ARI	14 TAU
18 ARI	17 TAU	19 GEM	18 CAN	19 VIR	18 LIB	17 SCO	18 CAP	16 AQU	16 PIS	17 TAU	17 GEM
21 TAU	20 GEM	21 CAN	20 LEO	21 LIB	20 SCO	19 SAG	20 AQU	19 PIS	18 ARI	20 GEM	19 CAN
23 GEM	22 CAN	24 LEO	22 VIR	23 SCO	22 SAG	21 CAP	22 PIS	21 ARI	21 TAU	22 CAN	22 LEO
26 CAN	24 LEO	26 VIR	24 LIB	25 SAG	24 CAP	24 AQU	25 ARI	24 TAU	23 GEM	24 LEO	24 VIR
28 LEO	26 VIR	28 LIB	26 SCO	27 CAP	26 AQU	26 PIS	27 TAU	26 GEM	26 CAN	27 VIR	26 LIB
30 VIR	28 LIB	30 SCO	28 SAG	30 AQU	29 PIS	28 ARI	30 GEM	29 CAN	28 LEO	29 LIB	28 SCO
			30 CAP			31 TAU			30 VIR		30 SAG

2003

JAN	FEB	MAR	APR	MAY	JUN	JUL	AUG	SEP	OCT	NOV	DEC
1 CAP	2 PIS	1 PIS	3 TAU	2 GEM	1 CAN	1 LEO	2 LIB	2 SAG	1 CAP	2 PIS	2 ARI
3 AQU	5 ARI	4 ARI	5 GEM	5 CAN	4 LEO	3 VIR	4 SCO	4 CAP	4 AQU	5 ARI	4 TAU
6 PIS	7 TAU	6 TAU	8 CAN	7 LEO	6 VIR	5 LIB	6 SAG	6 AQU	6 PIS	7 TAU	7 GEM
8 ARI	10 GEM	9 GEM	10 LEO	9 VIR	8 LIB	7 SCO	8 CAP	9 PIS	8 ARI	10 GEM	9 CAN
11 TAU	12 CAN	11 CAN	12 VIR	12 LIB	10 SCO	10 SAG	10 AQU	11 ARI	11 TAU	12 CAN	12 LEO
13 GYM	14 LEO	14 LEO	14 LIB	14 SCO	12 SAG	12 CAP	13 PIS	14 TAU	13 GEM	15 LEO	14 VIR
16 CAN	16 VIR	16 VIR	16 SCO	16 SAG	14 CAP	14 AQU	15 ARI	16 GEM	16 CAN	17 VIR	16 LIB
18 LEO	18 LIB	18 LIB	18 SAG	18 CAP	16 AQU	16 PIS	17 TAU	19 CAN	18 LEO	19 LIB	18 SCO
20 VIR	21 SCO	20 SCO	20 CAP	20 AQU	19 PIS	18 ARI	20 GEM	21 LEO	21 VIR	21 SCO	21 SAG
22 LIB	23 SAG	22 SAG	23 AQU	22 PIS	21 ARI	21 TAU	22 CAN	23 VIR	23 LIB	23 SAG	23 CAP
24 SCO	25 CAP	24 CAP	25 PIS	25 ARI	24 TAU	23 GEM	24 LEO	25 LIB	25 SCO	25 CAP	25 AQU
26 SAG	27 AQU	26 AQU	27 ARI	27 TAU	26 GEM	26 CAN	27 VIR	27 SCO	27 SAG	27 AQU	27 PIS
29 CAP		29 PIS	30 TAU	30 GEM	28 CAN	28 LEO	29 LIB	29 SAG	29 CAP	29 PIS	29 ARI
31 AQU		31 ARI				30 VIR	31 SCO		31 AQU		

2004

JAN	FEB	MAR	APR	MAY	JUN	JUL	AUG	SEP	OCT	NOV	DEC
1 TAU	2 CAN	3 LEO	1 VIR	1 LIB	2 SAG	1 CAP	1 PIS	2 TAU	2 GEM	1 CAN	1 LEO
3 CEM	4 LEO	4 VIR	4 LIB	3 SCO	4 CAP	3 AQU	4 ARI	5 GEM	5 CAN	3 LEO	3 VIR
6 CAN	7 VIR	7 LIB	6 SCO	5 SAG	6 AQU	5 PIS	6 TAU	7 CAN	7 LEO	6 VIR	6 LIB
8 LEO	9 LIB	9 SCO	9 SAG	7 CAP	8 PIS	7 ARI	8 GEM	10 LEO	10 VIR	8 LIB	8 SCO
10 VIR	11 SCO	12 SAG	11 CAP	9 AQU	10 ARI	10 TAU	11 CAN	12 VIR	12 LIB	10 SCO	10 SAG
13 LIB	13 SAG	14 CAP	13 AQU	11 PIS	12 TAU	12 GEM	13 LEO	15 LIB	14 SCO	13 SAG	12 CAP
15 SCO	15 CAP	16 AQU	15 PIS	14 ARI	15 GEM	15 CAN	16 VIR	17 SCO	16 SAG	15 CAP	14 AQU
17 SAG	17 AQU	18 PIS	17 ARI	16 TAU	17 CAN	17 LEO	18 LIB	19 SAG	18 CAP	17 AQU	16 PIS
19 CAP	20 PIS	20 ARI	19 TAU	19 GEM	20 LEO	20 VIR	20 SCO	21 CAP	20 AQU	19 PIS	18 ARI
21 AQU	22 ARI	23 TAU	21 GEM	21 CAN	22 VIR	22 LIB	23 SAG	23 AQU	23 PIS	21 ARI	21 TAU
23 PIS	24 TAU	25 GEM	24 CAN	24 LEO	25 LIB	24 SCO	25 CAP	25 PIS	25 ARI	23 TAU	23 GEM
25 ARI	27 GEM	28 CAN	26 LEO	26 VIR	27 SCO	26 SAG	27 AQU	27 ARI	27 TAU	26 GEM	25 CAN
28 TAU	29 CAN	30 LEO	29 VIR	28 LIB	29 SAG	28 CAP	29 PIS	30 TAU	30 GEM	28 CAN	28 LEO
30 GEM				31 SCO		30 AQU	31 ARI				31 VIR

2005

JAN	FEB	MAR	APR	MAY	JUN	JUL	AUG	SEP	OCT	NOV	DEC
2 LIB	1 SCO	2 SAG	3 AQU	2 PIS	3 TAU	2 GEM	1 CAN	2 VIR	2 LIB	1 SCO	2 CAP
4 SCO	3 SAG	4 CAP	5 PIS	4 ARI	5 GEM	5 CAN	3 LEO	5 LIB	4 SCO	3 SAG	4 AQU
6 SAG	5 CAP	6 AQU	7 ARI	6 TAU	7 CAN	7 LEO	6 VIR	7 SCO	7 SAG	5 CAP	6 PIS
8 CAP	7 AQU	8 PIS	9 TAU	9 GEM	10 LEO	10 VIR	8 LIB	9 SAG	9 CAP	7 AQU	9 ARI
10 AQU	9 PIS	10 ARI	11 GEM	11 CAN	12 VIR	12 LIB	11 SCO	12 CAP	11 AQU	9 PIS	11 TAU
12 PIS	11 ARI	13 TAU	14 CAN	14 LEO	15 LIB	15 SCO	13 SAG	14 AQU	13 PIS	11 ARI	13 GEM
15 ARI	13 TAU	15 GEM	16 LEO	16 VIR	17 SCO	17 SAG	15 CAP	16 PIS	15 ARI	14 TAU	15 CAN
17 TAU	16 GEM	17 CAN	19 VIR	18 LIB	19 SAG	19 CAP	17 AQU	18 ARI	17 TAU	16 GEM	18 LEO
19 GEM	18 CAN	20 LEO	21 LIB	21 SCO	21 CAP	21 AQU	19 PIS	20 TAU	19 GEM	18 CAN	20 VIR
22 CAN	21 LEO	23 VIR	23 SCO	23 SAG	23 AQU	23 PIS	22 ARI	22 GEM	22 CAN	21 LEO	23 LIB
24 LEO	23 VIR	25 LIB	25 SAG	25 CAP	25 PIS	25 ARI	24 TAU	24 CAN	24 LEO	23 VIR	25 SCO
27 VIR	25 LIB	27 SCO	28 CAP	27 AQU	28 ARI	27 TAU	26 GEM	27 LEO	27 VIR	26 LIB	28 SAG
29 LIB	28 SCO	29 SAG	30 AQU	29 PIS	30 TAU	29 GEM	28 CAN	29 VIR	29 LIB	28 SCO	30 CAP
		31 CAP		31 ARI			31 LEO			30 SAG	

2006

JAN	FEB	MAR	APR	MAY	JUN	JUL	AUG	SEP	OCT	NOV	DEC
1 AQU	1 ARI	1 ARI	1 GEM	1 CAN	2 VIR	2 LIB	1 SCO	2 CAP	1 AQU	2 ARI	1 TAU
3 PIS	3 TAU	3 TAU	4 CAN	3 LEO	5 LIB	5 SCO	3 SAG	4 AQU	4 PIS	4 TAU	3 GEM
5 ARI	6 GEM	5 GEM	6 LEO	6 VIR	7 SCO	7 SAG	6 CAP	6 PIS	6 ARI	6 GEM	6 CAN
7 TAU	8 CAN	7 CAN	8 VIR	8 LIB	9 SAG	9 CAP	8 AQU	8 ARI	8 TAU	8 CAN	8 LEO
9 GEM	10 LEO	10 LEO	11 LIB	11 SCO	12 CAP	11 AQU	10 PIS	10 TAU	10 GEM	10 LEO	10 VIR
12 CAN	13 VIR	12 VIR	14 SCO	13 SAG	14 AQU	13 PIS	12 ARI	12 GEM	12 CAN	13 VIR	13 LIB
14 LEO	16 LIB	14 LIB	16 SAG	15 CAP	16 PIS	15 ARI	14 TAU	14 CAN	14 LEO	15 LIB	15 SCO
17 VIR	18 SCO	17 SCO	18 CAP	18 AQU	18 ARI	17 TAU	16 GEM	17 LEO	17 VIR	18 SCO	18 SAG
19 LIB	20 SAG	20 SAG	20 AQU	20 PIS	20 TAU	19 GEM	18 CAN	19 VIR	19 LIB	20 SAG	20 CAP
22 SCO	23 CAP	22 CAP	22 PIS	22 ARI	22 GEM	22 CAN	21 LEO	22 LIB	22 SCO	23 CAP	22 AQU
24 SAG	25 AQU	24 AQU	25 ARI	24 TAU	25 CAN	24 LEO	23 VIR	24 SCO	24 SAG	25 AQU	24 PIS
26 CAP	27 PIS	26 PIS	27 TAU	26 GEM	27 LEO	27 VIR	26 LIB	27 SAG	26 CAP	27 PIS	27 ARI
28 AQU		28 ARI	29 GEM	28 CAN	29 VIR	29 LIB	28 SCO	29 CAP	29 AQU	29 ARI	29 TAU
30 PIS		30 TAU		31 LEO			31 SAG		31 PIS		31 GEM

2007

JAN	FEB	MAR	APR	MAY	JUN	JUL	AUG	SEP	OCT	NOV	DEC
2 CAN	1 LEO	2 VIR	1 LIB	1 SCO	2 CAP	2 AQU	2 ARI	1 TAU	2 CAN	3 VIR	3 LIB
4 LEO	3 VIR	5 LIB	3 SCO	3 SAG	4 AQU	4 PIS	4 TAU	3 GEM	4 LEO	5 LIB	5 SCO
7 VIR	5 LIB	7 SCO	6 SAG	5 CAP	6 PIS	6 ARI	6 GEM	5 CAN	7 VIR	8 SCO	8 SAG
9 LIB	8 SCO	10 SAG	8 CAP	8 AQU	9 ARI	8 TAU	8 CAN	7 LEO	9 LIB	10 SAG	10 CAP
12 SCO	10 SAG	12 CAP	11 AQU	10 PIS	11 TAU	10 GEM	11 LEO	9 VIR	12 SCO	13 CAP	13 AQU
14 SAG	13 CAP	14 AQU	13 PIS	12 ARI	13 GEM	12 CAN	13 VIR	12 LIB	14 SAG	15 AQU	15 PIS
16 CAP	15 AQU	17 PIS	15 ARI	14 TAU	15 CAN	14 LEO	15 LIB	14 SCO	17 CAP	18 PIS	17 ARI
19 AQU	17 PIS	19 ARI	17 TAU	16 GEM	17 LEO	17 VIR	18 SCO	17 SAG	19 AQU	20 ARI	19 TAU
21 PIS	19 ARI	21 TAU	19 GEM	18 CAN	19 VIR	19 LIB	20 SAG	19 CAP	21 PIS	22 TAU	21 GEM
23 ARI	21 TAU	23 GEM	21 CAN	21 LEO	22 LIB	22 SCO	23 CAP	21 AQU	23 ARI	24 GEM	23 CAN
25 TAU	23 GEM	25 CAN	23 LEO	23 VIR	24 SCO	24 SAG	25 AQU	24 PIS	25 TAU	26 CAN	25 LEO
27 GEM	25 CAN	27 LEO	26 VIR	25 LIB	27 SAG	27 CAP	27 PIS	26 ARI	27 GEM	28 LEO	27 VIR
29 CAN	28 LEO	29 VIR	28 LIB	28 SCO	29 CAP	29 AQU	29 ARI	28 TAU	29 CAN	30 VIR	30 LIB
				31 SAG		31 PIS		30 GEM	31 LEO		

2008

JAN	FEB	MAR	APR	MAY	JUN	JUL	AUG	SEP	OCT	NOV	DEC
1 SCO	3 CAP	1 CAP	2 PIS	2 ARI	2 GEM	2 CAN	2 VIR	1 LIB	3 SAG	2 CAP	2 AQU
4 SAG	5 AQU	4 AQU	4 ARI	4 TAU	4 CAN	4 LEO	4 LIB	3 SCO	5 CAP	4 AQU	4 PIS
6 CAP	7 PIS	6 PIS	6 TAU	6 GEM	6 LEO	6 VIR	7 SCO	5 SAG	8 AQU	7 PIS	6 ARI
9 AQU	10 ARI	8 ARI	8 GEM	8 CAN	8 VIR	8 LIB	9 SAG	8 CAP	10 PIS	9 ARI	9 TAU
11 PIS	12 TAU	10 TAU	10 CAN	10 LEO	11 LIB	10 SCO	12 CAP	10 AQU	13 ARI	11 TAU	11 GEM
13 ARI	14 GEM	12 GEM	13 LEO	12 VIR	13 SCO	13 SAG	14 AQU	13 PIS	15 TAU	13 GEM	13 CAN
15 TAU	16 CAN	14 CAN	15 VIR	15 LIB	16 SAG	15 CAP	17 PIS	15 ARI	17 GEM	15 CAN	15 LEO
18 GEM	18 LEO	16 LEO	17 LIB	17 SCO	18 CAP	18 AQU	19 ARI	17 TAU	19 CAN	17 LEO	17 VIR
20 CAN	20 VIR	19 VIR	19 SCO	19 SAG	21 AQU	20 PIS	21 TAU	19 GEM	21 LEO	19 VIR	19 LIB
22 LEO	23 LIB	21 LIB	22 SAG	22 CAP	23 PIS	23 ARI	23 GEM	22 CAN	23 VIR	21 LIB	21 SCO
24 VIR	25 SCO	23 SCO	25 CAP	24 AQU	25 ARI	25 TAU	25 CAN	24 LEO	25 LIB	24 SCO	24 SAG
26 LIB	28 SAG	26 SAG	27 AQU	27 PIS	28 TAU	27 GEM	27 LEO	26 VIR	28 SCO	27 SAG	26 CAP
29 SCO		28 CAP	30 PIS	29 ARI	30 GEM	29 CAN	30 VIR	28 LIB	30 SAG	29 CAP	29 AQU
31 SAG		31 AQU		31 TAU		31 LEO		30 SCO			31 PIS

2009

JAN	FEB	MAR	APR	MAY	JUN	JUL	AUG	SEP	OCT	NOV	DEC
3 ARI	1 TAU	2 GEM	1 CAN	2 VIR	1 LIB	3 SAG	2 CAP	3 PIS	3 ARI	1 TAU	1 GEM
5 TAU	3 GEM	5 CAN	3 LEO	5 LIB	3 SCO	5 CAP	4 AQU	5 ARI	5 TAU	4 GEM	3 CAN
7 GEM	5 CAN	7 LEO	5 VIR	7 SCO	6 SAG	8 AQU	7 PIS	7 TAU	7 GEM	6 CAN	5 LEO
9 CAN	7 LEO	9 VIR	7 LIB	9 SAG	8 CAP	10 PIS	9 ARI	10 GEM	9 CAN	8 LEO	7 VIR
11 LEO	10 VIR	11 LIB	10 SCO	12 CAP	11 AQU	13 ARI	11 TAU	12 CAN	12 LEO	10 VIR	9 LIB
13 VIR	12 LIB	13 SCO	12 SAG	14 AQU	13 PIS	15 TAU	14 GEM	14 LEO	14 VIR	12 LIB	11 SCO
15 LIB	14 SCO	16 SAG	14 CAP	17 PIS	16 ARI	17 GEM	16 CAN	16 VIR	16 LIB	14 SCO	13 SAG
18 SCO	17 SAG	18 CAP	17 AQU	19 ARI	18 TAU	19 CAN	18 LEO	18 LIB	18 SCO	17 SAG	16 CAP
20 SAG	19 CAP	21 AQU	19 PIS	21 TAU	20 GEM	21 LEO	20 VIR	20 SCO	20 SAG	19 CAP	19 AQU
23 CAP	21 AQU	23 PIS	22 ARI	24 GEM	22 CAN	23 VIR	22 LIB	22 SAG	23 CAP	21 AQU	21 PIS
25 AQU	24 PIS	26 ARI	24 TAU	26 CAN	24 LEO	26 LIB	24 SCO	25 CAP	25 AQU	24 PIS	24 ARI
28 PIS	26 ARI	28 TAU	26 GEM	28 LEO	26 VIR	28 SCO	26 SAG	28 AQU	28 PIS	26 ARI	26 TAU
30 ARI	28 TAU	30 GEM	28 CAN	30 VIR	28 LIB	30 SAG	29 CAP	30 PIS	30 ARI	29 TAU	28 GEM
			30 LEO		30 SCO		31 AQU				30 CAN

Mercury Ephemeris:
How To Find the Mercury Sign

Under the year of the birth, find the birth date. If birth was on the first or last day of a particular time period, it's possible that Mercury might be posited in the preceding or following Sign. For example, if the time period is from August 6 to September 10, and birth occurred on September 10, then Mercury might be in the next Sign. The only way to be absolutely sure is to have a chart done by a computer service (see appendix 2 for resources) or by a professional astrologer. If you are not sure, read the adjacent Sign, which may indicate the applicable Sign.

In the tables below, the periods when Mercury is in retrograde motion are indicated by the symbol (R).

1950

Jan 1 – Jan 8	AQU
Jan 9 – Jan 14	AQU (R)
Jan 15 – Jan 29	CAP (R)
Jan 30 – Feb 14	CAP
Feb 15 – Mar 7	AQU
Mar 8 – Mar 24	PIS
Mar 25 – Apr 7	ARI
Apr 8 – May3	TAU
May 4 – May 24	TAU (R)
May 25 – Jun 14	TAU
Jun 15 – Jul 2	GEM
Jul 3 – Jul 16	CAN
Jul 17 – Aug 1	LEO
Aug 2 – Aug 27	VIR
Aug 28 – Sep 4	LIB
Sep 5 – Sep 10	LIB (R)
Sep 11– Sep 26	VIR (R)
Sep 27 – Oct 9	VIR
Oct 10– Oct 26	LIB
Oct 27– Nov 14	SCO
Nov 15 – Dec4	SAG
Dec 5 – Dec 23	CAP
Dec 24 – Dec 31	CAP (R)

1951

Jan 1 – Jan 12	CAP (R)
Jan 13 – Feb 9	CAP
Feb 10 – Feb 28	AQU
Mar 1 – Mar 15	PIS
Mar 16 – Apr 1	ARI
Apr2 – Apr 14	TAU
Apr 15 – May 1	TAU (R)
May 2– May 8	ARI (R)
May 9 – May 14	ARI
May 15 – Jun 8	TAU
Jun 9 – Jun 23	GEM
Jun.24 – Jul 8	CAN
Jul 9 – Aug 1	LEO
Aug 2 – Aug 17	VIR
Aug 18 – Sep 9	VIR (R)
Sep 10 – Oct 1	VIR
Oct 2 – Oct 19	LIB
Oct 20 – Nov 7	SCO
Nov 8 – Dec 1	SAG
Dec 2 – Dec 7	CAP
Dec 8 – Dec 12	CAP (R)
Dec 13 – Dec 27	SAG (R)
Dec 28 – Dec 31	SAG

1952

Jan 1 – Jan 12	SAG
Jan 13 – Feb 1	CAP
Feb 2 – Feb 20	AQU
Feb 21 – Mar 7	PIS
Mar 8 – Mar 26	ARI
Mar 27 – Apr 19	ARI (R)
Apr 20 – May 14	ARI
May 15 – May 31	TAU
Jun 1 – Jun 14	GEM
Jun 15 – Jun 29	CAN
Jun 30 – Jul 29	LEO
Ju1 30 – Aug 22	LEO (R)
Aug 23 – Sep 6	LEO
Sep 7 – Sep 23	VIR
Sep 24 – Oct 11	LIB
Oct 12 – Oct 31	SCO
Nov 1 – Nov 20	SAG
Nov 21 – Dec 10	SAG (R)
Dec 11 – Dec 31	SAG

1953

Jan 1 – Jan 6	SAG
Jan 7 – Jan 25	CAP
Jan 26 – Feb 11	AQU
Feb 12 – Mar 2	PIS
Mar 3 – Mar 9	ARI
Mar 10 – Mar 15	ARI (R)
Mar 16 – Apr 1	PIS (R)
Apr 2 – Apr 17	PIS
Apr 18 – May 7	ARI
May 8 – May 22	TAU
May 23 – Jun 5	GEM
Jun 6 – Jun 25	CAN
Jun 26 – Jul 11	LEO
Jul 12 – Jul 28	LEO (R)
Jul 29 – Aug 4	CAN (R)
Aug 5 – Aug 11	CAN
Aug 12 – Aug 30	LEO
Aug 31– Sep 15	VIR
Sep 16 – Oct 4	LIB
Oct 5 – Oct31	SCO
Nov 1 – Nov 3	SAG
Nov 4 – Nov 6	SAG (R)
Nov 7 – Nov 23	SCO (R)
Nov 24 – Dec 10	SCO
Dec 11 – Dec 30	SAG
Dec 31 – Dec 31	CAP

1954

Jan 1 – Jan 17	CAP
Jan 18 – Feb 4	AQU
Feb 5 – Feb 20	PIS
Feb 21 – Mar 14	PIS (R)
Mar 15 – Apr 12	PIS
Apr 13 – Apr 29	ARI
Apr 30 – May 14	TAU
May 15 – May 30	GEM
May 31 – Jun 23	CAN
Jun 24 – Jul 17	CAN (R)
Jul 18 – Aug 7	CAN
Aug 8 – Aug 22	LEO
Aug 23 – Sep 7	VIR
Sep 8 – Sep 28	LIB
Sep 29 – Oct 18	SCO
Oct 19 – Nov 4	SCO (R)
Nov 5 – Nov 7	LIB (R)
Nov 8 – Nov 10	LIB
Nov 11 – Dec 3	SCO
Dec 4 – Dec 22	SAG
Dec 23 – Dec 31	CAP

1955

Jan 1 – Jan 10	CAP
Jan 1 – Feb 3	AQU
Feb 4 – Feb 25	AQU (R)
Feb 26 – Mar 17	AQU
Mar 18 – Apr 6	PIS
Apr 7 – Apr 21	ARI
Apr 22 – May 6	TAU
May 7 – Jun 3	GEM
Jun 4 – Jun 27	GEM (R)
Jun 28 – Jul 13	GEM
Jul 14 – Jul 28	CAN
Jul 29 – Aug 14	LEO
Aug 15 – Aug 31	VIR
Sep 1 – Oct 1	LIB
Oct 2 – Oct 22	LIB (R)
Oct 23 – Nov 7	LIB
Nov 8 – Nov 26	SCO
Nov 27 – Dec 15	SAG
Dec 16 – Dec 31	CAP

1956

Jan 1 – Jan 3	CAP
Jan 3 – Jan 18	AQU
Jan 19 – Feb 2	AQU (R)
Feb 3 – Feb 7	CAP (R)
Feb 8 – Feb 14	CAP
Feb 5 – Mar 10	AQU
Mar 11 – Mar 28	PIS
Mar 29 – Apr 12	ARI
Apr 13 – Apr 29	TAU
Apr 30 – May 14	GEM
May 15 – Jun 7	GEM (R)
Jun 8 – Jul 6	GEM
Jul 7 – Jul 20	CAN
Jul 21 – Aug 5	LEO
Aug 6 – Aug 26	VIR
Aug 27 – Sep 13	LIB
Sep 14 – Sep 29	LIB (R)
Sep 30 – Oct 5	VIR (R)
Oct 6 – Oct 10	VIR
Oct 11 – Oct 30	LIB
Oct 31 – Nov 18	SCO
Nov 19 – Dec 7	SAG
Dec 8 – Dec 31	CAP

1957

Jan 1 – Jan 1	CAP
Jan 2 – Jan 21	CAP (R)
Jan 22 – Feb 12	CAP
Feb 13 – Mar 3	AQU
Mar 4 – Mar 20	PIS
Mar 21 – Apr 4	ARI
Apr 5 – Apr 25	TAU
Apr 26 – May 19	TAU (R)
May 20 – Jun 12	TAU
Jun 13 – Jul 28	GEM
Jun 29 – Jul 12	CAN
Jul 13 – Jul 29	LEO
Jul 30 – Aug 27	VIR
Aug 28 – Sep 19	VIR (R)
Sep 20 – Oct 5	VIR
Oct 6 – Oct 23	LIB
Oct 24 – Nov 11	SCO
Nov 12 – Dec 1	SAG
Dec 2 – Dec 16	CAP
Dec 17 – Dec 28	CAP (R)
Dec 29 – Dec 31	SAG (R)

1958

Jan 1 – Jan 5	SAG (R)
Jan 6 – Jan 13	SAG
Jan 14 – Feb 6	CAP
Feb 7 – Feb 24	AQU
Feb 25 – Mar 12	PIS
Mar 13 – Apr 2	ARI
Apr 3 – Apr 6	TAU
Apr 7 – Apr 10	TAU (R)
Apr 11 – May 1	ARI (R)
May 2 – May 16	ARI
May 17 – Jun 5	TAU
Jun 6 – Jun 19	GEM
Jun 20 – Jul 4	CAN
Jul 5 – Jul 25	LEO
Jul 26 – Aug 9	VIR
Aug 10 – Aug 23	VIR (R)
Aug 24 – Sep 2	LEO (R)
Sep 3 – Sep 10	LEO
Sep 11 – Sep 28	VIR
Sep 29 – Oct 15	LIB
Oct 16 – Nov 4	SCO
Nov 5 – Dec 1	SAG
Dec 2 – Dec 20	SAG (R)
Dec 21 – Dec 31	SAG

1959

Jan 1 – Jan 10	SAG
Jan 11 – Jan 30	CAP
Jan 31 – Feb 16	AQU
Feb 17 – Mar 4	PIS
Mar 5 – Mar 19	ARI
Mar 20 – Apr 12	ARI (R)
Apr 13 – May 12	ARI
May 13 – May 28	TAU
May 29 – Jun 11	GEM
Jun 12 – Jun 28	CAN
Jun 29 – Jul 22	LEO
Jul 23 – Aug 15	LEO (R)
Aug 16 – Sep 4	LEO
Sep 5 – Sep 20	VIR
Sep 21 – Oct 8	LIB
Oct 9 – Oct 30	SCO
Oct 31 – Nov 14	SAG
Nov 15 – Nov 24	SAG (R)
Nov 25 – Dec 3	SCO (R)
Dec 4 – Dec 13	SCO
Dec 14 – Dec 31	SAG

1960

Jan 1 – Jan 3	SAG
Jan 4 – Jan 22	CAP
Jan 23 – Feb 8	AQU
Feb 9 – Mar 1	PIS
Mar 2 – Mar 24	PIS (R)
Mar 25 – Apr 15	PIS
Apr 16 – May 4	ARI
May 5 – May 18	TAU
May 19 – Jun 2	GEM
Jun 3 – Jun 30	CAN
Jul 1 – Jul 3	LEO
Jul 4 – Jul 5	LEO (R)
Jul 6 – Jul 27	CAN (R)
Jul 28 – Aug 10	CAN
Aug 11 – Aug 26	LEO
Aug 27 – Sep 11	VIR
Sep 12 – Oct 1	LIB
Oct 2 – Oct 27	SCO
Oct 27 – Nov 16	SCO (R)
Nov 17 – Dec 7	SCO
Dec 8 – Dec 26	SAG
Dec 27 – Dec 31	CAP

1961

Jan 1 – Jan 14	CAP
Jan 15 – Feb 1	AQU
Feb 2 – Feb 12	PIS
Feb 13 – Feb 24	PIS (R)
Feb 25 – Mar 6	AQU (R)
Mar 7 – Apr 17	AQU
Mar 18 – Apr 9	PIS
Apr 10 – Apr 26	ARI
Apr 27 – May 10	TAU
May 11 – May 28	GEM
May 29 – Jun 14	CAN
Jun 15 – Jul 8	CAN (R)
Jul 9 – Aug 3	CAN
Aug 4 – Aug 18	LEO
Aug 19 – Sep 4	VIR
Sep 5 – Sep 27	LIB
Sep 28 – Oct 10	SCO
Oct 11 – Oct 21	SCO (R)
Oct 22 – Nov 1	LIB (R)
Nov 2 – Nov 10	LIB
Nov 11 – Nov 30	SCO
Dec 1 – Dec 19	SAG
Dec 20 – Dec 31	CAP

1962

Jan 1 – Jan 7	CAP
Jan 8 – Jan 27	AQU
Jan 28 – Feb 17	AQU (R)
Feb 18 – Mar 14	AQU
Mar 15 – Apr 2	PIS
Apr 3 – Apr 17	ARI
Apr 18 – May 2	TAU
May 3 – May 26	GEM
May 27 – Jun 19	GEM (R)
Jun 20 – Jul 10	GEM
Jul 11 – Jul 26	CAN
Jul 27 – Aug 10	LEO
Aug 11 – Aug 29	VIR
Aug 30 – Sep 24	LIB
Sep 25 – Oct 15	LIB
Oct 16 – Nov 4	LIB
Nov 5 – Nov 23	SCO
Nov 24 – Dec 12	SAG
Dec 13 – Dec 31	CAP

1963

Jan 1 – Jan 1	CAP
Jan 2 – Jan 11	AQU
Jan 12 – Jan 19	AQU (R)
Jan 20 – Feb 1	CAP (R)
Feb 2 – Feb 14	CAP
Feb 15 – Mar 8	AQU
Mar 9 – Mar 25	PIS
Mar 26 – Apr 9	ARI
Apr 10 – May 2	TAU
May 3 – May 6	GEM
May 7 – May 10	GEM (R)
May 11 – May 30	TAU (R)
May 31 – Jun 14	TAU
Jun 15 – Jul 6	GEM
Jul 7 – Jul 17	CAN
Jul 18 – Aug 2	LEO
Aug 3 – Aug 26	VIR
Aug 27 – Sep 6	LIB
Sep 7 – Sep 16	LIB (R)
Sep 17 – Sep 29	VIR (R)
Sep 30 – Oct 10	VIR
Oct 11 – Oct 28	LIB
Oct 29 – Nov 15	SCO
Nov 16 – Dec 5	SAG
Dec 6 – Dec 26	CAP
Dec 27 – Dec 31	CAP (R)

1964

Jan 1 – Jan 15	CAP (R)
Jan 16 – Feb 10	CAP
Feb 10 – Feb 29	AQU
Mar 1 – Mar 16	PIS
Mar 17 – Apr 1	ARI
Apr 2 – Apr 16	TAU
Apr 17 – May 10	TAU (R)
May 11 – Jun 9	TAU
Jun 10 – Jun 24	GEM
Jun 25 – Jul 8	CAN
Jul 9 – Jul 26	LEO
Jul 27 – Aug 19	VIR
Aug 20 – Sep 11	VIR (R)
Sep 12 – Oct 2	VIR
Oct 3 – Oct 19	LIB
Oct 20 – Nov 7	SCO
Nov 8 – Nov 30	SAG
Dec 1 – Dec 9	CAP
Dec 10 – Dec 16	CAP (R)
Dec 17 – Dec 29	SAG (R)
Dec 30 – Dec 31	SAG

1965

Jan 1 – Jan 12	SAG
Jan 13 – Feb 2	CAP
Feb 3 – Feb 20	AQU
Feb 21 – Mar 8	PIS
Mar 9 – Mar 29	ARI
Mar 30 – Apr 22	ARI (R)
Apr 23 – May 15	ARI
May 16 – Jun 1	TAU
Jun 2 – Jun 15	GEM
Jun 16 – Jul 1	CAN
Jul 12 – Jul 30	LEO
Jul 31 – Aug 1	VIR
Aug 2 – Aug 2	VIR (R)
Aug 3 – Aug 19	LEO (R)
Aug 20 – Sep 8	LEO
Sep 9 – Sep 24	VIR
Sep 25 – Oct 12	LIB
Oct 13 – Nov 1	SCO
Nov 8 – Nov 23	SAG
Nov 24 – Dec 12	SAG (R)
Dec 13 – Dec 31	SAG

1966

Jan 1 – Jan 7	SAG
Jan 8 – Jan 26	CAP
Jan 27 – Feb 12	AQU
Feb 13 – Mar 2	PIS
Mar 3 – Mar 12	ARI
Mar 13 – Mar 21	ARI (R)
Mar 22 – Apr 4	PIS (R)
Apr 5 – Apr 17	PIS
Apr 18 – May 9	ARI
May 10 – May 24	TAU
May 25 – Jun 7	GEM
Jun 8 – Jun 26	CAN
Jun 27 – Jul 14	LEO
Jul 15 – Aug 7	LEO (R)
Aug 8 – Aug 31	LEO
Sep 1 – Sep 16	VIR
Sep 17 – Oct 5	LIB
Oct 6 – Oct 29	SCO
Oct 30 – Nov 6	SAG
Nov 7 – Nov 11	SAG (R)
Nov 13 – Nov 26	SCO (R)
Nov 27 – Dec 11	SCO
Dec 12 – Dec 31	SAG

1967

Jan 1 – Jan 19	CAP
Jan 20 – Feb 5	AQU
Feb 6 – Feb 23	PIS
Feb 24 – Mar 17	PIS (R)
Mar 18 – Apr 14	PIS
Apr 15 – May 1	ARI
May 2 – May 15	TAU
May 16 – May 31	GEM
Jun 1 – Jun 26	CAN
Jun 27 – Jul 20	CAN (R)
Jul 21 – Aug 8	CAN
Aug 9 – Aug 23	LEO
Aug 24 – Sep 9	VIR
Sep 10 – Sep 29	LIB
Sep 30 – Oct 21	SCO
Oct 22 – Nov 10	SCO (R)
Nov 11 – Dec 5	SCO
Dec 6 – Dec 24	SAG
Dec 25 – Dec 31	CAP

1968

Jan 1 – Jan 11	CAP
Jan 12 – Feb 1	AQU
Feb 2 – Feb 6	PIS
Feb 7 – Feb 11	PIS (R)
Feb 12 – Feb 28	AQU (R)
Feb 29 – Mar 17	AQU
Mar 18 – Apr 6	PIS
Apr 7 – Apr 22	ARI
Apr 23 – May 6	TAU
May 7 – May 29	GEM
May 30 – Jun 6	CAN
Jun 7 – Jun 13	CAN (R)
Jun 14 – Jul 1	GEM(R)
Jul 2 – Jul 12	GEM
Jul 13 – Jul 30	CAN
Jul 31 – Aug 14	LEO
Aug 15 – Sep 1	VIR
Sep 2 – Sep 28	LIB
Sep 29 – Oct 3	SCO
Oct 4 – Oct 7	SCO (R)
Oct 8 – Oct 24	LIB (R)
Oct 25 – Nov 7	LIB
Nov 8 – Nov 27	SCO
Nov 28 – Dec 16	SAG
Dec 17 – Dec 31	CAP

1969

Jan 1 – Jan 4	CAP
Jan 5 – Jan 20	AQU
Jan 21 – Feb 10	AQU (R)
Feb 11 – Mar 12	AQU
Mar 13 – Mar 29	PIS
Mar 30 – Apr 13	ARI
Apr 14 – Apr 30	TAU
May 1 – May 17	GEM
May 18 – Jun 10	GEM (R)
Jun 11 – Jul 7	GEM
Jul 8 – Jul 22	CAN
Jul 23 – Aug 6	LEO
Aug 7 – Aug 26	VIR
Aug 27 – Sep 16	LIB
Sep 17 – Oct 6	LIB (R)
Oct 7 – Oct 8	VIR (R)
Oct 9 – Oct 9	VIR
Oct 10 – Nov 1	LIB
Nov 2 – Nov 19	SCO
Nov 20 – Dec 9	SAG
Dec 10 – Dec 31	CAP

1970

Jan 1 – Jan 4	CAP
Jan 5 – Jan 24	CAP (R)
Jan 25 – Feb 13	CAP
Feb 14 – Mar 5	AQU
Mar 6 – Mar 21	PIS
Mar 22 – Apr 5	ARI
Apr 6 – Apr 28	TAU
Apr 29 – May 22	TAU (R)
May 23 – Jun 13	TAU
Jun 14 – Jun 29	GEM
Jun 30 – Jul 13	CAN
Jul 14 – Jul 30	LEO
Jul 31 – Aug 30	VIR
Aug 31 – Sep 22	VIR (R)
Sep 23 – Oct 7	VIR
Oct 8 – Oct 24	LIB
Oct 25 – Nov 12	SCO
Nov 13 – Dec 2	SAG
Dec 3 – Dec 19	CAP
Dec 20 – Dec 31	CAP (R)

1971

Jan 1 – Jan 2	CAP (R)
Jan 3 – Jan 8	SAG (R)
Jan 9 – Jan 13	SAG
Jan 14 – Feb 7	CAP
Feb 8 – Feb 25	AQU
Feb 26 – Mar 13	PIS
Mar 14 – Apr 1	ARI
Apr 2 – Apr 9	TAU
Apr 10 – Apr 18	TAU (R)
Apr 19 – May 3	ARI (R)
May 4 – May 16	ARI
May 17 – Jun 6	TAU
Jun 7 – Jun 21	GEM
Jun 22 – Jul 5	CAN
Jul 6 – Jul 26	LEO
Jul 27 – Aug 12	VIR
Aug 13 – Aug 29	VIR (R)
Aug 30 – Sep 5	LEO (R)
Sep 6 – Sep 10	LEO
Sep 11 – Sep 29	VIR
Sep 30 – Oct 17	LIB
Oct 18 – Nov 5	SCO
Nov 6 – Dec 3	SAG
Dec 4 – Dec 22	SAG (R)
Dec 23 – Dec 31	SAG

1972

Jan 1 – Jan 11	SAG
Jan 12 – Jan 31	CAP
Feb 1 – Feb 18	AQU
Feb 19 – Mar 5	PIS
Mar 6 – Mar 21	ARI
Mar 22 – Apr 14	ARI (R)
Apr 15 – May 12	ARI
May 13 – May 28	TAU
May 29 – Jun 11	GEM
Jun 12 – Jun 28	CAN
Jun 29 – Jul 24	LEO
Jul 25 – Aug 17	LEO (R)
Aug 18 – Sep 4	LEO
Sep 5 – Sep 21	VIR
Sep 22 – Oct 8	LIB
Oct 9 – Oct 30	SCO
Oct 31 – Nov 15	SAG
Nov 16 – Nov 28	SAG (R)
Nov 29 – Dec 5	SCO (R)
Dec 6 – Dec 12	SCO
Dec 13 – Dec 31	SAG

1973

Jan 1 – Jan 4	SAG
Jan 5 – Jan 23	CAP
Jan 24 – Feb 9	AQU
Feb 10 – Mar 4	PIS
Mar 5 – Mar 27	PIS (R)
Mar 28 – Apr 16	PIS
Apr 17 – May 5	ARI
May 6 – May 20	TAU
May 21 – Jun 3	GEM
Jun 4 – Jun 26	CAN
Jun 27 – Jul 6	LEO
Jul 7 – Jul 15	LEO (R)
Jul 16 – Jul 30	CAN (R)
Jul 31 – Aug 11	CAN
Aug 12 – Aug 28	LEO
Aug 29 – Sep 13	VIR
Sep 14 – Oct 2	LIB
Oct 3 – Oct 30	SCO
Oct 31 – Nov 19	SCO (R)
Nov 20 – Dec 8	SCO
Dec 9 – Dec 28	SAG
Dec 29 – Dec 31	CAP

1974

Jan 1 – Jan 15	CAP
Jan 16 – Feb 2	AQU
Feb 3 – Feb 15	PIS
Feb 16 – Mar 2	PIS (R)
Mar 3 – Mar 9	AQU (R)
Mar 10 – Mar 17	AQU
Mar 18 – Apr 11	PIS
Apr 12 – Apr 27	ARI
Apr 28 – May 11	TAU
May 12 – May 28	GEM
May 29 – Jun 17	CAN
Jun 18 – Jul 12	CAN (R)
Jul 13 – Aug 4	CAN
Aug 5 – Aug 19	LEO
Aug 20 – Sep 5	VIR
Sep 6 – Sep 27	LIB
Sep 28 – Oct 13	SCO
Oct 14 – Oct 26	SCO (R)
Oct 27 – Nov 3	LIB (R)
Nov 4 – Nov 11	LIB
Nov 12 – Dec 1	SCO
Dec 2 – Dec 20	SAG
Dec 21 – Dec 31	CAP

1975

Jan 1 – Jan 8	CAP
Jan 9 – Jan 30	AQU
Jan 31 – Feb 20	AQU (R)
Feb 21 – Mar 15	AQU
Mar 16 – Apr 4	PIS
Apr 5 – Apr 19	ARI
Apr 20 – May 3	TAU
May 4 – May 29	GEM
May 30 – Jun 22	GEM (R)
Jun 23 – Jul 12	GEM
Jul 12 – Jul 27	CAN
Jul 28 – Aug 11	LEO
Aug 12 – Aug 30	VIR
Aug 31 – Sep 26	LIB
Sep 27 – Oct 18	LIB (R)
Oct 19 – Nov 5	LIB
Nov 6 – Nov 24	SCO
Nov 25 – Dec 13	SAG
Dec 14 – Dec 31	CAP

1976

Jan 1 – Jan 2	CAP
Jan 3 – Jan 14	AQU
Jan 15 – Jan 24	AQU (R)
Jan 25 – Feb 3	CAP (R)
Feb 4 – Feb 15	CAP
Feb 16 – Mar 8	AQU
Mar 9 – Mar 26	PIS
Mar 27 – Apr 9	ARI
Apr 10 – Apr 29	TAU
Apr 30 – May 9	GEM
May 10 – May 19	GEM (R)
May 20 – Jun 2	TAU (R)
Jun 3 – Jun 13	TAU
Jun 14 – Jun 4	GEM
Jul 5 – Jul 18	CAN
Jul 19 – Aug 3	LEO
Aug 4 – Aug 25	VIR
Aug 26 – Sep 8	LIB
Sep 9 – Sep 20	LIB (R)
Sep 21 – Oct 1	VIR (R)
Oct 2 – Oct 10	VIR
Oct 11 – Oct 28	LIB
Oct 29 – Nov 16	SCO
Nov 17 – Dec 5	SAG
Dec 6 – Dec 28	CAP
Dec 29 – Dec 31	CAP (R)

1977

Jan 1 – Jan 17	CAP (R)
Jan 18 – Feb 10	CAP
Feb 11 – Mar 1	AQU
Mar 2 – Mar 17	PIS
Mar 18 – Apr 2	ARI
Apr 3 – Apr 20	TAU
Apr 21 – May 13	TAU (R)
May 14 – Jun 10	TAU
Jun 11 – Jun 25	GEM
Jun 26 – Jul 9	CAN
Jul 10 – Jul 27	LEO
Jul 28 – Aug 22	VIR
Aug 23 – Sep 14	VIR (R)
Sep 15 – Oct 3	VIR
Oct 4 – Oct 21	LIB
Oct 22 – Nov 9	SCO
Nov 10 – Nov 30	SAG
Dec 1 – Dec 12	CAP
Dec 13 – Dec 20	CAP (R)
Dec 21 – Dec 31	SAG (R)

1978

Jan 1 – Jan 1	SAG (R)
Jan 2 – Jan 13	SAG
Jan 14 – Feb 4	CAP
Feb 5 – Feb 22	AQU
Feb 23 – Mar 10	PIS
Mar 11 – Apr 1	ARI
Apr 2 – Apr 25	ARI (R)
Apr 26 – May 15	ARI
May 16 – Jun 3	TAU
Jun 4 – Jun 17	GEM
Jun 18 – Jul 2	CAN
Jul 3 – Jul 26	LEO
Jul 27 – Aug 4	VIR
Aug 5 – Aug 12	VIR (R)
Aug 13 – Aug 28	LEO (R)
Aug 29 – Sep 9	LEO
Sep 10 – Sep 26	VIR
Sep 27 – Oct 13	LIB
Oct 14 – Nov 2	SCO
Nov 3 – Nov 25	SAG
Nov 26 – Dec 15	SAG (R)
Dec 16 – Dec 31	SAG

1979

Jan 1 – Jan 8	SAG
Jan 9 – Jan 28	CAP
Jan 29 – Feb 14	AQU
Feb 15 – Mar 3	PIS
Mar 4 – Mar 15	ARI
Mar 16 – Mar 27	ARI (R)
Mar 28 – Apr 7	PIS (R)
Apr 8 – Apr 17	PIS
Apr 18 – May 10	ARI
May 11 – May 25	TAU
May 26 – Jun 8	GEM
Jun 9 – Jun 26	CAN
Jun 27 – Jul 17	LEO
Jul 18 – Aug 11	LEO (R)
Aug 12 – Sep 2	LEO
Sep 3 – Sep 18	VIR
Sep 19 – Oct 6	LIB
Oct 7 – Oct 29	SCO
Oct 30 – Nov 9	SAG
Nov 10 – Nov 17	SAG (R)
Nov 18 – Nov 29	SCO (R)
Nov 30 – Dec 12	SCO
Dec 13 – Dec 31	SAG

1980

Jan 1 – Jan 1	SAG
Jan 2 – Jan 20	CAP
Jan 21 – Feb 6	AQU
Feb 7 – Feb 26	PIS
Feb 27 – Mar 19	PIS (R)
Mar 20 – Apr 14	PIS
Apr 15 – May 1	ARI
May 2 – May 16	TAU
May 17 – May 31	GEM
Jun 1 – Jun 28	CAN
Jun 29 – Jul 22	CAN (R)
Jul 23 – Aug 8	CAN
Aug 9 – Aug 24	LEO
Aug 25 – Sep 9	VIR
Sep 10 – Sep 29	LIB
Sep 30 – Oct 23	SCO
Oct 24 – Nov 12	SCO (R)
Nov 13 – Dec 5	SCO
Dec 6 – Dec 24	SAG
Dec 25 – Dec 31	CAP

1981

Jan 1 – Jan 12	CAP
Jan 13 – Jan 31	AQU
Feb 1 – Feb 8	PIS
Feb 9 – Feb 15	PIS (R)
Feb 16 – Mar 2	AQU (R)
Mar 3 – Mar 17	AQU
Mar 18 – Apr 7	PIS
Apr 8 – Apr 23	ARI
Apr 24 – May 7	TAU
May 8 – May 28	GEM
May 29 – Jun 9	CAN
Jun 10 – Jun 22	CAN (R)
Jun 23 – Jul 3	GEM (R)
Jul 4 – Jul 12	GEM
Jul 13 – Aug 1	CAN
Aug 2 – Aug 16	LEO
Aug 17 – Sep 2	VIR
Sep 3 – Sep 26	LIB
Sep 27 – Oct 6	SCO
Oct 7 – Oct 13	SCO (R)
Oct 14 – Oct 27	LIB (R)
Oct 27 – Nov 9	LIB
Nov 10 – Nov 28	SCO
Nov 29 – Dec 17	SAG
Dec 18 – Dec 31	CAP

1982

Jan 1 – Jan 5	CAP
Jan 6 – Jan 23	AQU
Jan 24 – Feb 13	AQU (R)
Feb 14 – Mar 13	AQU
Mar 14 – Mar 31	PIS
Apr 1 – Apr 15	ARI
Apr 16 – May 1	TAU
May 2 – May 21	GEM
May 22 – Jun 13	GEM (R)
Jun 14 – Jul 8	GEM
Jul 9 – Jul 23	CAN
Jul 24 – Aug 8	LEO
Aug 9 – Aug 27	VIR
Aug 28 – Sep 19	LIB
Sep 20 – Oct 11	LIB (R)
Oct 12 – Nov 18	SCO
Nov 19 – Dec 12	SAG
Dec 13 – Dec 31	CAP

1983

Jan 1 – Jan 1	CAP
Jan 2 – Jan 7	AQU
Jan 8 – Jan 11	AQU (R)
Jan 15 – Jan 27	CAP (R)
Jan 28 – Feb 13	CAP
Feb 14 – Mar 6	AQU
Mar 7 – Mar 23	PIS
Mar 24 – Apr 7	ARI
Apr 8 – May 1	TAU
May 2 – May 25	TAU (R)
May 26 – Jun 13	TAU
Jun 14 – Jul 1	GEM
Jul 2 – Jul 15	CAN
Jul 16 – Jul 31	LEO
Aug 1 – Aug 28	VIR
Aug 29 – Sep 2	LIB
Sep 3 – Sep 5	LIB (R)
Sep 6 – Sep 24	VIR (R)
Sep 25 – Oct 8	VIR
Oct 9 – Oct 26	LIB
Oct 27 – Nov 13	SCO
Nov 14 – Dec 3	SAG
Dec 4 – Dec 22	CAP
Dec 23 – Dec 31	CAP (R)

1984

Jan 1 – Jan 11	CAP (R)
Jan 12 – Feb 8	CAP
Feb 9 – Feb 27	AQU
Feb 28 – Mar 14	PIS
Mar 15 – Mar 31	ARI
Apr 1 – Apr 11	TAU
Apr 12 – Apr 24	TAU (R)
Apr 25 – May 5	ARI (R)
May 6 – May 15	ARI
May 16 – Jun 7	TAU
Jun 8 – Jun 21	GEM
Jun 22 – Jul 6	CAN
Jul 7 – Jul 25	LEO
Jul 26 – Aug 14	VIR
Aug 15 – Sep 7	VIR (R)
Sep 8 – Sep 30	VIR
Oct 1 – Oct 17	LIB
Oct 18 – Nov 5	SCO
Nov 6 – Dec 1	SAG
Dec 2 – Dec 4	CAP
Dec 5 – Dec 7	CAP (R)
Dec 8 – Dec 24	SAG (R)
Dec 25 – Dec 31	SAG

1985

Jan 1 – Jan 11	SAG
Jan 12 – Jan 31	CAP
Feb 1 – Feb 18	AQU
Feb 19 – Mar 6	PIS
Mar 7 – Mar 24	ARI
Mar 25 – Apr 17	ARI (R)
Apr 18 – May 13	ARI
May 14 – May 30	TAU
May 31 – Jun 13	GEM
Jun 14 – Jun 29	CAN
Jun 30 – Jul 28	LEO
Jul 29 – Aug 20	LEO (R)
Aug 21 – Sep 6	LEO
Sep 7 – Sep 22	VIR
Sep 23 – Oct 10	LIB
Oct 11 – Oct 31	SCO
Nov 1 – Nov 18	SAG
Nov 19 – Dec 4	SAG (R)
Dec 5 – Dec 8	SCO (R)
Dec 9 – Dec 11	SCO
Dec 12 – Dec 31	SAG

1986

Jan 1 – Jan 5	SAG
Jan 6 – Jan 24	CAP
Jan 25 – Feb 10	AQU
Feb 11 – Mar 2	PIS
Mar 3 – Mar 7	ARI
Mar 8 – Mar 11	ARI (R)
Mar 12 – Mar 30	PIS (R)
Mar 31 – Apr 17	PIS
Apr 18 – May 7	ARI
May 8 – May 21	TAU
May 22 – Jun 5	GEM
Jun 6 – Jun 26	CAN
Jun 27 – Jul 9	LEO
Jul 10 – Jul 22	LEO (R)
Jul 23 – Aug 3	CAN (R)
Aug 4 – Aug 11	CAN
Aug 12 – Aug 29	LEO
Aug 30 – Sep 14	VIR
Sep 15 – Oct 3	LIB
Oct 4 – Nov 2	SCO
Nov 3 – Nov 22	SCO (R)
Nov 23 – Dec 9	SCO
Dec 10 – Dec 29	SAG
Dec 30 – Dec 31	CAP

1987

Jan 1 – Jan 17	CAP
Jan 18 – Feb 3	AQU
Feb 4 – Feb 18	PIS
Feb 19 – Mar 11	PIS (R)
Mar 12 – Mar 12	AQU (R)
Mar 13 – Mar 13	AQU
Mar 14 – Apr 12	PIS
Apr 13 – Apr 29	ARI
Apr 30 – May 13	TAU
May 14 – May 29	GEM
May 30 – Jun 21	CAN
Jun 22 – Jul 15	CAN (R)
Jul 16 – Aug 6	CAN
Aug 7 – Aug 21	LEO
Aug 22 – Sep 7	VIR
Sep 8 – Sep 28	LIB
Sep 29 – Oct 16	SCO
Oct 17 – Oct 31	SCO (R)
Nov 1 – Nov 6	LIB (R)
Nov 7 – Nov 11	LIB
Nov 12 – Dec 3	SCO
Dec 4 – Dec 22	SAG
Dec 23 – Dec 31	CAP

1988

Jan 1 – Jan 9	CAP
Jan 10 – Feb 2	AQU
Feb 3 – Feb 23	AQU (R)
Feb 24 – Mar 15	AQU
Mar 16 – Apr 4	PIS
Apr 5 – Apr 19	ARI
Apr 20 – May 4	TAU
May 5 – Jun 1	GEM
Jun 2 – Jun 24	GEM (R)
Jun 25 – Jul 11	GEM
Jul 12 – Jul 28	CAN
Jul 29 – Aug 12	LEO
Aug 13 – Aug 30	VIR
Aug 31 – Sep 28	LIB
Sep 29 – Oct 20	LIB (R)
Oct 21 – Nov 6	LIB
Nov 7 – Nov 24	SCO
Nov 25 – Dec 13	SAG
Dec 14 – Dec 31	CAP

1989

Jan 1 – Jan 2	CAP
Jan 10 – Jan 16	AQU
Jan 17 – Jan 28	AQU (R)
Jan 29 – Feb 5	CAP (R)
Feb 6 – Feb 14	CAP
Feb 15 – Mar 10	AQU
Mar 11 – Mar 27	PIS
Mar 28 – Apr 11	ARI
Apr 12 – Apr 29	TAU
Apr 30 – May 12	GEM
May 13 – May 28	GEM (R)
May 29 – Jun 5	TAU (R)
Jun 6 – Jun 11	TAU
Jun 12 – Jul 5	GEM
Jul 6 – Jul 19	CAN
Jul 20 – Aug 4	LEO
Aug 5 – Aug 25	VIR
Aug 26 – Sep 11	LIB
Sep 12 – Sep 26	LIB (R)
Sep 27 – Oct 3	VIR (R)
Oct 4 – Oct 10	VIR
Oct 11 – Oct 30	LIB
Oct 31 – Nov 17	SCO
Nov 18 – Dec 7	SAG
Dec 8 – Dec 30	CAP
Dec 31 – Dec 31	CAP (R)

1990

Jan 1 – Jan 20	CAP (R)
Jan 21 – Feb 11	CAP
Feb 12 – Mar 3	AQU
Mar 4 – Mar 19	PIS
Mar 20 – Apr 3	ARI
Apr 4 – Apr 23	TAU
Apr 24 – May 17	TAU (R)
May 18 – Jun 11	TAU
Jun 12 – Jun 27	GEM
Jun 28 – Jul 11	CAN
Jul 12 – Jul 28	LEO
Jul 29 – Aug 25	VIR
Aug 26 – Sep 17	VIR (R)
Sep 18 – Oct 5	VIR
Oct 6 – Oct 22	LIB
Oct 23 – Nov 10	SCO
Nov 11 – Dec 1	SAG
Dec 2 – Dec 14	CAP
Dec 15 – Dec 25	CAP (R)
Dec 26 – Dec 31	SAG (R)

1991

Jan 1 – Jan 3	SAG (R)
Jan 4 – Jan 13	SAG
Jan 21 – Feb 5	CAP
Feb 6 – Feb 23	AQU
Feb 24 – Mar 11	PIS
Mar 12 – Apr 4	ARI
Apr 5 – Apr 28	ARI (R)
Apr 29 – May 16	ARI
May 17 – Jun 4	TAU
Jun 5 – Jun 18	GEM
Jun 19 – Jul 3	CAN
Jul 4 – Jul 26	LEO
Jul 27 – Aug 8	VIR
Aug 9 – Aug 19	VIR (R)
Aug 20 – Sep 1	LEO (R)
Sep 2 – Sep 10	LEO
Sep 11 – Sep 27	VIR
Sep 28 – Oct 15	LIB
Oct 16 – Nov 3	SCO
Nov 4 – Nov 28	SAG
Nov 29 – Dec 18	SAG (R)
Dec 19 – Dec 31	SAG

1992

Jan 1 – Jan 9	SAG
Jan 10 – Jan 29	CAP
Jan 30 – Feb 15	AQU
Feb 16 – Mar 3	PIS
Mar 4 – Mar 17	ARI
Mar 18 – Apr 3	ARI (R)
Apr 4 – Apr 9	PIS (R)
Apr 10 – Apr 14	PIS
Aprl 5 – May 10	ARI
May 11 – May 26	TAU
May 27 – Jun 9	GEM
Jun 10 – Jun 26	CAN
Jun 27 – Jul 20	LEO
Jul 21 – Aug 13	LEO (R)
Aug 14 – Sep 2	LEO
Sep 3 – Sep 18	VIR
Sep 19 – Oct 6	LIB
Oct 7 – Oct 29	SCO
Oct 30 – Nov 11	SAG
Nov 12 – Nov 21	SAG (R)
Nov 22 – Dec 1	SCO (R)
Dec 2 – Dec 11	SCO
Dec 12 – Dec 31	SAG

1993

Jan 1 – Jan 2	SAG
Jan 3 – Jan 20	CAP
Jan 21 – Feb 7	AQU
Feb 8 – Feb 27	PIS
Feb 28 – Mar 22	PIS (R)
Mar 23 – Apr 15	PIS
Apr 16 – May 3	ARI
May 4 – May 17	TAU
May 18 – Jun 1	GEM
Jun 2 – Jul 1	CAN
Jul 2 – Jul 25	CAN (R)
Jul 26 – Aug 9	CAN
Aug 10 – Aug 25	LEO
Aug 26 – Sep 10	VIR
Sep 11 – Sep 30	LIB
Oct 1 – Oct 25	SCO
Oct 26 – Nov 15	SCO (R)
Nov 16 – Dec 6	SCO
Dec 7 – Dec 26	SAG
Dec 27 – Dec 31	CAP

1994

Jan 1 – Jan 13	CAP
Jan 14 – Jan 31	AQU
Feb 1 – Feb 11	PIS
Feb 12 – Feb 21	PIS (R)
Feb 22 – Mar 5	AQU (R)
Mar 6 – Mar 17	AQU
Mar 18 – Apr 9	PIS
Apr 10 – Apr 25	ARI
Apr 26 – May 9	TAU
May 10 – May 28	GEM
May 29 – Jun 12	CAN
Jun 13 – Jul 2	CAN (R)
Jul 3 – Jul 6	GEM (R)
Jul 7 – Jul 10	GEM
Jul 11 – Aug 2	CAN
Aug 3 – Aug 17	LEO
Aug 18 – Sep 3	VIR
Sep 4 – Sep 26	LIB
Sep 27 – Oct 9	SCO
Oct 10 – Oct 18	SCO (R)
Oct 19 – Oct 30	LIB (R)
Oct 31 – Nov 10	LIB
Nov 11 – Nov 29	SCO
Nov 30 – Dec 18	SAG
Dec 19 – Dec 31	CAP

1995

Jan 1 – Jan 6	CAP
Jan 7 – Jan 26	AQU
Jan 27 – Feb 16	AQU (R)
Feb 17 – Mar 14	AQU
Mar 15 – Apr 1	PIS
Apr 2 – Apr 16	ARI
Apr 17 – May 2	TAU
May 3 – May 24	GEM
May 25 – Jun 17	GEM (R)
Jun 18 – Jul 10	GEM
Jul 11 – Jul 25	CAN
Jul 26 – Aug 9	LEO
Aug 10 – Aug 28	VIR
Aug 29 – Sep 22	LIB
Sep 23 – Oct 14	LIB (R)
Oct 15 – Nov 2	LIB
Nov 3 – Nov 22	SCO
Nov 23 – Dec 11	SAG
Dec 12 – Dec 31	CAP

1996

Jan 1 – Jan 1	CAP
Jan 2 – Jan 9	AQU
Jan 10 – Jan 16	AQU (R)
Jan 17 – Jan 30	CAP (R)
Jan 31 – Feb 14	CAP
Feb 15 – Mar 6	AQU
Mar 7 – Mar 23	PIS
Mar 24 – Apr 7	ARI
Apr 8 – May 3	TAU
May 4 – May 27	TAU (R)
May 28 – Jun 13	TAU
Jun 14 – Jul 1	GEM
Jul 2 – Jul 15	CAN
Jul 16 – Aug 1	LEO
Aug 2 – Aug 25	VIR
Aug 26 – Sep 4	LIB
Sep 5 – Sep 11	LIB (R)
Sep 12 – Sep 26	VIR (R)
Sep 27 – Oct 8	VIR
Oct 9 – Oct 26	LIB
Oct 27 – Nov 14	SCO
Nov 15 – Dec 4	SAG
Dec 5 – Dec 23	CAP
Dec 24 – Dec 31	CAP (R)

1997

Jan 1 – Jan 12	CAP (R)
Jan 13 – Feb 8	CAP
Feb 9 – Feb 27	AQU
Feb 28 – Mar 15	PIS
Mar 16 – Apr 1	ARI
Apr 2 – Apr 15	TAU
Apr 16 – May 4	TAU (R)
May 5 – May 8	ARI (R)
May 9 – May 11	ARI
May 12 – Jun 8	TAU
Jun 9 – Jun 23	GEM
Jun 24 – Jul 7	CAN
Jul 8 – Jul 26	LEO
Jul 27 – Aug 17	VIR
Aug 18 – Sep 10	VIR (R)
Sep 11 – Oct 1	VIR
Oct 2 – Oct 18	LIB
Oct 19 – Nov 7	SCO
Nov 8 – Nov 30	SAG
Dec 1 – Dec 7	CAP
Dec 8 – Dec 13	CAP (R)
Dec 14 – Dec 27	SAG (R)
Dec 28 – Dec 31	SAG

1998

Jan 1 – Jan 12	SAG
Jan 13 – Feb 2	CAP
Feb 3 – Feb 19	AQU
Feb 20 – Mar 7	PIS
Mar 8 – Mar 27	ARI
Mar 28 – Apr 20	ARI (R)
Apr 21 – May 14	TAU
May 15 – May 31	ARI
Jun 1 – Jun 14	GEM
Jun 15 – Jun 30	CAN
Jul 1 – Aug 1	LEO
Aug 2 – Aug 23	LEO (R)
Aug 24 – Sep 7	LEO
Sep 8 – Sep 23	VIR
Sep 24 – Oct 11	LIB
Oct 12 – Nov 1	SCO
Nov 2 – Nov 21	SAG
Nov 22 – Dec 11	SAG (R)
Dec 12 – Dec 31	SAG

1999

Jan 1 – Jan 6	SAG
Jan 7 – Jan 25	CAP
Jan 26 – Feb 12	AQU
Feb 13 – Mar 2	PIS
Mar 3 – Mar 10	ARI
Mar 11 – Mar 17	ARI (R)
Mar 18 – Apr 2	PIS (R)
Apr 3 – Apr 17	PIS
Apr 18 – May 8	ARI
May 9 – May 23	TAU
May 24 – Jun 6	GEM
Jun 7 – Jun 26	CAN
Jun 27 – Jul 12	LEO
Jul 13 – Jul 31	LEO (R)
Aug 1 – Aug 6	CAN (R)
Aug 7 – Aug 10	CAN
Aug 11 – Aug 31	LEO
Sep 1 – Sep 16	VIR
Sep 17 – Oct 4	LIB
Oct 5 – Oct 30	SCO
Oct 31 – Nov 5	SAG
Nov 6 – Nov 9	SAG (R)
Nov 10 – Nov 25	SCO (R)
Nov 26 – Dec 10	SCO
Dec 11 – Dec 30	SAG
Dec 31 – Dec 31	CAP

2000

Jan 1 – Jan 18	CAP
Jan 19 – Feb 4	AQU
Feb 5 – Feb 20	PIS
Feb 21 – Mar 13	PIS (R)
Mar 14 – Apr 12	PIS
Apr 13 – Apr 29	ARI
Apr 30 – May 13	TAU
May 14 – May 29	GEM
May 30 – Jun 22	CAN
Jun 23 – Jul 16	CAN (R)
Jul 17 – Aug 6	CAN
Aug 7 – Aug 21	LEO
Aug 22 – Sep 7	VIR
Sep 8 – Sep 28	LIB
Sep 29 – Oct 17	SCO
Oct 18 – Nov 6	SCO (R)
Nov 7 – Nov 7	LIB (R)
Nov 8 – Nov 8	LIB
Nov 9 – Dec 3	SCO
Dec 4 – Dec 22	SAG
Dec 23 – Dec 31	CAP

2001

Jan 1 – Jan 10	CAP
Jan 11 – Feb 1	AQU
Feb 2 – Feb 3	PIS
Feb 4 – Feb 6	PIS (R)
Feb 7 – Feb 24	AQU (R)
Feb 25 – Mar 17	AQU
Mar 18 – Apr 6	PIS
Apr 7 – Apr 21	ARI
Apr 22 – May 6	TAU
May 7 – Jun 3	GEM
Jun 4 – Jun 27	GEM (R)
Jun 28 – Jul 12	GEM
Jul 13 – Jul 30	CAN
Jul 31 – Aug 14	LEO
Aug 15 – Sep 1	VIR
Sep 2 – Sep 30	LIB
Oct 1 – Oct 22	LIB (R)
Oct 23 – Nov 7	LIB
Nov 8 – Nov 26	SCO
Nov 27 – Dec 15	SAG
Dec 16 – Dec 31	CAP

2002

Jan 1 – Jan 3	CAP
Jan 4 – Jan 17	AQU
Jan 18 – Feb 4	AQU (R)
Feb 5 – Feb 7	CAP (R)
Feb 8 – Feb 13	CAP
Feb 14 – Mar 11	AQU
Mar 12 – Mar 29	PIS
Mar 30 – Apr 13	ARI
Apr 14 – Apr 30	TAU
May 1 – May 14	GEM
May 15 – Jun 7	GEM (R)
Jun 8 – Jul 7	GEM
Jul 8 – Jul 21	CAN
Jul 22 – Aug 6	LEO
Aug 7 – Aug 26	VIR
Aug 27 – Sep 13	LIB
Sep 14 – Oct 2	LIB (R)
Oct 3 – Oct 5	VIR (R)
Oct 6 – Oct 11	VIR
Oct 12 – Oct 31	LIB
Nov 1 – Nov 19	SCO
Nov 20 – Dec 8	SAG
Dec 9 – Dec 31	CAP

2003

Jan 1 – Jan 1	CAP
Jan 2 – Jan 22	CAP (R)
Jan 23 – Feb 13	CAP
Feb 14 – Mar 5	AQU
Mar 6 – Mar 21	PIS
Mar 22 – Apr 5	ARI
Apr 6 – Apr 25	TAU
Apr 26 – May 19	TAU (R)
May 20 – Jun 13	TAU
Jun 14 – Jun 29	GEM
Jun 30 – Jul 13	CAN
Jul 14 – Jul 30	LEO
Jul 31 – Aug 27	VIR
Aug 28 – Sep 19	VIR (R)
Sep 20 – Oct 7	VIR
Oct 8 – Oct 24	LIB
Oct 25 – Nov 12	SCO
Nov 13 – Dec 2	SAG
Dec 3 – Dec 16	CAP
Dec 17 – Dec 30	CAP (R)
Dec 31 – Dec 31	SAG (R)

2004

Jan 1 – Jan 5	SAG (R)
Jan 6 – Jan 14	SAG
Jan 15 – Feb 7	CAP
Feb 8 – Feb 25	AQU
Feb 26 – Mar 12	PIS
Mar 13 – Apr 1	ARI
Apr 2 – Apr 5	TAU
Apr 6 – Apr 13	TAU (R)
Apr 14 – Apr 29	ARI (R)
Apr 30 – May 16	ARI
May 17 – Jun 5	TAU
Jun 6 – Jun 19	GEM
Jun 20 – Jul 4	CAN
Jul 5 – Jul 25	LEO
Jul 26 – Aug 10	VIR
Aug 11 – Aug 25	VIR (R)
Aug 26 – Sep 1	LEO (R)
Sep 2 – Sep 10	LEO
Sep 11 – Sep 28	VIR
Sep 29 – Oct 15	LIB
Oct 16 – Nov 4	SCO
Nov 5 – Nov 29	SAG
Nov 30 – Dec 18	SAG (R)
Dec 19 – Dec 31	SAG

2005

Jan 1 – Jan 10	SAG
Jan 11 – Jan 30	CAP
Jan 31 – Feb 16	AQU
Feb 17 – Mar 5	PIS
Mar 6 – Mar 19	ARI
Mar 20 – Apr 11	ARI (R)
Apr 12 – May 12	ARI
May 13 – May 28	TAU
May 29 – Jun 11	GEM
Jun 12 – Jun 28	CAN
Jun 29 – Jul 22	LEO
Jul 23 – Aug 15	LEO (R)
Aug 16 – Sep 4	LEO
Sep 5 – Sep 20	VIR
Sep 21 – Oct 8	LIB
Oct 9 – Oct 30	SCO
Oct 31 – Nov 13	SAG
Nov 14 – Nov 26	SAG (R)
Nov 27 – Dec 3	SCO (R)
Dec 4 – Dec 12	SCO
Dec 13 – Dec 31	SAG

2006

Jan 1 – Jan 3	SAG
Jan 4 – Jan 22	CAP
Jan 23 – Feb 9	AQU
Feb 10 – Mar 1	PIS
Mar 2 – Mar 24	PIS (R)
Mar 25 – Apr 16	PIS
Apr 17 – May 5	ARI
May 6 – May 19	TAU
May 20 – Jun 3	GEM
Jun 4 – Jun 28	CAN
Jun 29 – Jul 3	LEO
Jul 4 – Jul 10	LEO (R)
Jul 11 – Jul 28	CAN (R)
Jul 29 – Aug 11	CAN
Aug 12 – Aug 27	LEO
Aug 28 – Sep 12	VIR
Sep 13 – Oct 2	LIB
Oct 3 – Oct 27	SCO
Oct 28 – Nov 17	SCO (R)
Nov 18 – Dec 8	SCO
Dec 9 – Dec 27	SAG
Dec 28 – Dec 31	CAP

2007

Jan 1 – Jan 15	CAP
Jan 16 – Feb 2	AQU
Feb 3 – Feb 13	PIS
Feb 14 – Feb 17	PIS (R)
Feb 18 – Mar 7	AQU (R)
Mar 8 – Mar 18	AQU
Mar 19 – Apr 10	PIS
Apr 11 – Apr 27	ARI
Apr 28 – May 11	TAU
May 12 – May 29	GEM
May 30 – Jun 14	CAN
Jun 15 – Jul 9	CAN (R)
Jul 10 – Aug 4	CAN
Aug 5 – Aug 19	LEO
Aug 20 – Sep 5	VIR
Sep 6 – Sep 27	LIB
Sep 28 – Oct 11	SCO
Oct 12 – Oct 24	SCO (R)
Oct 25 – Oct 31	LIB (R)
Nov 1 – Nov 11	LIB
Nov 12 – Dec 1	SCO
Dec 2 – Dec 20	SAG
Dec 21 – Dec 31	CAP

2008

Jan 1 – Jan 9	CAP
Jan 10 – Jan 27	AQU
Jan 28 – Feb 18	AQU (R)
Feb 19 – Mar 14	AQU
Mar 15 – Apr 2	PIS
Apr 3 – Apr 17	ARI
Apr 18 – May 2	TAU
May 3 – May 25	GEM
May 26 – Jun 18	GEM (R)
Jun 19 – Jul 10	GEM
Jul 11 – Jul 26	CAN
Jul 27 – Aug 10	LEO
Aug 11 – Aug 29	VIR
Aug 30 – Sep 23	LIB
Sep 24 – Oct 14	LIB (R)
Oct 15 – Nov 4	LIB
Nov 5 – Nov 23	SCO
Nov 24 – Dec 12	SAG
Dec 13 – Dec 31	CAP

2009

Jan 1 – Jan 1	CAP
Jan 2 – Jan 10	AQU
Jan 11 – Jan 21	AQU (R)
Jan 22 – Jan 31	CAP (R)
Feb 1 – Feb 14	CAP
Feb 15 – Mar 8	AQU
Mar 9 – Mar 25	PIS
Mar 26 – Apr 9	ARI
Apr 10 – Apr 30	TAU
May 1 – May 6	GEM
May 7 – May 13	GEM (R)
May 14 – May 30	TAU (R)
May 31 – Jun 14	TAU
Jun 15 – Jul 3	GEM
Jul 4 – Jul 17	CAN
Jul 18 – Aug 2	LEO
Aug 3 – Aug 25	VIR
Aug 26 – Sep 6	LIB
Sep 7 – Sep 18	LIB (R)
Sep 19 – Sep 28	VIR (R)
Sep 29 – Oct 10	VIR
Oct 11 – Oct 28	LIB
Oct 29 – Nov 16	SCO
Nov 17 – Dec 5	SAG
Dec 6 – Dec 25	CAP
Dec 26 – Dec 31	CAP (R)

2010

Jan 1 – Jan 14	CAP (R)
Jan 15 – Feb 10	CAP
Feb 11 – Mar 1	AQU
Mar 2 – Mar 17	PIS
Mar 18 – Apr 2	ARI
Apr 3 – Apr 17	TAU
Apr 18 – May 10	TAU (R)
May 11 – Jun 10	TAU
Jun 11 – Jun 25	GEM
Jun 26 – Jul 9	CAN
Jul 10 – Jul 27	LEO
Jul 28 – Aug 19	VIR
Aug 20 – Sep 11	VIR (R)
Sep 12 – Oct 3	VIR
Oct 4 – Oct 20	LIB
Oct 21 – Nov 8	SCO
Nov 9 – Dec 1	SAG
Dec 2 – Dec 9	CAP
Dec 10 – Dec 18	CAP (R)
Dec 19 – Dec 29	SAG (R)
Dec 30 – Dec 31	SAG (R)

Venus Ephemeris:
How To Find the Venus Sign

Under the year of birth, find the birth date. If birth was on the first or last day of a particular time period, it's possible that Venus might be posited in the preceding or following Sign. For example, if the time period is from August 6 to September 10, and birth occurred on September 10, then Venus might be in the next Sign. The only way to be absolutely sure is to have a chart done by a computer service (see appendix 2 for resources) or by a professional astrologer. If you are unsure, read the adjacent Sign to decide which is more applicable.

Before checking the following Venus tables, first look at the Venus Retrograde table on the next page to determine if the Planet was in retrograde motion at the time of birth. Look up the year in the left-hand column, then check the retrograde period, marked R, noticing the "backward" movement of the Planet from one Sign to the previous Sign. At the end of each entry, D indicates the planet's return to direct motion.

Example:

1975 R Aug 6 in Virgo, into Leo Sep 3, D Sep 18 at which point refer to the ephemeris to find 1975 Sep 3–Oct 4 Leo. Thus, if birth occurred between Sep 3–17, Venus would be in Leo Retrograde; but if birth occurred between Sep 18–Oct 4, Venus, while still in Leo, would be direct.

Venus does not retrograde every year.

Venus Retrograde Table

1950 R Jan 20 in Aqu	D Feb 20 1950
1951 R Aug 13 in Vir	D Sep 25 1951
1953 R Mar 23 in Tau, into Ari Apr 1	D May 4 1953
1954 R Oct 25 in Sag, into Sco Oct 28	D Nov 7 1954
1956 R May 30 in Can, into Gem Jun 24	D Jul 13 1956
1958 R Jan in Aqu	D Feb 18 1958
1959 R Aug 10 in Vir, into Leo Sep 21	D Sep 22 1959
1961 R Mar 20 in Ari	D May 2 1961
1962 R Oct 23 in Sco	D Dec 3 1962
1964 R May 29 in Can, into Gem Jun 18	D Jul 11 1964
1966 R Jan 5 in Aqu, into Cap Feb 7	D Feb 15 1966
1967 R Aug 8 in Vir, into Leo Sep 10	D Sep 20 1967
1969 R Mar 18 in Ari	D Apr 10 1969
1970 R Oct 20 in Sco	D Dec 2 1970
1972 R May 27 in Can, into Gem Jun 28	D Jul 9 1972
1974 R Jan 3 in Aqu, into Can Jan 30	D Feb 13 1974
1975 R Aug 6 in Vir, into Leo Sep 3	D Sep 18 1975
1977 R Mar 16 in Ari	D Apr 27 1977
1978 R Oct 18 in Sco	D Nov 28 1978
1980 R May 24 in Can, into Gem Jun 6	D Jul 6 1980
1982 R Jan 1 in Aqu, into Cap Jan 24	D Feb 10 1982
1983 R Aug 3 in Vir, into Leo Aug 28	D Sep 15 1983
1985 R Mar 13 in Ari	D Apr 25 1985
1986 R Oct 15 in Sco	D Nov 26 1986
1988 R May 22 in Can, into Gem May 28	D Jul 4 1988
1989 R Dec 29 in Aqu, into Cap Jan 17 1990	D Feb 9 1990
1991 R Aug 2 in Vir, into Leo Aug 22	D Sep 13 1991
1993 R Mar 11 in Ari	D Apr 22 1993
1994 R Oct 13 in Sco	D Nov 23 1994
1996 R May 20 in Gem	D Jul 2 1996
1997 R Dec 26 in Aqu, into Cap Jan 19 1998	D Feb 5 1998
1999 R Aug 2 in Vir, into Leo Aug 16	D Sep 11 1999
2001 R Mar 9 in Ari	D Apr 20 2001
2002 R Oct 10 in Sco	D Nov 21 2002
2004 R May 17 in Gem	D Jun 29 2004
2005 R Dec 24 in Aqu, into Cap Jan 2 2006	D Feb 3 2006
2007 R Jul 27 in Vir, into Leo Aug 10	D Sep 8 2007
2009 R Mar 6 in Ari, into Pis Apr 12	D Apr 17 2009
2010 R Oct 8 in Sco, into Lib Nov 9	D Nov 18 2010

1950

Jan 1 – Apr 6	AQU
Apr 7 – May 5	PIS
May 6 – Jun 1	ARI
Jun 2 – Jun 26	TAU
Jun 27 – Jul 22	GEM
Jul 23 – Aug 16	CAN
Aug 17 – Sep 9	LEO
Sep 10 – Oct 3	VIR
Oct 4 – Oct 27	LIB
Oct 28 – Nov 20	SCO
Nov 21 – Dec 14	SAG
Dec 15 – Dec 31	CAP

1951

Jan 1 – Jan 6	CAP
Jan 7 – Jan 30	AQU
Jan 31 – Feb 24	PIS
Feb 25 – Mar 20	ARI
Mar 21 – Apr 14	TAU
Apr 15 – May 10	GEM
May 11 – Jun 6	CAN
Jun 7 – Jul 7	LEO
Jul 8 – Nov 7	VIR
Nov 8 – Dec 8	LIB
Dec 8 – Dec 31	SCO

1952

Jan 1	SCO
Jan 2 – Jan 26	SAG
Jan 27 – Feb 20	CAP
Feb 21 – Mar 16	AQU
Mar 17 – Apr 8	PIS
Apr 9 – May 3	ARI
May 4 – May 28	TAU
May 29 – Jun 21	GEM
Jun 22 – Jul 15	CAN
Jul 16 – Aug 8	LEO
Aug 9 – Sep 2	VIR
Sep 3 – Sep 26	LIB
Sep 27 – Oct 21	SCO
Oct 22 – Nov 15	SAG
Nov 16 – Dec 9	CAP
Dec 10 – Dec 31	AQU

1953

Jan 1 – Jan 4	AQU
Jan 5 – Feb 1	PIS
Feb 2 – Mar 14	ARI
Mar 15 – Mar 30	TAU
Mar 31 – Jun 4	ARI
Jun 5 – Jul 6	TAU
Jul 7 – Aug 3	GEM
Aug 4 – Aug 29	CAN
Aug 30 – Sep 23	LEO
Sep 24 – Oct 18	VIR
Oct 19 – Nov 11	LIB
Nov 12 – Dec 5	SCO
Dec 6 – Dec 29	SAG
Dec 30 – Dec 31	CAP

1954

Jan 1 – Jan 21	CAP
Jan 22 – Fob 14	AQU
Feb 15 – Mar 10	PIS
Mar 11 – Apr 3	ARI
Apr 4 – Apr 28	TAU
Apr 29 – May 23	GEM
May 24 – Jun 17	CAN
Jun 18 – Jul 12	LEO
Jul 13 – Aug 8	VIR
Aug 9 – Sep 6	LIB
Sep 7 – Oct 22	SCO
Oct 23 – Oct 26	SAG
Oct 27 – Dec 31	SCO

1955

Jan 1 – Jan 5	SCO
Jan 6 – Feb 5	SAG
Feb 6 – Mar 4	CAP
Mar 5 – Mar 29	AQU
Mar 30 – Apr 24	PIS
Apr 25 – May 19	ARI
May 20 – Jun 12	TAU
Jun 13 – Jul 7	GEM
Jul 8 – Jul 31	CAN
Aug 1 – Aug 25	LEO
Aug 26 – Sep 18	VIR
Sep 19 – Oct 12	LIB
Oct 13 – Nov 5	SCO
Nov 6 – Nov 29	SAG
Nov 30 – Dec 23	CAP
Dec 24 – Dec 31	AQU

1956

Jan 1 – Jan 17	AQU
Jan 18 – Feb 10	PIS
Feb 11 – Mar 7	ARI
Mar 8 – Apr 3	TAU
Apr 4 – May 7	GEM
May 8 – Jun 22	CAN
Jun 23 – Aug 3	CAN
Aug 4 – Sep 7	CAN
Sep 8 – Oct 5	LEO
Oct 6 – Oct 31	VIR
Nov 1 – Nov 25	LIB
Nov 26 – Dec 19	SCO
Dec 20 – Dec 31	SAG

1957

Jan 1 – Jan 12	SAG
Jan 13 – Feb 5	CAP
Feb 6 – Mar 1	AQU
Mar 2 – Mar 25	PIS
Mar 26 – Apr 18	ARI
Apr 19 – May 12	LEO
May 13 – Jun 6	GEM
Jun 7 – Jul 1	CAN
Jul 2 – Jul 25	LEO
Jul 26 – Aug 19	VIR
Aug 20 – Sep 13	LIB
Sep 14 – Oct 9	SCO
Oct 10 – Nov 5	SAG
Nov 6 – Dec 6	CAP
Dec 7 – Dec 31	AQU

1958

Jan 1 – Apr 6	AQU
Apr 7 – May 4	PIS
May 5 – May 31	ARI
Jun 1 – Jun 26	TAU
Jun 27 – Jul 21	GEM
Jul 22 – Aug 15	CAN
Aug 16 – Sep 9	LEO
Sep 10 – Oct 3	VIR
Oct 4 – Oct 27	LIB
Oct 28 – Nov 20	SCO
Nov 21 – Dec 13	SAG
Dec 14 – Dec 31	CAP

1959

Jan 1 – Jan 6	CAP
Jan 7 – Jan 30	AQU
Jan 31 – Feb 24	PIS
Feb 25 – Mar 20	ARI
Mar 21 – Apr 14	TAU
Apr 15 – May 10	GEM
May 11 – Jun 6	CAN
Jun 7 – Jul 8	LEO
Jul 9 – Sep 19	VIR
Sep 20 – Sep 24	LEO
Sep 25 – Nov 9	VIR
Nov 10 – Dec 7	LIB
Dec 8 – Dec 31	SCO

1960

Jan 1	SCO
Jan 2 – Jan 26	SAG
Jan 27 – Feb 20	CAP
Feb 21 – Mar 15	AQU
Mar 16 – Apr 8	PIS
Apr 9 – May 3	ARI
May 4 – May 27	TAU
May 28 – Jun 21	GEM
Jun 22 – Jul 15	CAN
Jul 16 – Aug 8	LEO
Aug 9 – Sep 2	VIR
Sep 3 – Sep 26	LIB
Sep 27 – Oct 21	SCO
Oct 22 – Nov 15	SAG
Nov 16 – Dec 9	CAP
Dec 10 – Dec 31	AQU

1961

Jan 1 – Jan 4	AQU
Jan 5 – Feb 1	PIS
Feb 2 – Jun 5	ARI
Jun 6 – Jul 6	TAU
Jul 7 – Aug 3	GEM
Aug 4 – Aug 29	CAN
Aug 30 – Sep 23	LEO
Sep 24 – Oct 17	VIR
Oct 18 – Nov 10	LIB
Nov 11 – Dec 4	SCO
Dec 5 – Dec 28	SAG
Dec 29 – Dec 31	CAP

1962

Jan 1 – Jan 21	CAP
Jan 22 – Feb 14	AQU
Feb 15 – Mar 10	PIS
Mar 11 – Apr 3	ARI
Apr 4 – Apr 27	TAU
Apr 28 – May 22	GEM
May 23 – Jun 16	CAN
Jun 17 – Jul 12	LEO
Jul 13 – Aug 8	VIR
Aug 9 – Sep 6	LIB
Sep 7 – Dec 31	SCO

1963

Jan 1 – Jan 6	SCO
Jan 7 – Feb 5	SAG
Feb 6 – Mar 3	CAP
Mar 4 – Mar 29	AQU
Mar 30 – Apr 23	PIS
Apr 24 – May 18	ARI
May 19 – Jun 11	TAU
Jun 12 – Jul 6	GEM
Jul 7 – Jul 31	CAN
Aug 1 – Aug 24	LEO
Aug 25 – Sep 17	VIR
Sep 18 – Oct 11	LIB
Oct 12 – Nov 4	SCO
Nov 5 – Nov 28	SAG
Nov 29 – Dec 23	CAP
Dec 24 – Dec 31	AQU

1964

Jan 1 – Jan 16	AQU
Jan 17 – Feb 9	PIS
Feb 10 – Mar 6	ARI
Mar 7 – Apr 3	TAU
Apr 4 – May 8	GEM
May 9 – Jun 16	CAN
Jun 17 – Aug 4	GEM
Aug 5 – Sep 7	CAN
Sep 8 – Oct 4	LEO
Oct 5 – Oct 30	VIR
Oct 31 – Nov 24	LIB
Nov 25 – Dec 18	SCO
Dec 19 – Dec 31	SAG

1965

Jan 1 – Jan 11	SAG
Jan 12 – Feb 4	CAP
Feb 5 – Feb 28	AQU
Mar 1 – Mar 24	PIS
Mar 25 – Apr 17	ARI
Apr 18 – May 11	TAU
May 12 – Jun 5	GEM
Jun 6 – Jun 30	CAN
Jul 1 – Jul 24	LEO
Jul 25 – Aug 18	VIR
Aug 19 – Sep 13	LIB
Sep 14 – Oct 8	SCO
Oct 9 – Nov 5	SAG
Nov 6 – Dec 6	CAP
Dec 7 – Dec 31	AQU

1966

Jan 1 – Feb 6	AQU
Feb 7 – Feb 25	CAP
Feb 26 – Apr 6	AQU
Apr 7 – May 5	PIS
May 6 – May 31	ARI
Jun 1 – Jun 26	TAU
Jun 27 – Jul 21	GEM
Jul 22 – Aug 15	CAN
Aug 16 – Sep 8	LEO
Sep 9 – Oct 3	VIR
Oct 4 – Oct 27	LIB
Oct 28 – Nov 20	SCO
Nov 21 – Dec 13	SAG
Dec 14 – Dec 31	CAP

1967

Jan 1 – Jan 6	CAP
Jan 7 – Jan 30	AQU
Jan 31 – Feb 23	PIS
Feb 24 – Mar 20	ARI
Mar 21 – Apr 14	TAU
Apr 15 – May 10	GEM
May 11 – Jun 6	CAN
Jun 7 – Jul 8	LEO
Jul 9 – Sep 9	VIR
Sep 10 – Oct 1	LEO
Oct 2 – Nov 9	VIR
Nov 10 – Dec 7	LIB
Dec 8 – Dec 31	SCO

1968

Jan 1 – Jan 26	SAG
Jan 27 – Feb 20	CAP
Feb 21 – Mar 15	AQU
Mar 16 – Apr 8	PIS
Apr 9 – May 3	ARI
May 4 – May 27	TAU
May 28 – Jun 21	GEM
Jun 22 – Jul 15	CAN
Jul 16 – Aug 8	LEO
Aug 9 – Sep 2	VIR
Sep 3 – Sep 26	LIB
Sep 27 – Oct 21	SCO
Oct 22 – Nov 14	SAG
Nov 15 – Dec 9	CAP
Dec 10 – Dec 31	AQU

1969

Jan 1 – Jan 4	AQU
Jan 5 – Feb 2	PIS
Feb 3 – Jun 6	ARI
Jun 7 – Jul 6	TAU
Jul 7 – Aug 3	GEM
Aug 4 – Aug 29	CAN
Aug 30 – Sep 23	LIB
Sep 24 – Oct 17	VIR
Oct 18 – Nov 10	LIB
Nov 11 – Dec 4	SCO
Dec 5 – Dec 28	SAG
Dec 29 – Dec 31	CAP

1970

Jan 1 – Jan 21	CAP
Jan 22 – Feb 14	AQU
Feb 15 – Mar 10	PIS
Mar 11 – Apr 3	ARI
Apr 4 – Apr 27	TAU
Apr 28 – May 22	GEM
May 23 – Jun 16	CAN
Jun 17 – Jul 12	LEO
Jul 13 – Aug 8	VIR
Aug 9 – Sep 7	LIB
Sep 8 – Dec 31	SCO

1971

Jan 1 – Jan 7	SCO
Jan 8 – Feb 5	SAG
Feb 6 – Mar 4	CAP
Mar 5 – Mar 29	AQU
Mar 30 – Apr 23	PIS
Apr 24 – May 18	ARI
May 19 – Jun 12	TAU
Jun 13 – Jul 6	GEM
Jul 7 – Jul 31	CAN
Aug 1 – Aug 24	LEO
Aug 25 – Sep 17	VIR
Sep 18 – Oct 11	LIB
Oct 12 – Nov 5	LEO
Nov 6 – Nov 29	SAG
Nov 30 – Dec 23	CAP
Dec 24 – Dec 31	AQU

1972

Jan 1 – Jan 16	AQU
Jan 17 – Feb 10	PIS
Feb 11 – Mar 7	ARI
Mar 8 – Apr 3	TAU
Apr 4 – May 10	GEM
May 11 – Jun 11	CAN
Jun 12 – Aug 6	GEM
Aug 7 – Sep 7	CAN
Sep 8 – Oct 5	LEO
Oct 6 – Oct 30	VIR
Oct 31 – Nov 24	LIB
Nov 25 – Dec 18	SCO
Dec 19 – Dec 31	SAG

1973

Jan 1 – Jan 11	SAG
Jan 12 – Feb 4	CAP
Feb 5 – Feb 28	AQU
Mar 1 – Mar 24	PIS
Mar 25 – Apr 18	ARI
Apr 19 – May 12	TAU
May 13 – Jun 5	GEM
Jun 6 – Jun 30	CAN
Jul 1 – Jul 25	LEO
Jul 26 – Aug 19	VIR
Aug 20 – Sep 13	LIB
Sep 14 – Oct 9	SCO
Oct 10 – Nov 5	SAG
Nov 6 – Dec 7	CAP
Dec 8 – Dec 31	AQU

1974

Jan 1 – Jan 29	AQU
Jan 30 – Feb 28	CAP
Mar 1 – Apr 6	AQU
Apr 7 – May 4	PIS
May 5 – May 31	ARI
Jun 1 – Jun 25	TAU
Jun 26 – Jul 21	GEM
Jul 22 – Aug 14	CAN
Aug 15 – Sep 8	LEO
Sep 9 – Oct 2	VIR
Oct 3 – Oct 26	LIB
Oct 27 – Nov 19	SCO
Nov 20 – Dec 13	SAG
Dec 14 – Dec 31	CAP

1975

Jan 1 – Jan 6	CAP
Jan 7 – Jan 30	AQU
Jan 31 – Feb 23	PIS
Feb 24 – Mar 19	ARI
Mar 20 – Apr 13	TAU
Apr 14 – May 9	GEM
May 10 – Jun 6	CAN
Jun 7 – Jul 9	LEO
Jul 10 – Sep 2	VIR
Sep 3 – Oct 4	LEO
Oct 5 – Nov 9	VIR
Nov 10 – Dec 7	LIB
Dec 8 – Dec 31	SCO

1976

Jan 1	SCO
Jan 2 – Jan 26	SAG
Jan 27 – Feb 19	CAP
Feb 20 – Mar 15	AQU
Mar 16 – Apr 8	PIS
Apr 9 – May 2	ARI
May 3 – May 27	TAU
May 28 – Jun 20	GEM
Jun 21 – Jul 14	CAN
Jun 15 – Aug 8	LEO
Aug 9 – Sep 1	VIR
Sep 2 – Sep 26	LIB
Sep 27 – Oct 20	SCO
Oct 21 – Nov 14	SAG
Nov 15 – Dec 9	CAP
Dec 10 – Dec 31	AQU

1977

Jan 1 – Jan 4	AQU
Jan 5 – Feb 2	PIS
Feb 3 – Jun 6	ARI
Jun 7 – Jul 6	TAU
Jul 7 – Aug 2	GEM
Aug 3 – Aug 28	CAN
Aug 29 – Sep 22	LEO
Sep 23 – Oct 17	VIR
Oct 18 – Nov 10	LIB
Nov 11 – Dec 4	SCO
Dec 5 – Dec 27	SAG
Dec 28 – Dec 31	CAP

1978

Jan 1 – Jan 20	CAP
Jan 21 – Feb 13	AQU
Feb 14 – Mar 9	PIS
Mar 10 – Apr 2	ARI
Apr 3 – Apr 27	TAU
Apr 28 – May 22	GEM
May 23 – Jun 16	CAN
Jun 17 – Jul 12	LEO
Jul 13 – Aug 8	VIR
Aug 9 – Sep 7	LIB
Sep 8 – Dec 31	SCO

1979

Jan 1 – Jan 7	SCO
Jan 8 – Feb 5	SAG
Feb 6 – Mar 3	CAP
Mar 4 – Mar 29	AQU
Mar 30 – Apr 23	PIS
Apr 24 – May 18	ARI
May 19 – Jun 11	TAU
Jun 12 – Jul 6	GEM
Jul 7 – Jul 30	CAN
Jul 31 – Aug 24	LEO
Aug 25 – Sep 17	VIR
Sep 18 – Oct 11	LIB
Oct 12 – Nov 4	SCO
Nov 5 – Nov 28	SAG
Nov 29 – Dec 22	CAP
Dec 23 – Dec 31	AQU

1980

Jan 1 – Jan 16	AQU
Jan 17 – Feb 9	PIS
Feb 10 – Mar 6	ARI
Mar 7 – Apr 3	TAU
Apr 4 – May 12	GEM
May 13 – Jun 5	CAN
Jun 6 – Aug 6	GEM
Aug 7 – Sep 7	CAN
Sep 8 – Oct 4	LEO
Oct 5 – Oct 30	VIR
Oct 31 – Nov 24	LIB
Nov 25 – Dec 18	SCO
Dec 19 – Dec 31	SAG

1981

Jan 1 – Jan 11	SAG
Jan 12 – Feb 4	CAP
Feb 5 – Feb 28	AQU
Mar 1 – Mar 24	PIS
Mar 25 – Apr 17	ARI
Apr 18 – May 11	TAU
May 12 – Jun 5	GEM
Jun 6 – Jun 29	CAN
Jun 30 – Jul 24	LEO
Jul 25 – Aug 18	VIR
Aug 19 – Sep 12	LIB
Sep 13 – Oct 9	SCO
Oct 10 – Nov 5	SAG
Nov 6 – Dec 8	CAP
Dec 9 – Dec 31	AQU

1982

Jan 1 – Jan 23	AQU
Jan 24 – Mar 2	CAP
Mar 3 – Apr 6	AQU
Apr 7 – May 4	PIS
May 5 – May 30	ARI
May 31 – Jun 25	TAU
Jun 26 – Jul 20	GEM
Jul 21 – Aug 14	CAN
Aug 15 – Sep 7	LEO
Sep 8 – Oct 2	VIR
Oct 3 – Oct 26	LIB
Oct 27 – Nov 18	SCO
Nov 19 – Dec 12	SAG
Dec 13 – Dec 31	CAP

1983

Jan 1 – Jan 5	CAP
Jan 6 – Jan 29	AQU
Jan 30 – Feb 22	PIS
Feb 23 – Mar 18	ARI
Mar 19 – Apr 12	TAU
Apr 13 – May 8	GEM
May 9 – Jun 5	CAN
Jun 6 – Jul 9	LEO
Jul 10 – Aug 26	VIR
Aug 27 – Oct 5	LEO
Oct 6 – Nov 8	VIR
Nov 14 – Dec 6	LIB
Dec 7 – Dec 31	SCO

1984

Jan 1 – Jan 25	SAG
Jan 26 – Feb 18	CAP
Feb 19 – Mar 14	AQU
Mar 15 – Apr 7	PIS
Apr 8 – May 1	ARI
May 2 – May 26	TAU
May 27 – Jun 19	GEM
Jun 20 – Jul 13	CAN
Jul 14 – Aug 7	LEO
Aug 8 – Aug 31	VIR
Sep 1 – Sep 25	LIB
Sep 26 – Oct 19	SCO
Oct 20 – Nov 13	SAG
Nov 14 – Dec 8	CAP
Dec 9 – Dec 31	AQU

1985

Jan 1 – Jan 3	AQU
Jan 4 – Feb 1	PIS
Feb 2 – Jun 5	ARI
Jun 6 – Jul 5	TAU
Jul 6 – Aug 1	GEM
Aug 2 – Aug 27	CAN
Aug 28 – Sep 21	LEO
Sep 22 – Oct 16	VIR
Oct 17 – Nov 9	LIB
Nov 10 – Dec 3	SCO
Dec 4 – Dec 26	SAG
Dec 27 – Dec 31	CAP

1986

Jan 1 – Jan 19	CAP
Jan 20 – Feb 12	AQU
Feb 13 – Mar 8	PIS
Mar 9 – Apr 1	ARI
Apr 2 – Apr 26	TAU
Apr 27 – May 21	GEM
May 22 – Jun 15	CAN
Jun 16 – Jul 11	LEO
Jul 12 – Aug 7	VIR
Aug 8 – Sep 6	LIB
Sep 7 – Dec 31	SCO

1987

Jan 1 – Jan 6	SCO
Jan 7 – Feb 4	SAG
Feb 5 – Mar 2	CAP
Mar 3 – Mar 28	AQU
Mar 29 – Apr 22	PIS
Apr 23 – May 16	ARI
May 17 – Jun 10	TAU
Jun 11 – Jul 5	GEM
Jul 6 – Jul 29	CAN
Jul 30 – Aug 23	LEO
Aug 24 – Sep 16	VIR
Sep 17 – Oct 10	LIB
Oct 11 – Nov 3	SCO
Nov 4 – Nov 27	SAG
Nov 28 – Dec 21	CAP
Dec 22 – Dec 31	AQU

1988

Jan 1 – Jan 15	AQU
Jan 16 – Feb 9	PIS
Feb 10 – Mar 5	ARI
Mar 6 – Apr 3	TAU
Apr 4 – May 17	GEM
May 18 – May 26	CAN
May 27 – Aug 6	GEM
Aug 7 – Sep 6	CAN
Sep 7 – Oct 4	LEO
Oct 5 – Oct 29	VIR
Oct 30 – Nov 23	LIB
Nov 24 – Dec 17	SCO
Dec 18 – Dec 31	SAG

1989

Jan 1 – Jan 10	SAG
Jan 11 – Feb 3	CAP
Feb 4 – Feb 27	AQU
Feb 28 – Mar 23	PIS
Mar 24 – Apr 16	ARI
Apr 17 – May 10	TAU
May 11 – Jun 4	GEM
Jun 5 – Jun 28	CAN
Jun 29 – Jul 23	LEO
Jul 24 – Aug 17	VIR
Aug 18 – Sep 12	LIB
Sep 13 – Oct 8	SCO
Oct 9 – Nov 4	SAG
Nov 5 – Dec 9	CAP
Dec 10 – Dec 31	AQU

1990

Jan 1 – Jan 16	AQU
Jan 17 – Mar 3	CAP
Mar 4 – Apr 5	AQU
Apr 6 – May 3	PIS
May 4 – May 29	ARI
May 30 – Jun 24	TAU
Jun 25 – Jul 19	GEM
Jul 20 – Aug 13	CAN
Aug 14 – Sep 6	LEO
Sep 7 – Sep 30	VIR
Oct 1 – Oct 24	LIB
Oct 25 – Nov 17	SCO
Nov 18 – Dec 11	SAG
Dec 12 – Dec 31	CAP

1991

Jan 1 – Jan 4	CAP
Jan 5 – Jan 28	AQU
Jan 29 – Feb 21	PIS
Feb 22 – Mar 18	ARI
Mar 19 – Apr 12	TAU
Apr 13 – May 8	GEM
May 9 – Jun 5	CAN
Jun 6 – Jul 10	LEO
Jul 11 – Aug 21	VIR
Aug 22 – Oct 6	LEO
Oct 7 – Nov 8	VIR
Nov 9 – Dec 5	LIB
Dec 6 – Dec 31	SCO

1992

Jan 1 – Jan 24	SAG
Jan 25 – Feb 18	CAP
Feb 19 – Mar 13	AQU
Mar 14 – Apr 6	PIS
Apr 7 – May 1	ARI
May 2 – May 25	TAU
May 26 – Jun 18	GEM
Jun 19 – Jul 13	CAN
Jul 14 – Aug 6	LEO
Aug 7 – Aug 31	VIR
Sep 1 – Sep 24	LIB
Sep 25 – Oct 19	SCO
Oct 20 – Nov 13	SAG
Nov 14 – Dec 8	CAP
Dec 9 – Dec 31	AQU

1993

Jan 1 – Jan 3	AQU
Jan 4 – Feb 2	PIS
Feb 3 – Jun 5	ARI
Jun 6 – Jul 5	TAU
Jul 6 – Aug 1	GEM
Aug 2 – Aug 27	CAN
Aug 28 – Sep 21	LEO
Sep 22 – Oct 15	VIR
Oct 16 – Nov 8	LIB
Nov 9 – Dec 2	SCO
Dec 3 – Dec 26	SAG
Dec 27 – Dec 31	CAP

1994

Jan 1 – Jan 19	CAP
Jan 20 – Feb 12	AQU
Feb 13 – Mar 8	PIS
Mar 9 – Apr 1	ARI
Apr 2 – Apr 25	TAU
Apr 26 – May 20	GEM
May 21 – Jun 14	CAN
Jun 15 – Jul 10	LEO
Jul 11 – Aug 7	VIR
Aug 8 – Sep 7	LIB
Sep 8 – Dec 31	SCO

1995

Jan 1 – Jan 7	SCO
Jan 8 – Feb 4	SAG
Feb 5 – Mar 2	CAP
Mar 3 – Mar 27	AQU
Mar 28 – Apr 21	PIS
Apr 22 – May 16	ARI
May 17 – Jun 10	TAU
Jun 11 – Jul 4	GEM
Jul 5 – Jul 29	CAN
Jul 30 – Aug 22	LEO
Aug 23 – Sep 15	VIR
Sep 16 – Oct 9	LIB
Oct 10 – Nov 2	SCO
Nov 3 – Nov 27	SAG
Nov 28 – Dec 21	CAP
Dec 22 – Dec 31	AQU

1996

Jan 1 – Jan 14	AQU
Jan 15 – Feb 8	PIS
Feb 9 – Mar 5	ARI
Mar 6 – Apr 3	TAU
Apr 4 – Aug 6	GEM
Aug 7 – Sep 6	CAN
Sep 7 – Oct 3	LEO
Oct 4 – Oct 28	VIR
Oct 29 – Nov 22	LIB
Nov 23 – Dec 16	SCO
Dec 17 – Dec 31	SAG

1997

Jan 1 – Jan 9	SAG
Jan 10 – Feb 2	CAP
Feb 3 – Feb 26	AQU
Feb 27 – Mar 22	PIS
Mar 23 – Apr 15	ARI
Apr 16 – May 10	TAU
May 11 – Jun 3	GEM
Jun 4 – Jun 28	CAN
Jun 29 – Jul 23	LEO
Jul 24 – Aug 17	VIR
Aug 18 – Sep 11	LIB
Sep 12 – Oct 7	SCO
Oct 8 – Nov 4	SAG
Nov 5 – Dec 11	CAP
Dec 12 – Dec 31	AQU

1998

Jan 1 – Jan 9	AQU
Jan 10 – Mar 4	CAP
Mar 5 – Apr 5	AQU
Apr 6 – May 3	PIS
May 4 – May 29	ARI
May 30 – Jun 24	TAU
Jun 25 – Jul 19	GEM
Jul 20 – Aug 12	CAN
Aug 13 – Sep 6	LEO
Sep 7 – Sep 30	VIR
Oct 1 – Oct 24	LIB
Oct 25 – Nov 17	SCO
Nov 18 – Dec 11	SAG
Dec 12 – Dec 31	CAP

1999

Jan 1 – Jan 4	CAP
Jan 5 – Jan 28	AQU
Jan 29 – Feb 21	PIS
Feb 22 – Mar 17	ARI
Mar 18 – Apr 12	TAU
Apr 13 – May 8	GEM
May 9 – Jun 5	CAN
Jun 6 – Jul 12	LEO
Jul 13 – Aug 15	VIR
Aug 16 – Oct 7	LEO
Oct 8 – Nov 8	VIR
Nov 9 – Dec 5	LIB
Dec 6 – Dec 30	SCO
Dec 31 – Dec 31	SAG

2000

Jan 1 – Jan 24	SAG
Jan 25 – Feb 17	CAP
Feb 18 – Mar 12	AQU
Mar 13 – Apr 6	PIS
Apr 7 – Apr 30	ARI
May 1 – May 25	TAU
May 26 – Jun 18	GEM
Jun 19 – Jul 12	CAN
Jul 13 – Aug 6	LEO
Aug 7 – Aug 30	VIR
Aug 31 – Sep 24	LIB
Sep 25 – Oct 18	SCO
Oct 19 – Nov 12	SAG
Nov 13 – Dec 7	CAP
Dec 8 – Dec 31	AQU

2001

Jan 1 – Jan 2	AQU
Jan 3 – Feb 1	PIS
Feb 2 – Jun 5	ARI
Jun 6 – Jul 4	TAU
Jul 5 – Jul 31	GEM
Aug 1 – Aug 25	CAN
Aug 26 – Sep 19	LEO
Sep 20 – Oct 14	VIR
Oct 15 – Nov 7	LIB
Nov 8 – Dec 1	SCO
Dec 2 – Dec 25	SAG
Dec 26 – Dec 31	CAP

2002

Jan 1 – Jan 17	CAP
Jan 18 – Feb 10	AQU
Feb 11 – Mar 6	PIS
Mar 7 – Mar 31	ARI
Apr 1 – Apr 24	TAU
Apr 25 – May 19	GEM
May 20 – Jun 13	CAN
Jun 14 – Jul 9	LEO
Jul 10 – Aug 6	VIR
Aug 7 – Sep 6	LIB
Sep 7 – Dec 31	SCO

2003

Jan 1 – Jan 6	SCO
Jan 7 – Feb 3	SAG
Feb 4 – Mar 1	CAP
Mar 2 – Mar 26	AQU
Mar 27 – Apr 20	PIS
Apr 21 – May 15	ARI
May 16 – Jun 8	TAU
Jun 9 – Jul 13	GEM
Jul 14 – Jul 27	CAN
Jul 28 – Aug 21	LEO
Aug 22 – Sep 14	VIR
Sep 15 – Oct 8	LIB
Oct 9 – Nov 1	SCO
Nov 2 – Nov 25	SAG
Nov 26 – Dec 20	CAP
Dec 21 – Dec 31	AQU

2004

Jan 1 – Jan 13	AQU
Jan 14 – Feb 7	PIS
Feb 8 – Mar 4	ARI
Mar 5 – Apr 2	TAU
Apr 3 – Aug 6	GEM
Aug 7 – Sep 5	CAN
Sep 6 – Oct 2	LEO
Oct 3 – Oct 27	VIR
Oct 28 – Nov 21	LIB
Nov 22 – Dec 15	SCO
Dec 16 – Dec 31	SAG

2005

Jan 1 – Jan 8	SAG
Jan 9 – Feb 1	CAP
Feb 2 – Feb 25	AQU
Feb 26 – Mar 21	PIS
Mar 22 – Apr 14	ARI
Apr 15 – May 8	TAU
May 9 – Jun 2	GEM
Jun 3 – Jun 27	CAN
Jun 28 – Jul 21	LEO
Jul 22 – Aug 15	VIR
Aug 16 – Sep 10	LIB
Sep 11 – Oct 6	SCO
Oct 7 – Nov 4	SAG
Nov 5 – Dec 14	CAP
Dec 15 – Dec 31	AQU

2006

Jan 1 – Mar 4	CAP
Mar 5 – Apr 4	AQU
Apr 5 – May 2	PIS
May 3 – May 28	ARI
May 29 – Jun 22	TAU
Jun 23 – Jul 17	GEM
Jul 18 – Aug 11	CAN
Aug 12 – Sep 5	LEO
Aug 6 – Sep 29	VIR
Sep 30 – Oct 23	LIB
Oct 24 – Nov 16	SCO
Nov 17 – Dec 10	SAG
Dec 11 – Dec 31	CAP

2007

Jan 1 – Jan 2	CAP
Jan 3 – Jan 26	AQU
Jan 27 – Feb 20	PIS
Feb 21 – Mar 16	ARI
Mar 17 – Apr 10	TAU
Apr 11 – May 7	GEM
May 8 – Jun 4	CAN
Jun 5 – Jul 13	LEO
Jul 14 – Aug 7	VIR
Aug 8 – Oct 7	LEO
Oct 8 – Nov 7	VIR
Nov 8 – Dec 4	LIB
Dec 5 – Dec 29	SCO
Dec 30 – Dec 31	SAG

2008

Jan 1 – Jan 23	SAG
Jan 24 – Feb 16	CAP
Feb 17 – Mar 11	AQU
Mar 12 – Apr 5	PIS
Apr 6 – Apr 29	ARI
Apr 30 – May 23	TAU
May 24 – Jun 17	GEM
Jun 18 – Jul 11	CAN
Jul 12 – Aug 4	LEO
Aug 5 – Aug 29	VIR
Aug 30 – Sep 22	LIB
Sep 23 – Oct 17	SCO
Oct 18 – Nov 11	SAG
Nov 12 – Dec 6	CAP
Dec 7 – Dec 31	AQU

2009

Jan 1 – Jan 2	AQU
Jan 3 – Feb 1	PIS
Feb 2 – Apr 10	ARI
Apr 11 – Apr 23	PIS
Apr 24 – Jun 5	ARI
Jun 6 – Jul 4	TAU
Jul 5 – Jul 30	GEM
Jul 31 – Aug 25	CAN
Aug 26 – Sep 19	LEO
Sep 20 – Oct 13	VIR
Oct 14 – Nov 6	LIB
Nov 7 – Nov 30	SCO
Dec 1 – Dec 24	SAG
Dec 25 – Dec 31	CAP

2010

Jan 1 – Jan 17	CAP
Jan 18 – Feb 10	AQU
Feb 11 – Mar 6	PIS
Mar 7 – Mar 30	ARI
Mar 31 – Apr 23	TAU
Apr 24 – May 18	GEM
May 19 – Jun 13	CAN
Jun 14 – Jul 9	LEO
Jul 10 – Aug 5	VIR
Aug 6 – Sep 7	LIB
Sep 8 – Nov 6	SCO
Nov 7 – Nov 28	LIB
Nov 29 – Dec 31	SCO

Mars Ephemeris:
How to Find the Mars Sign

Under the year of birth, find the birth date. If birth was on the first or last day of a particular period, it's possible that Mars might be posited in the preceding or following Sign. The only way to be absolutely sure is to have a chart done by a computer service (see appendix 2 for resources) or by a professional astrologer. If you are unsure, read the adjacent Sign to decide which is applicable.

Before checking the Mars Ephemeris, first look at the Mars Retrograde table on the next page to determine if the Planet was in retrograde motion at the time of birth. Look up the year in the left-hand column, then check the retrograde period, marked R, noticing the "backward" movement of the Planet from one Sign to the previous Sign. At the end of each entry, D indicates the Planet's return to direct motion.

Example:

1975 R Nov 6 in Cancer, into Gemini Nov 26, D Jan 20 1976 at which point refer to the ephemeris to find 1975 Oct 18–Nov 25 Cancer.

Thus, if birth occurred between Oct 18–Nov 5, Venus would be in CANCER direct; but if birth occurred between Nov 6–Nov 25, Venus, while still in Cancer, would be retrograde.

Mars Retrograde Tables

1950 R Feb 12 in Lib, into Vir Mar 29	D May 3 1950
1952 R Mar 25 in Sco	D Jun 10 1952
1954 R May 23 in Cap, into Sag Jul 4	D Jul 29 1954
1956 R Aug 20 in Pis	D Oct 10 1956
1958 R Oct 10 in Gem, into Tau Oct 30	D Dec 20 1958
1960 R Nov 20 in Can, into Gem Feb 6 1961	D Feb 7 1961
1962 R Dec 26 in Leo	D Mar 16 1963
1965 R Jan 28 in Vir	D Apr 19 1965
1967 R Mar 8 in Sco, into Lib Apr 1	D May 26 1967
1969 R Apr 27 in Sag	D Jul 8 1969
1971 R Jul 11 in Aqu	D Sep 9 1971
1973 R Sep 19 in Tau, into Ari Oct 30	D Nov 26 1973
1975 R Nov 6 in Can, into Gem Nov 26	D Jan 20 1976
1977 R Dec 12 in Leo, into Can Jan 27 1978	D Mar 2 1978
1980 R Jan 16 in Vir, into Leo Mar 12	D Apr 6 1980
1982 R Feb 20 in Lib	D May 11 1982
1984 R Apr 5 in Sco	D Jun 19 1984
1986 R Jun 8 in Cap	D Aug 12 1986
1988 R Aug 26 in Ari, into Pis Oct 24	D Oct 28 1988
1990 R Oct 20 in Gem, into Tau Dec 15	D Jan 2 1991
1992 R Nov 28 in Can	D Feb 15 1993
1995 R Jan 2 in Vir, into Leo Jan 23	D Mar 24 1995
1997 R Feb 6 in Lib, into Vir Mar 9	D Apr 27 1997
1999 R Mar 18 in Sco, into Lib May 6	D Jun 4 1999
2001 R May 22 in Sag	D Jul 19 2001
2003 R Jul 29 in Pis	D Sep 27 2003
2005 R Oct 2 in Tau	D Dec 10 2005
2007 R Nov 26 in Can, into Gem Jan 1 2008	D Jan 30 2008
2009 R Dec 20 in Leo	D Mar 10 2010

1950

Jan 1 – Mar 27	LIB
Mar 28 – Jun 10	VIR
Jun 11 – Aug 9	LIB
Aug 10 – Sep 24	SCO
Sep 25 – Nov 5	SAG
Nov 6 – Dec 14	CAP
Dec 15 – Dec 31	AQU

1951

Jan 1 – Jan 21	AQU
Jan 22 – Feb 28	PIS
Mar 1 – Apr 9	ARI
Apr 10 – May 20	TAU
May 21 – Jul 2	GEM
Jul 3 – Aug 17	CAN
Aug 18 – Oct 3	LEO
Oct 4 – Nov 23	VIR
Nov 24 – Dec 31	LIB

1952

Jan 1 – Jan 19	LIB
Jan 20 – Aug 26	SCO
Aug 27 – Oct 11	SAG
Oct 12 – Nov 20	CAP
Nov 21 – Dec 29	AQU
Dec 30 – Dec 31	PIS

1953

Jan 1 – Feb 7	PIS
Feb 8 – Mar 19	ARI
Mar 20 – Apr 30	TAU
May 1 – Jun 13	GEM
Jun 14 – Jul 29	CAN
Jul 30 – Sep 14	LEO
Sep 15 – Nov 1	VIR
Nov 2 – Dec 19	LIB
Dec 20 – Doc 31	SCO

1954

Jan 1 – Feb 8	SCO
Feb 9 – Apr 11	SAG
Apr 12 – Jul 2	CAP
Jul 3 – Aug 23	SAG
Aug 24 – Oct 20	CAP
Oct 21 – Dec 3	AQU
Dec 4 – Dec 31	PIS

1955

Jan 1 – Jan 14	PIS
Jan 15 – Feb 25	ARI
Feb 26 – Apr 9	TAU
Apr 10 – May 25	GEM
May 26 – Jul 10	CAN
Jul 11 – Aug 26	LEO
Aug 27 – Oct 12	VIR
Oct 13 – Nov 28	LIB
Nov 29 – Dec 31	SCO

1956

Jan 1 – Jan 13	SCO
Jan 14 – Feb 27	SAG
Feb 28 – Apr 13	CAP
Apr 14 – Jun 2	AQU
Jun 3 – Dec 5	PIS
Dec 6 – Dec 31	ARI

1957

Jan 1 – Jan 27	ARI
Jan 28 – Mar 16	TAU
Mar 17 – May 3	GEM
May 4 – Jun 20	CAN
Jun 21 – Aug 7	LEO
Aug 8 – Sep 23	VIR
Sep 24 – Nov 7	LIB
Nov 8 – Dec 22	SCO
Dec 23 – Dec 31	SAG

1958

Jan 1 – Feb 2	SAG
Feb 3 – Mar 16	CAP
Mar 17 – Apr 26	AQU
Apr 27 – Jun 6	PIS
Jun 7 – Jul 20	ARI
Jul 21 – Sep 20	TAU
Sep 21 – Oct 28	GEM
Oct 29 – Dec 31	TAU

1959

Jan 1 – Feb 9	TAU
Feb 10 – Apr 9	GEM
Apr 10 – May 31	CAN
Jun 1 – Jul 19	LEO
Jul 20 – Sep 4	VIR
Sep 5 – Oct 20	LIB
Oct 21 – Dec 2	SCO
Dec 3 – Dec 31	SAG

1960

Jan 1 – Jan 13	SAG
Jan 14 – Feb 22	CAP
Feb 23 – Apr 1	AQU
Apr 2 – May 10	PIS
May 11 – Jun 19	ARI
Jun 20 – Aug 1	TAU
Aug 2 – Sep 20	GEM
Sep 21 – Dec 31	CAN

1961

Jan 1 – Feb 5	CAN
Feb 6 – Feb 7	GEM
Feb 8 – May 5	CAN
May 6 – Jun 27	LEO
Jun 28 – Aug 16	VIR
Aug 17 – Sep 30	LIB
Oct 1 – Nov 12	SCO
Nov 13 – Dec 23	SAG
Dec 24 – Dec 31	CAP

1962

Jan 1 – Jan 31	CAP
Feb 1 – Mar 11	AQU
Mar 12 – Apr 18	PIS
Apr 19 – May 27	ARI
Mar 28 – Jul 8	TAU
Jul 9 – Aug 21	GEM
Aug 22 – Oct 10	CAN
Oct 11 – Dec 31	LEO

1963

Jan 1 – Jun 2	LEO
Jun 3 – Jul 26	VIR
Jul 27 – Sep 11	LIB
Sep 12 – Oct 24	SCO
Oct 25 – Dec 4	SAG
Dec 5 – Dec 31	CAP

1964

Jan 1 – Jan 12	CAP
Jan 13 – Feb 19	AQU
Feb 20 – Mar 28	PIS
Mar 29 – May 6	ARI
May 7 – Jun 16	TAU
Jun 17 – Jul 29	GEM
Jul 30 – Sep 14	CAN
Sep 15 – Nov 5	LEO
Nov 6 – Dec 31	VIR

1965

Jan 1 – Jun 28	VIR
Jun 29 – Aug 19	LIB
Aug 20 – Oct 3	SCO
Oct 4 – Nov 13	SAG
Nov 14 – Dec 22	CAP
Dec 23 – Dec 31	AQU

1966

Jan 1 – Jan 29	AQU
Jan 30 – Mar 8	PIS
Mar 9 – Apr 16	ARI
Apr 17 – May 27	TAU
Jul 11 – Aug 24	CAN
Aug 25 – Oct 11	LEO
Oct 12 – Dec 3	VIR
Dec 4 – Dec 31	LIB

1967

Jan 1 – Feb 11	LIB
Feb 12 – Mar 31	SCO
Apr 1 – Jul 18	LIB
Jul 19 – Sep 9	SCO
Sep 10 – Oct 22	SAG
Oct 23 – Nov 30	CAP
Dec 1 – Dec 31	AQU

1968

Jan 1 – Jan 8	AQU
Jan 9 – Feb 16	PIS
Feb 17 – Mar 26	ARI
Mar 27 – May 7	TAU
May 8 – Jun 20	GEM
Jun 21 – Aug 4	CAN
Aug 5 – Sep 20	LEO
Sep 21 – Nov 8	VIR
Nov 9 – Dec 28	LIB
Dec 29 – Dec 31	SCO

1969

Jan 1 – Feb 24	SCO
Feb 25 – Sep 20	SAG
Sep 21 – Nov 3	CAP
Nov 4 – Dec 13	AQU
Dec 14 – Dec 31	PIS

1970

Jan 1 – Jan 23	PIS
Jan 24 – Mar 6	ARI
Mar 7 – Apr 17	TAU
Apr 18 – Jun 1	GEM
Jun 2 – Jul 17	CAN
Jul 18 – Sep 2	LEO
Sep 3 – Oct 19	VIR
Oct 20 – Dec 5	LIB
Dec 6 – Dec 31	SCO

1971

Jan 1 – Jan 23	SCO
Jan 24 – Mar 12	SAG
Mar 13 – May 3	CAP
May 4 – Nov 6	AQU
Nov 7 – Dec 26	PIS
Dec 27 – Dec 31	ARI

1972

Jan 1 – Feb 10	ARI
Feb 11 – Mar 27	TAU
Mar 28 – May 12	GEM
May 13 – Jun 28	CAN
Jun 29 – Aug 15	LEO
Aug 16 – Sep 30	VIR
Oct 1 – Nov 15	LIB
Nov 16 – Dec 30	SCO
Dec 31	SAG

1973

Jan 1 – Feb 12	SAG
Feb 13 – Mar 26	CAP
Mar 27 – May 8	AQU
May 9 – Jun 20	PIS
Jun 21 – Aug 12	ARI
Aug 13 – Oct 29	TAU
Oct 30 – Dec 24	ARI
Dec 25 – Dec 31	TAU

1974

Jan 1 – Feb 27	TAU
Feb 28 – Apr 20	GEM
Apr 21 – Jun 9	CAN
Jun 10 – Jul 27	LEO
Jul 28 – Sep 12	VIR
Sep 13 – Oct 28	LIB
Oct 29 – Dec 10	SCO
Dec 11 – Dec 31	SAG

1975

Jan 1 – Jan 21	SAG
Jan 22 – Mar 3	CAP
Mar 4 – Apr 11	AQU
Apr 12 – May 21	PIS
May 22 – Jul 1	ARI
Jul 2 – Aug 14	TAU
Aug 15 – Oct 17	GEM
Oct 18 – Nov 25	CAN
Nov 26 – Dec 31	GEM

1976

Jan 1 – Mar 18	GEM
Mar 19 – May 16	CAN
May 17 – Jul 6	LEO
Jul 7 – Aug 24	VIR
Aug 25 – Oct 8	LIB
Oct 9 – Nov 20	SCO
Nov 21 – Dec 31	SAG

1977

Jan 1	SAG
Jan 2 – Feb 9	CAP
Feb 10 – Mar 20	AQU
Mar 21 – Apr 27	PIS
Apr 28 – Jun 6	ARI
Jun 7 – Jul 17	TAU
Jul 18 – Sep 1	GEM
Sep 2 – Oct 26	CAN
Oct 27 – Dec 31	LEO

1978

Jan 1 – Jan 26	LEO
Jan 27 – Apr 10	CAN
Apr 11 – Jun 14	LEO
Jun 15 – Aug 3	VIR
Aug 4 – Sep 18	LIB
Sep 19 – Nov 3	SCO
Nov 4 – Dec 12	SAG
Dec 13 – Dec 31	CAP

1979

Jan 1 – Jan 20	CAP
Jan 21 – Feb 27	AQU
Feb 28 – Apr 7	PIS
Apr 8 – May 16	ARI
May 17 – Jun 26	TAU
Jun 27 – Aug 8	GEM
Aug 9 – Sep 24	CAN
Sep 25 – Nov 19	LEO
Nov 20 – Dec 31	VIR

1980

Jan 1 – Mar 11	VIR
Mar 12 – May 4	LEO
May 5 – Jul 10	VIR
Jul 11 – Aug 29	LIB
Aug 30 – Oct 12	SCO
Oct 13 – Nov 22	SAG
Nov 23 – Dec 30	CAP
Dec 31	AQU

1981

Jan 1 – Feb 6	AQU
Feb 7 – Mar 17	PIS
Mar 18 – Apr 25	ARI
Apr 26 – Jun 5	TAU
Jun 6 – Jul 18	GEM
Jul 19 – Sep 1	CAN
Sep 2 – Oct 21	LEO
Oct 22 – Dec 16	VIR
Dec 17 – Dec 31	LIB

1982

Jan 1 – Aug 3	LIB
Aug 4 – Sep 20	SCO
Sep 21 – Oct 31	SAG
Nov 1 – Dec 10	CAP
Dec 11 – Dec 31	AQU

1983

Jan 1 – Jan 17	AQU
Jan 18 – Feb 24	PIS
Feb 25 – Apr 5	ARI
Apr 6 – May 16	TAU
May 17 – Jun 28	GEM
Jun 29 – Aug 13	CAN
Aug 14 – Sep 29	LEO
Sep 30 – Nov 17	VIR
Nov 18 – Dec 31	LIB

1984

Jan 1 – Jan 10	LIB
Jan 11 –Aug 17	SCO
Aug 18 – Oct 4	SAG
Oct 5 – Nov 15	CAP
Nov 16 – Dec 24	AQU
Dec 25 – Dec 31	PIS

1985

Jan 1 – Feb 2	PIS
Feb 2 – Mar 14	ARI
Mar 15 – Apr 25	TAU
Apr 26 – Jun 8	GEM
Jun 9 – Jul 24	CAN
Jul 25 – Sep 9	LEO
Sep 10 – Oct 27	VIR
Oct 28 – Dec 14	LIB
Dec 15 – Dec 31	SCO

1986

Jan 1 – Feb 1	SCO
Feb 2 –Mar 27	SAG
Mar 28 – Oct 8	CAP
Oct 9 – Nov 25	AQU
Nov 26 – Dec 31	PIS

1987

Jan 1 – Jan 8	PIS
Jan 9 – Feb 20	ARI
Feb 21 – Apr 5	TAU
Apr 6 – May 20	GEM
May 21 – Jul 6	CAN
Jul 7 – Aug 22	LEO
Aug 23 – Oct 8	VIR
Oct 9 – Nov 23	LIB
Nov 24 – Dec 31	SCO

1988

Jan 1 – Jan 8	SCO
Jan 9 – Feb 21	SAG
Feb 22 – Apr 6	CAP
Apr 7 – May 21	AQU
May 22 – Jul 13	PIS
Jul 14 – Oct 23	ARI
Oct 24 – Nov 1	PIS
Nov 2 – Dec 31	ARI

1989

Jan 1 – Jan 18	ARI
Jan 19 – Mar 10	TAU
Mar 11 – Apr 28	GEM
Apr 29 – Jun 16	CAN
Jun 17 – Aug 3	LEO
Aug 4 – Sep l9	VIR
Sep 20 – Nov 3	LIB
Nov 4 – Dec 17	SCO
Dec 18 – Dec 31	SAG

1990

Jan 1 – Jan 29	SAG
Jan 30 – Mar 11	CAP
Mar 12 – Apr 20	AQU
Apr 21 – May 30	PIS
May 31 – Jul 12	ARI
Jul 13 – Aug 30	TAU
Aug 31 – Dec 13	GEM
Dec 14 – Dec 31	TAU

1991

Jan 1 – Jan 20	TAU
Jan 21 – Apr 2	GEM
Apr 3 – May 26	CAN
May 27 – Jul 15	LEO
Jul 16 – Aug 31	VIR
Sep 1 – Oct 16	LIB
Oct 17 – Nov 28	SCO
Nov 29 – Dec 31	SAG

1992

Jan 1 – Jan 8	SAG
Jan 9 – Feb 17	CAP
Feb 18 – Mar 27	AQU
Mar 28 – May 5	PIS
May 6 – Jun 14	ARI
Jun 15 – Jul 26	TAU
Jul 27 – Sep 11	GEM
Sep 12 – Dec 31	CAN

1993

Jan 1 – Apr 27	CAN
Apr 28 – Jun 22	LEO
Jun 23 – Aug 11	VIR
Aug 12 – Sep 26	LIB
Sep 27 – Nov 8	SCO
Nov 9 – Dec 19	SAG
Dec 20 – Dec 31	CAP

1994

Jan 1 – Jan 27	CAP
Jan 28 – Mar 6	AQU
Mar 7 – Apr 14	PIS
Apr 15 – May 23	ARI
May 24 – Jul 3	TAU
Jul 4 – Aug 16	GEM
Aug 17 – Oct 4	CAN
Oct 5 – Dec 11	LEO
Dec 12 – Dec 31	VIR

1995

Jan 1 – Jan 22	VIR
Jan 23 – Mar 25	LEO
Mar 26 – Jul 20	VIR
Jul 21 – Sep 6	LIB
Sep 7 – Oct 20	SCO
Oct 21 – Nov 30	SAG
Dec 1 – Dec 31	CAP

1996

Jan 1 – Jan 7	CAP
Jan 8 – Feb 14	AQU
Feb 15 – Mar 24	PIS
Mar 25 – May 2	ARI
May 3 – Jun 12	TAU
Jun 13 – Jul 25	GEM
Jul 26 – Sep 9	CAN
Sep 10 – Oct 29	LEO
Oct 30 – Dec 31	VIR

1997

Jan 1 – Jan 2	VIR
Jan 3 – Mar 8	LIB
Mar 9 – Jun 18	VIR
Jun 19 – Aug 13	LIB
Aug 14 – Sep 28	SCO
Sep 29 – Nov 8	SAG
Nov 9 – Dec 17	CAP
Dec 18 – Dec 31	AQU

1998

Jan 1 – Jan 24	AQU
Jan 25 – Mar 4	PIS
Mar 5 – Apr 12	ARI
Apr 13 – May 23	TAU
May 24 – Jul 5	GEM
Jul 6 – Aug 20	CAN
Aug 21 – Oct 7	LEO
Oct 8 – Nov 26	VIR
Nov 27 – Dec 31	LIB

1999

Jan 1 – Jan 25	LIB
Jan 26 – May 5	SCO
May 6 – Jul 4	LIB
Jul 5 – Sep 2	SCO
Sep 3 – Oct 16	SAG
Oct 17 – Nov 25	CAP
Nov 26 – Dec 31	AQU

2000

Jan 1 – Jan 3	AQU
Jan 4 – Feb 11	PIS
Feb 12 – Mar 22	ARI
Mar 23 – May 3	TAU
May 4 – Jun 16	GEM
Jun 17 – Jul 31	CAN
Aug 1 – Sep 16	LEO
Sep 17 – Nov 3	VIR
Nov 4 – Dec 23	LIB
Dec 24 – Dec 31	SCO

2001

Jan 1 – Feb 13	SCO
Feb 14 – Sep 7	SAG
Sep 8 – Oct 26	CAP
Oct 27 – Dec 7	AQU
Dec 8 – Dec 31	PIS

2002

Jan 1 – Jan 17	PIS
Jan 18 – Feb 28	ARI
Mar 1 – Apr 12	TAU
Apr 13 – May 27	GEM
May 28 – Jul 12	CAN
Jul 13 – Aug 28	LEO
Aug 29 – Oct 14	VIR
Oct 15 – Nov 30	LIB
Dec 1 – Dec 31	SCO

2003

Jan 1 – Jan 15	SCO
Jan 16 – Mar 3	SAG
Mar 4 – Apr 20	CAP
Apr 21 – Jun 15	AQU
Jun 16 – Dec 15	PIS
Dec 16 – Dec 31	ARI

2004

Jan 1 – Feb 2	ARI
Feb 3 – Mar 20	TAU
Mar 21 – May 6	GEM
May 7 – Jun 22	CAN
Jun 23 – Aug 9	LEO
Aug 10 – Sep 25	VIR
Sep 26 – Nov 9	LIB
Nov 10 – Dec 24	SCO
Dec 25 – Dec 31	SAG

2005

Jan 1 – Feb 5	SAG
Feb 6 – Mar 19	CAP
Mar 20 – Apr 29	AQU
Apr 30 – Jun 10	PIS
Jun 11 – Jul 26	ARI
Jul 27 – Dec 31	TAU

2006

Jan 1 – Feb 16	TAU
Feb 17 – Apr 12	GEM
Apr 13 – Jun 2	CAN
Jun 3 – Jul 21	LEO
Jul 22 – Sep 6	VIR
Sep 7 – Oct 22	LIB
Oct 23 – Dec 4	SCO
Dec 5 – Dec 31	SAG

2008

Jan 1 – Mar 3	GEM
Mar 4 – May 8	CAN
May 9 – Jun 30	LEO
Jul 1 – Aug 18	VIR
Aug 19 – Oct 2	LIB
Oct 3 – Nov 15	SCO
Nov 16 – Dec 26	SAG
Dec 27 – Dec 31	CAP

2009

Jan 1 – Feb 3	CAP
Feb 4 – Mar 13	PIS
Mar 14 – May 30	ARI
May 31 – Jul 10	TAU
Jul 11 – Aug 24	GEM
Aug 25 – Oct 15	CAN
Oct 16 – Dec 31	LEO

2010

Jan 1 – Jun 6	LEO
Jun 7 – Jul 28	VIR
Jul 29 – Sep 13	LIB
Sep 14 – Oct 27	SCO
Oct 28 – Dec 6	SAG
Dec 7 – Dec 31	CAP

2007

Jan 1 – Jan 15	SAG
Jan 16 – Feb 24	CAP
Feb 25 – Apr 5	AQU
Apr 6 – May 14	PIS
May 15 – Jun 23	ARI
Jun 24 – Aug 6	TAU
Aug 7 – Sep 27	GEM
Sep 28 – Dec 30	CAN
Dec 31 – Dec 31	GEM

Ingresses

Because Planets beyond Mars move so slowly, the following tables give only the date that the Planet moves into a particular Sign. As these tables use the glyph system, please refer to the following conversion table. An R following the glyph entry indicates retrograde.

Glyph	Sign
♈	Aries
♉	Taurus
♊	Gemini
♋	Cancer
♌	Leo
♍	Virgo
♎	Libra
♏	Scorpio
♐	Sagittarius
♑	Capricorn
♒	Aquarius
♓	Pisces

Jupiter Ingress

Year	Date		Sign	R		Year	Date		Sign	R		Year	Date		Sign	R
1950	APR	15	♓			1967	JAN	15	♋	R		1984	JAN	19	♑	
1950	SEP	14	♒	R		1967	MAY	23	♌			1985	FEB	6	♒	
1950	DEC	1	♓			1967	OCT	19	♍			1986	FEB	20	♓	
1951	APR	21	♈			1968	FEB	26	♌	R		1987	MAR	2	♈	
1952	APR	28	♉			1968	JUN	15	♍			1988	MAR	8	♉	
1953	MAY	9	♊			1968	NOV	15	♎			1988	JUL	21	♊	
1954	MAY	23	♋			1969	MAR	30	♍	R		1988	NOV	30	♉	R
1955	JUN	12	♌			1969	JUL	15	♎			1989	MAR	10	♊	
1955	NOV	16	♍			1969	DEC	16	♏			1989	JUL	30	♋	
1956	JAN	17	♌	R		1970	APR	30	♎	R		1990	AUG	18	♌	
1956	JUL	7	♍			1970	AUG	15	♏			1991	SEP	12	♍	
1956	DEC	12	♎			1971	JAN	14	♐			1992	OCT	10	♎	
1957	FEB	19	♍	R		1971	JUN	4	♏	R		1993	NOV	10	♏	
1957	AUG	6	♎			1971	SEP	11	♐			1994	DEC	9	♐	
1958	JAN	13	♏			1972	FEB	6	♑			1996	JAN	3	♑	
1958	MAR	20	♎	R		1972	JUL	24	♐	R		1997	JAN	21	♒	
1958	SEP	7	♏			1972	SEP	25	♑			1998	FEB	4	♓	
1959	FEB	10	♐			1973	FEB	23	♒			1999	FEB	12	♈	
1959	APR	24	♏	R		1974	MAR	8	♓			1999	JUN	28	♉	
1959	OCT	5	♐			1975	MAR	18	♈			1999	OCT	23	♈	R
1960	MAR	1	♑			1976	MAR	26	♉			2000	FEB	14	♉	
1960	JUN	9	♐	R		1976	AUG	23	♊			2000	JUN	30	♊	
1960	OCT	25	♑			1976	OCT	16	♉			2001	JUL	14	♋	
1961	MAR	15	♒			1977	APR	3	♊			2002	AUG	2	♌	
1961	AUG	12	♑	R		1977	AUG	20	♋			2003	AUG	28	♍	
1961	NOV	3	♒			1977	DEC	30	♊	R		2004	SEP	26	♎	
1962	MAR	25	♓			1978	APR	11	♋			2005	OCT	27	♏	
1963	APR	3	♈			1978	SEP	5	♌			2006	NOV	25	♐	
1964	APR	12	♉			1979	FEB	28	♋	R		2007	DEC	19	♑	
1965	APR	22	♊			1979	APR	20	♌			2009	JAN	6	♒	
1965	SEP	20	♋			1979	SEP	29	♍			2010	JAN	19	♓	
1965	NOV	16	♊	R		1980	OCT	27	♎			2010	JUN	7	♈	
1966	MAY	5	♋			1981	NOV	26	♏			2010	SEP	10	♓	
1966	SEP	27	♌			1982	DEC	25	♐							

Saturn Ingress

Year	Date		Sign	R		Year	Date		Sign	R		Year	Date		Sign	R
1950	NOV	20	♎			1973	AUG	1	♋			1991	FEB	6	♒	
1951	MAR	7	♍	R		1974	JAN	7	♊	R		1993	MAY	21	♓	
1951	AUG	13	♎			1974	APR	18	♋			1993	JUN	30	♒	R
1953	OCT	22	♏			1975	SEP	17	♌			1994	JAN	28	♓	
1956	JAN	12	♐			1976	JAN	14	♋			1996	APR	7	♈	
1956	MAY	13	♏	R		1976	JUN	5	♌			1998	JUN	9	♉	
1956	OCT	10	♐			1977	NOV	16	♍			1998	OCT	25	♈	R
1959	JAN	5	♑			1978	JAN	4	♌			1999	FEB	28	♉	
1962	JAN	3	♒			1978	JUL	26	♍			2000	AUG	9	♊	
1964	MAR	23	♓			1980	SEP	21	♎			2000	OCT	15	♉	R
1964	SEP	16	♒			1982	NOV	29	♏			2001	APR	21	♊	
1964	DEC	16	♓			1983	MAY	6	♎			2003	JUN	5	♋	
1967	MAR	3	♈			1983	AUG	24	♏			2005	JUL	17	♌	
1969	APR	29	♉			1985	NOV	16	♐			2007	SEP	3	♍	
1971	JUN	18	♊			1988	FEB	13	♑			2009	OCT	30	♎	
1972	JAN	9	♉	R		1988	JUN	10	♐	R		2010	APR	8	♍	
1972	FEB	21	♊			1988	NOV	12	♑			2010	JUL	22	♎	

URANUS INGRESS

1949	JUN	9	♋		1969	JUN	24	♎		1988	DEC	2	♑
1955	AUG	24	♌		1974	NOV	21	♏		1995	APR	1	♒
1956	JAN	27	♋ R		1975	MAY	1	♎ R		1995	JUN	8	♑ R
1956	JUN	9	♌		1975	SEP	8	♏		1996	JAN	12	♒
1961	NOV	1	♍		1981	FEB	17	♐		2003	MAR	11	♓
1962	JAN	10	♌ R		1981	MAR	20	♏ R		2003	SEP	16	♒
1962	AUG	9	♋		1981	NOV	16	♐		2003	DEC	31	♓
1968	SEP	28	♎		1988	FEB	14	♑		2010	MAY	29	♈
1969	MAY	20	♍ R		1988	MAY	26	♐		2010	AUG	15	♓

NEPTUNE INGRESS

1943	AUG	2	♎		1970	JAN	4	♐		1984	NOV	21	♑
1955	DEC	24	♏		1970	MAY	2	♑ R		1998	JAN	28	♒
1956	MAR	11	♎ R		1970	NOV	6	♐		1998	AUG	22	♑ R
1956	OCT	19	♏		1974	MAR	23	♓		1998 }	None		
1957	JUN	15	♎ R		1984	JAN	18	♑		2010 }			
1957	AUG	6	♏		1984	JUN	22	♐ R					

PLUTO INGRESS

1939	JUN	13	♌		1971	OCT	5	♎		1995	JAN	17	♐
1956	OCT	20	♍		1972	APR	17	♍ R		1995	APR	20	♏ R
1957	JAN	14	♌ R		1972	JUL	30	♎		1995	NOV	10	♐
1957	AUG	18	♍		1983	AUG	18	♍		2008	JAN	27	♑
1958	APR	11	♌ R		1984	APR	11	♌ R		2008	JUN	15	♐
1958	JUN	10	♍		1984	AUG	28	♏		2008	NOV	28	♑

BOOKS OF RELATED INTEREST

Tarot for Teens
by M. J. Abadie

The Goddess in Every Girl
Develop Your Teen Feminine Power
by M. J. Abadie

Teen Dream Power
Unlock the Meaning of Your Dreams
by M. J. Abadie

The Thundering Years
Rituals and Sacred Wisdom for Teens
by Julie Tallard Johnson

Teen Psychic
Exploring Your Intuitive Spiritual Powers
by Julie Tallard Johnson

Spiritual Journaling
Writing Your Way to Independence
by Julie Tallard Johnson

I Ching for Teens
Take Charge of Your Destiny with the Ancient Chinese Oracle
by Julie Tallard Johnson

Teen Feng Shui
Design Your Space, Design Your Life
by Susan Levitt

Inner Traditions • Bear & Company
P.O. Box 388
Rochester, VT 05767
1-800-246-8648
www.InnerTraditions.com

Or contact your local bookseller